CRANES
of the
WORLD

CRANES
of the
WORLD

Paul A. Johnsgard

INDIANA UNIVERSITY PRESS

BLOOMINGTON

Manufactured in the United States of America

Library of Congress Cataloging in Publication Data

Johnsgard, Paul A.
    Cranes of the world.

    Includes bibliographical references and index.
    1. Cranes (Birds)   I. Title.
QL696.G84J6   1983   598′.31   82-49015
ISBN 0-253-11255-9
1 2 3 4 5 87 86 85 84 83

Contents

CONTENTS

LIST OF PLATES

FOREWORD

Cranes have stalked earth's wetlands for some 60 million years. Since time untold mankind has been inspired by their primeval calls, elaborate dances, impressive migrations, and graceful beauty. Demoiselle cranes adorn the walls of ancient Egyptian tombs, statues of red-crowned cranes guard the Imperial Throne in Beijing's Forbidden City, and native Africans, Australians, and North Americans still mimic crane movements in their rituals. Paradoxically, modern man is threatening the demise of seven crane species. The proliferation of humanity has devastated the shallow wetlands in which cranes breed, and in some regions human ignorance and hunger continue to haunt these majestic creatures.

Settlers in North America obliterated the whooping cranes from the heart of the continent. By 1941 only 15 birds survived. Through decades of cooperative efforts among private organizations and the Canadian and U.S. governments, whoopers were protected and slowly increased to 72 birds by 1983 in the Aransas flock. Likewise, in Japan and West Germany remnant flocks of Japanese and Eurasian cranes are now recovering from perilously low numbers as a result of widespread conservation initiatives. In Asia and Africa, however, six crane species are in peril. Worst hit is the Siberian crane, which is now reduced to fewer than 200 birds and in continued decline. Their survival rests on conservation initiatives in Afghanistan, China, India, Iran, Pakistan, and the USSR. One flock is still hunted while traversing the Hindu Kush mountains of Afghanistan and Pakistan. In addition, the Siberian cranes are specialized aquatic vegetarians and have made a rapid retreat before the destruction of wetlands in south Asia. Likewise, in Africa many of the great floodplains that provide sanctuary for the wattled cranes are being destroyed by various development projects—and the range of the cranes contracts. And political and socio-economic difficulties in Asia and Africa compound the threats facing these birds, which regularly move across tense political boundaries.

We are faced with the challenge of protecting relict habitats, educating local peoples to protect the cranes, developing cooperative conservation efforts among politically polarized nations, and breeding cranes in captivity as a safeguard against extinction in the wild. Encouragingly, efforts are expanding to help the wild cranes, and all endangered species except the black-necked cranes are now well established in captivity.

Paul Johnsgard's excellent book brings us a comprehensive and current account of crane biology. His sketches, range maps, photographs, and informative text will help to improve man's understanding of these remarkable birds and thereby enhance their chances for survival.

GEORGE ARCHIBALD
Director
International Crane Foundation

PREFACE

It has now been little more than a decade since Lawrence Walkinshaw published his *Cranes of the World,* the only monograph on the family Gruidae to appear in the twentieth century. That being the case, it might seem premature to consider the publication of another book covering the same group of birds. However, the precarious state of all the crane species of the world, including no less than five endangered or vulnerable species and another of indeterminate status, according to the most recent assessment by the International Council for Bird Preservation, makes an up-to-date summary of the biology, distributions, and status of the Gruidae an important issue. Furthermore, Walkinshaw did not attempt to undertake comparative biological analyses, nor did he include range maps or recent population data for most species.

Walkinshaw's monograph appeared at about the time that the International Crane Foundation was being established, and together they provided a new source of interest in and centralized concern for the conservation and understanding of the cranes of the world. The growth of the Foundation's activities, including the sponsorship and publication of several workshops on crane biology, has provided a rich source of recent information on the cranes of the world and their biology.

In North America, the endangered whooping crane has been in the public eye for many decades. Its large size, its magnificent appearance, its well-publicized annual migrations between its Canadian breeding grounds and its Gulf Coast wintering area, its near brush with extinction, and its long and painfully slow population recovery since the 1940s have made the whooping crane the symbol for wildlife conservation in the minds of many people. In many areas too the smaller sandhill crane was extirpated as a breeding species early in the present century, and it is still absent as a breeding species in some of these regions. However, sandhill cranes have generally responded well to protection, and they now provide some of the most spectacular concentrations of large birds to be found in all of North America on some of their migratory staging areas and wintering grounds.

Cranes are a group of birds that can lift the human spirit as few other wild animals can do; their great size, marvelous soaring abilities, humanoid traits such as "dancing," and penetrating voices, all strike deep into the human psyche and forcefully remind us of the beauty and mystery of the natural world around us. We cannot lose even a single species of crane without seriously rendering our own existence that much poorer. It is in that spirit that I decided to write the present book, which I hope will be of value to ecologists, ethologists, conservationists, aviculturalists, and anyone else who has any interest in this splendid group of birds.

In the course of writing the book I had to rely on the help of various persons. One of the most important of these was Elizabeth C. Anderson, who provided me with a considerable number of Russian translations that she had produced for the International Crane Foundation; she also translated one or two additional items at my suggestion. Inasmuch as several of the rare or endangered cranes are largely or entirely associated with the USSR during the breeding season, access to this information was of particular value to me. Library facilities of the Edward Grey Institute, Oxford, England, and the ornithological library of the Peabody Museum of Natural History at Yale University were made available to me, and were of particular value in locating obscure citations. I was also given access to the reprint files of the International Crane Foundation, and was provided advice by Dr. George Archibald, Ronald Sauey, and others of their staff. Similarly, Dr. Lawrence Walkinshaw provided me with reprints, unpublished information, and a large number of photographs that he encouraged me to use in whatever manner might be desired. Dr. Walkinshaw's lifetime commitment to cranes and their conservation has been a source of great admiration for me, and I am pleased and honored that I am able to follow his landmark publications with a contribution of my own. Other persons who have aided me by providing unpublished information, supplying photographs, or offering other assistance include Joseph Blossom, Gregory Brown, Paul Conrad, William Conway, Prakash Gole, Guy

PREFACE

Greenwell, Tom Mangelsen, Christopher Marler, Kenneth Newman, Yuri Pukinskii, Christine Sheppard, David Skead, Warwick Tarboton, Stephen R. Wylie, and Donald Young. Dr. Myra Mergler Niemeier contributed a section on tracheal development and syringeal function for the chapter on crane vocalizations. To all of these people I offer my sincere thanks and appreciation.

* * IMPORTANT NOTICE * *

The International Crane Foundation, Baraboo, Wisconsin, is the world center for the study and preservation of cranes. Incorporated as a non-profit institution in 1973, ICF has distinguished itself as a vigorous force in the coordination of international efforts to save these regal and most endangered birds. Research in captive breeding techniques at ICF is enabling establishment of a "species bank" in which genetic resources will be secure, and from which cranes may eventually be released back into the wild as local conditions become favorable. ICF has made major advances in raising public awareness in many parts of the world, and has been influential in decisions to save tracts of wetlands for wildlife habitat in parts of Asia and Africa. An active education program at home provides tours for a growing number of school children, garden clubs, senior citizen groups, families, and bird lovers from all over the world. People wishing to participate in the effort to save cranes should get in touch with ICF (Route 1, Box 230C, Shady Lane Road, Baraboo, Wisconsin 53913, U.S.A.).

CRANES
of the
WORLD

Classification and Evolution

1 Cranes and their relatives the limpkins and trumpeters are fairly closely related members of the order of birds (Gruiformes) that also includes rails, gallinules, coots, and other marsh-adapted birds. Cranes, limpkins, and trumpeters are usually included within a superfamily, Gruoidea, although at least one recent authority (Cracraft, 1973) has suggested that the three groups all be included within a single family, Gruidae. However, traditionally only the cranes have been included within the Gruidae, and only the cranes will be dealt with in detail in this book. Nevertheless, the limpkins and trumpeters must be considered if the evolution of cranes is to be discussed, and thus it is perhaps desirable to define each of these three groups in a semiformal way, so that their similarities and differences are at once apparent.

Cranes can be defined as large, long-legged and long-necked members of the Gruiformes, with a small and elevated hind toe, an elongated and tapering bill that is often longer than the head, and nostrils that are oval or nearly linear and are open (pervious) from side to side. In most species the upper half of the head is nearly naked in adults, exposing colorful skin areas. The toes are not webbed, but are connected at the base by a membrane, and are moderately long. The wings are rounded in profile and have 10 functional primaries (and a vestigial eleventh in most), with the seventh or eighth primary the longest. The wing molt is relatively simultaneous, so that in most species at least the birds may be flightless for a time. There are from 18 to 25 secondaries, with the inner ones longer and curved, often even longer than the primaries, and usually with noncoherent vanes that break up into airy plumes. The tail is moderately long and is composed of 12 feathers (rectrices). There are 17 to 20 cervical vertebrae, 6 or 7 complete ribs, and the trachea is usually looped back to touch or even invade the keel of the sternum, sometimes coiling extensively within it. The sexes are alike in plumage, and all species are monogamous but usually are gregarious outside the breeding season. Their calls are loud and often resonant. From one to four spotted buffy or pale bluish eggs are laid in nests that are located on dry land or in marshy vegetation. Both sexes incubate and care for the young, which are mostly cinnamon brown and require two to three months to fledge. Most species are probably predominantly vegetarian, but all to some degree eat animal materials. There are fourteen species (fifteen if the crowned cranes are considered as two species), and cranes are found in all continents except South America and the Antarctic.

Limpkins are medium-sized, long-legged and long-necked members of the Gruiformes, having a large hind toe that is placed at the same level as the anterior toes, an elongated bill that is much longer than the head, and nostrils that are elongated and pervious. The head is entirely feathered, and the toes lack webbing at their bases and are relatively long and slender. The wings are strongly rounded, with the sixth and seventh primaries the longest. The secondaries are progressively longer inwardly, with the inner ones as long as the longest primaries, but their vanes are coherent. The wing molt is apparently gradual, so that the birds are never flightless. There are 12 rectrices in the long and rounded tail. There are 16 cervical vertebrae, and 6 or 7 complete ribs. The trachea is doubly looped in the lower neck of adult males but is not in contact with the keel of the sternum. The sexes are alike in plumage, and the single species is rather solitary, forming monogamous pairs. Limpkin calls are loud, and are reminiscent of human crying or wailing. Four to eight pale buffy eggs spotted with brown are laid in nests located among marsh vegetation, on bushes or vines, or in low trees (Kale, 1978). Incubation is by both sexes, and the downy young are almost uniformly brown and rather crane-like in appearance (Harrison, 1978). The young are cared for by both sexes, and continue to be fed for an extended period, even after they have fledged. Both adults and young feed to some degree on aquatic insects and amphibians, but they forage mainly on freshwater snails (*Pomacea*), to which their bills are highly adapted (Snyder and Snyder, 1969). The single species occurs from Florida through the West Indies and Mexico to southern South America.

Trumpeters are medium-sized members of the Gruiformes, with legs and neck of medium length, a small and elevated hind toe, a short and decurved bill, and nostrils that are somewhat oval and pervious. The head is entirely covered with feathers, and the toes are relatively short and unwebbed. The wings are strongly rounded, with 10 primaries (no vestigial eleventh), and the 16 secondaries are relatively long. Together with some of the longer scapulars, the secondaries are conspicuously tipped in each of the three species with green, gray, or white, forming a distinctive patch. The tail is fairly short and has 12 rectrices. There are 17 or 18 cervical vertebrae and 8 complete ribs. The trachea has been reported to form a long subcutaneous loop extending back nearly to the vent. However, this tracheal condition has been reported lacking in some specimens, suggesting that it might be limited to adult males. The sexes are alike in plumage, and adult trumpeters produce an extremely low-pitched booming or rumbling call, probably because of the specialized tracheal condition. "Singing" by groups is often performed from tree roosts at night. The birds are gregarious, but adults establish monogamous pairs and perform crane-like dancing displays during courtship (Sick, 1972). Six to ten rough white or pale greenish eggs are laid in ground nests, in tree holes, or in the crowns of palms. Nesting evidently occurs in small colonies, with five or six nests in adjoining trees. Incubation may be performed by the female alone (observations in captivity) or by both sexes (reported in the wild). The downy young are grayish to blackish, uniquely patterned with cinnamon lines on the back and brownish on the crown and wings. The young evidently grow very slowly, with chicks two months old still largely downy. The birds are mostly vegetarians, but about a fifth of their diet may be of insects (Beebe, Hartley, and Howes, 1917). There are three very similar species, all of which are confined to tropical South American forests.

In their general skeletal structure (fig. 1) cranes and limpkins have much in common; indeed, the two groups might be considered part of a common family on skeletal grounds (Beddard, 1898). In cranes, as in the limpkin, the skull has small gaps, or fontanels, in the occipital area, and the septum that separates the orbits has large "windows," or fenestrae. Trumpeters lack occipital fontanels, and have smaller interorbital fenestrae. Further, the skull of trumpeters has a group of about five small supraorbital bones, a condition otherwise found in only a few other "primitive" groups of birds. Finally, the maxillopalatine bones are convex, rather than concave as in cranes (fig. 2).

By contrast, the skull of the limpkin is remarkably similar to that of a typical crane, although the bill is much more elongated. Two other unusual features of the limpkin bill include the fact that the lower mandible is typically slightly twisted to the right, which enables the bird to reach into the aperture of a snail and around the bend of the shell to cut the columellar muscle. There is also a slight gap remaining between the mandibles a short distance back from the tip, a condition that may be useful for grasping snails and for carrying them in the bill (Snyder and Snyder, 1969) (fig. 2).

In the rest of its skeleton, the crane's only remarkable characteristic is the fact that in all the species of *Grus* the trachea is extensively convoluted within the keel of the sternum. The acoustic significance of this feature will be discussed in the chapter on vocalizations, but at this point it need only be noted that the sternum of the limpkin approaches the condition exhibited in the crowned cranes. In both of these groups the furcula (or "wishbone") does not reach the keel of the sternum, and the trachea passes through its opening toward the lungs in an essentially direct fashion. Yet, in both of these groups there is an indentation in the upper portion of the keel, the apparent homolog of the extensively excavated opening found in the keel among species of the genus *Grus* (fig. 3). In Beddard's (1902) view this condition suggests that in these forms the trachea was once coiled in front of the sternum. As noted earlier, the trachea of the male limpkin does exhibit coiling, but it occurs in the lower portion of the neck, well anterior to the sternum (Wetmore, 1965; Rüppell, 1933).

In the genus *Grus*, the furcula is extended to fuse with the keel of the sternum, and the entire keel is both widened and extensively excavated to receive the trachea, which coils within it for varying distances according to the species. The syringeal anatomy of the limpkin has not yet been carefully described, but another major difference that separates cranes from the trumpeter seems to be present in the syrinx and bronchi. Judging from the illustration of Beddard (1890), the bronchi of the trumpeter appear to be connected by a thin membrane, which probably effectively eliminates acoustical contribution by internal tympaniform membranes. This limits vocal activity to the external tympaniform membranes, which appear to be relatively poorly developed. On the other hand, in the genera *Grus* and *Bugeranus* at least, the internal tympaniform membranes are very large and triangular, and extend from the first bronchial semiring nearly to the lungs. Additionally in *Grus* and *Bugeranus* the paired intrinsic tracheal muscles extend back along the sides of the

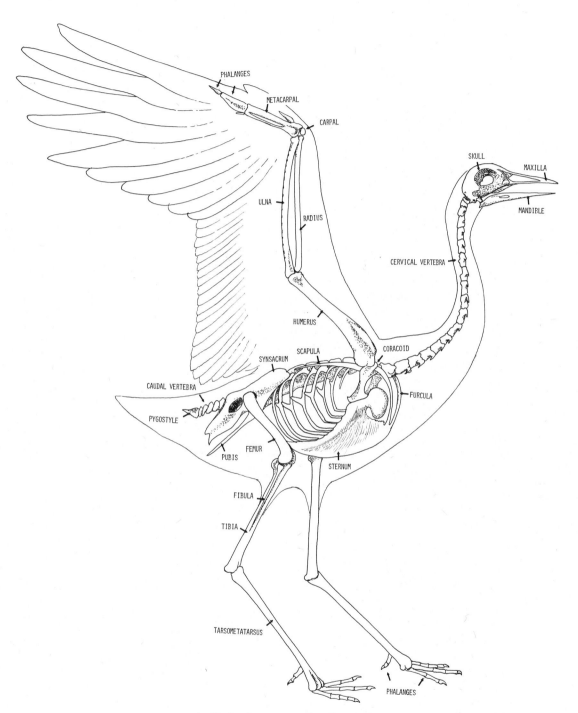

1. Skeletal anatomy of a *Grus* crane.

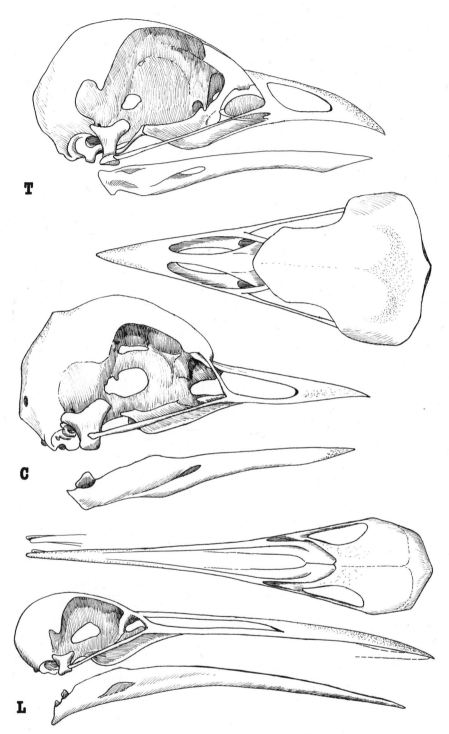

2. Lateral view of a trumpeter skull (T), dorsal and lateral views of a crowned crane skull (C), and dorsal and lateral views of a limpkin skull (L). Tip of limpkin bill is also shown in ventral view, to illustrate asymmetry.

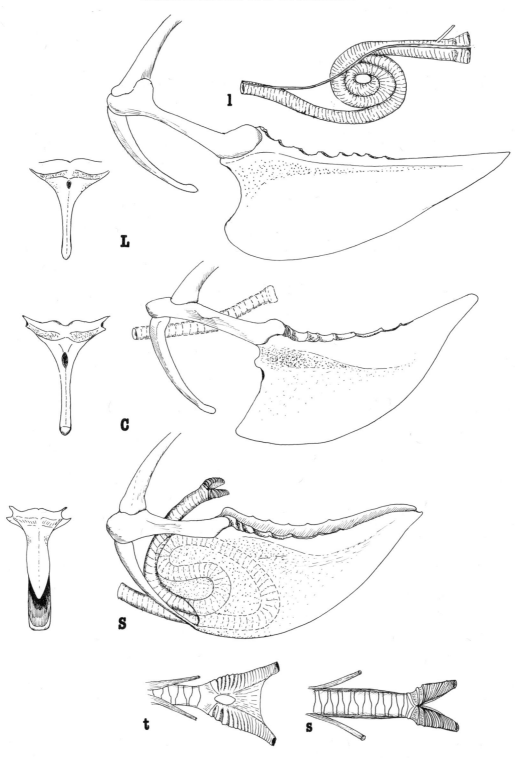

3. Sternum and pectoral girdle of limpkin (L), crowned crane (C), and sandhill crane (S) in lateral and frontal view, and ventral views of the tracheae of the limpkin (l), trumpeter (t), and sandhill crane (s). In part after Beddard (1890, 1902) and Rüppell (1923).

trachea to reach the first bronchial semirings, while in *Balearica* they terminate about 14 rings anterior to the end of the trachea (fig. 3). Evidently the latter condition also prevails in *Psophia* (Beddard, 1890, 1891).

The evolutionary and fossil history of the cranes and their relatives is still surprisingly unsettled, in spite of a rather large number of known fossil forms. As an example of this uncertainty, one might consider the divergent methods of crane classification that have appeared in the last few decades. Thus, in Wetmore's (1960) classification of the birds of the world, the crane-like forms are classified as follows:

Superfamily Gruoidea
  [Family Geranoididae (fossil)]
  [Family Eogruidae (fossil)]
  Family Gruidae
  Family Aramidae
  Family Psophiidae

Not many years later, in cataloging fossil bird groups, Brodkorb (1967) provided an arrangement that took a rather different form:

Family Gruidae
  [Subfamily Geranoidinae (fossil)]
  Subfamily Balearicinae
  [Subfamily Eogruinae (fossil)]
  Subfamily Gruinae
[Family Ergilornithidae (fossil)]
Family Aramidae
Family Psophiidae

In a similar review of fossil material, Cracraft (1973) proposed a classification that differs considerably from these two, and also from other recent groups, especially in the inclusion of both the trumpeters and the limpkins within the crane family:

Superfamily Geranoidea
  [Family Geranoididae (fossil)]
  [Family Bathornithidae (fossil)]
Superfamily Gruoidea
  [Family Eogruidae (fossil)]
  Family Gruidae
    Subfamily Gruinae
    Subfamily Psophiinae
      Tribe Psophiini
      Tribe Aramini

It is thus apparent that there is still no complete agreement as to the phylogeny and relationships of the crane-like birds. Cracraft judged that the crane-like birds (infraorder Grui) evolved during the Cenozoic period (that is, in the last 60 million years), and developed along two distinct phyletic lines. One of these lineages (the superfamily Geranoidea) subsequently died out, while the other (superfamily Gruoidea) gave rise to the contemporary groups that include the present-day cranes, trumpeters, and limpkin. In Cracraft's view, both of these major lineages had a common ancestor with the typical rails (Rallidae) during Cretaceous times. Jacob, Plawer, and Rosenfeldt (1979) also suggest a close relationship between cranes and rails.

As a group, the Gruiformes show a good deal of anatomical similarity to the shorebird order Charadriiformes, and it is very probable that these two major orders evolved from common ancestral stock (Beddard, 1891; Lowe, 1931; Howard, 1950; Feduccia, 1980). Thus, not only do some gruiform birds show characteristics in common with the Charadriiformes, such as the sunbitterns and the bustards, but also some charadriiform groups such as the jacanas have distinct similarities to the Gruiformes (Johnsgard, 1981).

Cracraft (1973) believed that the trumpeters are more closely related to the limpkin than to typical cranes, and that within the aramid-psophiid lineage the trumpeters' characteristics are relatively primitive. Although there is no fossil record of the trumpeters, Cracraft thought it likely that they arose about the same time as did the aramids, in the late Eocene or early Oligocene. Sibley (1960) believed that on the basis of egg-white proteins the trumpeters might be considered somewhat intermediate between cranes and rails, and later (Sibley and Ahlquist, 1972) noted a strong resemblance to rails in the egg-white characteristics of trumpeters, with a less striking similarity to *Balearica*. Cranes, trumpeters, and gallinules are also very similar in chromosome characteristics (Sasaki and Takagi, 1981).

Likewise the aramids are believed by Cracraft to be clearly closer to the cranes than to the rails, and in particular their skeletal features show strong similarities to such primitive cranes as *Balearica*. Fossil evidence indicates that the limpkin group goes back at least to the middle of the Oligocene, and perhaps originated as early as the late Eocene. Yet, some features of the aramids are distinctly raillike, and several writers (Fürbinger, 1888; Shufeldt, 1915) have commented on the intermediacy of the limpkin between the cranes and the rails. However, Beddard (1902) emphasized the strong skeletal similarities between the limpkin and cranes, as did also Mitchell (1915), while Garrod (1876) judged the limpkin to be most closely affiliated with the cranes, but more distantly similar to trumpeters and other gruiform groups.

A somewhat different view of crane evolution has been presented by Stegmann (1978), who judged that the cranes are closest to the bustards (Otididae) in their wing morphology, but have become more specialized for long flights. He imagined the sequence of evolution to proceed from the rails through the bustards to the cranes. He also thought that the trumpeters might be more closely related to the galliform birds than to the Gruiformes, or perhaps are nearest the cariamids, an obscure South American group usually placed close to the bustard family. Cracraft (1973) also believed that the cariamids might offer the nearest phylogenetic group to the trumpeters, but he did not extend his own studies to include this group.

However the cranes evolved, it is clear that by Eocene times they were well established in the Old World (genus *Paleogrus*, three species from England and Europe; *Geranopsis*, one species from England), while in North America the primitive and divergent crane-like *Geranoides* was present (Cracraft, 1969). Fragmentary remains of a questionable form, *Eubalearica tugarinovi*, have also been described from the Eocene of Usbek Soviet Socialist Republic. Both *Paleogrus* and *Geranopsis* more closely approach *Balearica* than *Grus* in their skeletal characteristics, and in some respects are hardly separable from that genus, suggesting that forms resembling the modern crowned cranes were already present in Eocene times. By late Oligocene and early Miocene times the genus *Probalearica* was present in both the Old World (France) and the New World (Florida). This also was a *Balearica*-like crane, and likewise distinctly similar to *Paleogrus*. Finally, by Pliocene times the genus *Pliogrus* was present in Europe. It evidently closely approached *Grus* in at least some of its characteristics, but *Pliogrus* is still only very poorly documented (Cracraft, 1973). A summary of fossil crane species is provided in table 1.

Most fossil cranes are known but from a few fragmentary and poorly preserved remains. Yet, a veritable treasure of fossil cranes has recently been unearthed in late Miocene deposits of northern Nebraska, among beds of volcanic ash nearly 10 million years old. Upwards of thirty crane specimens, some of them nearly complete, have been discovered in association with a rich assortment of rhinos, horses, and other fauna similar to that of a present-day African savanna community (Voorhies, 1981). Although these cranes have yet to be carefully studied and named, it is obvious that they are very close in skeletal features to the modern *Balearica* forms, with a simple sternum and a relatively straight trachea. This adds additional evidence to the view that the crowned crane type was once a widespread form and probably preceded *Grus* as a major crane type. It should perhaps also be noted that a Miocene crane fossil from Nebraska that has been estimated as of about the same age (Upper Snake Creek) has a humeral structure identical to the modern sandhill crane (Wetmore, 1928). As such, this would represent the oldest known fossil evidence of any bird species still surviving. However, a close comparison of this specimen with the newly discovered Nebraska form that was essentially contemporaneous with it will have to be made to eliminate the possibility that they are members of the same genus, and that both genera occurred in central North America at that time. In the same paper, Wetmore (1928) described a fossil *Aramus*, also from the Upper Snake Creek beds, that closely approaches the modern limpkin. The fossil *Grus* described by Wetmore is considered by Skinner, Skinner and Gooris (1977) to

TABLE 1

Synopsis of Fossil Gruidae of the World*

Geologic Period	Balearicinae (of Brodkorb, 1967)	Gruinae (of Brodkorb, 1967)
Pleistocene & Recent		*Grus bohatshevi* (Asia)
		Grus melitensis (Europe)
		Baeopteryx latipes (North America)
		Baeopteryx cubensis (Cuba)
Pliocene	*Pliogrus pentelici* (Europe)	*Grus nannodes* (North America)
	Pliogrus germanicus (Europe)	*Grus conferta* (North America)
Miocene	*Probalearica crataegensis* (North America)	*Grus ?canadensis* (North America)
	Paleogrus excelsus (Europe)	*Grus miocenicus* (Europe)
	Probalearica problematica (Europe)	
Eocene	*Eubalearica tugarinovi* (Asia)†	
	Geranopsis hastingsi (Europe)	
	Paleogrus hordweilliensis (Europe)	
	Paleogrus princeps (Europe)‡	
	Paleogrus geiseltalensis (Europe)	

*After Brodkorb (1967) and Cracraft (1973), but excluding neospecies from prehistoric or Pleistocene sites, and those forms removed from Brodkorb's list of Gruidae by Cracraft. *Grus miocenicus* (Grigorescu and Kessler, 1977) added.
†Of questionable gruiform status, according to Cracraft.
‡*Ornitocnemus robustus* of Brodkorb (1967).

be part of the type fauna of the Snake Creek formation, and of Late Clarendonian age, or of the same age as the *Balearica*-like fossils recently found by Voorhies.

The present-day species of the cranes of the world have generally been placed in 4 genera and 14 species, at least since the publication of Peters's (1934) widely adopted system. He recognized a single species of *Balearica*, two of *Anthropoides*, one of *Bugeranus*, and ten of *Grus*. Previously, Blaauw (1897) had recognized 16 species in three genera (*Grus*, *Anthropoides*, and *Balearica*), and Blyth and Tegetmeier (1881) had accepted 16 species in 2 genera (*Grus* and *Balearica*). By comparison, Sharpe (1894) recognized 9 genera (6 of which were monotypic) and 19 species. Archibald (1975, 1976) reevaluated the Gruidae from a behavioral standpoint and proposed a classification very similar to that of Peters's, except that two species of *Balearica* were recognized and the Siberian crane was shifted from *Grus* to *Bugeranus*. The same sequence of genera proposed by Peters was followed. Wood (1979) came to

very similar conclusions after a phenetic study of the morphology of cranes, and in particular judged that the Siberian crane might be considered congeneric with *Bugeranus carunculatus*. He did not deal directly with the question of the number of acceptable species of *Balearica*, but recently Dowsett and Dowsett-Lemaire (1980) judged that the crowned cranes should be considered conspecific, and also believed that the wattled cranes might be included in the genus *Grus*, as earlier treated by Snow (1978). I agree that the crowned cranes have not yet been proven to consist of two species, but I have followed Archibald and Wood in recognizing two species of *Bugeranus*. Beyond that, I have adopted Archibald's views on the relationships within the genus *Grus*, and the sequence of species and genera used in this book is derived from his conclusions, except that *Balearica* is used to begin the sequence rather than to terminate it, to conform to the weight of evidence suggesting that the crowned cranes are the most primitive of the living Gruidae.

Individualistic and Social Behavior

2 Like all higher organisms, cranes perform a variety of behavior patterns throughout their lives that have evolved to fulfill diverse functions. Much of their time is spent in self-directed activities necessary to maintain life and health. These individualistic or "egocentric" activities include such fundamental behaviors as breathing, eating, defecation, drinking, and sleeping or resting. Other activities, while not vital to life, are usually performed during "leisure time"; these include preening, shaking, stretching, oiling, and other actions that fall within a general umbrella of "comfort" activities. Still other activities, such as foraging and the seeking of shelter, result in aggregations of cranes drawn to the same environmental conditions, and such "quasi-social" behaviors may lead to actual social interactions. These truly social behaviors require the presence of another individual for their performance, with one individual serving as a "sender" of specific social signals (aggression, appeasement, sexual attractions, solicitation of food, etc.), while one or more other individuals serve as "receivers" of such signals. Frequently the "receiver" also becomes a "sender," and the simultaneous or sequential exchange of signals between individuals often results in complex social interactions that provide the basis for integration of pairs, families, and flocks. The following summary of egocentric and social behavior patterns in cranes is primarily based on Voss's (1976) inventory of behavior patterns in the greater sandhill crane; with little variation most or all of these patterns can be regarded as characteristic of cranes in general.

Egocentric Behavior Patterns

Resting and sleeping positions of cranes are achieved in several ways. Rarely, resting or sleeping may occur with the bird in a sitting posture, with legs completely folded underneath and the abdomen resting on the substrate. Incubating adults also assume this posture. More frequently, resting cranes, especially young cranes, assume a "hock posture," with the "heel" or tarsal joint bearing the weight of the bird, and the body raised about 30 degrees above the horizontal. Frequently the toes are slightly flexed in this posture, so that only their tips touch the ground.

Resting on a single leg is frequent in adults, with one leg locked in a vertical position and the other lifted and hidden in the flank and belly feathers. Resting or sleeping on two legs is similar, but both legs bear the body's weight. In either case the head and neck may be held fairly erect, may be nearly resting on the breast, or may be drawn to the side and rear, with the bill tucked into the scapular feathers.

Walking and running are performed with a human-like movement, at rates of from less than one to more than three steps per second. When running fast, cranes achieve a bouncing gait, and occasionally a running crane will extend it wings and flap them to some extent, apparently to gain additional speed and maintain balance. In flight, the legs typically are held back in direct line with the body, but it is not uncommon to see cranes flying in cold weather with one or both legs tucked invisibly forward in the flank feathers, producing a goose-like flight profile.

Preening by cranes is a time-consuming activity that begins shortly after hatching and continues throughout life, especially during molting periods. Typically cranes preen a single region for up to about 20 seconds, then move to another area. Frequently the feather is nibbled at its base initially, and then the feather is gently drawn through the beak between the upper and lower mandibles. This is especially true of the longer body and wing feathers, the vanes of which must be kept in fine repair if they are to provide a suitable airfoil.

Bathing is performed by initially crouching in the

water and flapping the wings and is often accompanied with a bobbing movement of the body, which tends to spread water up and over the breast and back. Bathing periods may last for several minutes, and are followed by prolonged preening. Newly hatched cranes are able to swim surprisingly well, considering their absence of webbed feet, and even juveniles as old as three months have been observed swimming fairly easily (Walkinshaw, 1949).

A movement apparently derived from normal preening activities (fig. 4P) is "back-slicking." In this behavior, the head and bill are usually directed toward the uropygial gland at the base of the tail, apparently to obtain oil, and then the head and beak are vigorously rubbed over the surface of the back and wing, as well as over the underparts and rest of the body that can be reached by the bill. At least two species of cranes (the sandhill and Eurasian) perform a similar behavior after first digging in mud or a mixture of mud and grassy vegetation. The crane then performs "back-slicking," spreading the material over most of the body feathers and producing a stain that is usually a bright rusty brown. Such "feather-painting" was observed by Voss in cranes as young as 15 weeks old, but is especially characteristic of adult cranes on nesting territories. The functions of "feather-painting" are obscure at best, and at times feather stains have been considered to be only incidental effects of preening. However, as Walkinshaw (1949) and Drewien (1973) have observed, birds often perform these activities for hours, and it seems probable that the coloration has functional significance as a camouflaging device for nesting birds or, less probably, as an advertisement signal for reproductively active birds.

Ingestion of solid food is performed by pecking movements or by digging in the ground with the beak. Scratching with the feet is evidently rarely if ever used. Drinking is performed by dipping the bill in the water and quickly raising it upward and forward (fig. 4D). A single drinking sequence requires about five seconds, and it may be repeated up to seven times in succession.

Stretching by cranes occurs in three major forms. Frequently a single wing and the corresponding leg are stretched simultaneously (fig. 4W). At other times, both wings are stretched simultaneously as the back is held horizontal and the neck is held extended and nearly vertical. Finally, during "bow-stretching" (fig. 4B) the bird raises both wings simultaneously while extending the neck horizontally forward. The wings may be held in an extended position for several seconds before the head is raised and the wings are folded. At this time defecation often occurs. A yawnlike "jaw-stretching" also sometimes occurs in cranes, especially during periods of relative inactivity.

Miscellaneous egocentric behaviors include a fluffing of the plumage while in a relaxed posture, wing-flapping, a scratching of the head region with the middle toe, and a rapid ruffling of the body feathers accompanied by a vigorous rotary body-shaking, followed by a gradual lowering of the body feathers.

Social Behavior Patterns

A few postures, although perhaps incidental egocentric behaviors, indicate the internal state of the crane and thus its probable subsequent activity. For example, "feather-sleeking" while in seemingly tense posture is often performed in response to the approach of a human or a dog and probably communicates this awareness of potential danger to other cranes. Similarly, before taking flight the bird sleeks its body feathers, faces into the wind, extends its head and neck forward in a nearly horizontal position, and may utter a "flight-intention" call (fig. 4F). Voss observed this preflight posture in cranes only six weeks old, or about a month prior to their actual fledging.

When taking off or attacking an enemy, the crane rapidly runs forward, with wings flapping. As an attacking crane approaches its enemy it jumps strongly into the air, with legs thrust forward, kicking at the opponent (fig. 4A). Frequently both cranes jump and kick in this manner, until one finally retreats.

Such social interactions as threats and attacks are accompanied by a rather wide array of ritualized postures, which "announce" the bird's internal state and at least at times may serve to avoid or reduce the intensity of hostile encounters. All cranes seem to exhibit remarkably similar threat displays, and those described by Voss for the sandhill crane are probably applicable to most or all other species as well.

According to Voss, thirteen of the world's crane species have bare reddish or pink skin in the neck or head region, and in seven of the species this skin is limited to the forehead and crown area. In these species, the amount of bare skin can be varied by muscular contraction or relaxation, and there is also a variable amount of skin engorgement, affecting the intensity of the color exhibited. The reddish skin area is exposed under a variety of stressful stimuli, such as during threat display, while dancing, during unison calling, and during copulation. On the other hand, the area is small and inconspicuous during submission signals.

During intense aggressive threat or (thwarted?) attack in young cranes, or during defense of the nest by adult cranes (figs. 5D and 6N), a posture is assumed in which the wings are spread horizontally outward, drooping at the wrist to cause the primaries to actually or nearly

4. Behavior patterns in cranes, as illustrated by the sandhill crane, and including preening or back-slicking (P), wing-stretching (W), bow-stretching (B), flight-intention (F), drinking (D), and attack (A). After Voss (1976).

touch the ground. In such a posture the bird stands or walks about while facing the stressful object.

An unusual threat display, the "crouch" or "squat-threat" (fig. 7C), has been observed in sandhill cranes as young as eleven weeks old. In this posture the bird initially stands with expanded crown, beak pointing downward, and neck retracted. The tarsi are then bent, and the bird gradually lowers to a completely sitting posture. The beak is held strongly downward, the bare crown is expanded, and the wings remain loosely folded or slightly spread. After remaining nearly motionless in this attitude for several seconds, the bird typically stands up again.

In sandhill cranes, and probably in most other cranes as well, a major threat display is the "raised-tertial" posture (fig. 7T). In this posture the crown is expanded, the bill is horizontal or lowered, and the tertial feathers are raised to form a vertical fanlike shape. Under extreme conditions the bird will bend forward, so that its head is lowered and its bill points directly downward. This display is often followed by more intense threat signals. While in the "raised-tertial" position, the crane often performs a "parade walk," moving stiffly about at a rate of about one step per second, toward the threatened object or in a circular movement around it. At this time the engorged crown is tilted toward the opponent.

During such walking threats the "ruffle-preen" display (fig. 7R) is frequently performed. This display begins with a general erection of feathers on the neck, back, wings, and other surfaces. The wings are slightly opened and lowered, and the two wings are flapped alternately, giving the impression that the bird is shaking itself or "ruffling" rapidly from one side to the other. At this time the bill may be pointed downward and back toward the abdomen, finally touching the feathers of the leg or flanks in a ritualized preening movement, and a low growl is often uttered. In species such as the white-naped, Siberian, and demoiselle, preening is often directed toward the scapulars rather than the leg area (fig. 6D). In the Siberian crane this display has been called the "ruffle-bow-shoulder" display (Sauey, 1976). Finally, the bird stops ruffling and returns to a resting position, with its crown still expanded. A less elaborate "ruffle" display, in which the bill is scarcely lowered, is also sometimes used, and at times a ritualized foraging movement replaces the preening component. Voss observed the "ruffle" display in crane chicks as young as 14 weeks old, although at this age the display was not so fully ritualized as in adults.

A final ritualized form of aggression is the "charge" display (fig. 7Ch). This display often occurs immediately after a crane lands near a flock of cranes, while chasing another crane, or immediately after copulation. It may be performed while running, walking, or standing still. The crown is expanded, the neck and head are pointed directly downward, and the feathers at the base of the neck and back are strongly raised. This distinctive posture may be held for as much as 10 seconds, and jabbing at the ground or vegetation sometimes accompanies it. Voss observed the display in birds as young as 11 weeks old.

In contrast to these various threat displays, appeasement in cranes is indicated by the bird assuming a horizontal body posture with the neck retracted, the wings loosely folded, the bill more or less horizontal, and the bare crown area reduced and inconspicuous. The body feathers are slightly fluffed, and the bird seems to walk in a loose-jointed fashion, rather than in the stiff manner of the "parade march" (fig. 7A).

The dancing display of cranes is common to all species and is clearly an ancient type of behavior. Indeed, very similar behaviour occurs in trumpeters during apparent courtship. Although crane dancing is also generally believed to be associated with courtship, it is clearly much more complex than having that single function, and indeed may occur in birds less than two days old. Archibald (cited by Voss, 1976) noted that unpaired cranes from two to three years old seem to dance more than do any other age group, and that indeed dancing probably serves to thwart aggression and facilitate pair formation, but it also occurs in young birds as a normal part of motor development. He believes that dancing serves to synchronize pair members sexually prior to nesting, and noted that older pairs of cranes dance less than do younger birds, probably because of reduced needs for thwarting aggression and for sexual synchronization. Dancing also occurs in situations of limited danger, such as when humans are approaching from a distance, or while a person is retreating from a nesting site. Voss (1976) observed dancing in sandhill crane chicks from 82 days of age onward, and thereafter noted it in many situations. She divided dancing behavior into several component parts, which may occur in varying combinations. Flightless chicks dance by alternate wing-flapping, jumping or bouncing, and running movements. As the birds grow older, "bowing" (fig. 5B) and "stick-tossing" (fig. 5T) also become a part of the activity. Voss observed "bowing" in birds 14 weeks old, and stick-tossing at 17 weeks of age. During "bowing," the neck is retracted as the legs are bent, and the bird bends forward and extends or lifts its wings. It then quickly extends its neck and legs, followed by a return to the retracted position. "Bowing" is often interspersed with jumping or each bow may end with a jump. "Stick-tossing" is similar to bowing, but an object is quickly grasped

5. Behavior patterns in cranes, as illustrated by the sandhill crane (in part after Voss, 1976) and including bowing (B), tossing (T), and distraction (D) behavior.

6. Behavior patterns in cranes, including display-preening (D) in Eurasian
   crane (left), white-naped crane (middle), and Siberian crane (right)
   (based on personal photos), and nest-defense behavior (N) in the
   Australian crane (after a published photograph).

7. Behavior patterns in cranes, as illustrated by the sandhill crane, and including tertial-raising (T), appeasement (A), crouch-threat (C), ruffle-preen (R), and charge (Ch). After Voss (1976).

8. Copulatory behavior in the Eurasian crane, including preliminary male "parade march" posture (1), female receptive posture (2), and treading sequence (3-6). After drawings in Glutz (1973).

during the retraction phase, and as the bird extends its neck and legs it flings its bill upward, throwing the object into the air. The neck is then quickly retracted and the bird bows forward once again.

Copulatory behavior has been well described for the sandhill crane (Voss, 1976), the Japanese crane (Masatomi and Kitagawa, 1975), and the Eurasian crane (Glutz, 1973). Precopulatory behavior may be initiated by either sex, but usually seems to be started simultaneously. The male may be up to 50 meters from the female, and begins to walk toward her in "parade march," with tertials raised, crown expanded, bill pointed upward, and neck stretched nearly vertically. The female holds her body in much the same position, and as the male approaches her closely she extends her wings horizontally outward, drooping at the wrists. As the male comes nearer he lowers his bill until it is pointing slightly downward, and then flaps his wings once or twice as he leaps on her back. His toes are hooked over her forewings and his tarsi rest on her rump, as the female bends forward into a nearly horizontal position, with her head slightly raised. The male remains on the female's back for up to 5 seconds, while flapping his wings to maintain his balance. He dismounts by stepping off backward or hopping forward over her head (fig. 8).

Following a successful copulation there is a postcopulatory display that may last up to 20 seconds. The birds typically stand side by side, with their crowns expanded and their necks stretched vertically upward. They typically simultaneously perform a "charge" display, and then stand with their beaks horizontal and their crowns expanded for several seconds. Finally, a "ruffle-threat" or a "ruffle-leg-threat" may be performed. Foraging, preening, or dancing may follow later (Voss, 1976). In the Japanese crane bowing and neck-arching are invariable postcopulatory displays (Masatomi and Kitagawa, 1975).

Flight and Migratory Behavior

All cranes take flight after a running start, finally springing into the air and gradually building up speed. While in flight, the wings are moved in a distinctive manner, with a very rapid upstroke and a slower downstroke. This distinctively rapid upstroke is more noticeable among birds that are disturbed or frightened than during normal flight (fig. 9).

The flight speed of cranes has not been well studied, but radar studies of the Eurasian crane during spring migration over the southern Baltic area (Alerstam and Bauer, 1973) indicate that their airspeeds range from 37 to 52 miles per hour. Allen (1952) suggested that the cruising rate of the whooping crane was about 45 m.p.h. Unlike geese, however, cranes often sail for prolonged periods on set wings, especially when they are soaring in thermals. At such times the birds may remain aloft for hours on end, the flocks slowly turning in wide circles and gradually ascending until they are nearly lost from view. Pennycuick, Alerstam, and Larsson (1979) have studied the use of thermal-assisted soaring in the migration of Eurasian cranes. They observed cranes climbing in thermals to heights of up to 2,010 meters above sea level and noted that the best climbing range appeared to be between 500 and 1,300 meters. However, powered flight was the major method of migratory flight, with thermals used only as a supplemental energy source. Besides occurring in Eurasian and sandhill cranes, soaring has also been observed in the white-naped crane, but has not definitely been observed in crowned cranes (Pennycuick, Alerstam, and Larsson, 1979). It also occurs in the Japanese crane (Masatomi and Kitagawa, 1975), and perhaps even in the heavy sarus crane (Ali and Ripley, 1969).

Migration in the northern cranes follows a fairly predictable annual schedule, as is indicated in table 2 by the summary of whooping crane records during spring and fall migration periods in North America. Although sandhill cranes and Eurasian cranes typically migrate in rather large flocks, flock sizes in whooping cranes are relatively small, especially during fall (as is shown in the same table). These small flock sizes in the whooping crane are presumably a reflection of the extremely small total population size, although even in earlier days the sizes of migrating flocks of whooping cranes were not very large. In studies of sandhill cranes in Nebraska, Bliese (1976) reported that diurnal spring flocks also averaged relatively small, with about 77 percent consisting of 50 birds or less, and over 84 percent having no more than 100 birds present. Allen (1952) suggested that during spring migration the whooping crane flocks probably average about 112 to 120 miles of northward movement per day, perhaps the equivalent of only about three hours of flying time. Fall flocks, returning with young birds, probably move southward rather more slowly than do spring migrants. Melvin and Temple (1982) provide a recent review of migration behavior and ecology in sandhill cranes.

Roosting Behavior

With the exception of the crowned cranes, which regularly perch and roost at night in trees (Walkinshaw, 1973), cranes typically roost on the ground or while standing in shallow water. During spring migration, the broad and shallow Platte River in Nebraska provides a perfect roosting site for virtually all of the lesser and Canadian sandhill cranes east of the Rocky Mountains. Typically standing about four feet apart in water that is only deep enough to cover their toes, the birds

9. Take-off (T), flying (F), and landing (L) behavior in the Japanese crane. After Masatomi and Kitigawa (1975).

TABLE 2

Fall and Spring Whooping Crane Migration Records*

	Sept. (all)	October			November		
		1-10	11-20	21-31	1-10	11-20	21-30
Alberta, Saskatchewan, Manitoba	89	44	48	19	5	1	—
North Dakota, Montana	16	13	18	20	11	1	—
South Dakota	11	7	9	5	4	1	—
Nebraska	4	6	20	13	5	1	—
Kansas	—	3	13	23	7	2	—
Oklahoma, Texas	1	4	2	15	13	9	1

	March (all)	April			May			June (all)
		1-10	11-20	21-31	1-10	11-20	21-31	
Alberta, Saskatchewan, Manitoba	—	5	33	33	34	19	9	6
North Dakota, Montana	—	12	26	23	11	3	1	—
South Dakota	2	9	9	6	2	1	—	4
Nebraska	22	51	43	6	6	1	1	1
Kansas	10	6	7	1	—	—	—	—
Oklahoma, Texas	19	11	—	1	2	—	—	—

Migratory Flock Sizes of Whooping Cranes since mid-1940s†

	1	2	3	4	5	6	7	8	9+	Total	Mean
Spring	18	34	15	13	8	5	1	3	2	99	3.1
Fall	49	47	36	17	10	10	2	1	1	173	2.6

*Based mainly on records of Allen (1952) and Derrickson (1980); numbers indicate total sightings reported for each time period.
†Based on records of Derrickson (1980); numbers indicate total sightings for each flock size.

spend the night along the edges of sandy bars and islands near the middle of the river, well protected from terrestrial predators such as coyotes. In dense concentrations, up to about 100 cranes may occur in an area of 3,000 square feet, a density of roughly 30 square feet per crane. Submerged sandbars are favorite primary roosting sites in the Platte and are sometimes occupied by as many as 30,000 birds in a single roosting area. Frith (1974) described one such roost of 30,000 birds that "filled the river" to within some 30 feet from the nearer bank, and stretched out over a mile in linear distance. Although the birds use such primary roosts throughout the night, "secondary" roosts are used just after daybreak and immediately before sunset for preening, dancing, resting, and some foraging. These roosts are usually less than a half mile from the primary roosts, and are often moist fields or pastures near the river. Movements to and from the primary roosts are closely tied to the amount of light. In the morning, about 20 percent of the cranes typically leave the roost by sunrise, and nearly all are gone within 100 minutes after sunrise.

In the evening, about 80 percent of the birds arrive back on the roost during the hour of sunset, and nearly all are on the roost by 40 minutes after sunset. Cloud cover, fog, rain, and winds all strongly affect these schedules, and most movement seems to occur at light levels of 20 to 400 foot-candles (Lewis, 1979b).

Foraging Behavior

During daylight hours of the nonbreeding season, cranes spend nearly all of their time in fields or other habitats where foraging occurs. Studies of spring migrant flocks of sandhill cranes in Nebraska indicate that the daylight hours are spent almost entirely in croplands, native grasslands, and haylands; only 8 of more than 1,000 observations were in other habitat types (Fritzell, Krapu, and Jorde, 1979). All of these areas have unrestricted visibility, fairly low vegetation, and an abundance of foods. Thus in harvested cornfields corn is consumed almost exclusively, and invertebrates are eaten in native grasslands and hayfields (Reinecke and Krapu, 1979). Foraging in corn is evidently a more effective manner of obtaining food energy than is foraging for invertebrates, and thus corn probably provides more than 90 percent of the food matter by weight of the daily intake during spring migration. Some of the kernels are probably dug from the ground, while others are probably picked directly from ears still lying on the ground. Invertebrates such as earthworms are probably obtained by probing, and one can frequently find dried cow droppings that have been probed and broken apart by crane bills, presumably for the insect life within or underneath them.

On the other hand, foraging behavior of the whooping crane in its wintering grounds seems to be typically performed while wading, and much of its food consists of invertebrates that are actively stalked (Allen, 1952). The birds often move about in circles while stalking blue crabs (*Callinectes* sp.), and walk in single file along shallow edges of ponds while probing for mud shrimps (*Callianassa*) or marine worms (Neieridae).

Nesting and Incubation Behavior

All cranes construct substrate nests of herbaceous vegetation, usually close to water, although the demoiselle and blue cranes nest on dry ground among stubble, with only a few small stones and straws lining the shallow hollow in which they place the eggs. More typically, cranes nest in shallow water, constructing a rather haphazard pile of vegetation that is somewhat packed down and hollowed at the top to provide a cavity for the eggs. Drewien (1973) found that nests of the sandhill crane situated in dry or only semimoist areas tend to be smaller and more simply constructed than those in water, which were larger, more elaborate, and often contained considerable amounts of vegetational materials. He found that, in sandhill cranes, nest building required from about a day to more than a week, depending on nest complexity, and that both sexes participate in building the nest. In all cranes, incubation begins with the first egg, and both sexes share incubation duties. Drewien (1973) noted that all of five sandhill cranes captured on their nests at night were females. However, during daytime hours, the sexes probably share incubation duties about equally. Allen's (1952) studies of nesting whooping cranes indicate that early in incubation there were usually 6 nest exchanges per day between 5:00 a.m. and about 7:30 p.m., but later in incubation the average rose to 7.6 nest exchanges per day, with the male spending somewhat more time on the nest than the female. On the average, the male spent somewhat over two hours on the nest per sitting, while the female averaged slightly under an hour and a half.

During the entire incubation period, the male averaged about 70 percent of the total incubation time. Early observations by Cosgrave (1911) on the white-naped crane also suggested that the male took the initiative both in beginning incubation behavior and in feeding the newly hatched young.

Incubation behavior in probably essentially identical in all cranes, and has been analyzed into component categories by Masatomi and Kitagawa (1975). During much of the time, the bird sits in a head-erect posture. Periodically it may stand up in the nest and apparently gaze downward at the eggs, sometimes shifting the position of the eggs with the tip of the bill. Nest-repair is identical to nest-building behavior, except for the presence of eggs. The bird stretches its neck forward and downward to pick up a bit of vegetation and places the material at its side, or underneath it if it is standing. Unlike waterfowl, cranes sometimes also carry material to the nest site, as during nest-relief. While incubating, the sitting bird sometimes performs preening, head-shaking, painting, and yawning, (Masatomi and Kitagawa, 1975).

Parental Care

All cranes exhibit a prolonged period of parental care toward their young, sometimes lasting well beyond the period required for fledging. From the time of hatching the chicks are fed by both parents, which carry food to them by holding it in the tip of the bill. Then, with lowered head, they offer it to the chick or drop it in front of the chick. Gradually the adult begins to lead the young to the food sources, although for a considerable period the adults continue to carry some food to the chick. Thus, fish may be carried to the young of Japanese cranes even a few months after hatching (Masatomi and Kitagawa, 1975). Feeding of the young may begin almost immediately after the chick is out of the shell and dry; I have observed a greater sandhill crane break up bits of the eggshell and gently feed them to the newly hatched chick only an hour or so after the chick had escaped the shell.

Brooding of the young is performed in a posture similar to normal sitting. This is usually performed by the female if the pair has only one chick. The chick crawls into the feathers of the female from behind, and sometimes exposes its head from below the leading edge of the wing. When threatened, the chick may also be covered by the parent, which stands or stoops over it, spreading the wings over it (Masatomi and Kitagawa, 1975).

When adults are leading young, the male typically takes the lead, followed by the female, and finally the young. From shortly after hatching, bill-touching is

TABLE 3

Wing Molting Variations of Wild Sandhill Cranes*

	Number	Percent of Total	Percent of Subsample
1. Wings with all remiges of the same age	44	40.7	—
2. Wings with some remiges of different ages	64	59.3	—
Primaries of the same age	7	—	10.9
Primaries of different ages	57	—	89.1
Secondaries of the same age	24	—	37.5
Secondaries of different ages	40	—	62.5
3. Wings with aberrant primary molt†	104	—	—
Molt complete on 1 side	7	6.7	—
Molt incomplete on 1 or both sides	97	93.3	—
Molt continuous sequentially	51	—	52.6
Molt discontinuous, starting with primary #1	32	—	32.9
Molt discontinuous, not starting with primary #1	14	—	14.4
4. Wings with aberrant secondary molt†	120	—	—
Molt complete on 1 side	52	43.3	—
Molt incomplete on 1 or both sides	68	56.7	—
Molt continuous sequentially	26	—	38.2
Molt discontinuous, starting with secondary #1	22	—	32.3
Molt discontinuous, not starting with secondary #1	20	—	29.4

*Based on data of Lewis (1979c), from 108 specimens of three subspecies.
†Sample size is twice the number of cranes in the sample; each wing is considered separately.

fairly frequently performed between chicks and parents. This behavior, which may be associated with food-begging and direct feeding, sometimes occurs as late as the spring following hatching. It is normally initiated by the chick rather than the parents (Masatomi and Kitagawa, 1975).

When breeding cranes encounter enemies, either or both of two defensive behaviors may result. Animals such as feral cats, dogs, foxes, or deer may be "mobbed," a maneuver during which the adult cranes approach the intruder while uttering an "alarm" call and move around it at a safe distance until it retreats. When humans, dogs, or other animals approach a nest having eggs or young chicks, the parents may perform a diversionary display, moving away from the nest, with or without wing-spreading, and assuming a posture associated with intense aggressive threat (figs. 6 and 7). Sometimes one of the birds will fly away without making diversionary displays, and the other may run around the enemy while uttering alarm calls (Masatomi and Kitagawa, 1975).

Molting Behavior and Flightlessness

Like other birds, cranes molt their feathers periodically, in a fairly predictable and regular sequence. Discussion of the molting stages of chicks will be deferred until later, and at this point it need only be mentioned that adult cranes undergo a prolonged annual molt in late summer and fall. The feathers of the body, neck, and part of each wing are gradually molted between August and October in the sandhill crane (Walkinshaw, 1949), and it is likely that the same applies to cranes in general (Blaauw, 1897). However, the primaries, secondaries, and perhaps some of the tertials are molted earlier in the summer, and in several species the adult birds are unable to fly during this period. Blaauw (1897) indicated that this condition probably exists in the Eurasian, Japanese, whooping, Siberian, blue, sarus, and white-naped cranes, and it has since been observed in hooded and sandhill cranes. Moody (1932) stated that although flightlessness is regular in the Japanese, hooded, white-naped, sarus, blue, and Siberian cranes, the crowned and demoiselle never become flightless. He noted that the flightless period of a blue crane lasted for a month. Heinroth and Heinroth (1958) attributed the lack of a flightless period in the demoiselle crane to its adaptation to an arid, steppe-like environment, and perhaps the same might be applied to the crowned crane.

During the molting period the birds spend much time preening and rearranging their feathers. They also remain in heavy cover and are highly elusive throughout the flightless period (Walkinshaw, 1973).

It has recently become apparent that there are intermediate stages between the completely flightless condition of most cranes associated with a simultaneous molting of the flight feathers, and the progressive molting of the wing feathers reported for crowned and demoiselle cranes. Lewis (1979c) has reported a rather surprising variation in the extent of wing molt in wild sandhill cranes (table 3), and it is probable that similar sorts of variations occur among Eurasian cranes (Glutz 1973; Cramp and Simmons, 1980).

Vocalizations

3 Of all avian sounds, few have the power to catch the human imagination and thrill the senses as much as does the bugling of a flock of distant cranes. Leopold (1949) referred to the progressively louder sounds of an approaching flock of sandhill cranes as "a tinkling of little bells," the "baying of some sweet-throated hound," and finally as "a pandemonium of trumpets, rattles, croaks and cries." The Greeks called it "iangling," and most recent writers have compared the calls of typical *Grus* cranes to trumpets or bugles. In doing so, they have inadvertently drawn attention to the similarity of the calls to the sounds generated by musical instruments, and it is important to investigate the similarities and dissimilarities between the vocalizations of cranes and the sounds generated from man-made musical instruments.

Crane Vocabularies

The vocal repertoires of nonpasserine birds seem generally to be fairly limited, and rather infrequently exceed about fifteen distinctly different signals, or call types (Thorpe, 1961). In contrast to the songs of at least some passerine birds, the calls of cranes seem to represent innately acquired signal systems that are not subject to experiential modifications nor are they evidently dependent upon gradual acquisition of significance through associative learning during an individual's lifetime (Archibald, 1975). Rather, they are stereotyped vocal performances, instinctively performed and responded to, and, as such, they play an extremely important role in the integration of the complex social behavior patterns of cranes, which primarily rely on vision and hearing for evaluating their social and physical environments.

Based on his studies of blue, sandhill, Eurasian, and Japanese cranes, Archibald (1975) has provided a complete inventory of gruine vocalizations, and a less complete survey of crowned crane calls (table 4). The following summary of crane vocabularies is derived from his observations.

Cranes begin to vocalize at the time of hatching, uttering high-pitched peeping calls that subsequently persist for most of the first year of life. The first two types of calls uttered by hatching and newly hatched chicks are the contact call and the stress call. The contact call is a low-amplitude, purring call that indicates the chick's well-being and its proximity to its parents. It is uttered almost constantly during foraging or while being brooded. Separation from the adults, chilling, hunger, or other similar stressful conditions elicit the stress call, a loud, unbroken call likely to attract the attention of the adults.

A food-begging call is usually uttered within the first 24 hours after hatching, and is a plaintive peeping note that stimulates feeding of the young by its parents. It occurs with diminishing frequency until the young bird is about a year old, or well after actual feeding by the parents has terminated.

At about the time of fledging, the flight-intention call is first uttered. This is a brief, high-frequency unbroken call that is uttered as the bird stands erect and faces into the wind. At about this time the alarm call also appears. It is a lower-pitched, more broken, and rapidly uttered call that is given in response to a frightening stimulus.

For most of the first year of life, these five calls constitute the young crane's vocabulary, but in times of extreme threat the guard call may occasionally be heard. The guard call is often uttered during the collective threat of parents and chick toward other crane families, but at times it may also be directed toward somewhat frightening stimuli, such as a distant dog. It is a loud, single-syllable call.

At the age of about 8 or 9 months (Eurasian crane) or 10 to 11 months (blue, sandhill, and Japanese cranes), the chick begins to lose its peeping voice and to acquire the lower, more gutteral voice of the adult. The contact

TABLE 4

List of Call Types of *Balearica* and *Grus* Cranes*

Call Type	Age When Uttered	Balearica	Grus
Contact Call	Throughout life	Present	Present
Food-begging Call	Chicks only	Present	Present
Stress Call	Mainly in chicks	Present	Present
Flight-intention Call	From fledging onward	Absent	Present
Alarm Call	From fledging onward	?	Present
Guard Call	After voice change	Present	Present
Location Call	After voice change	Present	Present
Unison Call	After 24 months	Present	Present
Precopulation Call	After 24 months	Present	Present
Click Call	As adults	Present	Absent
Quack Call	As adults	Present	Absent
Booming Call	As adults	Present	Absent
Grunt Call	As adults	Present	Absent
Nesting Call	When nesting	Absent	Present
Total chick calls		3	3
Total adult calls		8	8
Total calls		11	10

*Based primarily on descriptions of Archibald (1975, and pers. comm.).

call then becomes more low-pitched, and is used subsequently as a signal between "familiar" birds. At this time the food-begging call disappears, and the stress call becomes only rarely uttered. The flight-intention, alarm, and guard calls all become much louder.

After the voice change, a few major new calls appear. One, the location call, resembles the guard call but is more plaintive, and is used to vocally locate other cranes after visual separation. A second new call is the precopulatory call. This consists of a series of purr-like notes uttered with the crane in a distinctive posture.

Perhaps the most significant new call to emerge with vocal maturity is the unison call. This is typically not uttered by cranes until their second or third year of life, when they begin to pair. Unlike the single-noted guard call, the unison call is a complex and extended series of temporally coordinated calls uttered by a pair with the birds standing in a specific posture and in a specific spatial relationship to one another.

While nest-building, paired cranes emit a low, moaning nesting call, often while arranging nesting materials, or while the female is sitting on the nest in preparation to laying an egg.

Although the crowned cranes exhibit many of these same calls, they also have some unique calls that do not appear to be shared with any of the more typical gruine cranes, according to Archibald. Chicks of *Balearica* utter a contact call similar to that of *Grus*, but it is of lower frequency and more broken. A call possibly comparable to the stress call of *Grus* has been heard in crowned crane chicks, and food-begging calls are also present in these chicks (G. Archibald, pers. comm.). Yearling crowned cranes have been heard uttering guard calls, and the unique "booming call" has been observed in birds as young as 17 months old. In this call the gular sac is inflated and apparently serves as an adjunct resonator as a low-pitched call is produced. A unique "quack call" also occurs in crowned cranes, and is apparently used for mate location. Likewise, a distinctive "click call" is uttered when investigating a novel object. The unison call of *Balearica* usually consists of a guard call duet followed by a boom duet.

Interspecific Differences in the Unison Call

Archibald (1975, 1976) has provided an excellent comparison of the unison calls of all crane species except the black-necked crane, and unless otherwise indicated the following discussion is based on his summary.

In all cranes, the unison call is uttered with the crane in an erect, alert posture, with folded wings. In the crowned cranes, the pair members may or may not be standing close together, and either sex can begin the call. Additionally, the display is of varied length, and may last for more than a minute. The wings are not moved during the sequence, and the birds remain standing at a single place throughout. Typically, crowned cranes begin the display as a series of guard calls, which sometimes occur during the later booming sequence or may follow it. In the West African form (*pavonina*) the guard calls are monosyllabic honks, but in the eastern and South African forms (*gibbericeps* and *regulorum*) these calls are distinctly disyllabic, and the booming calls are lower in pitch, in correlation with the larger gular sacs.

In all other species of cranes, the unison calls are shorter, more penetrating, and lack booming, although the upper throat area may be expanded. Further, the sexes usually stand side by side while calling, and the wings are often raised or drooped. The sexes call in synchrony, but the calls as well as the postures assumed by the two sexes are different from one another.

In the genera *Bugeranus* and *Anthropoides* the calls are of a determinate length (up to 7 seconds). The two species of *Bugeranus* (wattled and Siberian cranes) have several features in common, including a relatively high-pitched call in both sexes and a rapid uncoiling of the neck of the male as he begins his display. However, unlike other cranes, in the Siberian crane the male begins the display, and unlike the situation in the wattled crane the display is of indeterminate length (Archibald, 1976). Males, and sometimes also females, lower the black primaries in the Siberian crane, but in the wattled crane the wings are held tightly against the body (fig. 10).

In the genus *Anthropoides*, the unison call is typically introduced by the guard call, and both calls are low, grating, and tend to lack harmonic development. The female typically begins the display, and one female call is normally uttered for each male call. In the demoiselle crane, the female begins by calling while extending her head back behind the vertical axis, while the male holds his head nearly vertically. In the blue crane the female holds her extended neck and head slightly behind the vertical throughout the display, while the male holds his head back even further and droops his primaries while raising his humeri, exposing the dark flight feathers (fig. 10).

In the genus *Grus*, the display is of indeterminate length, depending on intensity of stimulation, with the female usually beginning the call. In most species the female utters two or even three calls per male call. According to Archibald, three species groups in the genus *Grus* can be recognized on the basis of variations in the unison call.

The species group *canadensis* consists of the sandhill crane alone. In it, both sexes keep their wings folded throughout the display, and there is little wing-raising on the part of the male. With each call by the female, her bill is elevated about 45 degrees and is returned to the horizontal between calls. Males vary considerably in their head and wing movements.

The species group *antigone* includes the sarus, Australian, and white-naped cranes. In these species the female begins the display, initially elevating her bill to or beyond the vertical but later returning the bill to a less extreme angle. The male extends his head and neck to an extreme posture beyond the vertical, and lowers the primaries while raising the humeri throughout the display. The pair typically stand side by side, sometimes even touching one another (fig. 10). In the Australian crane the large gular sac is inflated at the end of the display, and one or two long and very low-pitched calls are uttered, presumably homologous to the booming calls of *Balearica*.

The species group *americana* includes the hooded, Eurasian, whooping, and Japanese cranes. The display is usually initiated by the female, with a long scream-like call followed by a series of shorter calls that average two or three per male call. The female initially extends her head and neck beyond the vertical, but later moves it more forward, while the degree of the neck extension and angular position varies with species and situation. Likewise, the amount of wing elevation and feather erection in males varies with degree of stimulation and threat. Pair members often walk toward the threatened object during the display. According to Archibald, the unison call of the Japanese crane varies between populations, with the Japanese form typically producing a call in which the female utters two or three short calls for every male call, while the mainland population females utter a long call followed by a short call for every male call.

Crane Vocalizations and Tracheal Variations

It has long been known that there is a relationship between the structure of the trachea in cranes and their remarkably loud and penetrating calls. Topsell (1972) reported that the French naturalist Pierre Bollonius (1517-1564) determined by dissection that the "throat bole" of cranes differed from those of all other birds, in that it "is fastened to the fleshe, as deepe as the ribbes without dependance on the intralls," and that this is the "true cause why their voices be hearde, before their bodies be seene." By 1575 the tracheal configuration of the Eurasian crane had been illustrated by V. Coiter, and subsequently most of the cranes of the world were described as to their tracheal condition. The monographic review by Berndt (1938), which deals with tracheal coiling in cranes, swans, and the relatively few other groups of birds in which it occurs, is still the most complete coverage of this subject.

On the basis of the work of Berndt and others, it is clear that the cranes exhibit a series of interspecific variations that provide a probable evolutionary progression of tracheal modifications affecting both the total tracheal length and the relationships of the trachea to the keel of the sternum.

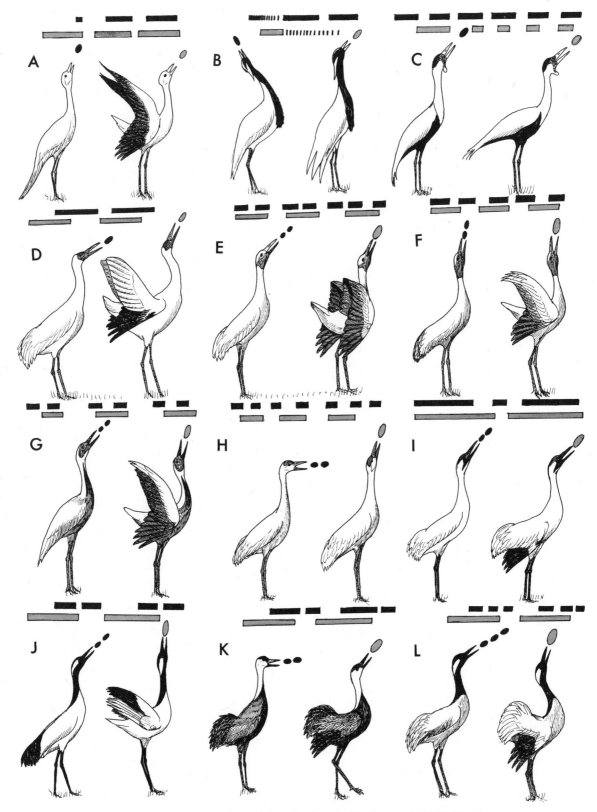

10. Unison-call posturing of blue (A), demoiselle (B), wattled (C), Siberian (D), Australian (E), sarus (F), white-naped (G), sandhill (H), whooping (I), Japanese (J), hooded (K), and Eurasian (L) cranes. Durations of male (shaded) and female (inked) vocalizations are indicated by bars above. "Balloons" indicate typical number of female calls per male call. After Archibald (1974).

In the generalized or "primitive" condition of the trachea in the crowned crane, the trachea passes back into the thoracic cavity directly (fig. 3). This is presumably the ancestral crane condition, and it might be noted that the recently found *Balearica*-like crane fossils from the late Miocene of Nebraska are sufficiently well preserved that many of the tracheal semirings are still intact, and these indicate a similar direct tracheal route (Gregory Brown, pers. comm.).

In all other surviving species of cranes the trachea of both sexes in the adult crane is looped downward to come into contact with the anterior edge of the sternum. In the wattled crane the loop is a simple S-shape, with the leading edge of the sternum recessed but not excavated to receive the tracheal tube (fig. 11). Evidently a very similar condition exists in the Siberian crane (Archibald, 1976).

In the genus *Anthropoides*, the condition is more like that of *Bugeranus* than of *Grus*. In the demoiselle crane a more extensive degree of tracheal invasion of the sternum may be seen (fig. 11), but the anterior edge of the trachea is still fully exposed to view. This is also the case with the blue crane (fig. 11).

Within the genus *Grus*, all species exhibit a relatively extensive excavation of the sternum by the trachea, which ranges from a relatively simple looping in the sandhill crane to a double looping that extends to the very posterior end of the keel in the whooping crane (fig. 11).

One of the obvious effects of such tracheal invasion of the sternum is a considerable increase in total tracheal length. This is well illustrated in table 5, in which the total average tracheal length may be seen to vary from about 50 centimeters in the crowned cranes and the demoiselle crane to more than 160 centimeters in the Japanese crane. The most obvious correlation of variations in tracheal lengths among crane species has to do with the vocalizations of adult cranes (table 5). It may be seen that, as the tracheal length is increased to increased tracheal invagination of the sternum, the adult vocalizations become progressively more penetrating and "whooping." On the other hand, there is no clear-cut direct relationship between tracheal length and the mean fundamental frequency of the unison call (table 6), or to the number of harmonics that are usually generated. What does seem to be true is that species with longer tracheae tend to show less fluctuation of frequencies when calling, and also tend to show better harmonic development than those species lacking tracheal elongation. Thus, harmonics are most poorly developed in the genus *Anthropoides*, which lacks both tracheal elongation and gular sacs, while as many as eight harmonics are developed in the crowned cranes (which have gular sacs) and from five to seven harmonics are typical of sarus, white-naped, hooded, Australian, Eurasian, and whooping cranes, all of which have greatly elongated tracheae. On the other hand, the Japanese crane exhibits little harmonic development, according to Archibald, in spite of its extremely elongated trachea. In common with the whooping crane, however, it shows a high degree of constancy of frequency during the unison and guard calls, especially among males.

Niemeier (1979b) has investigated the possible resonating role of the trachea in the vocalizations of sandhill cranes during ontogeny. She determined that calls after the "voice break" exhibited their greatest amplitude development at frequencies coincidental with the harmonic frequencies that would be generated from an open tube equal in length to the tracheal length of a bird. Thus, as in the swans and other Anatidae (Johnsgard, 1971), the crane's trachea evidently operates like an open-tube acoustical system. However, Niemeier also found that at the upper end of the trachea's length (in birds approaching a year or older), the trachea may be as much as 2.26 times longer than would be necessary to produce the fundamental frequencies actually generated by the birds. Adult-type bugling and similar calls were observed only after the trachea had reached a length in excess of 55 centimeters, and a diameter in excess of 1 centimeter.

It would thus seem that the cranes have "accepted" the respiratory penalties associated with an unusually long trachea (and thus an increased volume of "dead" tracheal air to be exchanged with each breath) for certain acoustical benefits. These benefits are evidently not lowered vocal frequencies *per se*, but instead may be associated with increased acoustic potential for harmonic development (and thus increased overall carrying power). Or more highly specific and individualized "tuning" of the syrinx may be possible, associated with individual differences in tracheal lengths, and possibly unique vocal characteristics might facilitate individual recognition. Both would have considerable advantages to birds such as cranes, which clearly rely heavily on vocalizations for their social signals. Evidently tracheal elongation must have certain acoustic advantages over the gular sacs for vocal resonance: otherwise one would have predicted that the latter device would have been retained and used in *Grus*, while in fact only the Australian crane seems to have retained or developed a functional gular sac.

Tracheal and Syringeal Development*

Elongated tracheae, arranged *in situ* in loops or coils, are presently known to occur in some 57 species of birds representing six orders (Gruiformes, Galliformes, Anseriformes, Ciconiiformes, Charadriiformes, and Passeriformes). There are actually four different types of anatomical associations of the coiled or looped tracheal tube in the class Aves. Tracheal coiling may be (1)

*This section contributed by Dr. Myra Mergler Niemeier, Iowa State University

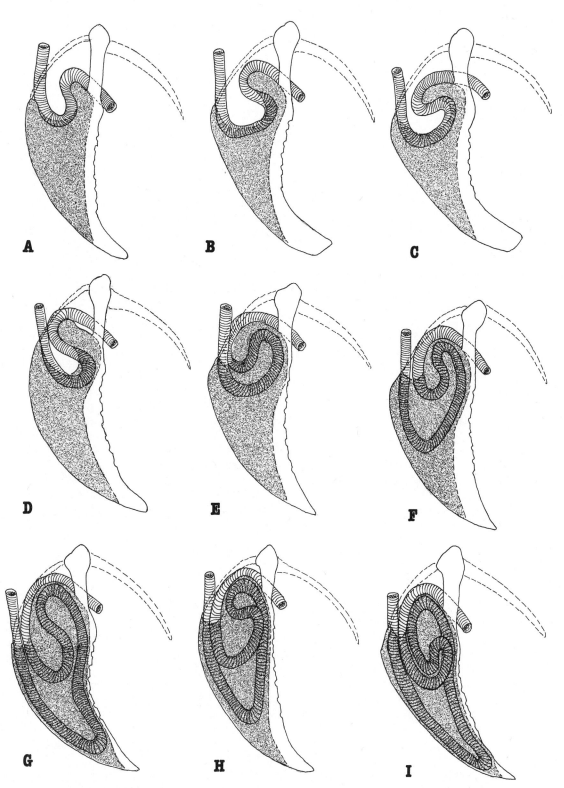

11. Adult tracheal and sternal anatomy of wattled (A), demoiselle (B and C), blue (D), sandhill (E), sarus (F), Eurasian (G), and whooping (H and I) cranes. In part after Berndt (1938).

TABLE 5

Crane Vocalizations and Sternal Characteristics

Species	Body Index*	Tracheal Invagination[†]	Vocal Characteristics[‡]
East African and South African Crowned Cranes	827	6.03	Mellow, disyllabic; also lower-pitched booming with gular sac, male lower than female, with fewer harmonics
West African Crowned Crane	763	7.04	Mellow, goose-like honk; higher-pitched booming with gular sac, male lower than female, and fewer harmonics
Blue Crane	887	57.44	Low-pitched, broken calls, little harmonic development, male lower than female
Demoiselle Crane	705	39.52	Low-pitched broken calls, no harmonic development, male lower than female
Wattled Crane	1,131	46.83	High-pitched scream, harmonics to ca. 5 kH., male lower than female
Siberian Crane	1,050	45.63	Musical call, harmonics to ca. 5 kH., male lower than female
Australian Crane	996	122.17	Very penetrating whooping, male calls lower than female and modified by gular sac, harmonics to ca. 5 kH. in female
Sarus Crane	1,105	109.9	Very penetrating whooping, most harmonics under 4 kH. in female, male lower than female
White-naped Crane	961	168.5	Very penetrating whooping, most harmonics under 4 kH., male lower than female
Sandhill Crane	797	64.53	Loud but less penetrating and pulsed calls, harmonics to ca. 6 kH., male lower than female
Whooping Crane	1,039	179.0	Very penetrating whooping, most harmonics under 4 kH., male lower than female
Japanese Crane	1,074	198.75	Very penetrating whooping, most harmonics under 3 kH., male lower than female
Hooded Crane	805	139.0	Loud but less penetrating whooping, male relatively high-pitched but lower than female, harmonics to ca. 5 kH.
Black-necked Crane	983	?**	Very penetrating whooping
Eurasian Crane	905	150.5	Very penetrating whooping, most harmonics under 4 kH., male lower than female

*Sum of exposed culmen, wing (chord), and tarsus in millimeters, from Wood (1976) except for black-necked crane.
[†]Based on measurements of Wood (1976); distance from anteriormost point of sternum to most posterior point of tracheal invagination, in millimeters.
[‡]Based on descriptions of Walkinshaw (1973) and Archibald (1975).
**Measurements not available, reported as "extensive" by Walkinshaw (1973).

TABLE 6

Tracheal Lengths and Fundamental Frequencies of Unison Calls, Various Cranes

Species	Average Tracheal Length (in centimeters)*			Fundamental Freq. (Hz)†	Tracheal References
	Intrasternal	Extrasternal	Total		
West African Crowned Crane	0	51.0(3)	51.0(3)	♂ 440-860 ♀ 590-920	Berndt, 1938 Archibald, 1975
East African Crowned Crane	0	53.5(2)	53.5(2)	♂ 470-970 ♀ 540-970	Archibald, 1975
Blue Crane	9.6(2)	55.0(2)	64.6(2) 58.7(3)	♂ 860 ♀ 1,240	Berndt, 1938 Archibald, 1975
Demoiselle Crane	9.7(1)	44.8(1)	54.5(1)	♂ 840 ♀ 1,400	Berndt, 1938
Wattled Crane	0	86.6(1)	86.6(1)	♂ 1,400 ♀ 1,700	Archibald, 1975
Australian Crane	—	—	106.9(8)	♂ 570 ♀ 880	Archibald, 1975
Sarus Crane	28.9(5)	—	88.1(4) 107.7(2)	♂ 1,090 ♀ 1,270	Berndt, 1938 Archibald, 1975
White-naped Crane	—	—	121.8(3)	♂ 770 ♀ 1,270	Archibald, 1975
Lesser Sandhill Crane	13.0(2)	43.0(1)	56.0(1)	♂ 510 ♀ 900	this study
Greater & Florida Sandhill Cranes	—	—	59.1(11)	♂ 500-550 ♀ 890-900	Niemeier, 1979b
Whooping Crane	71.0(1)	76.0(1)	147.0(1) 151.7(2)	♂ 790 ♀ 690-890	Coues, 1874 Archibald, 1975
Japanese Crane	—	—	162.8(1)	♂ 1,030 ♀ 1,110-1,190	Archibald, 1975
Hooded Crane	—	—	118.2(2)	♂ 770 ♀ 1,150-1,200	Archibald, 1975
Eurasian Crane	47.6(3)	—	109.6(3) 118.2(6)	♂ 1,030 ♀ 1,100-1,190	Berndt, 1938 Archibald, 1975

*Sample size indicated in parentheses, mean indicated for samples of more than one.
†Mean "basal frequency" of main portion of unison call, according to Archibald (1975).

superficial, that is, beneath the skin on the surface of the pectoral muscle or abdomen, (2) in association with the clavicle, (3) coiled within the thoracic cavity, or (4) within the sternum. Occurrence of this intrasternal housing of the trachea is second to the most common condition of superficial tracheal coiling. Intrasternal tracheal coiling is found in the majority of swan and crane species and is not found in any other avian family.

The order Gruiformes has received considerable attention in reference to tracheal structure. The most extreme degree of intrasternal tracheal elongation and convolution in this order is seen in various adult members of the family Gruidae.

Berndt's (1938) extensive review of the literature prior to the mid-1930s concerned tracheal and sternal anatomy in the cranes, excluding the white-naped crane, the hooded crane, the Japanese crane, and the black-necked crane. In 1973, Walkinshaw summarized the tracheal anatomy of all 15 species of cranes and presented subjective assessments of the tracheal length of one species relative to another (see table 5).

The relationship between the growth of the sternum and the trachea was documented by Schneider (1788-89, cited in Berndt, 1938), who showed that the sternum was not completely ossified in a pullet of the Eurasian crane, thus implying a developmental aspect to this sterno-tracheal relationship. In this example, only the "foremost and uppermost portions of the keel were ossified" (Schneider, 1788-89). Yarrell (1827) was apparently the first individual to note the developmental relationship between the sternum and the trachea in cranes with convoluted tracheae. In his examination of two specimens of the Eurasian crane he noted that one was "evidently a young bird by the state of the bones in which the insertion of the trachea is not carried so far as in the 'older bird'." Yarrell (1827) assumed that the greater "depth of insertion" (of the trachea) occurred only in male cranes. However, lack of sexual dimorphism relative to crane tracheal morphology is supported by Portmann (1959) and G. W. Archibald (pers. comm.).

W. K. Parker (1868) described and illustrated sternal and shoulder girdle structure in crowned cranes, in the Japanese crane, and in the sarus crane. Of particular interest is his description and illustration of the "shoulder bones and sternum of a recently hatched Manchourian [Japanese] Crane." Like Schneider (1788-89), Parker stated that the lateral parts of the sternum ossify first. Parker also described the association of the sternum and the trachea in developing Japanese and sarus cranes. The newly hatched Japanese crane showed only a shallow depression in the anterior surface of the sternum which accommodated a slight flection of the trachea. This depression was described as being much more extensive in a "half-grown" sarus, where "the tracheal loop turns suddenly upwards, apparently causing non-development and absorption of the bone, nearly to the lower coracoid lip" (Parker, 1868). Thus, Parker was the first to propose a possible mechanism by which the trachea is able to invade the sternum.

Roberts (1880) investigated the ontogeny of the tracheosternal apparatus in the sandhill crane. He examined an embryonic crane collected in Minnesota (probably a greater sandhill crane) that was about to hatch. Roberts described the trachea as "simple" (not entering the sternum) and described the sternum as being "entirely cartilaginous." Roberts was the first to state that tracheosternal development is an age-dependent phenomenon. He also described the adult position of the trachea within the sternum in both the sandhill crane and the whooping crane. (Tracheal coils extend to the posteriormost perimeter of the sternum in the whooping crane, but are confined to the anterior portion in sandhills.) He described the rest of the keel as being "composed of two frail plates separated by a thin layer of bony meshwork" (Roberts, 1880).

Coues (1892) referred to the tracheal structure of two "species" of sandhill crane, *canadensis*, the "Northern" sandhill crane and *pratensis*, the "Southern" sandhill crane, noting that "the trachea is at first simple and straight . . . [in the adult] the anterior half of the keel . . . is excavated to receive the [tracheal] folds." Pycraft (1913) described the same developmental phenomenon and speculated on the reciprocal processes involved in sternal excavation and tracheal invasion.

Age-dependent development of the sternum and trachea apparently caused Forbes (1882) to incorrectly assume that the female wattled crane possesses a highly convoluted trachea and that the male's is straight (as in both sexes of the Siberian crane).

Portmann (1959) was the first to correctly summarize tracheosternal development in swans and cranes. He explained that tracheal elongation and convolution attains the adult form "after several months" in the cranes (no species specified), unlike the swans, which do not attain the adult tracheal morphology until they are over one year of age. Portmann described the changes that take place in the cranial portion of the gruid sternum as a result of tracheal penetration, which was previously diagramed by Berndt (1938). G. W. Archibald (pers. comm.) also noted differences in tracheal structure in six newly hatched to newly fledged sandhill cranes.

Because the early, primarily anecdotal accounts of tracheal morphology in presumably immature cranes were chance findings for a variety of crane species of unknown age, no systematic study had been done to illustrate the process of tracheosternal development in known-age cranes with elongated tracheae. Niemeier (1979b) investigated this process in Florida cranes and greater sandhill cranes by x-raying captive-reared individuals with ages ranging from 3 days to 14 years.

Tracheal growth within the sandhill crane sternum was found to proceed as a gradual penetration of the initially cartilaginous tracheal loop into the cartilaginous sternum. The lateral portions of the sternum ossify first. The trachea reached its mature length (approximately 60 cm—see table 5) between 70 and 90 days of age, implying an average tracheal elongation rate of 0.6 cm per day.

The process of intrasternal tracheal elongation and coiling can be viewed as a dynamic interplay between the developing trachea and sternum. As the tracheal loop forces its way into the sternum, a concavity must be developed to allow for tracheal penetration. In early stages, this concavity is apparently the result of sternal growth. But, as the process of ossification begins, breaking down and rebuilding of sternal cartilage or bone is obviously necessary to accommodate the coiling of the tracheal loop.

Although tracheal development in these cranes is usually complete at two to three months of age, further coiling of the tracheal loop (found in 10, or 44 percent, of the 23 specimens examined) may be the result of a delay in sternal ossification or temporal extension of the building up and breaking down of intrasternal bone or cartilage. This may be especially true in the case of the greater sandhill crane, where intrasternal tracheal coiling is apparently more extensive but tracheal length is not significantly greater than it is in the Florida race. Tracheal elongation must be appreciably more rapid than sternal excavation for tracheal coiling to occur.

That is, the process of sternal enlargement must be slower than the process of tracheal elongation to force the tracheal loop to coil within this space. In fact, the rate of tracheal elongation is about five times that of sternal growth.

A space forms between the trachea at the point of flexure and the concavity on the anterior surface of the sternum. This indicates that the sternal excavation necessary for early penetration of the tracheal loop into the sternum is facilitated by sternal growth.

At various points during its ontogenetic development, the sandhill crane reflects the adult tracheal condition found in other species of cranes. This varies from the slight penetration of the trachea into the sternum in the unhatched chick (reflecting the tracheal condition of the adult Siberian crane and the wattled crane) to the moderately coiled trachea characteristic of adults of several species of *Grus*. Lastly, the adult status of extensive tracheal coiling is similar to (or even exceeded by) the tracheal coiling found in the Japanese, whooping, Eurasian, and black-necked cranes (Walkinshaw, 1973).

The problems of possible respiratory inefficiency associated with an elongated trachea have apparently been avoided in cranes by several means. The constant positive relationship between tracheal diameter and tracheal length (to 50 cm) indicates that, to this point at least, the sandhill crane avoids increased tracheal resistance to the airstream by increasing tracheal diameter relative to length. This idea has been suggested by Hinds and Calder (1971) for avian species whose tracheal volumes far exceeded those predicted by their body mass as a result of tracheal convolution; the sandhill crane's tracheal volume exceeds these predictions by 3.2:1 in males, second only to the 3.8:1 ratio of the trumpeter swan (*Cygnus buccinator*).

Unlike the mammalian larynx, which is a pre-bronchial structure (that is, it is located anterior to the bronchi), the most common type of avian syrinx is associated with the bronchi and is designated as a tracheobronchial type. Nonpasserine birds such as cranes have the most simplistic type of syrinx, formed of membranes in the inner and outer walls of the trachea at the point where it branches into the two bronchi. Tension on these two sets of tympaniform membranes is apparently controlled, in part, by only two sets of muscles, which are external to the trachea itself. Contraction of the sternotracheal musculature allows the syringeal membranes to bow into the lumina of the bronchi, creating slits through which air passes, thus setting the membranes into vibration (Sutherland and McChesney, 1965).

Because of their increasing size but consistent thinness (approximately 0.01 mm) during development, the internal tympaniform membranes are thought to be the primary sound-producing structures in cranes. The external tympaniform membranes were found by Niemeier (1979b) to be much smaller and thicker, with a high degree of variability in thickness. Both the internal and the external tympaniform membranes have been implicated as the sources of sound production in other types of birds.

The fundamental, or pitch-determining, frequencies emitted by the vibrating syringeal membranes (the voice of a bird) have historically been thought to be determined by tracheal length. This relationship, however, is not at all clear-cut, and evidence has been accumulated both for and against this effect in birds. Sandhill cranes show an independence of emitted carrier or pitch-determining frequencies and tracheal length during development.

1. South African crowned crane, adult. Photo by K. B. Newman.

2. West African crowned crane, adults. Photo by author.

3. South African crowned crane, adult at nest. Photo by W. R. Tarboton.

4. Blue crane, adult incubating. Photo by K. B. Newman.

5. Blue crane, adults at nest. Photo by K. B. Newman.

6. Demoiselle crane, adult. Photo by author.

7. Wattled crane, adult incubating. Photo by W. R. Tarboton.

8. Wattled crane, adult. Photo by author.

9. Siberian crane, adult. Photo by author.

10. Siberian crane, adult. Photo by author.

11. Australian crane, adult. Photo by author.

12. Sarus crane, adult. Photo by author.

13. White-naped crane, adult. Photo by author.

14. Greater sandhill crane, adult incubating. Photo by author.

15. Greater sandhill crane, family. Photo by author.

16. Whooping crane, adults in flight. Photo by Tom Mangelsen.

17. Whooping crane, adults in Saskatchewan. Photo by Tom Mangelsen.

18. Japanese crane, adult. Photo by author.

19. Japanese crane, yearling birds. Photo by author.

20. Black-necked crane, adult. Photo by William Conway.

21. Black-necked crane, adult. Photo by William Conway.

22. Hooded crane, juvenile. Photo by author.

23. Eurasian crane, adult at nest. Photo by L. H. Walkinshaw.

Ecology and Population Dynamics

Like other animals, cranes exist as natural populations that are dependent upon particular environmental conditions and that vary in population density between the absolute minimum numbers that have permitted survival to relatively dense populations that may approach or even temporarily exceed the carrying capacity of the habitat. Each species may also have an upper species-typical limit on population density, or "saturation point," which is independent of the carrying capacity of the habitat but which may be determined by such social adaptations as territorial requirements or individual distance characteristics. Within crane populations, individual birds or families remain within home ranges or geographic areas in which their movements are limited and within which they may spend much of their lives. Part of the occupied area may be defended from intrusion by conspecifics for varying periods; these areas of local social dominance range from individual distances to territories and probably play important roles in determining space requirements for crane populations. During periods of the year when breeding or wintering territories are not held, as during migration, dominance hierarchies serve to integrate the activities of the family and flock, and may likewise play important roles in population behavior and ecology. Interspecific differences in morphology and innate behavior patterns may further dictate specific foraging niches for each species, and these too may be of importance in regulating potential population sizes in cranes and in determining competition levels with other species.

Crane populations, whatever their densities, may be analyzed in terms of the individuals that make up the population unit. Thus, their sex composition, as defined by sex ratios, and their age composition, as similarly defined by age ratios, provide important information on the proportion of the population that represents potential breeders. The fall age-ratio, readily determined by field observations, provides critically important information on the rate of recruitment of young birds into the population and thus provides the best possible index to the success of the immediately past breeding season, and thus the maximum rate at which the population may be "harvested" by natural or other means while still maintaining the population size.

This recruitment rate is one of the statistics of importance in estimating the rate of population recycling, which is a result of mortality and survival rates. Mortality and survival are opposite sides of the same coin; as mortality rates increase, the average survival probabilities decrease, and life expectancy (or mean longevity) consequently decreases. Determining mortality rates in crane populations, which are only rarely banded in any numbers, is difficult at best. In rare cases (such as in extremely small populations) it may even be possible to account for every bird, and thus accurate estimates or mortality rates may be obtained for such limited populations. Regardless of the actual mortality rate, all animals in a population eventually die, and the length of time for a virtual 100 percent turning of the population age-class provides another useful population statistic, the turnover rate. In this chapter an attempt will be made to provide estimates of some of these important population characteristics for various cranes.

Feeding Ecology and Foraging Niches

Rather few species of cranes have been studied intensively as to their foraging niches and how these relate to those of other species of cranes or other possible competitors. As Walkinshaw (1973) has reported, cranes have been observed consuming a wide variety of foods, including frogs, snakes, small birds, birds' eggs, small mammals, snails, crustaceans, small fish, roots, tubers, earthworms, melons, sweet potatoes, insects, and other arthropods, so they clearly have broad dietary requirements. The best available information on foraging ecology comes from various studies on sandhill cranes. Early observations of these species indicated a predominance of vegetable foods in their diets, even on the breeding grounds (Allen, 1952). In an early study of 51 gizzards from lesser sandhill cranes shot during January on their New Mexican wintering areas, Boeker, Aldrich, and Huey (1961) reported that nearly 100 percent of the diet during that period consisted of various types of sorghum grains and green alfalfa.

Studies of sandhill cranes during fall in Saskatchewan (Stephen, 1967) indicate that grain was present in the digestive tracts of 93 percent of 190 specimens. This was predominantly wheat, although barley and oats were also found. The average amount of food found in the gullets was about 27 grams, or only about a fourth of the average amount of wheat and mash consumed per day by captive birds. Foraging density of the birds varied according to distance from their major roosts, and was as high as 248 birds per quarter-section (or 3.8 birds per hectare) in the mile nearest the roost. An average

distance of nearly 6 feet was observed between individual cranes foraging in grain fields.

Several other studies have confirmed the general principle that the major foods of sandhill cranes are vegetational materials, including grains, corn, tubers, stems, and leafy matter (table 7). Probably the overall content of such foods, as supplemented by a small amount of animal materials, contains about 10 percent protein (Reinecke and Krapu, 1979). During the spring period in Nebraska it is probable that corn makes up at least 90 percent of the total food consumed (Lewis, 1979a; Reinecke and Krapu, 1979; Iverson, Tacha, and Vohs, 1982). Grain such as ripening wheat is also a major food of fall staging flocks of sandhill cranes in southern Canada (Stephen, 1967), while in the Copper River delta area of Alaska the birds concentrate on the fleshy bulbs of arrow-grass (*Triglochin*)(Herter, 1982).

By comparison, the foraging niche of the larger whooping crane is clearly more closely associated with aquatic foods. During the early winter season in Texas the birds forage almost entirely on blue crabs (*Callinectes sapidus*), which are abundant in flooded tidal flats.

T A B L E 7

Major Foods of Sandhill Cranes at Various Seasons

	Summer (Idaho)*		Winter (Texas)†				Spring (Nebraska)‡	
	Digestive Tract		Gizzard		Esophagus		Esophagus	
	Vol. (%)	Freq. (%)	Vol. (%)	Freq. (%)	Vol. (%)	Freq. (%)	Vol. (%)	Freq. (%)
Plant Foods								
Timothy (corms)	68	55	—	—	—	—	—	—
Grass (leaves, tubers)	2	10	tr.	1	—	—	tr.	24
Lupinus (seeds)	1	2	—	—	—	—	—	—
Corn (grain)	—	—	—	—	—	—	93	100
Alfalfa (leaves, stems)	—	—	—	—	—	—	tr.	33
Cyperus (underground parts)	—	—	50.4	87	38.4	61	—	—
Nymphea (tubers)	—	—	8.7	9	4.8	14	—	—
Sorghum (grain?)	—	—	6.8	6	37.6	11	—	—
Animal Foods								
Orthopterans	11	35	2.1	9	0.2	11	2	27
Dipteran larvae	6	15	tr.	3	0.1	7	—	—
Lepidopteran larvae	3	40	6.8	9	3.9	11	—	—
Damselflies	1	30	—	—	—	—	—	—
Beetles	1	40	1.8	3.9	1.3	14	1	84
Earthworms	—	—	—	—	—	—	3	94
Snails	—	—	2.1	5.0	2.1	11	1	72

*Mullins and Bizeau, 1978 (entire digestive tract, 20 birds).
†Guthery, 1976 (esophagi of 28 birds, gizzards of 70 birds).
‡Reinecke and Krapu, 1979 (esophagi of 34 birds, adjusted for sampling bias).

During December and January these flats and sloughs become drained, and the birds then move into shallow bays and channels to probe for clams of at least six species, and only occasionally consume blue crabs. All the clams and crabs up to about 5 centimeters in width are swallowed whole, while large crabs are pecked into smaller pieces before being swallowed (Derrickson, 1980).

Like the whooping crane, the Siberian crane also consumes aquatic materials, obtained in water 25 to 68 centimeters deep (Sauey, 1979), but its food primarily consists of vegetation rather than animal sources. The demoiselle crane is evidently primarily a terrestrial forager, and extensively consumes ripening cereal grains, chick-peas, and lucerne (alfalfa) (Cramp and Simmons, 1980). The Eurasian crane consumes a diverse array of foods, with plant materials predominating, from the ground, from shallow water, in low vegetation, or from subsurface materials that are extracted by probing (Cramp and Simmons, 1980). The long-billed Australian crane prefers to forage on moist ground, by digging and grazing (Lavery and Blackman, 1969). The sarus crane similarly often digs for food with its bill, but also strips rice grains from their stalks effectively, sometimes kills and consumes snakes up to two feet in length, and otherwise seems to be quite omnivorous (Walkinshaw, 1973). Where it is in contact with wintering Siberian cranes, the sarus crane tends to forage in water no deeper than 30.5 centimeters, but it also contests more shallow areas with Siberian cranes, consistently dominating that species (Sauey, 1979). The African blue crane is apparently a ground-forager, with animal foods perhaps forming the majority of its diet, but it also at times eats grain or seeds and digs up and consumes roots. The crowned cranes also consume grain and grass seeds, but do not seem to dig as much as do the longer-billed species (Walkinshaw, 1973).

Territoriality and Home Ranges

Apart from breeding territories, which will be considered in the chapter on reproductive biology, cranes also exhibit territoriality outside of the nesting season. Thus the whooping crane exhibits strong winter territoriality, and during that time of year the birds exist as singles, pairs, or, at most, in family parties. Allen (1952) studied winter territoriality at Aransas Refuge and concluded that about 400 acres of salt flats, including ponds and estuaries, are required for the average pair or family of wintering whooping cranes. Of 14 territories actually mapped, the average was 436 acres. All of the 14 had frontage on one or more of the inside bays and included one or more types of salt flat ponds, which apparently are the optimum habitat type. The male is the defender of the territory, while the female and young remain close together and spend much time in foraging.

Nonbreeding territories have not been studied in any detail in the other species, but it seems likely that similar patterns exist in many but not all species. Bieniasz (1979) reported that a flock of 5 to 15 nonbreeding greater sandhill cranes occupied an area having a 3.2 to 4.8 kilometer radius, representing a total home range of several square miles. These birds fed, roosted, and loafed together, indicating that exclusive territoriality evidently was lacking. Walkinshaw (1973) noted that the Japanese crane and the white-naped crane exhibit more severe territorial hostility than does the smaller hooded crane, and besides territoriality associated with nests or young he recognized four additional types of crane territories. These included a crane's "territory around himself" (individual distance maintenance), similar defense of a mate, territories associated with the feeding area (especially during the breeding season), and territories maintained in a flock or at a roost (again perhaps an extension of individual distance attributes).

Sex Ratios and Age Ratios

The importance of obtaining reliable sex-ratio and age-ratio data in understanding population dynamics of cranes or other bird species is hard to exaggerate. Adult (or tertiary) sex ratios in monogamous species such as cranes should ideally be as close to equality as possible if maximum reproductive efficiency is to be obtained, and age-ratio data are of critical importance in judging the reproductive success for any given breeding season. Since cranes do not exhibit enough sexual dimorphism in size or voice to use reliably for field sexing, it is necessary to use samples of hunter kills to obtain an estimate of such ratios. For example, in a study of 109 lesser sandhill cranes killed on the wintering of New Mexico, the total sex ratio was 59 males to 60 females. If only adult birds are considered, the ratio was 46 males to 50 females. Both comparisons suggest that in this species at least the tertiary sex ratio does not diverge significantly from a 1:1 ratio. In a similar sample of 108 sandhill cranes collected between October and April and representing all three subspecies, Lewis (1979a) found a total of 56 males and 52 females. This also suggests that the adult sex ratio of the species does not diverge appreciably from equality.

A larger sample of age ratios is available from wild crane populations as a result of the relative ease of recognizing juvenile birds in fall crane flocks. The available data (table 8) indicate that the percentages of juveniles in various crane populations range from a minimum of about 8 percent to a maximum of about 18 percent, and average about 13.5 percent for all species. If this can be used as a reliable index of average recruitment rates in wild crane populations, and if the average pair of breeding adults successfully raises a single offspring to the fall period, it clearly means that only about a quarter of the nonjuvenile population of cranes

T A B L E 8

Percentages of Young in Various Crane Populations

Species	Percent Young in Population	Reference
Siberian Crane	8.5% of estimated 65 birds, 1969 (India)	Walkinshaw, 1973
	10.2% of 59 birds, 1974 (India)	Sauey, 1976
	7.3% of 41 birds, 1970s (USSR)	Flint and Kistchinski, 1981
Wattled Crane	4.2% of 784 birds	Konrad, 1981
Australian Crane	17% of flocks seen 1968-1970	Blackman, 1971a
Sarus Crane	16.7% of 137 birds	Blackman, 1971a
White-naped Crane	16.0% of 1,826 birds	Nishida, 1981
Sandhill Crane		
Lesser & Canadian	7.2% of 2,108 birds, Alaska, 1979-80	Herter, 1982
	10.5% of 24,086 birds, Canada, 1975	Buller, 1976
	11.5% of 30,393 birds, U.S., 1975	Buller, 1976
Greater	11.5% of 2,658 birds, New Mexico	Drewien, 1973
	11.5% of 14,442 birds, Wisconsin & Indiana	Crete and Grewe, 1982
Florida	15.6% of 192 birds	Walkinshaw, 1976
Whooping Crane	17.3% of wintering population, 1938-1952	Table 29
	15.1% of wintering population, 1953-1966	Table 29
	10.6% of wintering population, 1967-1980	Table 29
Japanese Crane	15.2% of 713 birds, 1965-1968	Walkinshaw, 1973
	12.8% of 3,339 birds, 1962-1978	Table 30
Hooded Crane	13.5% of 3,107 birds	Nishida, 1981
Eurasian Crane	12.0% of 5,808 birds	Libbert, 1969
	11.42% of 17,240 birds	Fernandez-Cruz, 1979-1980
	From 5 to 6.7% in various years	Swanberg, 1981

represents successfully breeding pairs, with the other 75 percent of adult birds either nonbreeders or unsuccessful breeders. Few if any of the other legally hunted game species in North America have such a low recruitment rate as this, and it poses serious and complex problems of management if cranes are to be legally hunted.

The data in table 8 suggest that there may be substantial inter-population differences in recruitment rates of cranes. For example, the Florida sandhill crane seemingly has a substantially higher recruitment rate than does either the greater or the lesser subspecies. Further, the recruitment rate of the whooping crane has dropped quite substantially since annual counts were first initiated (with the establishment of Aransas National Wildlife Refuge). Possible explanations and implications of this have been discussed elsewhere (Johnsgard, 1982). It seems likely that it may in part be related to the carrying capacity characteristics of the breeding grounds in Wood Buffalo National Park, which seem to support only a rather limited number of breeding pairs in the Sass and Klewi river areas of that park (Novakowski, 1966). Thus, increasing total population size of the species has not been accompanied by a major increase in known breeding birds, which for the period 1968 through 1979 averaged only 32 percent of the total nonjuvenile population (Kuyt, 1981a).

Another way of obtaining information relative to reproductive efficiency in crane populations is to determine the average brood size in populations of cranes with recently fledged young. Except for the crowned cranes, it may be taken as a basic assumption that the average clutch size in cranes is essentially two eggs, and that any family sizes of less than two young can be attributed to mortality of eggs or young among nesting birds. Obviously, such counts do not provide an estimate of those pairs that lost both of their eggs or young, but they do nevertheless provide a potentially useful index to the incidence of mortality among a substantial part of the egg or chick population. As may be seen in table 9, the percentage of pairs leading two fledged young in fall populations ranges from as little as about 11 percent to as high as nearly 40 percent. Thus, year-to-year variations in the raising of one or both youngsters do indeed produce a significant source of variation in annual productivity. The often-repeated statement that "cranes almost never raise more than one youngster" and that the second egg is thus biologically unimportant is therefore clearly subject to argument. For example, before the program of egg-removal from the nests of whooping cranes was instituted, nearly 15 percent of the families arriving at Aransas refuge each fall contained two young. It seems unlikely, however,

TABLE 9

Average Brood Size and Percent of Fledged "Twins" in Various Crane Populations

Wattled Crane:	Twins have never been reported in wild populations—Konrad, 1981
Sandhill Crane	
Lesser & Canada:	17% of 201 migrant families in the Central Flyway had two young in September (estimated average brood, 1.17 young)—Buller, 1976.
Greater (Oregon):	20.1% of 134 families in September had two young (estimated average brood size, 1.2 young)—Littlefield, 1976.
Greater (Idaho):	Average of 1.35 fledged young in 372 families in September (estimated 35% of all families with young)—Drewien, 1973.
Greater (New Mexico):	Average of 1.24 young in 282 families, late fall (estimated 24% of all families with young)—Drewien and Bizeau, 1974.
Greater (Michigan):	31% of 324 fall families had two young, or average brood size of 1.31 young per successful pair—Walkinshaw, 1973.
Florida:	Three of 27 family groups (11.1%) were groups of 4—Walkinshaw, 1976.
Whooping Crane:	14.5% of 48 broods arriving Aransas, 1949-1963, were of 2 young; average brood size, 1.15 young—Walkinshaw, 1973.
Eurasian Crane:	From 20% to 25% over four years; average of 24% or estimated 1.24 young per successful pair—Swanberg, 1981. Of 1,847 pairs, 17.62 percent had two young, or an average brood size of 1.18—Fernandez-Cruz, 1979-1980.
Hooded Crane:	48% of families observed in 1966-67 had two young—Nishida, 1981.
White-naped Crane:	27% of families observed in January 1980 had two young (estimated average brood size, 1.27 young)—Nishida, 1981.

that this program has directly resulted in the substantial reduction of recruitment rates just mentioned for the species, since the trend began well before the egg-removal program was initiated in 1967, but it has perhaps in a small part contributed to it.

Mortality and Survival Rates

It has been emphasized that populations of animals can vary in density, in spatial distribution patterns (territoriality favors dispersion, sociality favors clumping), and in sex and age composition. Not only can the population be analyzed for immature and adult components but the adults themselves have age composition characteristics, with the relative frequency of the various age classes depending on the rate at which the animals die. It is possible to gather such mortality information only by marking individuals (preferably while still young enough to determine their exact age at the time of marking), releasing them, and resampling the population at later times to determine how long the marked individuals survive. A review by Farner (1955) provides the theoretical concepts and practical methods that are required in the performance of such investigations with birds, and it is beyond the scope of this short review to mention them here. A few ideas, however, are so basic to the understanding of this aspect of population dynamics that they must be considered individually.

The relative rate at which individuals in a population die is usually expressed as an annual mortality rate (M), which is the ratio of those individuals dying during a year to the number that were alive at the beginning of the twelve-month period, whatever its starting point. The annual survival rate (S) is the opposite ratio: the proportion of the animals still surviving at the end of a twelve-month period to those that were alive at its start. Thus, $S + M = 1.0$ or $S = 1.0 - M$. The total population may be subdivided into different age classes according to the year in which each individual was hatched. The population thus consists of varying numbers of one-year-olds, two-year-olds, etc. For groups banded as birds of unknown ages, the population can alternatively be divided into year classes, representing groups of birds of unknown but varying minimum ages.

The length of time required for an entire age class of hatched young to be essentially eliminated from the population is referred to as the turnover period or turnover rate. This is perhaps properly estimated on the basis of time required for 100 percent of the age class to be reduced to 1 percent of its original size, but practice varies in this regard (Hickey, 1955; Petrides, 1949).

Mortality and survival rates in birds have usually been estimated on the basis of recovery rates of banded birds (Farner, 1955), but this technique requires a sample size large enough to provide a reasonable estimate of mortality rates throughout the entire potential longevity of a species. Banding recoveries often tend to overestimate mortality rates, particularly in long-lived species, where banded birds may survive for longer periods than are desirable for convenient analysis, or where the bands on long-lived birds may wear out and be lost before the birds actually die. Probably both of these conditions exist for cranes in general and introduce biases into the interpretation of banding data.

Until the introduction of legalized hunting of sandhill cranes in the United States in 1961, the intensity of banding activities was low and the incidence of banding recoveries was just about nil. Even as recently as 1977, Lewis commented on the low rate of banding recoveries on sandhill cranes through 1972, with first-year recoveries averaging less than 2 percent and total recoveries no greater than 3.5 percent. In recent years, however, the rate of banding recoveries for this species has increased, and in some cases has exceeded 7 percent (table 10). Thus, of 168 cranes banded in Texas in 1977, 13 had

been recovered in three years (7.7 percent). Of 33 total band recoveries from birds banded in Texas through 1979, 26 (79 percent) were recovered within a year of banding. These figures indicate an astonishingly high rate of first-year band recoveries for a species with a presumably very low natural mortality rate, and it is very possible that they reflect a serious degree of hunting overkill of sandhill cranes.

Since so few species of wild cranes have been banded in any numbers, it is only possible to apply the principles of population analysis by banding recoveries to a single species, the sandhill crane. In table 11 a tabulation of banding recoveries of all races of sandhill cranes banded in North America through 1979 and recovered through 1980 is provided. This total of nearly 200 banding recoveries provides a reasonably good basis

TABLE 10

Some Band Recovery Rates for Sandhill Cranes

Years of Banding	Location	Birds Banded	Bands Recovered	Recovery Years	Reference
1959-69	Texas	134	4(3.0%)*	3—13	Lewis, 1977
1965-68	Nebraska	542	37(6.8%)†	12—15	Lewis, 1977
1977	Texas	168	13(7.7%)†	3	Ramakka, 1979

*Recoveries to 1972
†Recoveries to 1981

TABLE 11

Survival of Sandhill Cranes Based on Banding Recoveries through 1980

Banding Year	Years between banding and recovery														
	1	1-2	2-3	3-4	4-5	5-6	6-7	7-8	8-9	9-10	10-11	11-12	12-13	13-14	14-15
1960	—	1	—	—	—	—	2	—	—	—	—	—	—	—	—
1961	1	—	—	1	—	—	—	—	—	—	—	—	—	—	1
1962	—	—	—	—	—	1	—	—	—	—	—	—	—	—	—
1963	—	—	—	1	—	—	—	—	—	—	—	—	—	—	1
1964	—	—	—	—	—	—	1	1	—	—	—	—	—	—	—
1965	2	1	—	—	1	1	—	—	—	—	—	1	—	—	1
1966	1	—	—	—	—	—	—	1	—	—	—	—	—	—	—
1967	1	1	1	2	—	—	—	—	1	1	—	—	1	—	
1968	9	3	2	2	1	2	2	1	1	3	3	1	—		
1969	1	—	1	3	—	—	1	—	—	—	—				
1970	1	2	—	1	2	—	1	1	—	—	—				
1971	—	—	1	—	1	—	—	—	—						
1972	5	2	4	2	—	1	—	—	—						
1973	1	—	2	1	1	—	—	—							
1974	—	—	—	—	1	—	—								
1975	2	—	—	—	—										
1976	2	2	—	3	—										
1977	14	2	1	—											
1978	30	2	—												
1979	14	1													
Total	84	17	12	16	7	5	7	4	2	4	3	2	1	0	3

TABLE 12

Life Table for Wild Sandhill Cranes, Based on Banding Recoveries through 1980

Year Class*	Total Deaths	Deaths 1,000	Survivors 1,000	% Survival
1	84	506	494	49.4
2	17	102	390	79.3
3	12	72	318	81.5
4	15	90	228	71.7
5	7	42	186	81.6
6	5	30	156	83.9
7	7	42	114	73.1
8	4	24	90	78.9
9	2	12	78	86.7
10	4	24	54	69.2
11	3	18	36	66.7
12	2	12	24	66.7
13	1	6	18	75.0
14	0	0	18	100.0
15	3	18	0	0.0
			Ave. (years 2-14)	78.2

*Refers to year following banding rather than to the actual age of bird.

TABLE 13

Estimated Total Sporting Harvests of Sandhill Cranes, 1961-1979*

Year	Manitoba and Saskatchewan	New Mexico	Texas	Other States	Total States	Minimum Harvest
1961	—	542	—	2,633	2	3,146
1961 (fall)	—	1,385	1,200	2,633	3	2,847
1962	—	1,161	1,230	2,633	3	5,087
1963	—	1,064	1,230	2,633	3	4,905
1964	3,124	1,246	1,260	2,633	3	8,263
1965	625	631	1,350	2,633	3	5,239
1966	531	514	890	2,633	3	4,568
1967	3,604	697	1,070	2,633	4	8,006
1968	4,837	1,076	1,339	2,705	7	9,957
1969	4,444	1,212	991	2,980	7	9,627
1970	5,344	1,805	2,213	3,185	7	12,547
1971	2,943	2,183	3,076	8,350	7	10,790
1972	2,143	780	2,270	3,055	9	8,284
1973	4,275	420	7,500	3,780	9	15,975
1974	6,699	220	4,700	3,790	9	15,899
1975	6,165	710	7,010	4,480	9	18,365
1976	1,636	858	6,122	2,400	9	11,016
1977	5,388	1,459	6,094	6,600	9	19,541
1978	1,575	1,089	5,720	5,300	9	13,684
1979	3,798	1,170	5,917	5,300	9	16,185

*Excludes cripping losses (about 15 percent of total kill), Canadian native kill, and Siberian and Mexican kills. The 1961-1972 data are from Lewis (1977); 1972-1979 Canadian data are from *Canadian Wildlife Service Progress Notes* 101 (1979) and 115 (1980). U.S. data for 1973-1976 are from Marten (1979), and also exclude Alaskan native kill, estimated at 2,000 birds by Lewis (1977). U.S. data for 1976-1979 are based on information provided by individual states, and include an estimated Alaskan native kill of 2,000 birds. "Total states" represents number of states in which cranes were legal game that year.

for establishing a life table and tentative estimates of annual mortality rates for this species (table 12).

In table 12, the progressively older "year classes" do not represent specific age-classes, since all banded cranes are initially included in "year class" 1, regardless of their actual age. Only a relatively small (12.0) percentage of the total recovery sample comes from birds identified as juveniles or immatures at the time of banding, and most were identified as adult or unknown. By ignoring the results from the year immediately following banding, the effects of presumably higher first-year mortality rates can be eliminated. Even with such an adjustment, the indicated annual survival rates for the species averages less than 80 percent (or more than a 20 percent annual mortality rate), which is well in excess of the recruitment rates indicated for sandhill cranes in table 8. Like the high rate of banding recoveries, these figures strongly suggest that hunting mortality in the sandhill crane is certainly now equalling and probably exceeding the species' current recruitment rates. Similarly, the turnover period of approximately 15 years indicated in table 12 is indicative of annual mortality rates well in excess of the probable 10 to 15 percent recruitment rates suggested by age ratios in fall populations, which should result in a turnover rate well in excess of 20 years (Petrides, 1949).

Because of the recent development of legalized sandhill crane hunting in North America, it is perhaps worth summarizing some of the evidence as to the current harvest levels for that species. The early years of harvest have been summarized by various authors (Johnsgard, 1973; Miller, Hochbaum, and Botkin, 1972; Lewis, 1977), while the years 1966 to 1975 were summarized for each of the states by Marten (1979). Marten observed that during that time period there was an average increase in harvest of sandhill cranes of 8 percent annually, which would represent an approximate doubling of harvest every nine years if current trends continue. He also noted that during an eight-year period of analysis, the state of Texas accounted for 58 percent of the total sport harvest in the United States. An updated summary of estimated legal crane harvests is presented in table 13. To these minimum figures must be added a substantial mortality associated with crippled but unretrieved birds (which is believed to be about 15 percent of the retrieved kill), the kill by Canadian natives (Eskimo and Indian hunters), and the legal or illegal kills in Mexico and in Siberia. Sandhill crane hunting is legal in Mexico and gaining in popularity (Lewis, 1977; Marten, 1979), and a limited amount of hunting also occurs during spring in Siberia. There are no firm bases for judging the sizes of these kills, but 8 of 62 band recoveries from cranes banded in Nebraska have been recovered from Mexico. This would suggest that, in spite of the probable low rate of band reporting from there, probably at least 12 percent of the cranes harvested in the Central Flyway are killed in Mexico. There are still only 4 band recoveries from the USSR (all from the Anadyr Basin), and 3 of these are from birds banded in New Mexico, while the fourth is from a Texas-banded bird. Thus, the Siberian mortality can probably be considered insignificant or at least unmeasurable at present. It thus seems probable that at least an additional 25 percent mortality rate can be attributed to crippling losses and Mexican hunting beyond the reported kills for the United States and Canada, which in the five most recent years of data have averaged about 14,100 birds. If 3,500 birds are thus added to this kill, plus an estimated 2,000 birds killed annually by Alaskan natives, it is apparent that the annual harvest is now probably close to 20,000 birds a year. Given an average fall recruitment rate of approximately 10 percent, it would require a population of 200,000 cranes to replace these losses, not counting all other sources of nonhunting mortality.

The first persons to point out the seriousness of hunting to the sandhill crane population were Miller, Hochbaum, and Botkin (1972), who concluded nearly a decade ago that "further increases in hunting might seriously endanger the species, and that the population is not being monitored accurately enough to detect a major population decline if it did occur." Since then, two additional states have been opened to sandhill crane hunting, and the estimated annual harvest has more than doubled!

The current size of the lesser and Canadian sandhill crane populations (the only ones being hunted legally) is still open to considerable controversy, largely as a result of difficulties in making complete spring inventories. Spring surveys in the Platte Valley of Nebraska have been conducted since 1957 during late March and April, and in most years have averaged about 200,000 birds (Frith, 1974; Lewis, 1979b). The 1976 spring inventory provided a total count of 150,119 birds, but Lewis believed that because of biases in undercounting, the actual population there might have been close to 400,000 birds. This very substantial disagreement underlines the contention of Miller, Hochbaum, and Botkin (1972) that the U.S. Fish and Wildlife Service is increasingly permitting the harvesting of a species of bird with very limited reproductive potential, and on the basis of little knowledge of its actual population sizes or trends. A more recent computer simulation model of cranes by Johnson (1979), using considerably different assumptions than did Miller, Hochbaum, and Botkin, would suggest that the population is not yet being overharvested, but all of these sophisticated models basically must rely on relatively primitive spring census data that are still not adequate to provide faith in such conclusions. Recent data provided by Melvin and Temple (1980) on first-year hunting mortality in sandhill cranes from the area of southern Manitoba cause additional concern about possible over-hunting effects. Of 64 birds that were banded in that area (62 juveniles, 2 adults), 9 were shot by hunters during their first fall of life, representing an approximate 14 percent harvest of juvenile birds in this particular population. It is clear that insufficient attention is being paid to sandhill crane harvest rates at the present time. Similarly, Herter (1982) reported that although juveniles made up only 6.5 percent of the young counted in fall flocks of cranes in the Copper River delta area of Alaska, they comprised 21.7 percent of the young in a sample of 46 hunter-killed birds, also indicating a very high vulnerability of juvenile birds to hunting. This figure compares closely with juvenile age ratios in hunter kill samples of 21.9 percent in the 1961 New Mexico season and 22.6 percent in the 1961 Texas season (unpublished report of Texas Game and Fish Commission by A. J. Springs, undated).

Comparative Reproductive Biology

5 The reproductive biologies of cranes are surprisingly similar. All crane species are strictly monogamous, have long pair bonds and a prolonged period of juvenile dependency, and are highly territorial during the breeding season. All cranes also have an extremely limited reproductive potential, resulting from their deferred sexual maturity, low clutch size, and limited renesting tendencies following the loss of a clutch or hatched young.

Yet, within these specific characteristics, there is also a fair amount of species diversity, which is largely associated with adaptation to ecologically diverse breeding habitats and geographic distributions. The most obvious of these adaptations are perhaps the interspecific variations in length of the breeding season and its seasonal timing. This may be readily seen when the monthly distribution of egg records for various species and subspecies of cranes are compared (table 14). Among all the temperate-to-arctic-breeding Northern Hemisphere cranes the egg-laying period is timed to coincide with spring, so that hatching occurs in late spring or early summer. This allows for a maximum length of time for the young to grow and fledge before the first fall storms or snowfalls, and for the young to hatch at near the peak of the early summer emergence of insects and other invertebrate life that they forage on. Even within the sandhill cranes, not only is it apparent that more southerly forms, such as the Florida and Mississippi races, have earlier egg-laying periods, but also the total period during which eggs may be found is greatly prolonged. This period includes a maximum spread of about half a year in the case of the Florida race, and such a wide spread suggests that renesting abilities may be fairly well developed in this race. For example, 20 percent of the egg records occur in three months following the peak month (March) in the Florida race, and 41 percent occur in the two months following the same month in the Mississippi form, while in the

Canadian and Alaskan populations only 2 percent of the egg records occur following the peak month (June).

Somewhat similar trends may be seen in the other northern cranes, with all of the species having peaks in the egg records occurring in April (Japanese crane), May (demoiselle, Eurasian, white-naped, and whooping cranes), or June (black-necked crane). Only the Eurasian crane exhibits a range of egg records suggestive of possible renesting significance.

On the other hand, the wattled crane of Africa exhibits an egg-record pattern that covers the entire twelve-month period, although apparently peaking between May and August. Walkinshaw (1964) states that in South Africa the wattled crane is a dry-season (winter) nester, while elsewhere it is said to nest in the rainy season (Konrad, 1981). Only slightly less extended than the wattled crane records are the records for the similarly tropical sarus crane, with records extending from June to March but peaking between July and September, typically shortly after the summer monsoon period. The Australian crane primarily breeds between September and March, with an apparent nesting peak in February. In that general area, the first storms of the wet season occur in October or November, and the wet season typically ends in March or April.

The West African crowned cranes exhibit a remarkably abbreviated breeding season, which is centered in July. In East Africa, this species breeds during the rainy period in most areas, but in the wettest parts of East Africa the dry season is apparently preferred (Brown and Britton, 1980). Similarly, the northern population of the South African crowned crane nests only during the rainy season (April to July) in Zambia, in contrast to the less restricted nesting of the wattled crane (Benson et al., 1971). Farther south the season seems to be concentrated between December and March, which also points to rainy-season nesting. A similar seasonal pattern for nesting occurs in the blue crane, which exhibits a peak

TABLE 14

Percentage Monthly Distribution of Egg Records, Various Cranes*

	Dec.	Jan.	Feb.	Mar.	Apr.	May	June	July	Aug.
Sandhill crane									
Florida (108)	2	5	24	50	16	3	1	—	—
Mississippi (34)	—	—	3	56	32	9	—	—	—
Michigan (203)	—	—	—	—	62	36	1	1	—
Western U.S. (126)	—	—	—	—	40	55	4	1	—
Canada (43)	—	—	—	—	2	56	40	2	—
Alaska (70)	—	—	—	—	—	6	91	1	1

	Mar.	Apr.	May	June	July	Aug.
Other northern cranes						
Japanese crane (19)	5	63	32	—	—	—
Demoiselle crane (33)	—	9	78	9	3	—
Eurasian crane (69)	—	29	54	17	—	—
White-naped crane (9)	—	22	56	22	—	—
Whooping crane (Canada, est. 78)	—	—	65	33	—	1
Black-necked crane (10)	—	—	20	70	10	—

	May	June	July	Aug.	Sept.	Oct.	Nov.	Dec.	Jan.	Feb.	Mar.	Apr.
Tropical & southern cranes												
Sarus crane (63)	—	3	27	22	19	3	3	8	2	8	5	—
Wattled Crane (91)	18	19	13	14	3	9	3	7	4	3	2	4
W. African crowned (15)	—	—	27	67	7	—	—	—	—	—	—	—
Australian crane (27)	—	4	—	—	11	7	4	7	19	41	7	—
Blue crane (61)	—	—	—	—	—	17	26	39	11	6	2	—
S. African crowned (59)	—	—	—	—	—	7	2	22	35	20	12	2

*Data from *Cranes*, vol. 1, no. 1, 1973; sample size in parentheses.

in egg records during the summer months of November and December. In this species' nesting areas about 80 percent of the annual rainfall occurs during the summer months (Walkinshaw, 1973).

It seems to be a fundamental characteristic of all cranes that they are highly dispersed and territorial during the breeding season. Because of these extremely large territories, territorial limits tend to become diffuse, and accurate estimates of territory sizes are thus very difficult to obtain. It is perhaps more realistic to measure breeding densities rather than to estimate territorial sizes, but a sampling of both kinds of approaches is presented in table 15. It may be seen that under rare conditions territories may be as small as 1.2 hectares (about 3 acres), but the average in sandhill cranes is closer to 25 hectares, or well above 50 acres. Similarly, total nesting densities are generally no more than at least 10 square kilometers per pair. The remarkably high sandhill crane breeding densities and small average territorial sizes observed by Drewien (1973) at Gray's Lake, Idaho, were attributed by him to a variety of local factors, including isolation, freedom from disturbance, and abundant breeding habitat.

Within the genera *Grus*, *Bugeranus*, and *Anthropoides*, the clutch size of all species is fairly close to 2.0 eggs. Only very rarely are three eggs present in the nests of these species, and the relatively few records of single-egg clutches are mostly associated with the wattled crane, in which single-egg clutches are common. Thus, for all practical purposes it is fair to say that all cranes except the wattled and crowned cranes consistently lay two-egg clutches (table 16). The crowned cranes exhibit an interesting divergence from this strict pattern and approach three-egg clutches in most portions of their range. Perhaps the only exception is in East Africa, where the data suggest that a slightly smaller average clutch size might be typical there. However, Pomeroy (1980b) has suggested that in this area the clutch size is altitude-dependent, with highland populations having larger clutches than those of lowlands.

It is typical for the size of the eggs of birds to be inversely related to the adult size of the birds; smaller species tend to lay eggs relatively larger than those of larger relatives. Thus, it is not surprising that the largest egg laid by any crane is produced by the smallest species, the demoiselle crane (table 17). Similarly, the eggs laid by the very large species, such as the whooping crane, the Australian crane, and the sarus crane, are among the relatively smallest of all crane eggs. Among the sixteen forms tabulated in table 17, an average weight reduction of 40.6 percent occurs between the

TABLE 15

Breeding Densities and Territory Sizes, Various Crane Populations

Species	Territory Area (Hectares)	Breeding Density Nests or Pairs/km²	Reference
West African Crowned Crane	86-388	—	Walkinshaw, 1973
Demoiselle Crane	—	0.10	Grummt, 1961
Wattled Crane	over 100	under 0.05	Konrad, 1981
Siberian Crane	—	0.001-0.002	Flint and Kistchinski, 1981
Sandhill Crane			
Lesser (Canada)	—	under 0.8 / 0.06	Lewis, 1977 / Walkinshaw, 1981a
Lesser (Alaska)	—	0.91-1.3	Boise, 1976
Greater (Oregon)	Ave. of 8, 25 (1.2-68.0)	—	Littlefield and Ryder, 1968
Greater (Idaho)	Ave. of 10, 17 (10-23)	ca. 0.25	Drewien, 1973
Greater (Michigan)	Ave. of 89, 57.7 (3-194)	—	Walkinshaw, 1965b
Greater (Wisconsin)	Ave. of 17, 126 (63-168)	max. 0.07	Crete and Grewe, 1982
Florida (Kissimmee)	—	ca. 0.07-0.08	Walkinshaw, 1976
Whooping Crane	Ave. of 18, 720 (40-4, 710)	—	Kuyt, 1981a
Japanese Crane			
USSR	400-1,230	—	Viniter, 1981
China	—	ca. 0.34-0.36*	Ma and Xu, 1980
Japan	—	ca. 0.39*	Masatomi, 1981b
Hooded Crane (Lower Amur)	—	0.019-0.038	Neufeldt, 1981a
Black-necked Crane	45	0.38*	Cheng, 1981
Eurasian Crane			
Germany	—	0.001-0.005	Glutz, 1973
Norway	—	0.015-0.020	Glutz, 1973
Finland	—	0.001-0.018	Merikallio, 1958
Sweden	—	0.015-0.017	Nilsson, 1982

*Estimated (50 percent of reported cranes/km² during breeding season).

fresh-egg stage and the weight of the newly hatched chick, with a range of 34 to 47 percent. There seem to be no significant interspecific differences apparent in this statistic.

There are no obviously significant differences in incubation periods among the species of cranes (table 18). One would expect that the high-latitude cranes should exhibit the shortest incubation periods, and it seems to be true that such forms as the Siberian crane, the Canadian sandhill crane, and the Eurasian crane all exhibit relatively short incubation periods. However, the demoiselle crane, a desert-breeding type, has a surprisingly abbreviated breeding season, to judge from table 14. What does show a rather remarkable interspecific variation is the length of the fledging period. The shortest fledging periods, not surprisingly, seem to be associated with high-latitude nesting, as in

such species as the lesser sandhill crane and the Eurasian crane. Yet, the demoiselle has what seems to be the shortest of all crane fledging periods, although this may in part be attributable to its unusually small adult size. Likewise, the crowned crane seems to have a remarkably short fledging period, based on avicultural data, although Walkinshaw (1964) reported the fledging period of the South African form under wild conditions to be about three months. As might be expected, the longest fledging periods are those of the tropical forms, including the sarus crane and the wattled crane, and probably also the Australian crane. Rather remarkably, the blue crane seems to have an extremely variable but protracted fledging period, in spite of its essentially temperate distribution. No obvious explanation for this anomaly is apparent, although van Ee (1966) noted that initial flying by the young

TABLE 16

Clutch-size Variations in Various Crane Populations

Species	Nests	Total Number of Nests of Each Clutch-size				Total Eggs	Average Clutch	Reference
		1	2	3	4			
East African Crowned	41	—	—	—	—	—	2.56	Pomeroy, 1980b
West African Crowned	17	0	3	14	0	48	2.47	Walkinshaw, 1973
South African Crowned								
Zambia & Rhodesia	17	4	3	10	0	40	2.35	Walkinshaw, 1973
South Africa	34	3	10	16	5	91	2.67	Walkinshaw, 1973
Blue Crane	61	7	53	1	0	116	1.90	Walkinshaw, 1973
Wattled Crane	90	35	55	0	0	145	1.61	Walkinshaw, 1973
Siberian Crane	12	—	—	—	—	—	1.75	Flint and Sorokin, 1981
Australian Crane	27	6	20	1	0	49	1.82	Walkinshaw, 1973
Sarus Crane	132	4	126	2	0	262	1.985	Walkinshaw, 1973
Lesser Sandhill								
Alaska	71	—	—	—	—	—	1.76	Boise, 1976
Alaska	77	9	68	0	0	154	1.88	Walkinshaw, 1973
Canadian Sandhill								
Canada	53	5	48	0	0	101	1.94	Walkinshaw, 1973
Greater Sandhill								
Oregon	108	9	99	0	0	207	1.92	Littlefield and Ryder, 1968
Michigan	183	8	174	1	0	359	1.96	Walkinshaw, 1973
Idaho	337	24	310	3	0	653	1.94	Drewien, 1973;
Florida Sandhill								
Georgia	6	1	5	0	0	11	1.83	Walkinshaw, 1973
Kissimmee	67	5	62	0	0	129	1.92	Walkinshaw, 1973
Central Florida	121	7	114	0	0	235	1.94	Walkinshaw, 1982
Cuban Sandhill	10	0	10	0	0	20	2.0	Walkinshaw, 1973
Mississippi Sandhill	79	—	—	—	—	—	1.86	Valentine, 1982
Whooping Crane	203	16	184	9	0	393	1.94	Kuyt, 1981b
Japanese Crane	22	1	21	0	0	43	1.95	Walkinshaw, 1973
Eurasian Crane	52	—	—	—	—	—	1.83	Masatomi, 1980
Schleswig-Holstein	17	1	15	1	0	34	2.0	Glutz, 1973
Finland	19	2	17	0	0	36	1.89	Glutz, 1973

might occur earlier if the parents have by then completed their wing molts and again are able to fly. Yet, this does not seem to provide an adequate explanation for the seemingly deferred fledging of this species.

It is to be expected that nesting and fledging success rates (table 19) might be highly variable among species and from year to year in the same species, for these are largely dependent upon local and highly variable factors, such as weather conditions and degrees of local disturbance or predation. However, it would appear that in many cases the nesting success of wild crane populations is rather surprisingly high, occasionally with as many as 70 to 80 percent of the nests that are initiated being successfully terminated. This remarkably high rate of nesting success is probably associated with effective nest defense by the combined efforts of the two adults, which are large enough to deter all but the most persistent predators. The percentage of eggs hatched is similar to that of the percent of nests successfully terminated, suggesting a very low number

of eggs that fail to hatch as a result of infertility, dead embryos, or other factors that might reduce hatchability. The rate of fledging success, however, is highly variable and is a difficult statistic to obtain with any degree of certainty. The figures in table 19 suggest that anywhere from about 44 to 71 percent of the eggs laid may result in successfully fledged young under natural conditions. It is a general rule of thumb among crane biologists that no more than one of the two crane young that normally hatch from a clutch will be fledged successfully, owing to intersibling strife. This is clearly not an invariable rule, as the data of Walkinshaw (1976) indicate. Interestingly, the fledging success data for wild whooping cranes for the period 1967-1978 include the time during which single eggs have been removed from whooping crane nests, so that many clutches actually consisted of only a single egg to begin with. The limited data suggest that fledging success of the remaining offspring has increased somewhat during this period, although not so much as one would have predicted if this were a

TABLE 17

Egg, Hatchling, and Adult Weights, Various Cranes

Species	Estimated Egg Weight (grams)	Percent Adult Weight	Average Chick Weight (1 day)	Percent Adult Weight	Estimated Adult Female Weight (kg)
Crowned Crane	156	4.3	91.7*	2.5	3.6
Blue Crane	181	4.9	120.1[†]	3.7	3.2
Demoiselle Crane	134	5.7	73.4*	3.1	2.35
Siberian Crane	202	3.8	121.7*	2.3	5.3
Sarus Crane	238	3.5	134.2*	2.0	6.8
Australian Crane	185	3.2	102.3[†]	1.8	5.7
White-naped Crane	207	4.1	116.3*	2.3	5.0
Sandhill Crane					
Lesser	164	4.8	104.0*	3.1	3.35
Canadian	178	4.7	107.7[†]	2.8	4.3
Florida	180	4.8	116.4*	3.1	3.75
Greater	204	4.7	119.2*	2.8	4.3
Whooping Crane	212	3.3	124.4[‡]	1.9	6.4
Japanese Crane	235	3.6	132.0*	2.0	6.5
Hooded Crane	175	5.0	113.7*	3.2	3.5
Eurasian Crane	189	3.7	121.1*	2.3	5.15
Black-necked Crane	222	3.7	118.1**	1.9	6.0

*Archibald and Viess (1979)
[†]Walkinshaw (1973)
[‡]Erickson and Derrickson (1981)
**Lu, Yao, and Liao (1980)

TABLE 18

Incubation and Fledging Periods, Various Cranes

Species	Incubation Period (in days)*	Fledging Period (in days)	Reference (Fledging Period)
Crowned Crane	28-31	63	Archibald and Viess, 1979
Blue Crane	28-35	at least 110	van Ee, 1966
Demoiselle Crane	27-30	55-65	Cramp and Simmons, 1980
Wattled Crane	35-40	about 150	Konrad, 1981
Siberian Crane	29	76	Michael Putnam (pers. comm.)
Sarus Crane	31-36	120	Rothschild, 1930
Australian Crane	35-36	about 98	Lavery and Blackman, 1969
White-naped Crane	28-32	at least 70	Archibald and Viess, 1979
Sandhill Crane			
Lesser	—	over 60	Boise, 1976
Canadian	27	—	—
Greater	31-32	67-75	Drewien, 1973
Florida	31-32	at least 70	Archibald and Viess, 1979
Whooping Crane	30-35	80-90	Kuyt, 1981b
Hooded Crane	—	75	Michael Putnam (pers. comm.)
Japanese Crane	30-34	about 95	Bartlett, 1861
Black-necked Crane	31-33	about 90	Lu, Yao and Liao, 1980
Eurasian Crane	28-31	63-70	Heinroth and Heinroth, 1926-28

*After Archibald (1974), except for the Siberian crane, which is from Michael Putnam (pers. comm.).

TABLE 19

Nesting and Fledging Success Rates in Various Crane Populations

Species	Total Nests	Total Eggs	Nests Successful	Eggs Hatched	Young Fledged*	Reference
Blue Crane	17	34	11(64.7%)	25(73.5%)	—	Walkinshaw, 1963
Lesser Sandhill						
Alaska	6	11	4(66.6%)	7(63.6%)	—	Boise, 1976
Greater Sandhill						
Various states	—	63	—	42(66.7%)	—	Walkinshaw, 1949
Michigan	133	252	(102)77%	(184)73%		Hoffman, 1979
Michigan (Lower)	204	380	161(78.9%)	294(77.4%)	284(96.6%)	Walkinshaw, 1981a
Idaho	326	—	255(78%)	—	—	Drewien, 1973
Oregon	456	—	201(44%)	—	—	Littlefield, 1976
Florida Sandhill						
Loxahatchee	25	44	22(88%)	31(70%)	—	Thompson, 1970
Central Florida	119	224	92(77.3%)	176(77.6%)	174(98.9%)	Walkinshaw, 1982
Whooping Crane						
N.W. Territories (1954-1965)	37	72	30(81.1%)	40(55.5%)	32(80%)	Novakowski, 1966
N.W. Territories (1966-1980)	211	260†	—	156(60%)†	96(61.5%)	Kuyt, 1981a
Eurasian Crane						
Schleswig-Holstein	22(1st)	—	17(77.3%)	—	—	Glutz, 1973
	4(2nd)	—	2(50%)	—	—	Glutz, 1973
	17	34	—	25(73.5%)	—	Glutz, 1973
	41	—	26(63.4%)	—	—	Glutz, 1973
Japanese Crane	—	63	74.4%	(50)79.4%	(22)44%	Masatoma, 1981b

*Fledging success calculated on basis of total eggs that hatched. †Minimum number, excluding eggs removed from the nest.

TABLE 20

Results of Cross-fostering of Whooping Cranes, 1975-1980*

	1975	1976	1977	1978	1979	1980	Totals
Eggs Incubated							
From Canada	14	15	16	13	19	12	89
From Patuxent	0	2	14	15	5	2	38
Total Eggs Incubated	14	17	30	28	24	14	127
Chicks Hatched							
From Canada	9	11	15	9	12	10	66
From Patuxent	—	0	5	5	4	2	16
Total Chicks Hatched	9	11	20	14	16	12	82
Total Egg Losses	5	6	10	14	10	2	47
Hatching Success (%)†	64	65	67	50	67	86	65
Young Fledged							
From Canada	5	4	4	3	6	4	26
From Patuxent	—	0	0	0	2	1	3
Total Young Fledged	5	4	4	3	8	5	29
Fledging Success (%)‡	55	36	20	21	50	42	35
Cranes Reaching Wintering Areas							
Young-of-year	4	3	2	3	7	4	23
Older Age-Classes	—	3	6	6	8	14	37
Total	4	6	8	9	15	18	60
Annual Post-juvenile Mortality	—	1	0	2	1	1	5
Annual Mortality (%)	—	25	0	25	11	6	11.9

*Data for 1975-1977 from Drewien and Bizeau (1978); more recent data from Derrickson (1980) and Drewien (1978-1981). Slightly different figures are provided by Erickson and Derrickson (1981). †Percentage of total eggs incubated. ‡Percentage of total chicks hatched.

critically important aspect of survival in young cranes.

Some of the best data on hatching and fledging success in wild cranes are now available as a result of the cross-fostering experiments involving the placing of whooping crane eggs in the nests of the greater sandhill crane (Drewien and Bizeau, 1978). These eggs have come from two very different sources: from wild whooping cranes in Wood Buffalo National Park, Canada, and from a small captive flock of whooping cranes at Patuxent Wildlife Research Center, Laurel, Maryland. As shown in table 20, hatching success and fledging success of offspring from wild-population eggs are similar to data for wild whooping cranes and other wild crane populations, at least during the first five years of this study. The eggs taken from the wild population exhibited a surprisingly high, 74 percent, hatchability. However, the fledging success of these young was only 29 percent, or appreciably less than available data for young from the wild population. Eggs from the Patuxent population exhibited a 42 percent hatchability and a fledging success of only 7.9 percent, suggesting some serious inherent problems in the viability of eggs and young from this captive stock. Mortality rates of birds following fledging seem to be relatively low, and are probably not significantly different from those of other wild whooping cranes, to judge from the still limited available data.

Aviculture and Hybridization

6 The keeping of cranes in captivity, either as pets or as animals to be fattened for the pot, is evidently a very old practice. Captive cranes are depicted on the walls of the Temple of Deir-el-Barari of the Nile Valley, where cranes are shown walking in stately fashion between slaves. Each crane's bill is tied down close to its neck, which would upset its balance and thus prevent it from flying away (Whymper, 1909). Armstrong (1979) noted that cranes were apparently domesticated in ancient Greece, and that Plutarch (c. A.D. 46-c. A.D. 120) mentions the nesting of tame cranes, presumably Eurasian cranes. According to Rothchild (1930), a diary of the Moghul emperor Jenangir (1605-1627) mentions the breeding of sarus cranes in captivity. Additionally, crowned cranes were being maintained in Rome by at least as early as the fifteenth century, and a Eurasian crane was maintained for some 40 years by Leonicus Tomaecus, an Italian professor at Padua, at about the beginning of the sixteenth century. Live specimens of the Japanese crane also reached the Vatican by about the sixteenth century, as a gift from Japanese royalty (Topsell, 1972). Cheng (1981) stated that cranes were raised by Chinese royalty as early as the West Chou dynasty, some 2,200 years ago.

Apart from the Eurasian crane, the demoiselle was perhaps the most commonly represented species in European zoos and collections in early years. Bennett (1831) noted that few had reached England by the time of his writing. They were also then rare in France, but toward the end of the seventeenth century the Versailles menagerie contained several individuals that nested there, and one of the young thus produced survived for 24 years. The demoiselle was also successfully bred prior to 1764 at Osterley Park, Middlesex (Hayes, cited by Wiley, 1978).

By the mid-1800s, most of the cranes of the world had been brought into captivity in the major zoological gardens. In 1868, the Zoological Society of London's collection included all the cranes of the world except the hooded, the white-naped, and the then still-undiscovered black-necked crane (*Proceedings Zoological Society of London*, 1868:567). By 1899, the Berlin Zoological Garden was exhibiting all the world's cranes except for the black-necked, the sarus, and the hooded (*loc. cit.* 1900:303), and in 1893 Lord Lilford's private collection was said to include virtually all of the world's cranes (Trevor-Battye, 1903). It is uncertain when the black-necked crane first was brought into captivity, but Delacour (1925) brought the species to Clères, France, in 1924. He suggested that this was the first European importation, although the black-necked crane had apparently been maintained in captivity in the Orient before that time. Archibald and Oesting (1981) have reviewed its avicultural history.

Breeding by captive cranes was attained much less regularly, but at least on the estate of W. H. St. Quinten in northern England the demoiselle was bred by 1903, the sarus by 1911, the Japanese by 1919, and the hooded reportedly nested in 1920 (Moody, 1932). Some of these early nestings were not well documented, but a listing of seemingly reliable early nestings of cranes in captivity is provided in table 21. Hopkinson (1926) provided a fairly complete listing of early breedings of cranes up to the early 1920s, and may be consulted for details.

AVICULTURAL TECHNIQUES

A complete recent review of crane avicultural methods has been provided by Wiley (1978), and the present discussion is based in large measure on his contribution, as well as on those of Sauey and Brown (1977), Archibald (1974), Archibald and Viess (1979), and Larue (1981).

TABLE 21

Early or Initial Breedings of Cranes in Captivity

Species	Date	Reference
"Black-necked" Crowned Crane	before 1914	Hopkinson, 1926
East African Crowned Crane	1975 (probably earlier)	Steel, 1977
Blue Crane	early 1900s	Hopkinson, 1926
Demoiselle Crane	late 1600s	Bennett, 1831
Wattled Crane	1944	Crandall, 1945
Siberian Crane	1977*	Archibald and Viess, 1979
Australian Crane	1908	Woburn Park records
Sarus Crane	early 1600s	Rothschild, 1930
White-naped Crane	1872	Hopkinson, 1926
Sandhill Crane	1899	Hopkinson, 1926
Whooping Crane	1950†	Allen, 1952
Japanese Crane	1861	Bartlett, 1861
Hooded Crane	1908	King, 1979
Black-necked Crane	Not yet bred‡	—
Eurasian Crane	latter 1800s	Hopkinson, 1926

*Eggs taken from the wild were hatched and chicks reared; first actual breeding in 1981 at International Crane Foundation.

†In semicaptive conditions at Aransas Refuge.

‡This species has been kept at the Peking (Beijing) Zoological Gardens since 1965, and at four other Chinese zoos, but has not yet bred.

Physical Environmental Requirements

Wiley points out that it has been traditional for crane aviculturists to provide as much space as possible for crane pairs, to reproduce their normal territorial spacing patterns as far as possible. However, at the present time, the average crane holding enclosure averages only about 800 square feet. Regardless of the size of the enclosure, visual isolation from adjoining pairs is critical. Cranes are prone to fight through wire fences, often with damage to their wings, breasts, or heads, until a visual barrier is established (Archibald and Viess, 1979). This can be provided by shrub or vine plantings, by placing debris such as old Christmas trees on both sides of a chain-link fence, or by using other opaque barriers. On the other hand, vocal isolation is not needed, and indeed the calls of adjacent pairs may stimulate reproductive behavior. Archibald and Viess stress that each breeding pair must have its own breeding territory, without which it cannot exhibit "confident" behavior that leads to normal breeding. Too much disturbance within the territory can lead to territorial abandonment or absence of nesting attempts altogether. Within the holding areas, a good cover of low-growing foliage, such as grass and weeds, is most desirable, and of course clean water should always be available. However, ponds or marshy areas are not necessary and perhaps are undesirable, as they may harbor disease organisms. In hot or sunny areas, a shade tree is desirable within the territory, and a heap of dried marsh vegetation should be provided for nest construction (Archibald, 1974).

In temperate latitudes of the United States, some special adjustments may be needed for photoperiodic control of breeding behavior. Thus, hooded cranes in Wisconsin have been artificially exposed to photoperiods that were gradually increased from 16 hours to 23 hours, within a two-month period starting the first of March. In 1976 and 1977, among a group of hooded cranes exposed to this light regime, two pairs were stimulated to lay fertile eggs. Apparently the actual intensity of light is less important than the ability to see and continue normal activity patterns associated with breeding for longer periods of the day (Archibald and Viess, 1979). Similar attempts were made to influence the environmental humidity of crowned cranes and Australian cranes, and it was apparent that the incidence of sexual displays was higher among crowned cranes on days of artificial showers (by hose and sprinklers) than on dry days. Similarly the Australian cranes were more active and their facial skin was brighter on wet days than during dry weather.

Nutrition

Wiley (1978) reported that in earlier times the diets of captive cranes were mostly grains and some poultry rations, supplemented seasonally by natural high-protein foods such as insects and fish. At present, several high-protein preparations are available, and these may be useful in stimulating breeding (Archibald, 1974). During the nonbreeding season a low-protein diet of about 16 to 18 percent protein is typically provided, but a higher protein food of 27 to 36 percent is begun about a month before the breeding season. Natural food items may also be offered at this time, but if these are high in protein this should be taken into account when estimating the total protein intake. Fish, crickets, and mealworms all are excellent high-protein natural foods, and live foods are especially useful in stimulating feeding by the chicks.

Archibald (1974) reported that at the International Crane Foundation newly hatched chicks are fed for the first month of life on a 26 percent protein commercial turkey starter preparation, to which the following are added per 100 grams of this food: corn meal 2,000 grams, vitamin B_1 50 g, magnesium sulfate 25 g, zinc carbonate 15 g, niacin 10 g, pyridoxine 500 milligrams, choline chloride 300 mg, folic acid 250 mg, biotin 50 mg. From 30 days after hatching until the end of the second year, the birds are fed 22 percent protein commercial food (turkey grower pellets). After that they are provided the adult mix, which is 16 percent protein outside the breeding season and 36 percent during breeding. Larue (1981) has provided more recent information on crane diets at the I.C.F., which now uses a 20.5 percent protein diet for breeders, supplemented by ground oyster shell for females. Maintenance diets outside the breeding season have 19.4 percent protein content.

Egg-laying and Incubation

In early years of aviculture, most cranes were normally allowed to incubate their own eggs and raise their own young. The success of this approach depends greatly on favorable weather, freedom from predation or human harassment, and similar conditions. If natural rearing is used, the aviculturist should be aware that in all cranes the eggs hatch at staggered intervals, and thus there is an age difference in the young that might result in sibling strife and possible death of the younger and weaker birds (Wiley, 1978).

In wild cranes, copulation usually begins about a month before egg-laying, and much the same is true of captive birds. Archibald and Viess (1979) reported that during this prelaying period captive females are regularly inseminated artificially to accustom them to human manipulation and to assure egg fertility. Techniques for artificial insemination have been provided by Archibald (1974) and Larue (1980). Gee and Sexton (1979) reported that semen can be effectively frozen and stored in liquid nitrogen for up to at least two months. In the second year of study, egg fertility by this method was 62 percent, and hatchability was 60 percent of the fertile eggs. Artificial insemination done up to eight days before egg-laying is apparently effective in achieving fertility, but if it is done more than ten days before laying, or less than two days before laying, it is apparently ineffective. Gee and Sexton reported that, of eggs obtained from 17 females of nine species, fertility ranged from 44 to 49 percent, and hatchability was from 58 to 91 percent. Rearing success ranged from 62 to 90 percent. Up to ten eggs were obtained in a single season from a female sarus crane (five of which were fertile and resulted in reared offspring), while seven Japanese cranes were raised from eight eggs laid in a single season. Koga (1976) determined that when successive clutches were taken from the nest before incubation, Japanese cranes would lay up to four clutches (rarely nine eggs), and white-naped cranes laid up to eight clutches (to seventeen eggs). Fertility and hatchability did not change significantly throughout the entire egg-laying period of nearly four months. Each egg should be removed as it is laid, and not replaced with a dummy egg, but excessive disturbance should be avoided. A variety of records of relative hatchability and survival of cranes bred in captivity is provided in table 22. Unincubated eggs may be stored in a refrigerator for up to ten days, but should be turned 180 degrees on a daily basis. They should be warmed to room temperature about a day before incubation (Archibald, 1974).

Incubation in artificial incubators or under broody hens provides an alternative to incubation by the parents, and the use of artificial forced-air incubators is probably now the most commonly chosen method. Eggs are incubated in a horizontal position and are turned at rates ranging from every two hours to three times per day. The best incubation temperatures seem to be those providing a relative humidity of 58 to 64 percent, with dry-bulb readings of 99.50 to 99.75° F (37.5-37.6° C) and wet bulb readings of 86-88° F (30-31° C). Within four days of hatching, the eggs are moved to a separate hatching incubator, which has a relative humidity at the saturation point. The eggs are no longer turned after this transfer. The chick is left in the hatcher until it is out of the shell and dried, and then is moved to a brooder. The hatching process usually requires about 36 hours, and the chick should be given assistance only if it has not completed hatching after 48 hours, to avoid damaging the yolk sac (Archibald, 1974). Larue and Hoffman (1981) recommended that the brooder should contain a feather duster for the chick to hide under, bowls for food and water, and a thermometer. The brooder should also have an adjustable floor in order to regulate inside height and to accommodate for growth, and should be covered by a soft carpet or other somewhat pliable surface that will help to avoid the development of crooked toes.

Care of Chicks

For the first few days of life, the weight of the newly hatched chick invariably declines, but by about the

TABLE 22

Hatchability and Survival of Cranes Bred in Captivity

Species	Eggs Laid	Chicks Hatched	Young Reared	Reference
West African Crowned Crane	5	5	4	Archibald and Viess, 1979
Blue Crane	10	0	0	Archibald and Viess, 1979
	56	35	23	Guy Greenwell, pers. comm.
Siberian Crane	9	0	0	Archibald and Viess, 1979
Sarus Crane	38	8	8	Archibald and Viess, 1979
	55	36	33	Guy Greenwell, pers. comm.
White-naped Crane	23	4	4	Archibald and Viess, 1979
	114	57	?	Koga, 1976
Whooping Crane	71	16	5	Maroldo, 1980
	42	20	9	Erickson and Derrickson, 1981
Japanese Crane	38	23	15	Archibald and Viess, 1979
	82	33	16	Takahaski and Nakamura, 1981
Hooded Crane	6	6	6	Archibald and Viess, 1979
Totals	549	243 (44.3%)	123 (28.3%)*	

*Excluding Koga, 1976.

TABLE 23

Mean Weights of Crane Chicks during First Week after Hatching*

Species	Mean Hatching Weight (grams)	Subsequent Weights (as % of hatching weight), Successive Days after Hatching					
		1	2	3	4	5	6
Crowned Crane[†]	91.7	85	85	92	95	104	121
Blue Crane	121.3	91	92	89	97	106	118
Demoiselle Crane	73.4	93	89	97	114	130	144
Siberian Crane	121.7	91	88	88	97	108	118
Sarus Crane	134.2	92	93	95	104	115	131
White-naped Crane	116.3	92	93	96	98	101	125
Japanese Crane	132.0	88	91	100	101	117	124
Hooded Crane	113.7	89	87	89	89	102	112
Eurasian Crane	121.1	93	92	94	96	104	114
Average	—	90.4	89.9	93.3	98.9	109.5	123.3

*Calculated from data presented by Archibald and Viess (1979) and Stephen Wylie (pers. comm.).
[†]Hybrid West African x East African.

fourth or fifth day after hatching, the chick typically reaches and exceeds the original hatching weight (table 23). Once this initial period has passed, the rate of chick growth normally increases rapidly (table 24, figure 12).

Brooding of newly hatched cranes requires a unit having a temperature of between 85 and 95° F, at least for the first few days. Normally the chicks are not fed for the first 36 to 48 hours after hatching, to allow for a complete resorbtion of the yolk sac, but water should be provided to prevent dehydration.

When raising chicks by hand, most aviculturists provide considerable quantities of such animal foods as live crickets, mealworms, bits of fish, ground raw meat, and hard-boiled eggs. Gradually these can be eliminated and a general high-protein chow is adequate. This prepared food, with protein levels of 22 to 26 percent, is used for the first three or four weeks, but too much feeding will result in too-rapid weight gain and possible serious leg problems (Wiley, 1978).

Archibald and Viess (1979) reported that the newly

TABLE 24

Weekly Mean Weights of Crane Chicks, First 10 Weeks after Hatching*

Species	Mean Hatching Weight (grams)	Subsequent weights (as % of hatching weight), by weeks									
		1	2	3	4	5	6	7	8	9	10
Crowned Crane[†]	91.7	121	300	568	1127	1976	—	2524	fledge	—	—
Demoiselle Crane	73.4	144	399	795	1339	1985	2476	2652	2823	2894	fledge
Siberian Crane	121.1	118	253	482	933	1794	2267	2652	2807	3082	3351
Sarus Crane	134.2	131	235	371	680	1146	1464	1882	2477	3129	3998
Lesser Sandhill	104.0	175	443	1052	1442	1695	2096	2373	2526	2684	2867
Florida Sandhill	116.4	193	355	600	972	1027	1748	1972	2352	2531	2651
Canadian Sandhill	103.0	156	347	773	1230	1743	2052	2181	2337	2539	2741
Greater Sandhill	119.2	121	241	539	962	1443	1710	2010	2314	2544	2742
White-naped Crane	116.3	125	220	461	731	985	1242	1709	2190	2527	2832
Whooping Crane	126.0	—	119	387	753	—	1686	2302	—	—	3412
Japanese Crane	132.0	124	294	548	863	1235	1611	1819	2560	2860	3192
Hooded Crane	113.7	112	258	464	778	1074	1554	1886	2193	2413	2681
Eurasian Crane	121.1	114	248	540	1153	—	—	—	2755	2943	3075
Average	—	136	299	644	1017	1421	1836	2150	2488	2740	2973

*Calculated from data presented by Archibald and Viess (1979) and Stephenson (1971); data of latter source (for whooping crane) excluded from average computations.
[†]Hybrid West African x East African.

hatched chick is placed in a small and carpeted enclosure, with a heat lamp that keeps the area no warmer than 37.7° C. When no visual contact with other chicks is possible, the cage is provided with a large mirror, so the chick can imprint on its own reflection. A small shallow dish is filled with stones and water, and a second one is provided with a special starter mix. A red dowel is suspended above the second dish to stimulate feeding, with the tip of the dowel just touching the food. The chick is taught to feed by dipping the dowel in water, and then in the food, and finally moving the dowel in front of the chick's head. Several days of such training may be needed before the chick begins to feed on its own. These authors recommend feeding the chick on the second day after hatching.

After the chick has begun to feed on its own, it is moved to a confine that has an inside cement floor with wood shavings, and an adjacent outside confine, again in visual contact with other chicks. During their first week, chicks often develop crooked toes, but these can be treated by bandaging them with a toothpick for support if needed. Such toe problems should be treated as they appear, for otherwise they may be followed by rotation of the entire leg and foot. Lateral displacement of the hock joint may be treated by a pair of plastic bands that are joined by a piece of elastic that provides the proper degree of leg alignment. Medial displacement of the joint is much more difficult to treat, according to Archibald and Viess.

If pinioning is to be done, it should be done at an early age, to avoid too severe stress on the chick. As the bird grows older it should be provided larger areas, and it is desirable to exercise the young birds frequently.

Care of Immatures and Juveniles

Archibald and Viess (1979) reported that the holding techniques for various age-groups of cranes can be

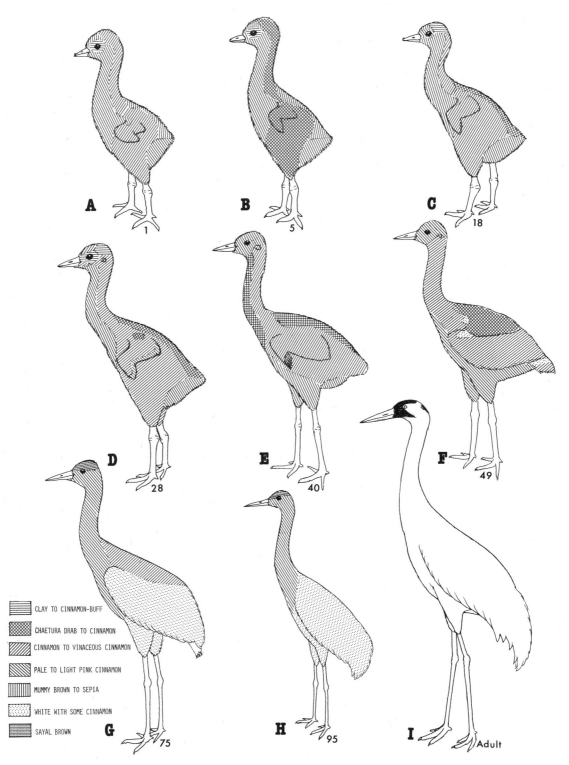

CLAY TO CINNAMON-BUFF

CHAETURA DRAB TO CINNAMON

CINNAMON TO VINACEOUS CINNAMON

PALE TO LIGHT PINK CINNAMON

MUMMY BROWN TO SEPIA

WHITE WITH SOME CINNAMON

SAYAL BROWN

12. Stages in plumage development of whooping cranes during first 95 days
    after hatching (A-H) and as adults (I). Numbers indicate days after
    hatching. Not drawn to uniform scale; after Stephenson (1971).

important in managing these birds. Crane chicks are wing-clipped at the time of fledging, and are then placed in a large enclosure with other young birds. These young birds are typically gregarious and show little conflict after a social hierarchy has been established. At the age of 22 months all the potential pairs are separated and placed in individual compounds for possible breeding. Pairing normally occurs soon after this separation, and the area is used by the birds as a breeding territory.

Sexing of cranes is generally quite difficult, as measurements of the sexes almost invariably overlap. Vent-sexing is relatively difficult, although for at least some species it seems fairly reliable in sexing older age-classes (Blackman, 1971a; Tacha and Lewis, 1979). An alternate, albeit expensive, method is that of chromosomal analysis (Sasaki and Takagi, 1981), and fecal samples may be chemically tested for estrogenic or androgenic hormones (Czekala and Lasley, 1977). However, direct observation of the gonads by surgical examination (laparotomy) is probably the simplest and most certain method of establishing the bird's sex, although it does place the bird under some stress. Adults of at least some species may be accurately sexed by a study of sex-specific posturing and vocalizations during the unison call (Archibald, 1974, 1975, 1976).

Initial Reproduction and Longevity of Adults

Although sexual maturity in hand-raised birds typically occurs within about three years of hatching, wild-caught birds often fail to exhibit sexual behavior after many years in captivity, if indeed they ever do. Archibald and Viess (1979) reported obtaining viable semen from three-year-old sandhill, Eurasian, and Japanese cranes, and semen has also been obtained from whooping

TABLE 25

Longevity Records for Cranes in Captivity

Species	Reported Life-span	Reference
Crowned Crane		
Sudan	15 years, 6 months, 18 days	Flower, 1925
	Average of 20, 84 months	Flower, 1925
West African	Average of 7, 50 months	Mitchell, 1911
South African	28 years	Whipsnade Zoo records
	Average of 14, 43 months	Mitchell, 1911
Blue Crane	At least 22 years, 10 months	Stephen Wylie, pers. comm.
	Average of 8, 58 months	Mitchell, 1911
Demoiselle Crane	At least 27.5 years*	Flower, 1925
	Average of 13, 45 months	Mitchell, 1911
Wattled Crane	At least 36 years (still fertile)*	Conway and Hamer, 1977
	Average of 9, 34 months	Mitchell, 1911
Siberian Crane	Over 61 years, 8 months*	Davis, 1969
	At least 65 years (still fertile)*	George Archibald, pers. comm.
Australian Crane	33 years	Lavery and Blackman, 1969
	Average of 10, 68 months	Mitchell, 1911
Sarus Crane	At least 25 years (still fertile)*	Guy Greenwell, pers. comm.
	Average of 7, 64 months	Mitchell, 1911
White-naped Crane	28 years	Flower, 1925
	At least 45 years (still fertile)*	George Archibald, pers. comm.
Sandhill Crane	24 years, 2 months, 18 days	Flower, 1925
Whooping Crane	40 years	Moody, 1931
	Average of 5, 34 months	Mitchell, 1911
Japanese Crane	25 years, 6 months	Mitchell, 1911
	Average of 8, 59 months	Mitchell, 1911
	3 still alive at 20, 21, & 22 years	Koga, 1976
Hooded Crane	19 years	Whipsnade Zoo records
Eurasian Crane	42 years, 10 months	Mitchell, 1911
	Average of 15, nearly 16 years	Flower, 1925

*Acquired as individuals of unknown age.

TABLE 26

Survey of Cranes Bred or Maintained in Captivity

	Total Reported Zoo Breedings 1969-1977*	Average Cumulative Total of Birds Reported per Year	Average Number of Zoos Reporting Species per Year
Crowned Crane			
Hybrids or sspp.?	24	—	—
West African & Sudan	21	—	—
South & East African	54	—	—
Blue Crane	116	—	—
Demoiselle Crane	77	—	—
Wattled Crane	10	66	12
Siberian Crane†	3	10.5	8
Australian Crane	17	27.6	9
Sarus Crane	208	—	—
White-necked Crane	29	54.4	16
Sandhill Crane†			
Greater Sandhill	4	—	—
Mississippi	2	10.8	1
Lesser	1	—	—
Florida	3	51.1	5.8
Cuban	0	1	1
Whooping Crane†	6	15	2.3
Japanese Crane	35	51.5	19
Hooded Crane	2	58.8	19
Black-necked Crane	0	3.3	1
Eurasian Crane	26	—	—

*Based on information in International Zoo Yearbook.
†Some "breedings" from hatching wild eggs included.

TABLE 27

Records of Hybridization among Cranes of the World*

	Blue	Wattled	Australian	Sarus	White-naped	Sandhill	Whooping	Japanese	Hooded	Eurasian
Crowned	C	—	—	—	—	—	—	—	—	—
Demoiselle	C	—	—	—	C	—	—	—	—	C
Blue		—	—	—	C	—	—	—	—	—
Wattled			—	—	—	C	—	—	—	—
Australian				C, W, (F)	—	—	—	—	—	—
Sarus					—	—	—	—	—	C
White-naped						C	—	?†	—	C
Sandhill							C	C	—	—
Whooping								—	—	—
Japanese									—	C
Hooded										W

*C = Captive-bred, W = Wild-bred, (F) = Fertile.
†A reported hybrid may have been a melanistic Japanese Crane (Austin, 1948).

cranes of this age-class (Derrickson, 1980). However, the age of initial successful breeding in 11 male individuals of cranes representing seven species ranged from 5 to 12 years and averaged 7.27 years (various zoo records). Similarly, of 14 female cranes representing ten species, the average age of initial captive breeding was 7.85 years, and the range was 4 to 16 years. A three-year-old female blue crane laid two eggs that proved fertile, although the embryos died before hatching (Christopher Marler, pers. comm.). It is thus clear that many cranes in zoos do not attempt to breed for several years after actual reproductive maturity. Similarly, some birds continue to breed until they are well over 20 years old, and sometimes until they are nearly 40 (table 25). Actual longevity is often much greater than this, especially in the species of the genus *Grus*, as is also indicated in table 25. Thus cranes are one of the more long-lived groups of birds in captivity, and one Siberian crane was known to have survived in excess of 61 years (Davis, 1969).

By the 1960s, all the cranes of the world had been brought into captivity, and as of 1981 all had been bred under captive conditions except for the black-necked crane. Indeed, some species, such as the sarus crane, are now being bred in quite remarkable numbers (table 26), and the zoo populations of this species and of the crowned cranes, the blue cranes, and the demoiselles are probably quite high, although exact numbers are unavailable. Zoo populations of the rarer species in captivity are much better known, however, and not only do such rare species as the Japanese crane, the hooded crane, and the white-naped crane have excellent captive populations but also the success in reproduction under captive conditions is improving constantly.

Hybridization

Hybridization among captive birds has been observed fairly frequently in the crane family, and a summary of hybrid records through the late 1950s was provided by Gray (1958). At that time the only intergeneric hybrid combinations known were one involving the blue crane and the white-naped crane and another between the wattled crane and the sandhill crane. No wild crane hybrids were mentioned in Gray's summary.

In addition to Gray's records, Rutgers and Norris (1970) reported intergeneric hybridization between the demoiselle crane and the white-naped. Furthermore, at least two interspecific combinations have now been reported from wild populations. Several individuals of hybrids between the Eurasian and hooded cranes have been seen on wintering areas of Kyushu, Japan (Nishida, 1981). In addition, in recent years wild hybrids between the Australian crane and the sarus crane have been reported in their area of recent sympatry in northern Australia. Furthermore, this hybrid combination is known to be fertile (Gray, 1958) and may produce introgressive hybridization in Australia (Archibald, 1981b).

A summary of available crane hybridization records is provided in table 27. A supposed hybrid between the white-naped crane and the Japanese crane, a specimen that was originally described as a black-necked crane (Gray, 1958), is probably not an actual hybrid and is perhaps simply a melanistic example of the Japanese crane (Austin, 1948). Hybrids between the sandhill crane and the whooping crane have been obtained only with the assistance of artificial insemination (Derrickson, 1980). Only a single case of hybridization involving the genus *Balearica* has so far been reported. A hybrid produced by a female South African crowned crane and a male blue crane was raised in Pretoria, South Africa, and survived for at least 16 months (*South African Digest*, 11 July 1975, p. 16).

Endangered Species and Conservation

7 Few families of birds, other than some associated with small island archipelagos, have such a large proportion of their species in danger of extinction as does the crane family. Of the 14 extant species of cranes, King (1979) regards two full species (whooping crane and Siberian crane) as endangered, three more (Japanese, hooded, and white-naped) as vulnerable, and the black-necked crane as of indeterminate status. Additionally, one race (the Mississippi) of the sandhill crane is classified as endangered, and the Cuban race is regarded as rare and local. Thus, more than a third of the world's crane species are currently considered vulnerable or endangered.

There is also good reason to believe that the wattled crane is rapidly declining and should perhaps be placed in the "vulnerable" category. The eastern sarus crane is probably also in a vulnerable situation. It is thus worth considering the current populations of each of these forms, and their prospects for survival in the future. A general summary of their estimated current population sizes is presented in table 28, and in the following discussion the endangered species are organized in a sequence reflecting their apparent relative rarity. The rare or endangered subspecies are discussed after the accounts of the full species.

RARE OR ENDANGERED SPECIES

Whooping Crane

The history of the endangered whooping crane is now so well known, as a result of the monograph by Allen (1952) and several more recent popular books (McNulty, 1966; McCoy, 1966; Zimmerman, 1975), that a detailed discussion seems unwarranted. Derrickson (1980) has summarized much of the population data for the species up to the late 1970s, and Johnsgard (1982) has also provided an analysis of the trends of the mortality and natality rates that are becoming evident.

The lowest known wild population size of the whooping crane was in 1945, when only 17 birds appeared at Aransas National Wildlife Refuge in Texas, and when only 2 more were known to be existing in Louisiana. The Louisiana population had disappeared by 1949, and in 1952 only 21 birds arrived and wintered at Aransas National Wildlife Refuge. The same number was present in the fall and winter of 1954, but the mid-1950s marked the beginning of a gradual increase in numbers that is still continuing. In the fall of 1975, the first fledged offspring resulting from the egg transplantation experiments at Gray's Lake, Idaho, reached the Rio Grande Valley of New Mexico, providing a secondary wintering population site (table 29). Numerical information on the success of this experiment through 1980 was provided earlier (table 20).

At present, the whooping crane population is slowly increasing, reaching nearly 100 birds by 1982, although the species' actual natality rates are the lowest in history (Johnsgard, 1982). Thus, there is little reason to feel secure about its long-term status, and more intensive efforts must be made to find ways of increasing the actual number and success of wild breeding pairs. These remain remarkably few, and perhaps have not significantly changed in the past 20 years, judging from the total numbers of fledged young reaching the wintering grounds annually (table 29).

Siberian Crane

In his summary of the status of this species in the USSR, Flint (1978a) suggested that the eastern Siberian breeding population then numbered no more than some 300 birds, and the western Siberian population

TABLE 28

Estimated Population Sizes of Endangered Populations of Cranes

Species or Race	Estimated Number in Wild	Number in Captivity, 1979 & 1980*	References
Wattled Crane	Endangered in Transvaal & Natal. Local in Zambia & Botswana, 1970s. Few in Namibia, Zimbabwe, Malawi, Ethiopia, Angola, Zaire, and Mozambique, 1970s.	69	West, 1976 Konrad, 1981 Konrad, 1981
Siberian Crane	ca. 24 breeding in western Siberia, 1980 (9 wintering in Iran, 15 in India). ca. 300 breeding in eastern Siberia, 60 in eastern Siberia, mid-1970s.	12	Archibald, 1981c Flint, 1978a
White-naped Crane	2,700 in late 1970s.	154	Yamashina, 1978
Cuban Sandhill Crane	ca. 100-150 in late 1970s.	—	King, 1979
Mississippi Sandhill Crane	ca. 40-50 in 1980.	24	Valentine, 1981
Whooping Crane	78 wintering in Texas, 1980-81. 16 wintering in New Mexico, 1981-82.	26	U.S.F.W.S. data
Japanese Crane	80 in Amur and Ussuri basins, late 1970s. ca. 200 in Hokkaido, late 1970s. Total world population ca. 300-400, late 1970s.	139	Yamashina, 1978
Hooded Crane	2,800 in late 1970s.	92	Yamashina, 1978
Black-necked Crane	ca. 600 on Tsaidam breeding grounds	8	Tso-hsin Cheng, pers. comm.

*Data from *International Zoo Yearbook*, vols. 20 and 21 (1980 and 1981); Chinese zoo data from 1979, remainder from 1980.

consisted of perhaps 60 individuals. There had been no noticeable reduction in numbers for the past 10 years, although in the past 100 to 150 years the population had exhibited a catastrophic reduction in numbers. This was especially true of the western population, and Flint suggested that as industrial development is built up in that area the entire population might disappear. Flint considered the major causes of population declines to be human encroachment on the breeding areas, poaching, unsatisfactory remaining habitat, mortality during migration and wintering, and general disturbance of the population structure.

King (1979) provided a population estimate of the eastern (Yakutia) component as numbering 300 birds as of 1974. He also noted that Afghanistan and India support transient or wintering populations of up to 200 birds, while a remnant wintering population of 9 birds was discovered in 1978 in the south Caspian coastlands at Feredookenar. In 1981 about 100 birds from the Yakutia population were found wintering along the Yangtze River, in eastern China.

Archibald (1981c) has reviewed this species' status,

and suggested that the 1979-80 population was 250 to 300 individuals, with an eastern component of about 200 birds and the remainder in the western Siberian group. The western group actually consists of two subpopulations. One of these winters in the Caspian lowlands and, as already noted, included only 9 birds in 1978. The other winters in the Keoladeo Ghana Sanctuary of north-central India, with a stopover in the Ab-i-Estada saline lake of Afghanistan. This flock declined from 77 birds in 1970 to only 15 in the winter of 1980-81, probably because of hunting on their stopover point in Afghanistan. The most recent population estimates are a 1980 estimate of 200 birds in the Yakutia population by Vladimir Flint, and 1981 counts of 16 birds in Iran and 34 in India (Ronald Sauey, pers. comm.).

Japanese Crane

King (1979) considered this species "vulnerable," and it is included in the Japanese *Red Data Book of Japanese Birds* (no date). Flint (1978a) considered it

TABLE 29

Whooping Crane Wintering Populations

Year (fall)	TEXAS Adults	TEXAS Juveniles	Sub-total	LOUISIANA Total		Grand Total
1938	14	4	18	11		29
1939	15	7	22	13		35
1940	21	5	26	6		32
1941	13	2	15	6		21
1942	15	4	19	5		24
1943	16	5	21	4		25
1944	15	3	18	3		21
1945	14	3	17*	2		19
1946	22	3	25	2		27
1947	25	6	31	1		32
1948	27	3	30	1		31
1949	30	4	34			34
1950	26	5	31			31
1951	20	5	25			25
1952	19	2	21			21
1953	21	3	24			24
1954	21	0	21			21
1955	20	8	28			28
1956	22	2	24			24
1957	22	4	26			26
1958	23	9	32			32
1959	31	2	33			33
1960	30	6	36			36
1961	34	5	39			39
1962	32	0	32			32
1963	26	7	33			33
1964	32	10	42			42
1965	36	8	44			44
1966	38	5	43			43
1967	39	9	48			48
1968	44	6	50			50
1969	48	8	56			56
1970	51	6	57			57
1971	54	5	59			57

Year (fall)	TEXAS Adults	TEXAS Juveniles	Sub-total	NEW MEXICO Adults	NEW MEXICO Juveniles	NEW MEXICO Subtotal	Grand Total
1972	46	5	51				51
1973	47	2	49				49
1974	47	2	49				49
1975	49	8	57		4		61
1976	57	12	69	3	3	6	75
1977	62	10	72	6	2	8	80
1978	68	7	75	6	3	9	84
1979	70	6	76	8	7	15	91
1980	72	6	78	14	4	18	96
1981	71	2	73	16	0	16	89
1982†	66	6	72	—	—	14	86

NB: "Adult" category includes all birds in nonjuvenile plumage (at least 1 year old).
*Incomplete count (based on counts during previous and following falls, 18 adults and 4 juveniles were probably alive in 1945).
†Based on December information.

TABLE 30

Japanese Crane Populations on Hokkaido*

Year	Adults	Juveniles	Total
1952	—	—	33
1953	—	—	42
1954	—	—	52
1955	—	—	61
1956	—	—	76
1957	—	—	92
1958	—	—	125
1959	—	—	139
1960	—	—	172
1961	—	—	175
1962	164	20	184
1963	128	19	147
1964	137	17	154
1965	148	24	172
1966	144	26	170
1967	171	34	205
1968	147	24	171
1969	188	24	212
1970	146	33	179
1971	129	18	147
1972	195	27	222
1973	204	29	233
1974	221	32	253
1975	180	14	194
1976	180	40	220
1977	229	28	257
1978	195	19	214
1979	215	34	249

*After Masatomi (1979, 1981b)

"very rare, and disappearing" in the *Red Data Book* of the USSR. In 1964, the USSR breeding population was some 200 to 300 birds, including 30 to 35 breeding on the southeastern shores of Lake Khanka (Fisher, Simon, and Vincent, 1969). However, Flint estimated that in the late 1970s there were no more than 25 to 30 breeding pairs in all of the USSR, and a known total world population of 282 birds, based on winter census data. Similarly, Yamashina (1978) estimated that about 80 birds occur on the known USSR breeding grounds (the east shore of Lake Khanka and the middle courses of the Amur and Ussuri rivers), and that there are some as yet unknown breeding numbers along the River Sungari in northern Manchuria, and in extreme northeastern Mongolia.

Although population sizes are unknown, the Japanese crane certainly once bred on both Hokkaido and Honshu, and perhaps also on Shikoku and Kyushu, but by the late 1800s it may have been confined to a single area in eastern Hokkaido. When this population was discovered in 1924 it was found to have less than 20 birds and only three known active nests. The area was made a

sanctuary in 1925 and was then believed to include 20 to 30 birds. By 1934 there were about 30 resident birds, and by 1949 about 35 were present. Since 1952 fairly complete counts have been made on a yearly basis (table 30). The large buildup of birds during the late 1950s and early 1960s is remarkable and seems too rapid to have been accounted for by normal reproductive potentials. It thus must in part have resulted from the attraction of cranes from elsewhere, presumably from the continent. Yet this population is essentially sedentary, although a few Japanese cranes turn up in the winter with other cranes in a crane sanctuary at Arasaki, Kagoshima Prefecture, Kyushu. Since the early 1970s the Hokkaido population has remained essentially stable at between 147 and 257 birds (table 30).

Compared to this Japanese population, the mainland population (which Archibald, 1975, 1976, considers a distinct race) is much more difficult to estimate accurately. The USSR breeding ground estimates have already been mentioned, and these birds now winter largely or entirely in Korea. Previously, wintering also occurred south to central China and on Taiwan.

Besides a few birds that winter each year in South Korea, there is also a small colony that both winters and apparently also breeds near Pyonguang Zoo, North Korea (King, 1979). The wintering population in China is unknown but may number in the hundreds. In Japan the species has been considered a National Monument since 1935, and a Special National Monument since 1952. It was designated as a National Monument in South Korea in 1968, and is also protected in North Korea and in the USSR. A history of its conservation in Japan was provided by Masatomi (1981a).

Hooded Crane

This species was reported as "vulnerable" by King (1979) and was included in the *Red Data Book* of the USSR (Flint, 1978a) and in that of Japan. Flint classified it "rare, little-studied," and considered it an endemic breeding species in the USSR.

Almost nothing can be said of the breeding population, as very few nests have been found. An estimated 12 to 15 pairs breed in the Bikin River marshes, Ussuri basin. Winter counts suggest a population of about 2,800 birds in the late 1970s. Of these, about 1,500 to 2,200 winter on Kyushu Island and about 75 to 100 on Honshu, and there are few if any still present in Korea (Flint, 1978a). There is no recent information as to numbers wintering in China. In Japan, the wintering population dropped from 3,435 in 1939 to only about 250 after the Second World War. However, by 1973 there were 2,793 reported in Kagoshima Prefecture and 137 more in Yamaguchi Prefecture. Thus, nearly all the hooded cranes of the world now winter in Japan, so far as can presently be judged (Yamashina, 1978). A listing of numbers observed at Arasaki, Kagoshima Prefecture, and in Yamaguchi Prefecture is provided in table 31. These two areas are the only significant wintering areas in Japan, and provide the best available estimates of the species' numbers. The Japanese wintering population has been protected since 1955, and the hooded crane has been considered a National Monument in South Korea since 1970 (King, 1979). Kawamura (1981) has summarized population data for Yamaguchi Prefecture, and Nishida (1981) has done the same for Kagoshima Prefecture.

White-naped Crane

This species is regarded by King (1979) as "vulnerable," and was classified by Flint (1978a) as "very rare, numbers decreasing" in the *Red Data Book* of the USSR. Although it formerly wintered throughout Japan, the species now is limited to the area of Sendai, Kyushu. It was formerly much more abundant in Japan, and 469 were counted in 1939. However, by 1947 the number was down to 25. By 1974 the species had increased to approximately 600 birds. Nearly 1,500 birds were counted in Japan in the winter of 1977-78 (table 32).

Flint (1978a) estimated the world population as 2,632 birds, based on winter counts. Numbers on the breeding grounds are still unknown, but it is believed that breeding occurs primarily in Mongolia and Manchuria, with possibly some breeding in the Tuvinskaya ASSR. No breeding is known to occur in the USSR (Flint, 1978a).

Certainly Korea is the most important single wintering area for this species, and in November 1961 a flock of at least 2,300 birds was found at the confluence of the Han and Imjin rivers. There were 1,500 birds in the same area in 1974, and 2,000 in 1977. A considerable number of these birds evidently continue on to Japan; as noted above, many were observed in Japan that same winter (King, 1979). At present, about 1,500 to 2,000 white-naped cranes are in the Han River estuary, and many of them scatter through the DMZ for the winter. About 1,000 now continue on to Kyushu, Japan (Won, 1981). The species has been protected in South Korea since 1970, and the Han River estuary was made a sanctuary in 1975, with additional areas (Gimpogun, Inchon) so designated in 1977. It is also given special protection at Sendai, Kyushu. Although the species has been recently reported from the lower Yangtze of China, there is no indication of the actual number of birds. The total number of wintering birds is far greater than the known breeding populations for this species, indicating that there are still unknown breeding areas to be found. These perhaps occur around the east shore of Lake Baikal, or around the Kerulen River and the Onon River basin in Mongolia (Yamashina, 1978). Their status in Korea has recently been summarized by Won (1981), Archibald (1981a), and Kyu and Oesting (1981).

Wattled Crane

Although not included in King's (1979) list, there is little doubt that the wattled crane is now suffering a substantial range retraction and has been locally eliminated from much of its originally widespread range in Africa. The species exists as two surprisingly widely disjunctive populations, which are not considered racially distinct. The northern population, restricted to a relatively small range in the Ethiopian highlands, is either small or declining (Konrad, 1981). The southern population has been reported from as far north and as low as the mouth of the Congo River, and south to the Cape of Good Hope. Actual breeding records seem to be almost entirely confined to areas east of 25° east longitude and south of 10° south latitude (Snow, 1978), although a small area of local breeding

TABLE 31

Wintering Hooded Crane Populations in Honshu and Kyushu*

Year	Yamaguchi Prefecture (Honshu)	Kagoshima Prefecture (Kyushu)	Total
1897	34	—	—
1907	55	—	—
1912	65	—	—
1921	100	—	—
1927	—	400	—
1929	—	600	—
1933	140	—	—
1936	—	2,381	—
1939	—	3,435	—
1940	355	—	—
1947	200	250	450
1950	160	265	425
1955	150	274	424
1960	132	376	508
1961	108	723	831
1962	111	811	922
1963	110	1,053	1,163
1964	109	1,127	1,136
1965	101	1,442	1,543
1966	125	1,447	1,572
1967	90	1,450	1,540
1968	78	1,452	1,530
1969	78	1,562	1,640
1970	91	2,072	2,163
1971	108	2,023	2,131
1972	106	2,286	2,392
1973	137	2,793	2,930
1974	90	2,158	2,248
1975	108	2,867	2,975
1976	110	2,813	2,923
1977	105	3,296	3,401
1978	87	3,179	3,266
1979	73	3,889	3,962

*After Koga (1974) and Nishida (1981)

also occurs in Ovamboland, South-West Africa (Namibia) (Winterbottom, 1971). Probably the largest part of its southern population now occurs in Zambia, Zimbabwe, the Transvaal, and Natal, according to West (1976). However, it now is extirpated from Cape Province and Swaziland and no longer occurs in western Transvaal (David Skead, pers. comm.). It is considered endangered in both Natal and Transvaal (Konrad, 1981). According to Konrad, it is also declining or present only in small numbers in Zimbabwe, Malawi, Namibia (South-West Africa), Angola, Zaire, and Mozambique. This would suggest that only Zambia and Botswana still support good wattled crane populations. In these two areas, six large wetlands provide feeding and nesting habitats for the species, with individual wetlands supporting between 250 and 3,000 birds. They include the Kafue Flats,

Bangweulu, Busanga, and Liuwa in Zambia, and the Okavango and Magadigadi in Botswana. Three of these areas (Kafue Flats, Okavango, Bangweulu) are targeted for damming or wetland reclamation, and in another (Luiwa) the human population pressures are affecting reproduction of a supposedly protected crane population (Konrad, 1981). Douthwaite (1974) reported that the Kafue Flats area supports less than 1,000 birds during flood periods, but some 3,000 birds in the latter half of the dry season. Breeding occurs during the rainy season in small wetland habitats, and toward the end of the wet season in larger wetlands, as floodwaters recede (Konrad, 1981). All told, it seems quite possible that the total wild population of this species is likely to be under 10,000 individuals. Konrad (1981) has made research and conservation recommendations for this rare species.

TABLE 32

Wintering White-naped Crane Populations in Kyushu, Japan*

Year	Total Cranes	Year	Total Cranes
1939	467	1961	71
1940	25	1962	96
1941	50	1963	45
1942	50	1964	121
1943	30	1965	129
1944-46	?	1966	181
1947	25	1967	221
1948	50	1968	203
1949	30	1969	233
1950	28	1970	257
1951	23	1971	287
1952	20	1972	401
1953	20	1973	449
1954	22	1974	582
1955	25	1975	781
1956	27	1976	1,021
1957	31	1977	1,220
1958	34	1978	1,448
1959	45	1979	670
1960	60		

*After Walkinshaw (1973), Archibald (1978), and Nishida (1981).

Black-necked Crane

Of all the crane species, this is certainly the least known, and any attempt to estimate its numbers can be little more than sheer guesswork. King (1979) considered it of "indeterminate" status, although he noted that during the 1930s it was still apparently fairly common on the wintering grounds of Yunnan, China (Schäfer, 1938). King noted that 15 had been seen during the winter in Bhutan in 1974, and a few adults plus one chick had been observed in Ladakh in 1976 (Ali, 1976). A nest was observed in the same area in 1978 (Gole, 1981), but the species is certainly extremely rare in Ladakh. Most recently, an estimate of about 600 birds seen during October 1979 in the Tsaidam Basin of China now provides a crude indication of its abundance (Cheng, 1981).

RARE OR ENDANGERED SUBSPECIES

Cuban and Mississippi Sandhill Cranes

The Cuban race of the sandhill crane is considered "rare and local" by King (1979), while the Mississippi race is considered an endangered population by King as well as by the U.S. Fish and Wildlife Service.

King estimated the Cuban population to total probably some 100 to 150 birds. These include about 30 on the Isle of Pines, about 30 in the Zapata Swamp area, and smaller numbers in the Pinar del Rio pine barrens. There are probably also some still present in the Camaguey prairie area. However, no hard information is available on any of these areas at present. Walkinshaw (1949) estimated that in the mid-1940s only 15 to 20 pairs occurred on the Isle of Pines, but no earlier good estimates are available for this race.

The Mississippi sandhill crane was first reported in 1928 and was believed at that time to number approximately 50 to 100 individuals. In 1940 Walkinshaw (1949) estimated that 25 pairs of birds might be then breeding in Jackson County. In 1972 it was recognized as a distinct race, and in 1973 it was designated as an endangered form. Valentine and Noble (1970) estimated that the population consisted of less than 40 birds in the late 1960s. The most recent available estimate is that of Valentine (1979, 1981), who suggested that as of 1978 there were 12 to 15 breeding pairs, and the total 1980 wild population was 40 to 50 birds. An area of some 6,070 hectares in Jackson County was declared a national wildlife refuge in 1974, and in 1977 an area of 10,552 hectares (26,000 acres) also was designated as critical habitat. Valentine has also outlined the recovery plan for this population, which includes the raising of 10 captive pairs to provide stock for supplementing the wild population and for translocating to other parts of the original range of this race. Such releases began in 1981 with apparent success (Valentine, 1982).

Recently Walkinshaw (1981a) has estimated the Cuban sandhill crane to number about 200 birds, the Mississippi population to be 40 to 50, and the Florida race to be about 4,800 individuals.

Burmese Sarus Crane

Although this subspecies is not included in King's (1979) listing, Archibald et al. (1981) reported that the eastern or Burmese sarus crane is now considered extirpated from Burma, Thailand, Malaysia, and the Philippines and is of undetermined status in Cambodia and Vietnam. On the other hand, it has recently colonized Queensland, Australia, and seems to be increasing there. Madsen (1981) was unable to locate any cranes on Luzon, of the Philippines, during searches in 1979, but believed that a few isolated individuals might still survive in the Tabuk area of Kalinga-Apayao Province. The Philippine government may begin a restocking program by releasing hand-raised birds (Archibald et al., 1981).

Major Sources of Mortality in Wild and Captive Cranes

If rare and endangered cranes are to be preserved effectively, then a few words on the probable major sources of crane mortality, both in the wild and in captivity, are warranted. There are few good summaries of actual sources of mortality in wild crane populations, since most deaths obviously go unobserved and unreported. Allen (1952) judged that of the 39 estimated whooping crane mortalities (of birds that had survived to reach Aransas at least once) between 1939 and 1949, 14 birds (representing 36 percent of the total) were known to have been killed, while the fate of the remainder was unknown. During this entire period the species was federally protected and its status was well publicized; thus illegal killing was a surprisingly high source of mortality.

A more complete documentation of losses in wild cranes is available for the Japanese crane on Hokkaido, for the period 1950-1979 (table 33). During this period a total of 245 cranes were known to have died. These deaths occurred during the total of 2,168 "crane years,"

TABLE 33

Mortality Sources in Various Crane Populations

| | Captive Populations | | | Wild |
	Chicks*	Immatures and Adults†	All Ages†	Japanese Cranes‡
Diseases				7.7%
Herpes	—	—	36.1%	—
Erysipelas	—	—	3.2%	—
Pneumonia	11.8%	—	3.2%	—
Staphylococcus	—	—	3.2%	—
Enteritis	8.8%	7.0%	—	—
Omphalitis	8.8%	—	—	—
Septicemia	5.9%	—	—	—
Miscellaneous	2.9%	1.8%	6.5%	—
Parasites	5.9%	3.5%	—	—
Traumatic Effects				
Fighting	4.4%	26.3%	16.4%	—
Collision with wires	—	—	—	70.9%
Injury or accident	7.3%	15.7%	6.5%	—
Shooting	—	—	—	2.0%
Cold stress	7.3%	—	6.5%	—
Unspecified trauma	—	—	3.2%	—
Age	—	—	3.2%	—
Anatomical Abnormality	20.6%	—	—	—
Predator	2.9%	1.7%	3.2%	—
Miscellaneous	19.4%	—	—	—
Unknown	2.9%	8.8%	8.2%	21.2%

*Based on 68 chicks and 57 immature or adult sandhill cranes at Patuxent Wildlife Research Center (Carpenter, Locke, and Miller, 1976).
†Based on 61 deaths of 13 crane species at the International Crane Foundation (Archibald and Viess, 1979).
‡Based on deaths of 245 cranes in Hokkaido (Akiyama, 1981).

judging from table 30, and thus represent a known mortality of about 1 percent per year. Of these deaths, much the largest single mortality source was trauma caused by collision with electric wires. It remains to be seen whether other crane populations are as vulnerable to wire collisions as these figures indicate, but there is evidence that utility highlines pose a potentially serious threat to sandhill cranes as well (Tacha, Martin, and Endicott, 1979). The presence or installation of utility lines through areas of critical habitat for endangered cranes should certainly be avoided if possible.

By comparison, mortality sources for captive crane populations seem to consist primarily of traumatic factors or disease pathogens, with accidental deaths being relatively insignificant (table 33). During the period from the establishment of the International Crane Foundation in 1973 to 1978, 61 of 195 captive cranes died, or roughly 6 percent per year. Of these losses, much the largest resulted from a herpes outbreak in 1978, emphasizing the danger of keeping captive birds on areas of continually used soil. Another important mortality source was "aggressive trauma" or "cranicide," caused when one crane attacked another, usually because of territorial intrusion. A few deaths of small or young cranes have been caused by avian predators such as great horned owls (*Bubo virginianus*), although probably most cranes, once they attain fledging, are relatively safe from such predators. Nonetheless, one juvenile crane on its fall migration between Gray's Lake and New Mexico was observed to be attacked in flight and killed by a golden eagle (*Aquila chrysaetos*).

Parasitic infections occasionally pose serious problems in both wild and captive bird populations. Thus, parasites contributed to 7 percent of the 135 sandhill crane mortalities at the Patuxent Wildlife Research Center between 1966 and 1975 (Carpenter, Locke, and Miller, 1976). Treatment methods for major parasitic infections of captive cranes have been outlined by Carpenter (1979). These included gapeworms, coccidiosis, and idiopathic protozoan infections, primarily of young birds. However, only gapeworms seem to cause significant adult mortality in cranes. In this combined sample of adults and young birds, trauma from aggression, injury, or accident was responsible for 30 percent of the deaths, infectious diseases 18 percent, anatomical abnormalities 13 percent, and nutritional problems 4 percent. Additionally, miscellaneous factors were responsible for 20 percent, 4 percent of the birds were subjected to euthanasia, and the deaths of 6

percent were from undetermined causes. Unlike the tabulations shown in table 33, these mortality figures include all age-groups from downy young (which accounted for half of the total deaths) to adults. The largest category (36 percent) of mortality factors of downy young consisted of diseases such as pneumonia, omphalitis, and septicemia, while for immatures and adults various traumatic factors caused the largest single source of mortality.

Summary of Distributional Status of Endangered Cranes

Archibald et al. (1981) recently summarized the distribution patterns and population trends of the endangered populations of cranes, and analyzed the present and past distributions of all crane species by countries. An abbreviated summary of their information is presented in table 34. It is apparent from this table that a multinational effort will be required for virtually all of the endangered cranes for effective conservation, since all of the endangered cranes depend on habitats in several countries for part or all of their life cycles. Of the threatened species, only the wattled crane is entirely nonmigratory, and thus only it is likely to be effectively managed by the actions of any single nation. The black-necked and Japanese cranes also have resident populations in China and Japan respectively, while the hooded and white-naped cranes must depend on the cooperative efforts of the several countries that encompass their breeding, migrational, and wintering areas. The future of the whooping crane is likewise essentially dependent upon the bilateral cooperation of the United States and Canada, although efforts are being made to establish a new breeding population confined within the limits of the United States and having a shorter and more fully protected migration route. Similarly, the Soviets and Iranians may cooperate in establishing a new and more secure population of Siberian cranes by substituting Siberian crane eggs into the nests of Eurasian cranes that breed in Siberia and winter in the Arjan National Park of Iran. A less likely possibility would be to place the eggs of Siberian cranes in nests of lesser sandhill cranes, which breed in Siberia but winter in the western United States. However, this latter population is now subjected to considerable hunting pressure, and thus there are many serious conservation problems associated with this option (Archibald, et al., 1981).

TABLE 34

Countries Represented in Current Distributions of Cranes of the World*

	Permanent Resident	Summer	Transient	Winter
Black-necked Crowned Crane	12	—	(2)	—
Gray-necked Crowned Crane	15	—	—	—
Demoiselle Crane	—	6	25 (3)	13
Blue Crane	4	1 (1)	—	—
Wattled Crane (Vulnerable?)	10	—	—	—
Siberian Crane (Endangered)	—	1	7	3 (2)
Australian Crane	3	—	—	—
Sarus Crane	5	—	—	—
White-naped Crane (Vulnerable)	—	3	6	4 (1)
Sandhill Crane (all races)	2	4	4	2 (1)
Mississippi Sandhill (Endangered)	1	—	—	—
Cuban Sandhill (Endangered)	1	—	—	—
Whooping Crane (Endangered)	—	2	2	1
Japanese Crane (Vulnerable)	1	2 (1)	2	3 (2)
Hooded Crane (Vulnerable)	—	2	6	2 (2)
Black-necked Crane (Vulnerable?)	1	2	5	5
Eurasian Crane	—	11	47 (1)	27 (4)

*Numbers indicate countries in which species currently is regularly present; additional irregular presence indicated by parentheses. Modified from Archibald et al. (1981).

Cranes in Myth and Legend

8 Wherever cranes occur in the world, their stature, intelligence, wariness, and sociality have captured the human imagination and have given rise to a variety of legends, myths, and folktales. Among the best sources of such information for England and southern Europe are the manuscript writings of Edward Topsell (1572-1625), which have been edited and recently republished (1972). Topsell reported that "when fables ruled the world" it was believed that a proud queen of Pygmies named Oenoe or Gerania was turned into a crane by Juno and Diana, because she taught her people to neglect other gods and worship her. Gerania thereafter began an irreconcilable war between cranes and Pygmies that has persisted ever since. Much the same story appears in the Iliad of Homer. From this legend perhaps came the Greek name *geranos* or *gereunos* for cranes. Likewise, they were sometimes known as the birds of Palamedes, since, at about the time of the Trojan Wars, the mythic hero Palamedes reputedly invented several Greek letters by watching the convolutions of flying cranes. The avian genus *Palamedea*, however, was subsequently applied to the South American crane-like birds known as screamers. On the other hand, the Romans called cranes *grues*, evidently because of their grunting voices.

According to Topsell, even the African crowned cranes were well known to Pliny and other early Roman writers, and the Eurasian crane was even more familiar to the early Romans, who were greatly impressed by its longevity. An Italian professor at Padua, Leonicus Tomaeus (1457-1533) reportedly maintained a crane in captivity for some forty years. Cranes were also evidently raised as pets or fattened for the pot in ancient Greece. Plutarch referred to the practice of fattening them by sewing shut their eyelids, which quiets the birds (from which practice the English term hoodwinking derives), and a design on an ancient Greek vase in the Hermitage Museum of Leningrad shows a seated woman offering a morsel of food to a crane (Armstrong, 1979). Aristotle and other early Greek writers believed that the feathers of cranes changed color with age. Thus, as humans age from black to gray and finally to white, so too were cranes thought to change from black through yellow to white. On the other hand, later writers used the absence of plumage changes in cranes as symbolic of constancy and singular endeavor.

Besides apparently contributing several letters to the Greek alphabet, cranes and their behavior are responsible for several words that have gained general use. The geranium plant is so named for the seed capsule's resemblance to a crane's bill. The Latin *congruere*, meaning an agreement, is the origin of the English word *congruence* (Topsell, 1972). Soon after the Norman Conquest of England there was a general interest developed in genealogy, and the branching form of a family tree was referred to as a "crane's foot," or *pied de grue*, from which is derived the present word *pedigree* (Ingersoll, 1923). The calling of cranes, or *iangling*, also gave rise to the modern English word *jangling*.

The migrations of cranes, marked by large flocks and clamoring calls, were well known to the Greeks and Romans, and were used to mark the changing of the seasons. Topsell noted that the birds have keen senses of sight, hearing, and smell. Further, like the kings of Persia, the cranes have both summer and winter dwellings, and they follow certain limited and determinate schedules during which they change their habitations. Thus, Pliny praised the regular order of crane and quail migrations, in which the quails regularly appeared one month before the cranes in spring and likewise departed a month before them during fall. When the cranes were about to leave Thrace they were believed to assemble in rank and order in the manner of soldiers. Before the flock finally left, the oldest of the cranes would fly about in a circle three times, after which he would fall down and die of exhaustion, to be buried by the others. After this ceremony the rest would take flight toward Africa to spend the winter.

Topsell noted that during flight, the birds attain unusual heights and fly in triangular formation, and that unlike other birds they fly both night and day. The high flight was attributed to the birds' desire to see great distances ahead, and perhaps foresee the onset of rains or storms in order that they might avoid them. Further, when at such heights the stragglers can better be observed and helped. The usual triangular formation, like the Greek letter lambda, allows the birds to cut the air more readily, while during high winds they tend to fly in the form of a half-moon. When set upon by eagles, the birds were believed to assume the shape of a ring, or that of a heart, in order that they might fly with greater courage and strength. It was noted that the birds sometimes change places in formation, and by this regular changing of formation various letters of the alphabet are imitated. More remarkably, Cicero believed that each crane rested its head on the back of the bird flying immediately ahead of it. The lead crane, having no bird to rest its head upon, eventually retired to the end of the line, to place its head on the back of the trailing bird, which had previously supported none.

Topsell noted that the three most likely letters to have been extracted from the flight of cranes, alpha, lambda, and upsilon, are probably not actually attributable to Palamedes, who was reputed to have invented several new Greek letters from watching the formations of cranes. Yet, M. Martial (A.D. 40-104), a Roman epigramist, and Flavius Cassiodorus (c. 490-575) both affirmed that the entire Greek alphabet was obtained from the flight of cranes by the god Mercury.

Topsell observed that while in flight, cranes always treat the foremost of them as captain and arrange themselves so as not to obscure the view of the lead bird. The older birds take turns being leader, and should any of the flock become weary before reaching their destinations two other birds will take the tired individual on their backs or wings, or support it with their outstretched legs. Topsell observed that cranes rarely fly against the wind, except when being chased, and they also avoid strong backwinds that might ruffle their feathers and weaken them; of the two they prefer to fly against the wind.

Many early writers believed that when cranes flew long distances they would swallow a heavy stone that served as ballast, to strengthen themselves against sudden gusts of wind. Others believed that the birds carried the stone so that when nearing the end of their journey they could drop the stone and on hearing it land could determine whether they had crossed the ocean or not. Yet others believed that the birds kept the stones in their mouths to stop their voices and thus escape detection from eagles. Some, such as Aristotle, denied this story, but Pliny believed that the birds filled their throats with sand and also carried stones. Some believed that the stone was carried by their feet, and Topsell suggested that perhaps the carrying of stones by the individuals that were swiftest of flight prevented them from flying so fast that they might outstrip and lose contact with the slower ones. Pliny reported that after the cranes had crossed the Sea of Pontus and had dropped the stones that they were carrying in the feet for ballast, they landed and cast up the sand carried in their throats, which had by then been transformed into a perfect yellow stone. Through the help of fire, this stone could then be transformed into gold.

On their fall flight to Egypt the cranes were believed to choose a captain, since they knew they would meet with enemies there, but on their return flight to Europe they neither chose a captain nor posted watches. In their choice of a guide, they select one of the strongest and oldest birds, which might be best able to find the proper way and strong enough to withstand the wind. In the middle of the flock the youngest and weakest birds fly, in order that they might be encouraged by those both in front and behind. Other watchmen and officers are placed at the rear, to call to the captain and inform him that all are following. The captain must not only fly in the foremost position and guide the flock properly, but must also help stand guard while the flock rests at night. Many watchmen are also posted, while each of the others in the flock sleeps with one leg lifted and its head under a wing. Plutarch stated that the birds stand their watch like Hercules, who leaned with his head and hand upon his club. Thus the crane stands on one leg and holds a stone in the claws of the other foot, so that if sleep should overtake the bird, it would drop the stone, awakening itself and the other sleeping birds (Topsell, 1972).

According to Topsell, when the cranes have reached three years of age they leave the cold climates for their breeding grounds. Then the birds form couples, and the males fertilize their mates while the latter are standing upright rather than lying on the earth. In addition to two eggs, a stone is also often "laid" in the nest, at least in captivity. In one account, a male and female crane that were being held in an orchard laid eggs and raised two young. As the female led the young about, the chicks would sometimes forsake her and follow the male instead. Once, after calling the young away from their father, the female was viciously attacked and killed by the male.

Topsell stated that cranes, like wild geese, eat all kinds of wild grain. He also noted that cranes feed on serpents, and that in Thessaly (central Greece) were it not for the storks and cranes the people would be forced to leave the country. Thus, people were forbidden by law to kill the birds, an immunity referred to as "antipelargia" (from the Greek *palargos*, or stork).

Aristotle, Homer, and many other early authors

believed that the cranes regularly engaged in warfare with Pygmies, or *geranomachian*. These Pygmies were believed to live in caves and were called Troglodytes, and at times were thought to ride on the backs of various animals. According to Pliny, the Pygmies were driven out of Geranea, their first city, by cranes, and later made warfare with them, attacking with iron weapons and darts or by riding on the backs of rams and holding in their hands a kind of clapper. They attacked the birds at the time of breeding, descending thus on their nesting areas and destroying the birds and their eggs. This was done only during the breeding period, for later in the fall the arrival of other cranes might overthrow the Pygmies by their very numbers.

Topsell noted that cranes exhibit hostility toward eagles and hawks, and when cranes see such predators they usually flee with haste and utter loud calls. Yet, when there are enough cranes present to resist, he noted that they would gather into a circle or ring and, with their heads lifted to the highest, would advance on the eagle or hawk and force it to depart. Besides protecting one another, cranes show a special love for their own young, and at times the pair will fight with one another over the education of their young. At such times, when the cranes are thus engaged in fighting, they are more easily captured by men. A more cunning method of capturing cranes was recounted by Topsell. A bottle or gourd is emptied and is coated with birdlime. Then a bee is placed inside. When the crane hears the humming of the bee it thrusts its head inside to capture the insect, only to be caught fast by the head feathers and blinded. Then the bird stands helplessly until it is captured alive. From this practice a Russian fable perhaps arose in which a fox invited a crane to supper but prepared a dish of broth, which the fox could readily lap up but which the crane was unable to take up with its beak. In return, the crane invited the fox to supper, putting meat into a deep pot with a thin neck into which the crane was able to reach but not the fox.

Wild cranes were also captured or killed by the use of falcons or small eagles. In Germany, such large falcons were called "crane falcons" or "girfalcons." Smaller falcons might also be used to force the cranes to the ground where they could be caught by dogs.

Topsell noted that cranes fly remarkably swiftly, although they fly so high that from the earth it would seem that they are actually flying very slowly. Further, by flying at night as well as during the day, they are able to cross great distances in a short time. At night they utter almost continuous calls to keep informed of their positions, and by flying high enough to escape the shadow of the earth they actually are able to see well enough to find their way. When the birds do sleep at night, they raise up one leg and place the head upon the wing, by which the heat of the body is transmitted to the brain; thus the bird is able to sleep more easily, according to Topsell.

Cranes occur in many historical and allegorical contexts, such as a city in Thrace (or Messinia) and a mountain on the Megaris Peninsula near Corinth that were called Gerania. Reportedly the latter, now called Yerania, was so named because the people followed the calls of flying cranes at the time of a flood, thus reaching higher ground and saving themselves from drowning. The death of Ibycus is probably the most famous of crane stories from ancient Greece. This poet of Rhegium (who lived about 550 B.C.) was set upon by robbers, and before expiring looked up to see cranes flying overhead. With his dying breath he told the robbers that the cranes would avenge him. Some time later, in the market place of Corinth the robbers saw the cranes flying overhead, and one fearfully exclaimed to the others, "Behold the cranes of Ibycus." On being thus overheard, the men were detained and questioned by the authorities, and later confessed their crime.

The sagacity of cranes, and the belief that they carried stones in their feet at night to keep them awake, are the basis for their frequent allegorical association with intelligence. The flight of a crane signified a wise man who had studied astronomy or any other "lofty and sublime" study. Yet, a fool who handled divine matters wickedly or without true wisdom was also at times compared to a flying crane, and Plotinus believed that such a man was eventually metamorphosed into a crane. The democratic form of government was compared to the orderly behavior associated with cranes, in which all the populace participates in elections. Thus the word *congruere*, to consent or agree, came from the unified and collective behavior of cranes. If a man should live his entire life in a consistent and singular manner, he was sometimes compared to a crane, for although many other birds change their colors with age, the crane remains much the same in appearance throughout its life. Cranes were believed to give equal honor to all, for their captains regularly give up their lead in flight to go to the rear of the flock, and thus the last becomes first, and the birds can live in freedom without king or tyrant. Christians were told that they must imitate cranes in their watchfulness, and avoid the fall of sin in much the way that a crane avoids sleep by holding a stone with its raised foot. Likewise, Christians must help one another, with a mutual concern for the weakest, in order that all might reach a final resting place safely. And, as a crane adds ballast for its flight, a Christian must ballast himself with the fear of God until he arrives in heaven, and at the end of the journey the ballast will turn to gold or to a precious stone (Topsell, 1972).

Cranes were often the sources of morality tales, as in the story of a group of cranes and geese feeding together in a field. They were soon approached by hunters. On seeing them, the cranes quickly took flight, but the heavier and fatter geese were unable to escape. Thus, in times of war, the poor that have little or nothing might easily flee while rich men cannot escape with all their possessions and are soon caught and killed by the enemy.

With all this symbolism, it is not surprising that cranes were believed to have special table and medicinal qualities. Their flesh was considered useful against cancers, ulcers, palsies, and "winde in the gutts." Dried powders of their flesh were used to treat cancers, ulcers, and fistulas, "nerves" from their wings and legs were believed to help a person recover his strength, and their bone marrow was used as an eye salve. Crane fat was placed in the ears to improve hearing and treat deafness, and their "gall" was variously used to treat forgetfulness or other maladies (Topsell, 1972).

Although not noted by Topsell, the dances of cranes have attracted the attention of many cultures. The somewhat circular movements of the crane's dance were associated by ancients with the sun's seasonal movements. The appearance of the cranes in the spring thus implied a resurgent sun-god, while their dancing epitomized both fertility and death. According to Plutarch, when Theseus returned to Delos from Crete after slaying the Minotaur, he and his friends danced the geranos or crane dance, going through the convoluted motions of entering and leaving the Cretan labyrinth (Rowland, 1979). Crane dancing has had its counterparts in both eastern and western cultures, for the Oskits of Siberia dressed in crane skins and performed funereal dances, and similar dances were associated with Chinese funerals. In Australia, many of the aboriginal tribes included crane dances in their corroborees.

In Chinese tradition the crane is a common symbol of longevity, and the soul of the dead is often represented as riding to heaven on a crane's back. Likewise in Chinese tradition, old pine trees sometimes turn into cranes, since both are long-lived, and the two are often associated in both Chinese and Japanese art (Armstrong, 1979; Rowland, 1979).

As the Chinese culture gradually came to influence Japan, the Japanese accepted the idea of a crane as a symbol of longevity and gradually modified it to be an emblem of joy. Since the ninth century, in Japan the cranes have been regarded as a symbol of happiness, and typically in the marriage ceremony a design incorporating both the crane and the tortoise is used to symbolize both happiness and longevity (Taka-Tsukasa, 1967; Hattori, 1928).

In many parts of the world, such as Russia, Sicily, and India, the crane serves as an animal guide in various folktales, usually leading a younger brother into various adventures. Often the slyness of cranes is emphasized, as when a crane offers to transport fish to a place where there are no fishermen, only to eat them. Or, according to the North American Indians, Old Grandfather Crane helps others to cross a river by using his long legs as a bridge, and then later dumps their pursuers in the water (Leach, 1972). Many cultures believe that cranes will sometimes carry small birds on their backs to help them on their long migrations. Thus the Siberian Tartars believed that cranes transport corncrakes southward, and Egyptians believed that both cranes and storks carry small birds across the Mediterranean. Similarly, the Crow Indians of Montana believed that the sandhill crane carries a small bird, the napite-shu-utl, or "crane's back," on its back. This small bird regularly accompanies the crane, and flutters up to settle on the bird's back when it takes off. At this time the bird utters a chattering whistle, which is the basis for the Crow warriors' blowing a small bone whistle when they go riding off to battle (Ingersoll, 1923).

Not only do cranes often carry small birds on their backs, but at times they even steal humans, according to the folklore of the Eskimos of the Bering Sea area:

> One autumn day, very long ago, the cranes were preparing to go southward. As they were gathered in the great flock they saw a beautiful young woman standing alone near the village. Admiring her greatly, the cranes gathered about, and lifting her on their widespread wings, bore her far up in the air and away. While the cranes were taking her up they circled below her so closely that she could not fall, and their loud, hoarse cries drowned out her calls for help, so she was carried away and never seen again. Ever since that time the cranes always circle about in autumn, uttering their loud cries while preparing to fly southward, as they did at that time. (Nelson, 1896-97)

The characteristic circling of the cranes was noted fearfully by the slaves of Alabama, who believed that if a crane circles over the house three times someone in the family will soon die (Leach, 1972). The similarity of this belief to Pliny's story of a crane circling three times and then dying prior to migration of the rest of the flock is noteworthy. A similar coincidence is the Egyptian belief that the god Toth, whose symbol was the crane-like ibis, was credited with inventing hieroglyphs (Rowland, 1979).

Two final crane legends from the Orient can be used to exemplify the strong emotional attachments between humans and cranes. The first, a Chinese legend, involves Tsêng Ts'ang, a disciple of Confucius who spared the life of a wounded crane. The crane flew away, and later returned with its mate, each of them carrying a pearl in its mouth, which they then presented to Tsêng Ts'ang (Hattori, 1928).

In a Japanese legend, a nobleman who had lost his wealth and retired to the country once saw a hunter who had captured a crane and was about to kill it. The nobleman begged the hunter to spare its life, but the hunter would only do so in return for the nobleman's precious sword, his last possession of value. The following night a young lady appeared at the door of the nobleman and asked him for shelter, explaining that she had been driven from her home by a cruel stepmother and needed a place to stay. The nobleman admitted her, and soon the two fell in love and were married. One day, the feudal lord decided to have a hunting party, and the woman was then forced to confess that she was really the crane that the nobleman had saved, and that she must flee. Together they left, and went to live in the palace of her parents (Hattori, 1928).

Lastly, in the words of the Italian poet Lodovico Ariosto (1474-1533), a brief poem on the majesty of cranes and their flight:

> And as wee see strainge Crane are wont to doe
> First stalke a while ere they their wings can finde,
> Then soare from ground not past a yard or two,
> Till in their wings they gathered have the winde;
> At last they mount the very cloudes vnto,
> Trianglewise according to their kind.
>
> (Topsell, 1972).

SPECIES
ACCOUNTS

Crowned Crane

Balearica pavonina (Linnaeus) 1758

Other Vernacular Names. Blue-necked or gray crowned crane (*regulorum* and *gibbericeps*), Black-necked or dark crowned crane (*pavonina* and *ceciliae*); Ma-hem (Afrikaan); Grue couronnee, Grue ronnee du Cap (French); Konigskranich (German); Minima kanmuri-zuru (Japanese); Makoka zhuravl (Russian); Grulla corona (Spanish); I-hem (Xhosa); U-Nohemu (Zulu).

Range. Resident in open country over most of Africa south of the Sahara, excepting the Congo Basin and the driest portions of southwestern Africa.

Subspecies or Semispecies.

B.p. pavonina: West African Crowned Crane. Resident north of the Congo Basin from Senegal east to Lake Chad, and south to Sierra Leone, Nigeria, and northern Cameroon.

B.p. ceciliae: Sudan Crowned Crane. Resident in the Nile Valley from Malakal south to Nimule and east to Lake Rudolf and the Ethiopian lakes.

B.(p.) gibbericeps: East African Crowned Crane. Resident in eastern Africa from extreme eastern Zaire, Uganda, and Kenya to central Tanzania. Sometimes considered (with *regulorum*) a separate species.

B.(p.) regulorum: South African Crowned Crane. Resident in southern Africa from Mozambique southward to about Port Elizabeth, South Africa. Sometimes considered (with *gibbericeps*) a separate species, here considered a semispecies.

Measurements. Wing, both sexes of *ceciliae* average 496.7 mm (range 470-565 mm), of *pavonina* average 547.5 mm (range 506-585mm), of *gibbericeps* 559.4 mm (range 458-615 mm) and of *regulorum* 565.2 mm (range 523-642 mm). Exposed culmen, both sexes of *ceciliae* average 56.1 mm (range 49-62 mm), of *pavonina* 56.5 mm (range 53-64 mm), of *gibbericeps* 59.4 mm (range 52-71 mm) and of *regulorum* 61.9 mm (range 57-68 mm). Tarsus, both sexes of *ceciliae* average 188 mm (range 172-205

mm), of *pavonina* 196 mm (range 190-203 mm), of *gibbericeps* 201.1 mm (range 170-207 mm), and of *regulorum* 207.1 mm (range 170-234 mm). Females generally average from 85 to 95 percent of male measurements, but rarely exceed male measurements. Eggs, average (in *pavonina*) 85.5 × 57.5 mm (82.3-89.5 × 55.8-58.9 mm); in *regulorum* 75.4 × 55.2 mm (70.4-78.4 × 52.0-58.8 mm) (Walkinshaw, 1973).

Weights. Walkinshaw (1973) lists a male and female of *ceciliae* as 3,628.8 grams each. Pomeroy (1980a) shows weights for four adults of *gibbericeps* ranging between 3 and 4 kilograms. Estimated egg weights are from 122 grams (*regulorum*) to 156 grams (*pavonina*).

Description

Adult males and females are alike. Those of *pavonina* and *ceciliae* are generally darker than the two southern forms, and have smaller red chin wattles. In these two northern forms the bare cheek patches are white above, and a much larger lower portion is pinkish to reddish, while in the southern forms the cheek patches are almost entirely white, with a small upper portion bright red. A large, straw yellow crown covers the top of the head (paler in the southern forms), with each feather in the crest black-tipped and ringed with whitish or brownish. There are black velvety feathers around the bare cheek patches, which are bounded below with reddish skin areas of varying size, becoming large wattles in the southern forms. The neck feathers are pearl gray (southern forms) to slate gray (northern forms), becoming elongated and pointed toward the base of the neck and grading into body feathers of the same color. The primaries are black, as are the outermost one or two secondaries; the next two or three secondaries have black inner webs and chestnut on the

Distribution of the South African (vertical hatching), East African (diagonal hatching), Sudan (vertical hatching), and West African (horizontal hatching) crowned cranes. Cross-hatching indicates areas of greatest abundance, and inked circles indicate breeding records (mainly after Snow, 1978).

exposed webs. The innermost secondaries are broad, long, and plume-like. The tail is black, and the upper and lower wing coverts are white, with the inner greater coverts becoming straw-colored and plume-like. The iris is grayish white to pale blue, the bill is black, and the legs and toes are black.

Juveniles are generally grayish, the upperpart feathers being edged with rufous, and those of the underparts with sandy buff. The crown and nape are brown, the face is feathered and buffy, and the crest is spiky and golden buff. The wing coverts are white, with buff tips or with varying amounts of gray and buff. The iris is brown, the legs and toes are pink initially, gradually changing to horn and finally to black. The throat wattle (which appears at about four months) is initially pink. The adult plumage is attained at about 12 months, but adult eye color and full development of the throat wattle and facial color may not occur for about another year (Pomeroy, 1980a).

Downy chicks (of *regulorum*) are pale buff, with the head pale ivory to light buff, and the back and dorsal stripe umber, and with dark flank spots, dark shoulders, and a dark caudal spot. The underparts are very pale buff, and the chest is a darker buff. The bill is gray, with a flesh color at the base of the lower mandible, and the base of the bill is light horn color. The iris is dark brown, the legs are flesh color, and the soles of the toes are pale yellow (Walkinshaw, 1973).

Identification

In the field, the distinctive white upper and under wing coverts, which contrast with darker brown or black flight feathers, allow this species to be identified at any distance. The yellow crown is also diagnostic. The calls are honking and hollow-sounding, of generally low pitch and with considerable harmonic development.

In the hand, the presence of a "crown" is diagnostic. The races *pavonina* and *ceciliae* typically have reddish on the lower part of the cheek patch (extending about halfway up in *pavonina* and more than halfway in *ceciliae*), and both have very small bare wattles. the races *regulorum* and *gibbericeps* typically have larger red throat wattles, and cheek patches that are mostly white with a small reddish area near the top. All these features appear to be somewhat variable. In *gibbericeps* the bare area typically extends upward well above the eyes into the velvety black forehead, forming a rounded knoblike process. The trachea does not penetrate the sternum; it passes directly back to the bronchial bifurcation without looping downward.

DISTRIBUTION AND HABITATS

Historical and Current Ranges

The historical ranges of the four populations of crowned cranes have been reviewed by Walkinshaw (1964, 1973), from which it would appear that no major range retractions have occurred in recent times. The form *ceciliae* once ranged north to Khartoum, where the type specimen was taken, but it rarely if ever occurs there now. Of the four populations, it is probable that the West African form *pavonina* may be the most vulnerable, in spite of its apparently broad distribution. Only two actual breeding records were indicated throughout the range of this subspecies by Snow (1978), and most records of breeding seem to be from Nigeria, where it is now becoming rare (Parker, 1971). The smallest apparent range is that of the Sudan race *ceciliae*, which was also the last subspecies to be described. This form occurs in the western provinces of Ethiopia only locally (Urban and Walkinshaw, 1967), and is otherwise largely restricted to the Upper Nile of Sudan, with the southernmost record apparently from extreme northern Uganda at Dufile, near Nimule. Cranes from northern Uganda reportedly often show intergradation between *ceciliae* and *gibbericeps*, although specimens from the critical areas seem to be lacking (Walkinshaw, 1964). *Ceciliae* has also been collected in extreme northern Kenya, at the northeastern end of Lake Rudolf (Owre, 1966). Except for these records, the crowned cranes of Uganda and Kenya all appear to be of the East African form *gibbericeps* (Pomeroy, 1980a). In Uganda, crowned cranes are most common in southeastern areas, where swamps are frequent, and are generally less numerous in the formerly forested areas of south central Uganda. This subspecies is likewise apparently most common in the southwestern portions of Kenya, east of Lake Victoria, becoming scarce in the drier areas to the north (Donald Young, pers. comm.). It also has been regularly reported in the Rift Valley lakes from Lake Albert southward through Lake Edward, Lake Bunyoni, and Lake Kivu, with nonbreeding records extending to about the south end of Lake Tanganyika. *Gibbericeps* is also the form ranging into Tanzania and Malawi, and extending southward an uncertain distance, where it evidently intergrades with *regulorum*. There are specimens attributed to the latter race from as far north as Zambia, Zimbabwe, and the Zambezi River (Walkinshaw, 1964). In Zambia the subspecies is fairly widespread, but is scarce in the Northern Province and is most common in the Kafue Basin and Luanga Valley (Benson et al., 1971). Breeding records from the South African crowned crane *regulorum* are largely limited to Zambia and South Africa, although nonbreeding records extend west all the way to the Cunene River of extreme southern Angola (Snow, 1978).

Habitat Requirements and Densities

Crowned cranes are associated with open country, especially grasslands near water, and they are apparently largely sedentary (Snow, 1978). The birds forage primarily in grasslands, but also require swamps for breeding, and wherever available they use large trees for roosting. However, where necessary, they will also use smaller trees for roosting, or may even roost in shallow water (Pomeroy, 1980b). In some areas they have been able to exploit croplands, where they sometimes do damage to crops such as groundnuts and soybeans. They may also destroy cotton seedlings by uprooting them while searching for insects. In areas where the rainfall is less than 700-800 mm per year the birds are sparse (Pomeroy, 1980b).

On their breeding grounds in Natal, South Africa, crowned cranes nest in marshes that have such associated grass genera as *Pennisetum, Andropogon, Arundo*, and *Miscanthidium*, and such sedges as *Carex, Cyperus, Scirpus, Pycreus*, and *Ascolepis*. Other typical genera are *Disa* (Orchidaceae), *Chironia* (Gentianaceae), and *Dierama* (Iridaceae). In Zambia, some of the grasses associated with breeding areas are *Panicum, Sporobolis, Chloris, Hyporrhinia, Setaria, Brachiaria, Digitaria*, and *Echinochloa*. A variety of herons, egrets, storks, ibis, ducks, and other marsh-breeding birds were also reported to be typical nesting associates by Walkinshaw (1964). He noted that both blue cranes and wattled cranes were found nesting in the same South African marshes; the blue crane occupied a different niche, and the wattled cranes tended to nest during a different season. In Zambia, however, there is a substantial overlap in the nesting periods of crowned and wattled cranes, with crowned cranes nesting mainly between December and March and wattled cranes primarily from March to October (Benson et al., 1971).

In South Africa, nesting habitats consist of open marshes having a few centimeters of standing water and knee-high to shoulder-high stands of sedges and grasses. According to Walkinshaw, the preferred South African breeding biotype consists of the shorelines of lakes or large marshes grown up to reeds, rushes, sedges, and papyrus, where the cover is extremely dense and tall enough to effectively hide the birds. These areas may be rather deep, with some floating islands of vegetation, or they may be fairly small and shallow. In the West African form the bird nests not only in such marshes but also in flooded fields of rice, atcha, or yams, and nesting may even occur on dry land, although always very close to water (Walkinshaw, 1973). In the Sudan race, typical breeding biotypes seem to be rather large and grassy marshes, from a few centimeters to a meter in depth, and with knee-high to hip-high vegetation dominated by *Cyperus, Eleocharis, Scirpus, Setaria, Cynodon*, and various legumes and rosaceous plants (Urban and Walkinshaw, 1967). In Uganda, the nesting habitat of the East African race consists of grassy swamps (Pomeroy, 1980b).

Population densities are not yet well verified in this species. Pomeroy (1980b) suggested that in southern Uganda large areas may support at least one crane per square kilometer, suggesting a total Ugandan population in the tens of thousands. Burke (1965) judged the population in the Kisii District of western Kenya to be about 1.14 birds per square mile (0.4 per square kilometer). Walkinshaw (1981a) found 7 pairs and 34 nonbreeders in an area of 21 square miles in Nigeria, or 2.28 birds per square mile.

FOODS AND FORAGING BEHAVIOR

Foods of Adults

Crowned cranes are relatively diverse in their foraging activities, and consume not only a diversity of vegetable materials but also such animal life as lizards, grasshoppers, other insects, millipedes, and earthworms. In Kenya they have been observed feeding on armyworms (*Spodoptera* spp.) and cutworms (noctuid moths), and in the Sudan on crickets (Pomeroy, 1980b). Walkinshaw (1973) reported that the West African form has been reported to eat crabs (*Potamon* sp.).

Vegetable material consumed by crowned cranes includes the seed heads of sedges (*Cyperus* spp.) and such grasses as *Cynodon* spp., and evidently long grasses growing around swamps that are in the process of seeding are preferred foods. The birds also have been observed pecking at old cobs of maize, and seem to prefer knocking seeds off heads of millet and maize cobs rather than picking up loose seeds. The birds often forage in croplands, especially of such types as soybeans and groundnuts, or consume the flowers and pods of bean plants. Damage to crops is sometimes indirect, as when the birds trample cotton crops while displaying, or dig up seedlings, apparently in search of insects (Pomeroy, 1980b).

Foraging Behavior

Several observers have commented on the tendency of crowned cranes to stamp their feet while walking through grassy vegetation, apparently to disturb and thus expose insects (Walkinshaw, 1964; Pomeroy, 1980b). These birds have also been seen walking among feeding cattle, much in the manner of cattle egrets (*Bubulcus ibis*), presumably catching the insects disturbed by the moving cattle. The birds are also attracted to freshly plowed fields, and they tend to feed in short grass rather than in long grassy cover, again presumably for the easily captured insect life. They are sometimes attracted to rubbish dumps, where insects are associated with waste food (Pomeroy, 1980b).

MIGRATIONS AND MOVEMENTS

No specific migrations have been documented in this species, although during the nonbreeding season the birds flock, and may then gather at favorable locations well away from nesting areas. Thus, during the nonbreeding season, large flocks of the West African race have been reported in the northern portion of Cameroon, and in the vicinity of Lake Chad, northeastern Nigeria, apparently dispersing to breed elsewhere during the rainy season (Walkinshaw, 1973). In Uganda the population appears to be essentially sedentary, and the birds seem to make only local movements (Pomeroy, 1980b). There is no good information suggesting significant movements from the other East African or South African populations.

GENERAL BIOLOGY

Sociality

In Uganda, a certain amount of breeding activity occurs throughout the entire year, although breeding is at a low point during September and October, and has distinct peaks at about November to February, and again from May to July, during relatively drier periods. Thus, the most common group size of cranes in Uganda is of paired birds (about 57 percent of 118 groups counted), while single birds are the next most common social unit (17 percent); most of the remaining birds were seen in groups of from 3 to 20 birds, with only a few observations of groups ranging from 51 to 150 birds (Pomeroy, 1980b).

Studies by Walkinshaw (1964) in Zambia (Northern Rhodesia) and in South Africa during December and January, during the breeding period, indicated that 59 percent of the birds were then in pairs, while the flocked birds were of nonbreeding individuals. In Natal, he observed twelve single birds, nineteen groups of 2, two groups of 3, one of 19, and two of 28 birds. Among the breeding birds, Walkinshaw noted that the mate of the incubating bird always roosted in the marsh near the nest, even if nearby trees were available.

According to Walkinshaw, crowned cranes that are successful in raising young retain their family group structure for as long as 9 or 10 months, after which the adults drive away the young and prepare to nest again. When the family breaks up, the young birds tend to join together in flocks, and spend much of their time feeding in fields. Some of the foods consumed by such groups of young birds are the seeds of grasses, sedges, and grains (Walkinshaw, 1964).

Daily Activities

Unlike other cranes, crowned cranes normally roost in trees. They exhibit a preference for open trees such as mvule (*Chlorphora*), which has high, bare lower branches that provide an excellent view, or the tops of leafless trees. The birds leave their roosts at dawn, or variably later during wet or misty mornings, and do not return until just before nightfall. During the daylight hours they feed from 50 to 75 percent of the time, being least active during the middle of the day. On especially hot days they may move into shade or pant visibly. Even within large flocks, the birds can be seen to move about in pairs, suggesting a prolonged pair bond. Within such flocks, displays are not infrequent, and mutual preening, especially of the neck feathers, has also been observed. Sometimes displays are stimulated by minor disturbances, and occasionally the entire flock may become involved in this activity. Such activities are more frequent as evening approaches, but rarely last more than a few minutes, and are typically interspersed with foraging behavior (Pomeroy, 1980b).

Interspecific Interactions

Crowned cranes are locally sympatric with wattled cranes and blue cranes. They are smaller than and subordinate to wattled cranes (Walkinshaw, 1964), and probably occur on rather wetter and more heavily vegetated habitats than are typically used by blue cranes. The bill shape of crowned cranes is quite different from the bills of wattled or blue cranes, suggesting quite different foraging niches.

When nesting, the birds are able to expel other crowned cranes, blue cranes, and spur-winged geese quite easily, and have been observed to cause a steer to retreat from their nesting site (Walkinshaw, 1973).

BREEDING BIOLOGY

Age of Maturity and Time of Breeding

The period of sexual immaturity in crowned cranes is still uncertain but full adult eye color and coloration of the bare face and neck areas are not attained until the birds are 20 to 24 months old (Pomeroy, 1980a). Steel (1977) reported that hand-raised East African cranes that he reared in 1967 did not attempt to breed until 1974.

The period of nesting in crowned cranes seems to be remarkably variable in different parts of Africa. The West African race breeds in Gambia in September and October, egg records in Nigeria are during the rainy season from July to early September, and there is a southern Mauritania breeding record for October (Mackworth-Pread and Grant, 1970; Walkinshaw, 1973). In the Sudan race, breeding records include nest-building in August, eggs in September and early

October, downy young in late October and November, and 6-week old young in February (Walkinshaw, 1973). Breeding records in Uganda extend throughout the year for the East African race, but there are peaks in the breeding activity associated with drier periods (Pomeroy, 1980b). According to Brown and Britton (1980), crowned cranes generally breed in the rainy season in most areas of East Africa, but in the wettest portions the dry period seems to be preferred. In Zambia the breeding records for *regulorum* extend from December to April, with the largest numbers occurring in December and February (Benson et al., 1971). This corresponds to the rainy season in Zambia. Breeding during the rainy season is also typical of Malawi (Nyasaland) and the Rhodesias (Zambia and Zimbabwe), with nearly half of the breeding records from January (Benson, 1960). In South Africa the breeding season is also associated with the rainy period, probably from mid-October to May 22, but probably peaking between December and February (Walkinshaw, 1973).

Pair Formation and Courtship

Courtship in this species is still only very poorly understood. One of the first good descriptions of display was that of Serle (1939), who described the "nuptial dance" of *pavonina* as follows:

> The birds would be walking sedately side by side when the performance began, which was heralded by both birds simultaneously bobbing the whole body up and down. Then they leapt forwards together, still side by side, and at each forward leap the wings were flapped. After a few leaps this prelude to the dance would conclude in a short forward run. Sometimes, when they appeared less excited, they would leap without opening their wings. Presently they would leap in opposite directions till they were some thirty yards apart, when they would turn and bound towards each other with great leaps and, when they had met, dance round each other in circles, all these movements being carried out with delightful grace and buoyancy. Towards the end of the performance one bird would get tired and, when the other came flapping towards it, only responded by dipping its head and indulging in a few demure hops without flapping its wings. When the dance was concluded they remained immobile for a while and then flew off to perch on a tree near the fadama.

A similar description was provided by Walkinshaw (1964) for crowned cranes in general:

> Both male and female participate, but usually the male is the aggressor. Crowned cranes begin their dance differently than do other cranes that I have observed. Without moving their body, they bob their heads up and down four to ten times. Some-times this is all they do, but often they begin to bow. Then, spreading their wings, they jump 6 to 8 feet into the air with legs drooping motionless beneath them. Sometimes between hops they pick up objects from the ground and toss them into the air. Sometimes they call, sometimes not. The dancing crane often goes completely around his mate doing all this and sometimes both birds dance opposite each other. Sometimes one does the dancing, again the other.

The sequence of drawings showing display in a pair of wild East African crowned cranes (figure 13) is based on a series of 35 mm transparencies taken in Kenya by Donald Young, and well illustrates the strong bowing component (with strongly ruffled neck feathers), as well as an apparent touching of the beaks at one point.

Copulatory behavior in the crowned crane is only incompletely described, but Walkinshaw (1973) observed a pair of West African cranes mating. The female suddenly raised her head forward and upward, and stood quietly in that position for about a minute. The male, standing some ten feet away, approached quickly, mounted her as she squatted slightly, and as they copulated he stood on her back with his wings slightly waving. Afterwards they began feeding. This description would suggest that copulatory behavior in *Balearica* is very much like that of *Grus*.

Adult vocalizations of the West African ("Nigerian"), East African ("Kenyan"), and South African ("Southern") crowned cranes were studied by Archibald (1975, 1976). He observed rather marked differences between the West African form and the other two populations studied, as well as marked differences between *Balearica* and typical gruine cranes. Thus, the guard call of *Balearica* is a hollow-sounding, honklike vocalization that is relatively low in pitch and rich in harmonic development. However, although the guard call of the West African races is a monosyllabic honk, that of the other forms studied is a disyllabic *ka-wonk*, with the second syllable higher in pitch. Further, in the unison display, guard calls predominated in the West African form, while "booming" dominated in the East African race. In both types, the gular sac is inflated during calling, but it is larger in the eastern and southern populations, and the calls are correspondingly lower in pitch.

Crowned cranes begin their unison display in varied ways. The pair may be standing close together or not, and either sex may begin or end the call sequence. The display is of variable length, and may last more than a minute. The birds stand in the same place throughout the display, and do not move their wings. The display is usually begun with a series of guard calls, during which the red gular sac is inflated and the head is slowly turned from side to side as the mandibles remained

13. Sequence of bowing (1-7) and dancing (8) behavior in the East African crowned crane, based on a series of photographs taken by Donald Young.

closed. The neck is held erect and the beak horizontal. Then, a series of booming calls is uttered, with the neck lowered, the beak elevated to about 45 degrees, and the head held at shoulder level. Guard calls may also be uttered during or following the booming sequence. During the display, the calls phase in and out of synchrony, since each bird calls at a fixed rate that is independent of that of its mate (Archibald, 1975, 1976).

Territoriality and Early Nesting Behavior

According to Walkinshaw (1973), territories of the West African crowned crane varied from 86 to 388 hectares (212-958 acres). The size was evidently smallest where cranes had territories adjoining those of other pairs, although typically each pair lacked close neighbors. The territories included both a nesting territory and a feeding area, and the birds paid little attention toward defending the latter. In fact, both cranes and other birds were allowed to forage in the feeding territory without disturbance. Feeding usually occurred from a half a mile to a mile from the nest site, and the birds would either walk or fly to their foraging grounds from the nesting site.

On the other hand, all birds, such as other crowned cranes, ducks, spur-winged geese, bustards, and owls, were quickly chased from the nesting territory. On two occasions a breeding pair of crowned cranes landed near the nest of another pair. In this case, both members of each pair approached until they were only a few meters apart, and the male of each pair assumed a display posture with its neck and head arched in a curve, the bill pointed downward, and stood almost motionless for ten to thirty minutes. Both males performed "false" preening during this period, but no actual fighting ensued. After a period of preening by all four birds, they gradually moved back into their respective territories.

During actual attack, the cranes spread their wings and approach with arched neck and lowered head, the two members of the pair usually approaching side by side. Fighting is done by jumping, wing-flapping, kicking, and stabbing with the beak. If humans, cattle, or snakes should approach the nest, distraction display is typical. This includes dancing on the part of one or both birds. Head-bobbing is done frequently, and the birds will sometimes spread their wings, run around the intruder, or jump up and down. At times they will also pick up objects from the ground and toss them into the air (Walkinshaw, 1964).

According to Walkinshaw (1973), crowned cranes can readily drive blue cranes out of their territories, or even spur-winged geese, but are distinctly fearful of wattled cranes and avoid approaching them very closely. However, he observed a pair frighten away a steer that approached the nest too closely.

The usual location of nests in crowned cranes is in standing water, or at least very near it, although on rare occasions the birds have been known to nest in trees (Steyn and Ellman-Brown, 1974).

Walkinshaw's (1973) accounts of the South African and East African crowned cranes indicate that nest construction is relatively simple. Both members of a pair begin pulling up marsh vegetation and trampling it down around the nest site, so that a circular area 5 to 15 meters in diameter is flattened. In the middle of this the birds toss grass and sedges into a haphazard pile, occasionally trampling it or sitting on it to flatten it and make a depression in the middle. Six nests of the South African race that Walkinshaw measured were from about 50 to 86 centimeters in diameter. The rim averaged about 12 centimeters. Of eight West African crane nests that he studied, seven were on dry land, but all were within 3 meters of water, and one was placed in water 2 feet deep. Six were placed among farm crops, and all were within 100 meters of higher and drier land where the birds fed. These nests averaged larger than did the South African nests, and ranged from nearly 70 to 140 centimeters across. The one that was built in deep water was raised so that the top was 33 centimeters above water. Nest materials are apparently not carried to the nest. If they are obtained out of reach of the nest, they are simply thrown toward the nest with a slight sideways action. If the material lands away from the nest, it may again be picked up later and tossed onto the nest. Scratching with the feet is a second although minor method of accumulating materials on the nest (Walkinshaw, 1973). In the case of the tree-nesting crowned crane described by Steyn and Ellman-Brown (1974), the nest was about 6 meters above ground, and was a relatively small and flat platform of twigs that had evidently been snipped from the tree.

Egg-laying and Incubation

The rate of egg-laying is evidently somewhat less than 1 egg per day. Steel (1977) noted that a pair of captive crowned cranes produced 3 eggs in 4 days in one year, and 4 eggs in 6 days in another year. On the latter occasion a replacement clutch of 4 eggs was laid after the loss of the original clutch. Walkinshaw (1973) found a nest in Nigeria in which 3 eggs were laid in a 5-day period, while all 3 eggs in a South African nest were laid during a 1-week period. Similarly, Wyndham (1940) reported that 3 eggs were laid in a 7-day period.

It is doubtful that significant differences in clutch sizes exist in the various forms of crowned cranes. Walkinshaw (1973) reported average clutch sizes of the South African crane as 2.67 eggs (34 clutches) for South Africa and 2.35 eggs (17 clutches) for Zambia and Rhodesia (Zimbabwe), while Pomeroy (1980b) noted that the average clutch size in Kenya and Uganda for the East African race was 2.56 eggs (41 nests). Pomeroy noted, however, that the clutch seems to vary with altitude; 12 nests from areas of generally below 1,500 meters averaged 2.17 eggs, while 29 nests from highland areas above 1,500 meters averaged 2.72 eggs. Records of 17 West African crane nests provided by Walkinshaw (1973) indicate an average clutch of 2.47 eggs.

Incubation begins with the first egg, with the birds changing incubation duties periodically. Walkinshaw, (1973) estimated that in a nest he studied in Nigeria the eggs were incubated 81.4 percent of the daylight hours in a 2-day period, although one or the other adult was present at the nest for 96.47 percent of this period. The smaller bird, presumably the female, incubated at night, while the other bird roosted up to a mile away in a tree. In a South African crane nest that he studied, the female incubated during 3 of 4 nights, while in another nest the eggs were incubated 90.5 percent of the time in a 2-day period, the male contributing slightly over half the total. Although the first and last eggs of a nest may be laid nearly a week apart, hatching of the entire clutch usually occurs within about a 24-hour period, suggesting that the early stages of incubation prior to clutch completion may not be very intense. Thus, while the incubation period of the first-laid egg may be about 31 days, the last-laid egg typically hatches 28 or 29 days after it is laid (Walkinshaw, 1973).

Hatching and Postbreeding Biology

Like other crane chicks, those of crowned cranes remain near their nest for the first day or so, but by the second day after hatching are prone to wander off with their parents in search of food. However, they remain near the general nesting area, and may return at night for brooding. Unlike the families of wattled and blue cranes, the young of crowned cranes are not led out into the nearby plains or veldt, and instead tend to remain in heavy cover (Walkinshaw, 1973).

A description of the development of the young has been provided by Pomeroy (1980a). He observed that the rate of growth of the tarsus and the increase in wing length were relatively rapid, while the weight increase as well as the growth rate of the bill, tail, and crest were relatively slow and only approach adult dimensions at 12 to 20 months of age. Pomeroy estimated that fledging occurred at about 100 days of age, and Walkinshaw (1973) stated that hand-reared West African cranes may not fly until they are 4 months old. However, Steel (1977) estimated that hand-reared East African birds were virtually fledged at 8 weeks of age, and Archibald and Viess (1979) reported fledging in hand-reared birds

at only 63 days after hatching. Clearly, these wide divergences in estimated fledging times must indicate an unknown source of considerable variation, perhaps in the amounts of food available to the young cranes.

Walkinshaw (1973) noted that in all of three South African nests he studied the young cranes were fed pieces of crabs (*Potamon* sp.) when about 24 hours old. The chicks seem to feed less on insects and more on grass seeds than do other crane chicks, and they also do not dig as much as do the longer-billed species of cranes.

RECRUITMENT RATES, POPULATION STATUS, AND CONSERVATION

Unfortunately, there are no good estimates of numbers for any of the races of this species. Pomeroy (1980b) judged that the Uganda population alone was probably in the tens of thousands, and might well be increasing. He judged that, for those nesting efforts producing young that survived beyond three months after hatching, the number of young per pair averaged 1.3. He noted that young birds make up a small proportion of the total birds seen, and the overall recruitment rate might be no greater than that estimated by Miller, Hochbaum, and Botkin (1972) for the sandhill crane (2-8 percent annually), in spite of the considerably larger average clutch size of the crowned crane. Parker (1971) reported that in Nigeria the crowned crane merits a conservation priority. Urban (1981) believed the Sudan race to be secure.

EVOLUTIONARY RELATIONSHIPS

The general evidence on the distinctive position of *Balearica* in the family Gruidae has already been offered in the chapter on classification and evolution, and so little needs to be added here. Wood (1979) reported that *Balearica* was anatomically divergent from all other species of extant cranes in six to ten analyses that he performed. In the remaining four analyses it was more similar to *Anthropoides* or *Bugeranus* than to *Grus*. The additional similarities of *Balearica* to such fossil genera as *Paleogrus* and *Probalearica* (Brodkorb, 1967; Cracraft, 1973) would suggest that *Balearica* is of a more generalized type than are these other modern genera, and should be listed first in taxonomic sequence.

Blue Crane

Anthropoides paradisea (Lichtenstein) 1793

Other Vernacular Names. Stanley crane; Bloukraan (Afrikaan); Grue bleue (French); Paradieskranich (German); Hagoromo zuru (Japanese); Chetyrekhkrydy zhuravl (Russian); Grulla azul (Spanish); Groote Sprinkhaan-vogel (Boers, Transvaal).

Range. Resident in the upland interior of South Africa and possibly adjacent Mozambique north almost to the Zambezi, and with a small isolated population near the Etosha Pan of Namibia (South-West Africa).

Subspecies. None recognized.

Measurements. Wing (both sexes), 514-590 mm (average of 10, 552.6 mm). Exposed culmen, 81-98 mm (average of 10, 88.8 mm). Tarsus, 205-252 mm (average of 10, 235.2 mm). Eggs, average 92.4 × 59.63 mm (80.6-101.0 × 55.1-66.5) (Walkinshaw, 1973).

Weights. Few weights are available, but a male and a female at the International Crane Foundation weighed 5,675 and 3,632 grams respectively. The estimated egg weight is 181 grams. Walkinshaw (1963) noted that six newly laid eggs averaged 185.3 grams (range 168.2-201.8).

Description

Adults of both sexes are almost uniformly bluish gray, becoming darker on the upper neck and the lower half of the head and nape, where the feathers are thick, dense, and decomposed. The crown, forehead, lores, and anterior cheeks are lighter, sometimes almost white, while the cheeks, ear coverts, and nape are dark ashy gray, with the feathers loose and lengthened, producing a distinctive "cobra-like" profile. The feathers of the lower foreneck are also elongated and pointed, and the secondaries, especially the inner ones, are extremely elongated, sometimes reaching the ground. The primaries are black or slate gray, with dark coverts, and the secondaries are blackish near the tips. The tail is black or nearly black. The iris is dark brown, the bill is ochre to grayish, tinged with pink basally, and the legs and toes are dark gray or black.

Juveniles are slightly lighter gray than adults, and are somewhat tawny on the top of the head. They also lack the long wing plumes of adults.

Downy chicks are buffy yellow over the entire head and most of the neck, with the shoulders, the upper portion of the wings, the back, the rump, and part of the sides pearly gray, with scattered buffy areas along the sides. The lower throat and the breast as well as the undersides of the wings are nearly white, and there is a pale buffy area around the eye. The iris is dark brown, the bill is pale bluish gray with a flesh-colored base, and the legs and toes are initially bluish gray, gradually becoming darker gray on the legs and tops of the toes (Walkinshaw, 1973).

Identification

In the field, this is the only African crane that is uniformly silvery bluish gray, with long, dangling inner secondaries that nearly touch the ground. In flight the birds appear to be almost entirely gray-bodied, with darker flight feathers and tail. The calls are raspy and pulsed, and are fairly low-pitched. The male often raises his wings and droops his primaries while calling in unison with the female.

In the hand, the distinctive bluish color, the greatly elongated inner secondaries, and a "cobra-like" head profile are all distinctive. The trachea does not penetrate the keel of the sternum.

Distribution of the blue crane in Africa (hatching), including peripheral area of nonbreeding occurrence (broken line). Inset indicates breeding records (after Snow, 1978).

DISTRIBUTION AND HABITATS

Historical and Current Ranges

Both historically and at the present time the range of the blue crane has been a remarkably restricted one, confined almost exclusively to open grassy habitats in the upland interior of South Africa. Additionally, there is a small disjunctive breeding population in Namibia, to the south and east of the Etosha Pan (Snow, 1978). The species is generally found at lower altitudes during the winter months, but evidently breeds most commonly at elevations of 1,300 to 1,800 meters, in areas where relatively few large mammals are present and where disturbance from human activities and cattle pasturing is not severe.

The northern end of its South African breeding range is in the Transvaal, with the northern limit for breeding records in the vicinity of Belfast and Middelburg, at about 26° south latitude. The species is evidently widely distributed in Orange Free State, breeding in nearly all districts; it also breeds commonly and widely in Natal. In the latter area the birds nest occasionally in the dry thornveld zone (914–1,219 meters), but breed primarily in the highland sourveld (1,372–1,829 meters) and in the lower parts of the bergveld (2,000 meters). In the Drakensberg Mountains of southwestern Natal the birds sometimes nest as high as 2,134 meters (Walkinshaw, 1963, 1973). Breeding records in Cape Province are less numerous, but extend west to the Little Karoo (Walkinshaw, 1973; Snow, 1978).

Habitat Requirements and Densities

The habitats of this species in Natal, where it is perhaps as abundant as anywhere in its range, consist mostly of pastured grass-covered hills, valleys, and plains having a few scattered tree plantings. The grass and sedge cover in favored nesting areas is relatively thick and fairly short, and consists of species of such grass genera as *Pennisetum, Andropogon, Arundo,* and *Miscanthidium,* and sedges such as *Ascolepis, Pycreus, Cyperus, Scirpus,* and *Carex.* The climate is temperate, with dry, cold winters, and with more than 80 percent of the rain coming during the summer months, often in the form of hailstorms. During the colder months the birds leave their high-altitude breeding grounds and move to lower altitudes (Walkinshaw, 1963, 1973).

Few estimates of densities are available for this species. Walkinshaw (1963, 1973) reported that in one Natal locality where nine pairs were breeding, the average distance between nests was 1,711 meters. In favorable situations the pairs were generally separated from one another by at least 400 meters, although in hilly areas, where visual isolation was enhanced by the topography, pairs would sometimes nest within sight of one another and would have contiguous foraging areas.

FOODS AND FORAGING BEHAVIOR

Foods of Adults

In Walkinshaw's (1963, 1973) observations, he noted that nesting blue cranes often fed from the ground, capturing insects such as grasshoppers, and also capturing frogs and crabs. However, more often they fed on seeds from the heads of grasses and sedges growing near their nests. At times the birds also ate crabs (*Potamon* sp.), parts of which they fed to their young.

As an incubating bird left its nest, it would walk to its regular feeding ground, stopping at times to drink or preen, and sometimes pecking at morsels. Occasionally the birds would walk as far as a kilometer from the nest to feed, but rarely did they fly.

Foods of Young

Van Ee (1966) noted that newly hatched birds at the Bloemfontein Zoo were initially offered small crickets, pieces of earthworms, ladybirds, pieces of grasshoppers, ant eggs, snails, and the like by the female. After the chicks were ten days old they began to consume frogs, toads, small lizards, and small snakes.

Foraging Behavior

Little has been written on foraging behavior, but it is apparent that the birds feed primarily from the surface of the ground and from low-growing vegetation. They have not been observed digging with their bills, nor is feeding in water evidently a normal mode of foraging. Blaauw (1897) does note that various plant bulbs are also consumed by the birds, suggesting that probing, or perhaps pulling of plants up by their roots, may be a method of foraging.

MIGRATIONS AND MOVEMENTS

Seasonal Movements

Although it is apparent that migration does occur in this species, rather little is known of its details. Walkinshaw (1963, 1973) notes that the birds are migratory in Natal, moving northwestward in March and returning in early September. However, he mentioned that in the Drakensberg Mountain region of Natal the migration is chiefly altitudinal, with the birds moving down in March and up in September.

During periods of winter concentration, up to as many as 200 or 300 birds may gather in favored areas. Among these are the Swartberg District, East Griqualand, near the Drakensberg Mountains, where up to 200 birds concentrate. In Orange Free State as many as 300 commonly occur during winter (Walkinshaw, 1973). The northern end of Orange Free State, on the Vaal River near Bloemhof, was a major wintering area according to Blaauw (1897). Here the birds would gather, in groups of 50 or even as many as 300 birds, and spend the daylight hours feeding among herds of springbok antelopes, and the nights sleeping in pools in the company of crowned cranes, flamingos, and storks. Evidently the cranes and springboks formed an integrated society, with the cranes often warning the antelopes of possible danger.

Daily Movements

Walkinshaw (1963, 1973) noted that breeding birds sometimes moved as far as a kilometer from the nest site for foraging, usually walking the entire distance. No other information is available on daily movements.

GENERAL BIOLOGY

Sociality

Although sociality in wild flocks is not well documented, some interesting observations of van Ee (1966) are perhaps relevant. He studied a flock of ten birds in the 35-acre grounds of the Bloemfontein Zoo. The flock consists of four two-year-old birds of unknown sex and six adult birds having an even sex ratio. The birds were released during July (winter), when the species is normally flocking. After a few weeks, the birds moved into nearby lucerne (alfalfa) fields, and remained there. During the first week of September, one of the adult males began to exhibit dominance and would lead the flock during foraging activities. A second bird began to exhibit dominance traits 13 days later than the first, and within 21 days the other full-grown birds were behaving similarly. On September 25 the adults began to attack the younger birds, striking them with their beaks and legs. This resulted in the death of one of the young birds on September 30. The other young birds escaped into the zoo grounds. On October 18 the group of remaining adults broke up, after pair-forming behavior had begun in one of the pairs. On October 24 the other four birds also left the fields for the zoo grounds.

During aggressive chases between the adults, a typical pattern occurred. One of the paired birds would lower its head to the ground, shake its wings, then raise its head. Or, it would stand in an erect posture, shake its tail, and sometimes call. The calling alone would usually cause retreat in the other four birds, but sometimes after calling the dominant male would attack them. During this period the male was typically the aggressor, but on two occasions the female was also observed performing the same aggressive behavior.

Daily Activities

Little has been written on daily cycles of activity. In one pair studied by Walkinshaw (1963, 1973), the female incubated at night, while in another pair the male did. In this area, sunrise occurred just before 5:00 a.m., and on two days the first morning exchange at the nest occurred at 5:30 and at 6:12. Sunset was at 7:00 p.m., and during three days the final nest exchange occurred at 6:15, 6:30, and 6:12 p.m. This would suggest that, as in other cranes, roosting times are closely tied to sunrise and sunset.

After the young birds are fledged and fully grown, they form large flocks, roosting as a group in shallow water at night, and flying out shortly after daylight to feed in nearby fields (Walkinshaw, 1963).

Interspecific Interactions

Blue cranes share their habitat with both wattled cranes and crowned cranes in eastern South Africa, and are appreciably smaller than wattled cranes but of about the same size as crowned cranes. To what extent they might compete for foods or interact socially is still undescribed.

Other large birds that nest in the same marshy areas sometimes used by blue cranes are various herons, egrets, ibises, the white stork (Ciconia ciconia), the spur-winged goose (Plectropterus gambensis), and the secretary bird (Sagittarius serpentarius). It is possible that some of these species also compete with blue cranes for foods, or represent threats to eggs or young. However, nesting birds evidently relentlessly attack any bird or mammal that approaches their nest, including cattle, tortoises, guinea fowls, plovers, and even sparrows. Whenever a human entered the nesting area he was attacked by the male of the pair. Initially the bird would begin a threat, with wings spread, the body held erect, and the beak directed toward the person. If the person approached the nest more closely, an outright attack would follow, with kicking so severe that at times the bird's claws would become lodged in the person's clothing. Waving a stick or hat did not deter the bird, but only increased its ferocity. During this period the female would crouch with her wings spread, giving the impression of being wounded, and the male would invariably try to place himself between his mate and the person. When the person finally turned away from the nest and had retreated far enough for the male to stop his attacks, the pair would join in a mutual calling display for several times before returning to the nest. However, these observations were made on relatively tame zoo birds, and Walkinshaw (1963) found that whenever a person approached the nest of wild birds they would simply walk away from it, or would circle the man while walking a few meters apart, sometimes with wings outstretched, sometimes dancing, and sometimes calling. However, whenever another blue crane entered their territory they would chase it away, driving it out in flight.

BREEDING BIOLOGY

Age of Maturity and Time of Breeding

Walkinshaw (1963) reported that one pair of captive blue cranes nested for the first time when they were five years old. Of two pairs that have bred at Flamingo Gardens, England, one initially bred when the male was nine and the female was seven years old, while a second bred when the male was eight and the female four (data from private survey by Joe B. Blossom, pers. comm.)

The breeding period is highly seasonal in this temperate-adapted species. Egg records are entirely limited to the period between October and March, with nearly half of the records occurring during December (see table 14). There is no evident variation in the nesting records from the Transvaal, Natal, or Orange Free State, judging from records mentioned by Walkinshaw (1973). Walkinshaw (1963) observed that of 17 nests studied in Natal 13 were in use during December, and only 2 were active after January 7. The latest nest record mentioned by him (1973) is from Cape Province, for a nest with eggs on March 1.

Pair Formation and Courtship

The only observations on pair-forming behavior are those of van Ee (1966). He observed that, among a group of six adult birds in which the sexes were evenly divided, apparent pair-forming behavior began in early October. This began with the birds running in circles, and it was not evident as to whether the activity was begun by the males or females. The running behavior lasted for as much as five minutes, intensified over a period of the next four days after it had begun, and was always followed by calling. On the following day, one of the males began to pick up bunches of grass, branches, and dried pieces of donkey-dung. He threw these items into the air, and jumped high in the air. He then ran around the other birds, stopped suddenly in front of one of the females, and then ran away from her and the other birds. After a run of about 150 yards he suddenly stopped and began calling. After two days, the "selected" female joined in the picking-up behavior, and jumped simultaneously into the air with him. The other four birds followed halfheartedly.

According to van Ee, the primary aspect of the courtship is the "dance." This might last for as much as one to four hours. It begins with the birds running around in circles, as if the male is chasing the female. However, there is no contact between them, and they are separated by a distance of about ten feet. Suddenly the two birds stop and call in unison.

The next phase is characterized by both birds simultaneously picking up bunches of grass, which are thrown into the air. The birds also jump high in the air, run in circles, again pick up grasses and toss them, kicking at them as they come down, and once again run in small circles. This ritual may last for half an hour. The birds then stop very near one another and resume calling. They then run straight across the field, remaining very close to one another. The final phase is once again the throwing up of bunches of grass. This phase never lasts more than ten minutes and is performed with the birds facing one another. At times one bird will snap up the grass that had been thrown up by its partner and toss it up again. All these phases are repeated many times, and after every phase there is calling. The shortest complete ritual observed by van Ee was 28 minutes, and the longest was four hours. He noted that the behavior lasted for nearly two weeks, and was not terminated by copulation.

After two weeks of this dancing behavior, copulation was observed by van Ee. He reported that the receptive female crouches low, spreads her wings somewhat, raises her tail, and stretches the neck forward while bending it somewhat. The male mounts, grips her neck feathers just behind the nape, and places his claws on her "elbows." The wings are flapped as copulation begins, and at the end he lowers them to the ground, so as to have "an extra pivot." As he dismounts both birds begin to call. In one pair the female was observed to remain erect during copulation, and the male flapped his wings to maintain balance. A maximum of three copulations were seen during one day.

Territoriality and Early Nesting Behavior

As noted earlier, territories of wild birds in Natal were relatively large, with birds usually separated from other pairs by a distance of at least 400 meters, and with an average distance of 1,711 meters between the nests of nine pairs (Walkinshaw, 1963, 1973).

In his 1966 study, van Ee observed that the male begins selecting a nest site a week prior to the laying of the first egg. After copulation, the male would wander off slowly, and start picking up objects, dropping them again immediately in front of the female. At this time he would utter a very low call, sounding like *kworr*. The female would watch in a seemingly uninterested manner and wander off, with the male remaining behind and repeating the ritual several times. If the female did not return he would follow her and begin the same ritual on another location. This might be repeated for several days, until the female responded by inspecting the site, lifting and putting down the objects that he had gathered, and uttering a similar but higher-pitched call than that of the male. After accepting the site, the female began to clean it, and both birds would call repeatedly from the site. Van Ee never observed copulation at the nest site, which was typically a bare spot of ground that was slightly higher than its surroundings.

Calling at the nesting site gradually intensified, finally reaching a rate of up to 13 times in 10 minutes.

Walkinshaw (1963) noted that nests were built in four habitat types. These included short grass and sedge-grown marshes (vleis), which extended through narrow valleys surrounded by grassy and pastured slopes, and grassy pastured fields themselves, marshy borders associated with dammed areas, and short-grass foothills. All nests found by Walkinshaw were only a few meters from dry land, if in wet situations, or not far from water if constructed in dry situations. In a pastured field, one nest was found with no nest material present at all, and when materials were present they were of grass or other materials adjacent to or very near the site. Nests in vleis were typically very small and of grassy material, while in marshy areas around dams a small pile of rushes was used for a site. However, in short-grass foothills the birds built rather elaborate nests of pebbles approximately a half-inch in diameter. These pebbles were placed side by side on a flat site that was surrounded by short green grass. Evidently this is the typical nest type in that habitat. Walkinshaw found older nests only a few meters away from active nests, suggesting a considerable fidelity to specific nest areas by individual birds from year to year.

Egg-laying and Incubation

According to van Ee (1966), the eggs are laid early in the morning, between 6:00 and 9:00, while Walkinshaw (1963) believed they are laid during midday. In two nests studied by Walkinshaw the two eggs were laid two days apart in one case and three days apart in the other. Van Ee found that in all of six nests the eggs were laid on successive days. The first eggs were not covered in van Ee's observations, while Walkinshaw noted that in the nests he studied incubation began with the first egg. Incubation is performed by both sexes, with rather frequent nest exchanges. In one of the nests studied by Walkinshaw the male incubated at night, and the female did so in the other. During three days of observation the male incubated 42.6 percent of the time and the female 54.3 percent. The eggs were left unattended for only 3.0 percent of the total period of observation. However, the eggs were actually incubated only 87.9 percent of the time, with the remainder associated with periods while the bird was standing on the nest. Incubation periods of the male averaged about an hour, and those of the female about 90 minutes.

In van Ee's observations, the male was observed incubating in only two of the six nests studied, and in both cases his activity was irregular. Van Ee observed periods of as long as four hours during which the eggs were unattended, and variations in egg-covering of from 41 to 89 percent of the total time. However, in spite of this, all the eggs hatched in all the nests. The eggs were turned regularly during daylight hours, from an average of 9 to 21 times a day in different nests. In all cases the incubation period was the same, namely 30 days. Walkinshaw reported incubation periods of from 30 to 33 days for various sources, including both captive and wild birds.

The clutch size of the blue crane is quite consistently of two eggs. Walkinshaw (1963) reported that 26 of 29 clutches were of two eggs, with one of three and two of one. He noted further that the coloration of the eggs varies considerably, especially as to the size and extent of dark streaks and spots, and to a very slight extent the second-laid egg tends to be larger than the initial egg of a clutch.

Hatching of the eggs is essentially synchronous, according to van Ee, with the average time elapsing between the hatching slightly less than three hours. In his observations the hatching always occurred in early morning, between 5:15 and 8:56. Walkinshaw noted that the chicks could be heard within the eggs about 24 hours prior to pipping, and that hatching occurred 12 to 24 hours after initial pipping. The young remained in the nest for about 12 hours normally, but when the chicks hatched on successive days the older chick remained in the nest longer.

Hatching and Postbreeding Biology

Van Ee reported that the first day after hatching was spent in and immediately around the nest, with the male attacking any intruder. On the second day, the chicks began to walk around with their parents, and at this time the female became as aggressive as the male in defending the brood. During the hottest part of the day the chicks would rest in the shade of their parents, flattening their necks to the ground and giving the impression of being dead.

Walkinshaw mentioned that the eggshells from which the young had just hatched were among the first foods offered the chicks. However, van Ee observed no feeding of the young on the day after hatching. On the second day, the female began picking up bits of food and touching the chick's beak with it until the youngster accepted it. He did not see the male bird feeding the young at all. For the first two days, food was provided nearly every five minutes, the female typically touching the chick's bill and uttering a soft *urrrrrr* sound. This was uttered until the third day. Later, the young birds took food more readily, and soon it would be taken as soon as it was offered. Food-offering was not continued after ten days, at which time the female began to point out food on the ground and let the chick pick it up itself. After fifteen days the young could pick up food without assistance of the female.

The young chicks were observed to be good swimmers, able to cross areas of as much as 35 feet of water.

Walkinshaw (1963) estimated that the young could fly when about three months old, but van Ee stated that in the case of three broods the fledging required from as little as three months and three weeks to six months. There is thus evidently considerable variation in the rate of growth of chicks.

Van Ee stated that the peeping call of the chicks was retained for more than a year, and that the adult call was first heard when the young were sixteen months old. According to him, the young are cared for until the next breeding season, when they are chased out of the breeding area by their parents.

RECRUITMENT RATES, POPULATION STATUS, AND CONSERVATION

No information is available on recruitment rates in this species. It is the national bird of the Republic of South Africa and is fully protected. According to van Ee (1981), this species has a healthy population throughout South and South-West Africa and is nowhere endangered in spite of local shooting.

EVOLUTIONARY RELATIONSHIPS

Wood (1979) reported that the blue crane and the demoiselle crane cluster together in all of his analyses except for the "skeletal measurements/humerus length" ratios, apparently because the demoiselle has evolved a humerus that is slightly different from that of other cranes. Collectively, the two species of *Anthropoides* were more often similar to *Grus* (five of eight analyses) than to either *Bugeranus* or *Balearica*.

The evolution of these two grassland-adapted species from a common ancestral type can be readily imagined on both ecological and zoogeographic grounds, and I certainly favor the idea that they are congeneric.

Demoiselle Crane

Anthropoides virgo (Linnaeus) 1758

Other Vernacular Names. None in General English use; Shuai-yu-hao (Chinese); Grue demoisella, Demoiselle de Numidae (French); Jungfernkranich (German); Karkarra (Hindi); Aneha-zuru (Japanese); Krasavka zhuravl (Russian); Grulla damisela, Grulla moruna (Spanish).

Range. Bred at least formerly in northwestern Africa (Algeria, Tunisia, possibly northern Morocco); currently breeds in Europe from the southern Ukraine and the Crimea through southeastern Russia (north to the region of Volgograd and south to the steppes to the east of the lower Volga), eastward through the steppes of the Kirghiz, western Siberia, southern Minusinsk, and the Altai, Lake Baikal, and of southern Transbaikalia, to the steppes of northwestern Manchuria. Breeds locally southward to the Sea of Aral, western Chinese Turkestan, and Mongolia, with isolated colonies in Armenia, northwestern Tadzhikistan, and Inner Mongolia. Also recently found breeding in eastern Turkey. Migratory, wintering in northwestern Africa (from Lake Chad to the White and Blue Niles), India, and Pakistan, and more rarely in Assam and Burma. Perhaps winters locally or rarely elsewhere (Iraq, Iran, Seistan, Baluchistan), with vagrants sometimes reaching Japan, Ussuriland, and western Europe.

Subspecies. None recognized.

Measurements. Wing, males 453-508 mm (average of 15, 484.4 mm); females 449-490 mm (average of 12, 469.8 mm). Exposed culmen, males 63-71mm (average of 15, 66.35 mm); females 60-68 mm (average of 12, 65.1 mm). Tarsus, 168-201 mm (average of 15, 180.1 mm); females 152-186 mm (average of 12, 170.4 mm). Eggs, average 83.6 × 53.8 mm (72.0-91.5 × 48.9-56.65 mm) (Walkinshaw, 1973).

Weights. Adult males (3) from the USSR weighed from 2,325 to 2,450 grams, and adult females ranged from 1,985 to 2,750 grams (Dementiev and Gladkov, 1968). Wintering birds in India ranged from 2,250 to 3,060 grams (Ali and Ripley, 1969). Two males in June weighed 2,325 grams and two females weighed 2,100 and 2,500 grams (Glutz, 1973). The estimated egg weight is 134 grams and the actual weight of fresh eggs is about 130 grams (Heinroth and Heinroth, 1926-28).

Description

Adults of both sexes are alike, with a light gray feathered area from the crown to the nape. A line over the ear coverts, a patch below the eye, and a long plume behind the coverts are pure white. The rest of the head and neck are black, with the feathers of the lower neck long and pointed, hanging below the breast. The primaries, greater coverts, and alula are black. The secondaries are black, with increasing amounts of gray basally on the inner webs. The inner secondaries are long, pointed, straight, and ashy gray, the outer and middle ones with darker tips and outer webs. The tail and upper tail coverts are gray, with darker tips, and the rest of the body plumage is pale bluish gray. The iris is red, the legs and toes are black, and the bill is greenish at the base, yellowish in the center, and pinkish at the tip.

Juveniles are pale ashy gray on the head, neck, body, and wing coverts, becoming nearly white on the head. The tufts on the ear coverts are grayish and only slightly elongated, as are the feathers of the lower neck. The flight feathers are like those of adults, but duller, and the inner secondaries are shorter than in adults and dull slate gray, with pale inner webs.

Immatures from their first autumn to spring are like adults, but the black of the head and neck is duller, the

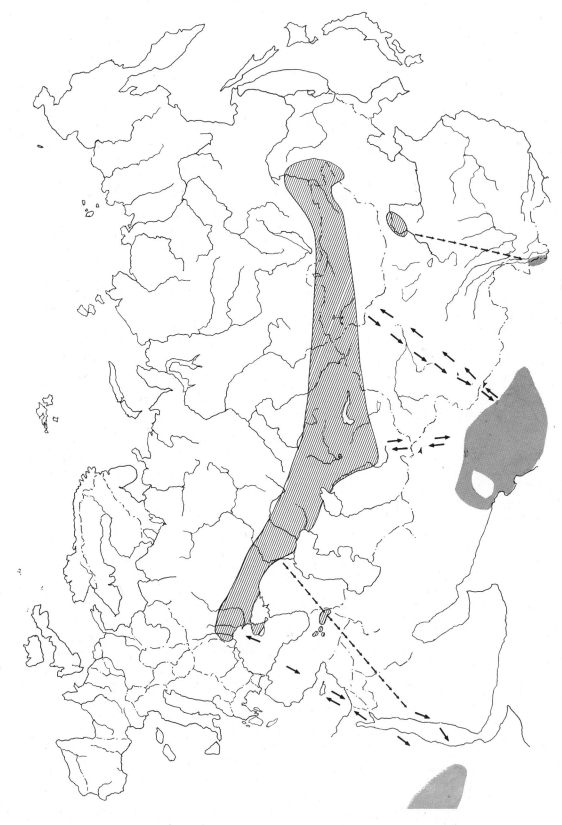

Breeding (hatched) and wintering (shaded) distributions of the demoiselle crane. Large arrows indicate major known migratory routes; smaller arrows indicate minor or presumptive routes. Arrowhead indicates location of Kali Gandaki Valley, Nepal.

feather tips of the head and neck are often tinged with rufous, the tertials and elongated head and neck feathers are shorter and less dense, and the ear tufts are tinged with gray. Many of the body feathers are tinged with ash brown or sepia at the tips, and the general color is less uniformly bluish gray than in adults.

Downy chicks have the crown and nape buff brown, the sides of the head, chin, and throat light buff, and the upperparts and sides gray brown or buff brown, with darker stripes on the back and on each wing. The underparts are pale gray to off-white (Cramp and Simmons, 1980; Walkinshaw, 1973). Downy young of this species are duller than those of *Grus grus*, with less rufous apparent. There is a second down coat that is light drab, with hair brown along the middle of the back (Fjeldså, 1977).

Identification

In the field, this small crane is the only one that exhibits a uniformly black neck and head, save for ornamental white ear tufts. Otherwise it is generally grayish in appearance. Its calls are surprisingly low-pitched, and are never performed with wing-drooping.

In the hand, this is the smallest crane (bill with culmen length of less than 75 mm), and the only one with white ear tufts that hang down behind the nape. Its trachea does not penetrate the keel of the sternum, but does pass along its anterior edge.

DISTRIBUTION AND HABITATS

Historical and Current Breeding Ranges

The range of this species has evidently retracted considerably in historical times, especially in its western sector. For example, it once bred near Kairouan in Tunisia, but was rare there by the 1930s and there have been no recent records. Breeding in Morocco occurred as recently as the 1930s. It also bred in small numbers in Algeria during the nineteenth century, at Boghari, Zahrez, and Zani. It regularly occurred during migration in southern Spain during that same period, but there is no evidence of its breeding there (Cramp and Simmons, 1980).

Similarly, the species bred in Romania in the late 1800s, and perhaps continued to nest in Dobrogea until as late as 1926. It may also have bred in Moldavia and Wallachia. In the adjacent USSR it once bred further north (to Kiev, Kharkhov, and Poltava) (Cramp and Simmons, 1980). It still evidently extends as a breeding species from the northern Caucasus (Manych, Mozodz, and Nogai steppes) and Transcaucasia (Lake Sevan) eastward through the Volga and Ural River steppes and

across Kazakhstan north of the Aral Sea, southeastwardly perhaps to northern Tadzhikstan (Leninabad region, near Tashkent), then eastwardly north of the Tian Shan Mountains to Mongolia and Inner Mongolia (Dementiev and Gladkov, 1968).

Besides this range, a small disjunctive breeding unit still occurs in eastern Turkey, where nesting has been documented on three occasions since 1966. The birds have also been observed during spring in the Middle Atlas Mountains of Morocco during the 1960s and 1970s, but no breeding has been proven (Cramp and Simmons, 1980). However, Archibald et al. (1981) recently reported the finding of a group of cranes "apparently breeding near Rez, Morroco."

The account of Kozlova (1975) provides the most detailed recent information on the species' central Asian distribution. She states that its primary nesting area is now in the Mongolian People's Republic, and that it nests less commonly in southern central Asia. Originally the species inhabited the entire Asian steppe region all the way to its western edge, but now except for Mongolia it is largely found in Kazakhstan (sporadically in Hirghisa), in the lower Volga Valley in Predkavkaz (near the Caucasus), and in the southern Ukraine. The northern limit extends to east of the region of Khailar, and the steppes along the rivers Argun and Aga. In southwestern Qabakail it still occurs near Kyakhta and is common in the Tuvinsk Minasinsk and Abakansk steppes and in the southern parts of Kulinda. In Kazakhstan it nests north to 50-52° north latitude, in the Volga region to 49°, while in the Ukraine it has survived only in the steppes near the Black Sea and in Sivash. Its eastern limits probably include the foothills of the Great Khingan Range of Manchuria, and beyond this may extend to the upper Sungari Basin. The most easterly nesting records are for Yakchikh, a short distance east of Khailar in the steppes of the River Yal Butekhatsi, in the Tungar hills near the border of Mongolia and Inner Mongolia, and in Alashan. Beyond the Altai Mountains of Mongolia the species becomes rare in the Gobi Desert (Kozlova, 1975). A recent estimate of the USSR population of demoiselle cranes is 45,000 to 50,000 birds, although this estimate is based on extremely limited data (USSR Crane Working Group Information Bulletin, November 1981).

In the western parts of its USSR range, the species apparently now occurs from the Issyk-Kul and Sonkyol lake valleys to the At-baski River, the edges of the Betapak-Dall Desert, the Telikulsk lakes, the upper reaches of the Emba River, the southern parts of the Middle Ural, and the Volga nearly to its mouth. It also occurs in the vicinity of Volgograd, the Kalmyk steppes, and the Predkaykaz steppes. It also still nests in the middle and lower Dom River basin on the Kerchensk Peninsula, and in the steppes near the Black Sea in the Crimea to the mouth of the Dnieper River (Kozlova,

1975). The Kalmyk steppes support the densest USSR nesting population of 6,000 to 8,000 nesting pairs.

Habitat Requirements and Densities

This species breeds mainly in steppe habitats, ranging altitudinally from inland sea level up to perhaps about 3,000 meters (Cramp and Simmons, 1980), as at Lake Sonkyol (Kirgiziya) USSR. Typically it inhabits hilly steppes that penetrate into mountains along wide river valleys, where it may even occupy forest edge habitats such as meadows. It prefers dry areas dominated by wormwood (*Artemisia*) and grassy steppes of feathergrass (*Stipa*) and fescue (*Festuca*). It occurs in shrubby steppes and in semi-deserts, but occupies damp marshes and swamps only during feeding. Evidently access to water is an essential requirement, and the birds use such diverse sources as rivers, streams, or even wells to drink (Kozlova, 1975). They will at times be found on unvegetated alkali flats, or on large expanses of rock or gravel. Foraging is often done in cultivated areas, especially after the young are well grown. In recent years, nesting in cultivated areas of the USSR has become more prevalent and may be an important conservation development.

Breeding densities are evidently quite low, although detailed estimates are not available. According to Chekmenev (1960), the birds are distributed widely in desert regions, with neither the topography nor vegetational characteristics affecting their distribution. However, the critical habitat requirement is a proximity to water, with no nests being located more than 1.3 kilometers from water, and most nests situated 200 to 500 meters from water. Spengenberg (in Dementiev and Gladkov, 1968) located ten nests within a 10-kilometer square area of the Volga River, some of which were no more than 200 or 300 meters apart. Grummt (1961) reports an average density of about 10 square kilometers per pair in northern Mongolia. Nests often average about 3 to 4 kilometers apart, but may be closer under favorable conditions, and in one instance six nests were found separated by distances of 300 to 1,500 meters (Glutz, 1973).

Wintering Range and Habitats

Wintering in Africa is mainly on the Blue and White Niles at about 9-15° north latitude, in river margins and dry acacia grass habitats, generally south of the wintering areas of the Eurasian crane. Some wintering also occurs in western Ethiopia, and another important wintering area is in Chad (Lakes Fitri, Iro, and Chad) (Cramp and Simmons, 1980). Wintering also occurs in the northwestern and west-central part of the Indian subcontinent, diffusing eastwardly occasionally to Assam and Bangladesh, and southward to Mysore. Bengal, Assam, and Burma are evidently minor wintering areas. In India the birds occur in winter crop fields, paddy stubble, sandy riverbeds, and on the flat and open margins of jheels and tanks (Ali and Ripley, 1969). The easternmost regular wintering grounds are in Burma (coastal and the Irrawaddy Valley); no wintering is believed to occur in China.

FOODS AND FORAGING BEHAVIOR

There is no detailed information on foods of the demoiselle crane, but plant materials are consumed for much of the year, supplemented by invertebrates, especially beetles, during summer (Chekmenev, 1960). According to Kozlova (1975), this species primarily consumes seeds, especially grass seeds, but also readily eats large insects, worms, and lizards. When foraging it walks slowly, in fits and starts, but sometimes while catching insects it makes quiet movements and is also an adept runner. In their wintering grounds in India, large flocks gather in cultivated areas, where they consume large amounts of wheat, chickpeas, and alfalfa. Ripening cereal crops are also favored, and the birds sometimes do considerable damage to such crops (Ali and Ripley, 1969). Likewise in the USSR during late summer and fall the birds often move into cereal fields to feed on the ripening grains, and they often do great damage to crops (Dementiev and Gladkov, 1968).

MIGRATIONS AND MOVEMENTS

Seasonal Movements

The migrations of this species consist of two major units. Probably most or all of the birds breeding west of the Volga River and the Caspian Sea winter in northeastern and north-central Africa; a juvenile banded in the Ukraine was recovered in the Sudan the following December (*Vogelwarte* 26:200; Cramp and Simmons, 1980). The major wintering area, however, occurs on the Indian subcontinent, which probably provides wintering for the major breeding populations of Mongolia and adjacent areas. Presumably the Burmese wintering grounds receive migrants from extreme eastern Asia.

Dementiev and Gladkov (1968) have summarized the fall migration in the USSR, stating that flocking begins as early as August, and at times the flock sizes may reach 400 or more birds. Most have departed from Dauria by late August and all by mid-September, and similarly in the Altai fall migration begins in late August and continues to mid-September. Maximum fall numbers in the Kalmykia area reach 26,000 to 29,000 birds, and spring numbers are 17,000 to 18,000 (USSR Crane Working Group Information Bulletin No. 2, 1981).

On the lower Irgiz River the local cranes begin leaving in August and continue to late September, leave Turkemenia from mid-September, and depart the Ukraine in early September.

Migrants in the Nile Valley have been observed through September. The main passage over Cyprus occurs before that of the Eurasian crane, during August and early September. The birds pass over the Red Sea between late August and late September, and are present in their African winter quarters between October and February, when the northward movement begins (Cramp and Simmons, 1980).

The spring migration from Africa moves north over the Red Sea during the second half of March, and over Cyprus from late March to mid-April. The first arrivals in southern Russia are usually reported near the end of March, although in cold springs the birds may be delayed until April. Some late spring movements over the Red Sea (late May and early June) may be of immature birds (Cramp and Simmons, 1980).

A major migratory route for the population of eastern Asian demoiselle cranes that winter in the Indian subcontinent crosses the Dhaykagiri-Annapurna range in north-central Nepal. This enormous range is partly bisected by the Kali Gandaki River (84° east longitude), and at least during the fall migration period this valley provides a major means of access for cranes wintering in northern and northeastern India. Martens (1971) reported that huge numbers of demoiselle cranes passed through this valley during early October of 1969. In less than ten days of observation he counted more than 30,000 cranes, and judged this to be an incomplete count. According to Fleming, Fleming, and Bangdel (1976), the demoiselle crane migrates in large groups through Nepal in October and November, and again in April and May.

A more recent study by Thiollay (1979) in the same area of the Kali Gandarki valley between September 24 and October 5, 1978, provides additional details on the magnitude of this fall flight. During this twelve-day period, which was certainly well before the peak migration period, he counted 61,000 cranes. He reported that during good weather conditions many birds were seen flying between 5,000 and 8,000 meters (16,500 to 26,400 feet) above sea level, and that they were really concentrated in the valley only during conditions of strong winds and heavy clouds. Few other migrants were observed during this time, but golden eagles (*Aquila chrysaetos*) regularly harassed the migrating cranes. The eagles not only disturbed the migration, but also killed some of the birds as well. Quite possibly this narrow corridor is the major migratory route for all of the demoiselle cranes breeding in Siberia and Mongolia, and thus systematic counts in the area would be

of great value in estimating the current world population of this species.

Little else is known of the migrations of the eastern half of the population. The fall migrants regularly appear over Kohat in northwestern Pakistan in late August, while their earliest reported arrival date in Mysore, India, is December 20. Their latest spring departure there is March 5 (Ali and Ripley, 1969). In Tadzhikstan spring migrants have been seen during the first half of April, on the lower Syr Darya during the second third of April, and in the vicinity of the Aral Sea at the end of April. In the Altai Mountains they arrive from mid-April to the first part of May, and in northern Mongolia between late April and early May (Dementiev and Gladkov, 1968).

Daily Movements

Ali and Ripley (1969) noted that while the birds are on the wintering grounds of India they spend mornings and early afternoons feeding in newly sown or stubble fields and in fields of ripening crops. The rest of the day and also the nighttime hours are spent lazing on open sandbars of large rivers or on the margins of jheels. Actual distances moved in the course of a day are still unreported.

GENERAL BIOLOGY

Sociality

Flock sizes during spring and fall migrations in central Kazakhstan are evidently fairly small; Chekmenev (1960) reports the first spring flocks are usually small groups of 4 to 10 birds, while larger flocks arrive later on in April. During the breeding season in May the birds sometimes feed in fields in groups of as many as 7 birds, according to Chekmenev.

During the fall migration, large flock sizes seem to be more common. As many as 400 birds have been reported in Ili, Kazakhstan. However, probably many large flocks go undetected during migration, as they fly relatively high (Dementiev and Gladkov, 1968) and are appreciably smaller than the other Eurasian cranes. Meinertzhagen (1954) suggests that demoiselle cranes generally fly at altitudes of 330 to 1330 meters, and thus might easily be overlooked.

On wintering areas large flocks are often typical; one flock in the Punjab area of India (apparently with a mixture of Eurasian cranes) consisted of a broad band of birds extending about 1.5 miles in length (Ali and Ripley, 1969). Similarly, in the Sudan, flocks of this species and of Eurasian cranes numbering up to 20,000 individuals have been reported south of Khartoum (Mathiasson, 1964). Where mixed with Eurasian cranes, the demoiselles evidently maintain separate social groups within the larger assemblage (Cramp and Simmons, 1980).

Daily Activities

The daily activities of this species are probably very much like those of the Eurasian crane, although specific details are lacking. As noted earlier, the birds typically forage in fields during mornings and early afternoons while in their wintering grounds, and roost on open sandbars or along the margins of jheels. According to Chekmenev (1960), during the incubating period the foraging period lasts about three or four hours, presumably by the nonincubating bird. The incubating bird will not leave the nest during the hottest and coldest portions of the day.

Interspecific Interactions

In spite of their rather small size, these cranes are evidently fierce protectors of their nests, and not only will give chase to dogs and foxes but also will attack eagles (*Aquila*) and bustards (*Otis tarda*) without hesitation (Baker, 1928). The birds often associate during wintering periods with Eurasian cranes, but the extent of their competition is unknown. The incubating cranes are tolerant of such domesticated animals as sheep that might pass within about 100 meters of the nest, but an incubating bird may leave the nest should such intruders approach within 40 or 50 meters (Chekmenev, 1960). At times as many as six birds will cooperatively drive predators away from the vicinity of the nest site. There has also been a case reported in which a bird assisted its mate when the latter was attacked by a peregrine (*Falco peregrinus*); the crane used its sharp inner claws for such aerial defense rather than the bill. On the other hand, a captive bird once reportedly killed a man by stabbing him through the eye (Cramp and Simmons, 1980).

BREEDING BIOLOGY

Age of Maturity and Time of Breeding

There are few records of known-age birds breeding in captivity. One pair bred initially in Flamingo Gardens, England, when the male and female were each five years old (from a private survey by Joe Blossom). However, it has been suggested that in the wild the birds may breed initially when only two years old (Glutz, 1973; Cramp and Simmons, 1980).

The breeding period is fairly extended over the species' broad geographic range. In the Crimea the egg records extend from the end of April to the middle of May. In northern Kazakhstan the records are from the middle of May to the end of June, and in northern Mongolia from the end of May to the end of June (Glutz, 1973; Dementiev and Gladkov, 1968). Hatching extends from late May (May 21 earliest date for central Kazakhstan) to the end of June (northern Mongolia) (Walkinshaw, 1973). There is no information available as to what if any incidence of renesting might occur under natural conditions.

Pair Formation and Courtship

As in all cranes, this species is monogamous and is believed to have a lifelong pair bond. Courtship is greatly prolonged, and occurs not only on the breeding grounds; dancing behavior has also been observed during fall migration (Dementiev and Gladkov, 1968) as well as during spring (*Ibis* 89:77-98).

According to Archibald (1975, 1976), the vocalizations of this species during the guard call and unison call sequence are similar to those of the blue crane; both have raspy calls with poor harmonic development. In both species of *Anthropoides* the female usually begins the call, and a single female call is uttered for each of the male's calls. The female begins the display by extending her head and neck from slightly behind the vertical backward to as much as 45 degrees, and utters the first of a series of calls at the rate of about two per second. The male soon joins in, with his neck held vertically and the bill tilted about 45 degrees below the vertical. The male's calls are somewhat lower than those of the female, and are somewhat longer and more broken than those of the female. During the sequence the female may remain in her extreme back-tilted neck position or may gradually return the head and neck to the vertical. The wings are not lowered and the tertials are not noticeably raised in either sex. The display lasts about three or four seconds (Walkinshaw, 1973).

During mutual display, dancing also occurs, in which the birds often bow with spread wings, and also may throw small objects up into the air (Kozlova, 1975). As the birds are relatively small, these movements are done with considerable grace and animation. The dancing is done with the inner wing feathers depressed rather than raised, and is more balletlike than in *Grus*, with the birds not jumping so high or so frequently as in other cranes. Occasionally the birds head-bob toward one another, either synchronously or alternately, and move in semicircles around each other, with the tail raised and the wings slightly opened. As in other cranes, there seems to be no differentiation of the sexes during such displays, which most often occur at dawn and especially at dusk. During group display, the birds often form a loose ring around dancing individuals; the participants raise their ear tufts and black neck plumes, and fan their tails while uttering their loud calls.

Occasionally the dancing birds are replaced by birds from the group of "spectators," and sometimes the entire group will "race" off in one direction. The activity is ended by the group flying up, circling the area, and breaking up into smaller groups or pairs (Baker, 1928; Cramp and Simmons, 1980).

Territoriality and Early Nesting Behavior

After their arrival on the breeding grounds, demoiselles tend to remain social for a time, the flocks reassembling at morning and evening, presumably for foraging and roosting. However, territorial behavior soon begins, and at that time the pairs become relatively scattered, with the nest sites rarely closer than 200 to 300 meters apart. Six nests in Kirgiz were spaced at distances of 300 to 1,500 meters apart (Glutz, 1973). The territories are established fairly near a source of water and in areas that are partially to entirely free of vegetation. Walkinshaw (1973) has suggested that the relative proximity of nests in this species may be related to their communal display tendencies, and is reflected in their relatively weak voices as compared with *Grus* species. Further, the small size of the birds no doubt makes them much more vulnerable to predators, and this may also encourage a greater degree of sociality.

The nest site is invariably simply a place in which small stones are present, and no attempt is made to find or construct a concavity. Sometimes rootlets are also found in the nest too. Occasionally old nest sites are present as well, suggesting a strong nest-site fidelity. Of four nests found in Kazakhstan and reported on by Chekmenev (1960), one was on a flat area of steppe with a soil foundation and vegetation present, one was on a bare hilltop otherwise covered with grass, one was on a bare area of a hill, and one was on a bare valley area between hills.

Egg-laying and Incubation

In Siberia the eggs are laid between the end of May to the end of June, while in central Kazakhstan egg-laying is appreciably earlier. There, hatching may occur as early as May 21, suggesting that egg-laying may begin in April in some cases (Chekmenev, 1960). The eggs are laid at intervals of 24 to 28 hours, and replacements may be laid after early loss of the eggs (Cramp and Simmons, 1980). On the other hand, Chekmenev noted that after a nest was destroyed the birds remained around for a time, and then began a wandering pattern of behavior. The clutch is normally two eggs, but rarely consists of one or three (Walkinshaw, 1973). Of eight completed clutches, seven had two eggs and one was of a single egg (Glutz, 1973). The eggs are generally pale olive yellow or olive green, with purplish lavender spotting, and, according to Chekmenev, blend very well into their background. The eggs are certainly incubated by both sexes, but mostly by the female. Chekmenev implies that it is the female that undertakes the incubation, with foraging by the adults never done closer than 300 meters from the nest. The incubating bird sits with its head held high, yet is often hard to see because of the surrounding grass. When it senses danger it rises from the nest, walks some distance, then takes flight and calls to its mate. Together the birds circle the nesting area. When the danger is past, the birds approach the nest, inspect the area, and resume incubation. Sometimes the nonincubating male will also walk by the nest, look it over, and wander away only when all is quiet. The incubating birds are tolerant of nearby sheep when they are at least 100 meters from the nest, but leave the nest if they approach within 40 or 50 meters. When flushed from the nest during early morning hours when the temperature is 6° C, the bird will return to the nest within an hour, but later when the temperature is 20° C the bird may stay away two or three hours.

The incubation period is 27 to 29 days, the shortest of all the crane species. Toward hatching, the incubating bird sits more tightly than earlier in incubation. At that time, the male may sometimes divert danger by calling and dancing, or the female may perform a distraction display if suddenly surprised on the eggs. Either or both adults may also feign disablement, walking with the head and body low to the ground, and dragging the tips of both wings on the ground (illustrated in Cramp and Simmons, 1980). Occasionally as many as six birds may cooperate in driving predators from a nesting area, further suggesting the value of small territories and somewhat clumped nesting behavior in these birds.

Hatching and Postbreeding Biology

Since incubation begins with the first egg, hatching is asynchronous, although at times the eggs evidently hatch nearly simultaneously. Thus, Chekmenev (1960) described a nest in which both newly hatched chicks were present and still quite helpless, while in another, one chick was dry and probably hatched the previous evening, while the other had already left the nest. Evidently the adults normally take the chicks from the nest as soon as they are fully dried. When they are approached by humans, the chicks huddle on the ground, like downy balls. Soon after hatching they begin to feed, and later, when approached by danger, they attempt to hide under grassy cover. After the birds become fairly mobile, the family begins a wandering life, but they do not stray more than two kilometers from water. Then, when the young are in danger the chicks hide while the adults fly ahead, or when older the young birds will also jump and attempt to fly.

The food of the chicks is probably mostly insect materials; captive chicks ate beetles, orthopterans, butterflies, and ants. Incubating adults that were examined were found to have consumed grain, other plant seeds, and a few beetles (Chekmenev, 1960). In late summer, the birds fly to nearby grainfields to feed. The fledging period is probably 55 to 65 days, which is extremely short for cranes (Cramp and Simmons, 1980).

Probably most fledging occurs in the Kazakhstan region by late July or early August, assuming that hatching normally occurs before the first of June. However, fall migration here usually occurs in October, so perhaps families spend a month or two after fledging in putting on weight and gathering into premigratory flocks. Unlike most other cranes, the adults do not molt their primary and secondary feathers simultaneously during this period, and thus remain able to fly continuously . However, wing molt does begin during the late summer and early fall. According to Dementiev and Gladkov (1968), primary replacement proceeds from the innermost and outermost primaries to the middle ones, and occurs over a period of four or five months, from late July until December. By September or October only the second or third primaries have yet to be replaced. Evidently the secondaries, "tertials," and tail feathers are replaced later, since specimens taken at this time show no trace of molt in these areas. Cramp and Simmons (1980) suggest that the primaries are molted in a centrifugal pattern from the middle ones, but with the outermost ones perhaps not molted during the same season but rather only in the next year, when the molt cycle begins again. Molt patterns in the young birds are still unstudied, but probably are similar to those of the Eurasian crane (Cramp and Simmons, 1980).

The young birds evidently leave on migration with their parents, and presumably remain with them through the winter. It is believed that the age of first breeding in this species may be as early as two years, so family bonds perhaps persist for at least a year.

RECRUITMENT RATES, POPULATION STATUS, AND CONSERVATION

Unfortunately, there is no good information on the incidence of juvenile birds in fall or winter flocks, although such information should be easily obtainable. Similarly, there are no estimates of population status except in Europe and northern Africa, where the species has been essentially exterminated. There are no precise data from the USSR, but there are suggestions of a marked decline there too (Cramp and Simmons, 1980). In Mongolia the species is still very common, widely distributed, and an abundant nester, and Mongolia probably has the largest population of demoiselle cranes in the world. The species is not hunted there, and so conditions are favorable for its conservation in Mongolia (Bold, 1981).

EVOLUTIONARY RELATIONSHIPS

The recent study by Wood (1979) supports the idea that *Anthropoides* is a valid genus, since the two *Anthropoides* species generally clustered together in nearly all the analyses he undertook. Wood noted that *Anthropoides* was more often (5 of 8 analyses) associated with *Grus* than with either *Bugeranus* or *Balearica*. However, *Anthropoides* ecologically resembles *Balearica* in that both are primarily vegetarians (as also is *Bugeranus leucogeranus*), and further both *Anthropoides* and *Balearica* tend to have relatively short or weak vocalizations and live where food is fairly abundant on plains or in fields (Walkinshaw, 1973). These similarities are certainly the result of ecological convergence rather than suggestive of evolutionary affinities.

1. West African crowned crane, adult. *Photo by L. H. Walkinshaw.*

2. South African crowned crane, adult at nest. *Photo by W. Tarboton.*

3. South African crowned crane, adult at nest. *Photo by W. Tarboton.*

4. Blue crane, adult at nest. *Photo by W. Tarboton.*

5. Demoiselle crane, adult. *Photo by author.*

6. Wattled crane, adult incubating. *Photo by W. Tarboton.*

7. Wattled crane, adults at nest. *Photo by W. Tarboton.*

8. Siberian cranes, adults taking off. *Photo by G. W. Archibald.*

9. White-naped cranes, adults in flight. *Photo by Eizi Takabayashi, courtesy International Crane Foundation.*

10. White-naped crane, adult male performing unison call. *Photo by author.*

11. White-naped cranes, adults dancing, Izumi, Japan. *Photo by Eizi Takabayashi, courtesy International Crane Foundation.*

12. Lesser sandhill cranes, adults landing at roost, Platte River, Nebraska. *Photo by author.*

13. Greater sandhill crane, territorial male calling, Grand Teton National Park. *Photo by author.*

14. Greater sandhill cranes, adult and juvenile in winter, New Mexico. *Photo by author.*

15. Whooping crane, juvenile plumage. *Photo by author.*

16. Whooping crane, adult female. *Photo by author.*

17. Japanese cranes, adults performing unison call. *Photo by Iwamatzo, courtesy International Crane Foundation.*

18. Japanese cranes, adults wintering in Demilitarized Zone, Korea. *Photo by G. W. Archibald.*

19. Japanese crane, adult in flight. *Photo by William Gause, courtesy International Crane Foundation.*

20. Hooded cranes, adults wintering in Kyushu, Japan. *Photo by Eizi Takabayashi, courtesy International Crane Foundation.*

21. Hooded cranes, adults wintering in Kyushu, Japan. *Photo by Eizi Takabayashi, courtesy International Crane Foundation.*

22. Hooded crane, adults at nest, USSR. *Photo by Yuri Pukinskii.*

23. Hooded crane, adult brooding young, Ussuriland, USSR. *Photo by Yuri Pukinskii.*

24. Black-necked cranes, adults in breeding habitat, Ladahk. *Photo by Prakash Gole.*

Wattled Crane

Bugeranus carunculatus (Gmelin) 1789

Other Vernacular Names. Great African wattled crane; Grue caroncule (French); Glockenkranich, Klunkerkranich (German); Hooka Zuru (Japanese); Asbrikanskiy Sorodavachaty (Russian); Mothlathomo (Sotho, Sesuto); Grulla zarzo (Spanish); Makalanga (Zambian).

Range. Resident in eastern and southern Africa, from Ethiopia in the north southward discontinuously through southern Tanzania (apparently absent from Kenya and northern Tanzania) and Mozambique to the Transvaal and Natal, and westward to southern Angola and Namibia (South West Africa), in the latter area breeding locally only. Now extirpated from Cape Province and Orange Free State, and probably declining elsewhere (West, 1976).

Subspecies. None recognized.

Measurements. Wing (chord), males 613-717 mm (average of 7, 669.7 mm); females 619-687 mm (average of 7, 634.1 mm). Exposed culmen, males 150-185 mm (average of 7, 174.0 mm); females 124-183 mm (average of 7, 161.4 mm). Tarsus, males 298-342 mm (average of 7, 321.6 mm); females 232-330 mm (average of 7, 309.8 mm). Eggs, average 101.9 mm × 65.3 mm (91.0-116.5 × 59.3-71.5 mm) (Walkinshaw, 1973).

Weights. An adult male and female at the International Crane Foundation weighed 8,966 and 8,285 grams (G. Archibald, pers. comm.). The estimated egg weight is 240 grams. Weights of 21 infertile eggs ranged from 199 to 258 grams (Conway and Hamer, 1977). One fresh egg weighed 265.3 grams (Walkinshaw, 1973). Sugita and Suzuki (1980) provide growth curves for three chicks to 135 days of age, when they averaged over 5,000 grams.

Description

Adults of both sexes are similar, but the bare skin of the male is darker red than that of the female. In both sexes this bare area is covered by small, rounded excrescences. The feathered portion of the head is dark slaty gray above the eyes and on the crown, but is otherwise white, including the wattles, which are almost fully feathered and hang down from the region of the upper throat. The mantle, breast, primaries, secondaries, tail coverts, and tail are black, and the remainder of the back and wings are ashy gray. The breast and neck are white, continuous with the head. The inner secondaries are elongated, reaching beyond the tail. The iris is dark orange to reddish, the bill is light reddish brown, and the legs and toes are black or dark gray.

Juveniles lack the bare skin on the face, and have less prominent wattles. The body plumage is more tawny and less contrasting than that of the adult.

Immatures in their first winter resemble adults but lack black crowns and are not so black on the back and underparts.

Downy chicks are pale buff on the head and neck, becoming dark brown on the lower neck, back, the back of the wings, and the thighs. The iris is brown, the bill is horn-colored, and the legs and feet are bluish black. The wattles are slightly evident and covered with pale buff down (Walkinshaw, 1973).

Identification

In the field, this is the only African crane that has an all-white neck, contrasting with a blackish crown, breast, and back. Like the blue crane, it has long and pointed secondaries that nearly reach the ground, but the blue crane lacks a wattle or red on the face. The wattled crane's calls are higher in pitch than those of any other cranes except the Siberian crane, and are usually begun from a coiled-neck posture, followed by vertical neck-stretching.

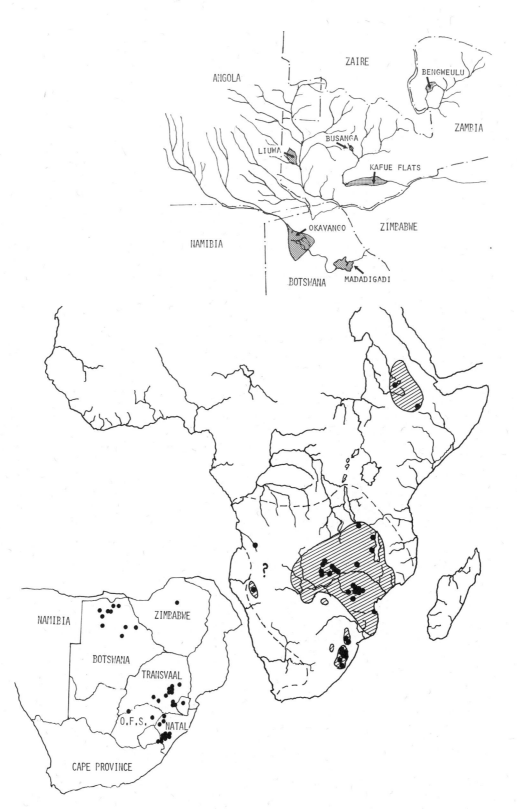

Distribution of the wattled crane in Africa, including known current distribution (hatching), probable maximum historical range (broken line), and breeding records (after Snow, 1978). Insets show 1980 sightings (after Day, 1980), and the locations of major breeding areas in upper Zambezi Basin (after Konrad, 1981).

In the hand, the pendent wattle immediately identifies this species. This trait is present even in downy young chicks. Internally, the trachea does not penetrate the sternum, but merely indents the keel with a vertical loop.

DISTRIBUTION AND HABITATS

Historical Range

There can be little doubt that the range of this species has retracted considerably in the current century, but even today its distribution is rather poorly known. The wattled crane is a bird of local and discontinuous distribution (Snow, 1978) and is largely limited to rather inaccessible wetlands. The northern population seems to have always been confined to the Ethiopian uplands, although there is an apparently undocumented occurrence in Somalia. Records from Ethiopia are fairly numerous and range in elevation from 7,000 feet (2,134 meters) to 12,000 feet (3,990 meters). The most northerly of these records is from the vicinity of Asmera, in Eritrea, and the most southerly from northern Sidamo Province (Snow, 1978; Walkinshaw, 1973). Breeding records exist for Dangila, Gojam (Gwejam) Province, in 1928, and for Adkoba, in Bale Province, in 1963 (Walkinshaw, 1973).

The other population of wattled cranes is separated by an equatorial gap of more than 1,000 kilometers from the northern birds; there are no records for either Uganda or Kenya. In Zaire there are but few records, including an old coastal record from Banana. There are also specimen records from Kasai Occidental, from Nieuwdorp in the upper Katanga drainage, from Kinda in the Lulua District, Elisabethville, and from Lalambwe and also 65 kilometers north of the Mwati River. No breeding records exist for Zaire.

To the south of Zaire, in Angola, one breeding record (1934) exists, for Andula, in the Bie District. At least in the late 1800s it was common in the interior of Benguela, and more recently,(Traylor, 1963) was widespread in the southern interior, north to Cuanza Sul and southern Lunda.

In northern Namibia (Ovamboland) there are several old records, and the species had probably long existed in the flats and intermittent rivers that flow north and east into Angola and Botswana. However, the only available breeding records are fairly recent ones, from Ovambo (West, 1976).

In Botswana, (previously Bechuanaland Protectorate) the species has probably always been confined to the northern areas (Ngamiland); nonbreeding records extend south to the vicinities of Lake Dow (Xau) and Lake Ngami (Snow, 1978).

Probably the greatest changes in historical ranges have occurred in South Africa. The species was once widespread from the Eastern Cape to as far south as Somerset West and Caledon in the Western Cape. However, Snow (1978) does not show any breeding records for anywhere west of the border area separating Cape Province from Natal. Walkinshaw (1973) likewise provides no breeding records for the Cape Province, but there is a possible breeding record for the Cape Town area from the 1800s (West, 1963). However, breeding is historically well-documented for Natal, Orange Free State (at Harrismith), and for the Transvaal (Belfast and the Vaal River).

The species is seen in Lesotho during migration, and in Swaziland its historic occurrence is undocumented. However, in Natal the species has apparently long been relatively common, especially among the vleis that lie directly below the low berg regions, at elevations of 1,524 to 1,829 meters. Breeding records exist for as early as 1895 for the Newcastle area, while other early records exist for the Mooi River area, Hidcot, and Nottingham Road. More recent Natal breeding records from the 1960s exist for the Dartmoor Forestry Reserve, Greytown, Himeville (Underberg), the Hlatikulu River area, and Howick, Sarsdon Hill (Walkinshaw, 1964).

In Mozambique, breeding has been documented for the mouth of the Sabi River, near Lourenco Marques. This seems to be the only sea-level breeding record for the species.

In Zimbabwe (previously Southern Rhodesia), a rather large number of breeding records exist (Walkinshaw, 1973), but in Tanzania there are but a few nonbreeding records (Burungi and Hhehe). The northernmost record from eastern Africa seems to be from the vicinity of Iringa, in southern Tanzania (Snow, 1978).

In Zambia (previously Northern Rhodesia),the species has apparently always been fairly common, and there are many breeding records (Benson et al., 1971; Walkinshaw, 1973). It is especially frequent in the west, but is scarce in the northeast and the Luangwa Valley, and evidently absent from the middle Zambezi. Breeding records there extend throughout the year, with a peak between May and July.

Current Range

The present status of the wattled crane in Ethiopia is totally unknown, but current political conditions there make it unlikely that the species is prospering.

The species' status in Zaire is scarcely better known, but Konrad (1981) suggested that the southeastern corner of this nation may support some birds, especially in the Upemba Basin region.

In Angola, the situation is likewise poorly studied, but Konrad (1981) believes that a significant population may still exist in the tributaries of the Zambezi River in the east, in the wetlands bordering Namibia in the south, and in the central highland and associated basins.

In Namibia, wattled cranes now occur only in the extreme northern grasslands and are probably decreasing as a result of human population pressures (West, 1977).

In South Africa the wattled crane has now been extirpated from Cape Province (West, 1976; Konrad, 1981). In Orange Free State the situation is scarcely better; West reported "no reliable records," and Konrad stated that only two pairs are known to exist there.

In Natal the species is said to be fairly widespread in areas above 1,282 meters, and is most common above 1,648 meters (West, 1963). However, Day (1980) estimated that only about 40 pairs are now known in all of Natal. In the Transvaal the wattled crane is declining, and perhaps the area supports no more than about 25 pairs (Konrad, 1981); about 18 pairs are in the Belfast area, and 3 other pairs occur south of Belfast between Lake Chrissie and Amsterdam (Day, 1980; Tarboton, in press).

In Swaziland the species is now considered to be extirpated (Konrad, 1981), although as recently as the 1970s a few pairs were believed to be resident in the western part of the country (West, 1976).

In Mozambique, the situation is uncertain. In the lower areas, the cranes appear to be nomadic, occurring during the summer and early autumn in Gorongosa, the Banhine, and the Delta grasslands. There are also records from various high-altitude grasslands, and there may be a migration of birds between these grassland types. Probably breeding birds are most likely to occur in the mountainous border country of Zimbabwe and Mozambique from Inyanga south to Chipinga (West, 1976).

In Malawi, there are resident wattled cranes on the highland plateaus, but these areas are being affected by afforestation of the plateau grasslands and by human population densities (West, 1976). This population may now be endangered (Konrad, 1981).

In Botswana, the primary wattled crane habitats are found in the Okavango Delta and the Magadigadi wetlands. The Okavango area, a permanent wetland with associated savannas within a 13,000 square kilometer area, supports several nesting pairs and perhaps as many as a thousand birds during February, in the nonbreeding period. Magadigadi likewise has large numbers (from several hundred to as many as 2,000) of cranes between January and May; these birds are believed to come from the Kafue Flats area of Zambia during high-water periods there, and many molt during this period.

In Zambia, the most important present wattled crane habitats are in the upper Zambezi and the nearby Kafue River, while the Bangweulu area of the Chambezi and Luapula rivers provides a secondary area of significance. On the upper Zambesi, the Liuwa floodplain is a 3,500 square kilometer area that attracts both nesting and nonbreeding cranes. In one November census, 145 wattled cranes were observed, and 58 percent of them were paired. The area is included in the Liuwa Plain National Park. To the east, the Kafue Flats area, a floodplain of some 6,000 square kilometers along the Kafue River, supports Africa's largest single population of wattled cranes, including about 300 breeding pairs and up to 3,000 birds during the peak season. Breeding here peaks in June and July, when from 3 to 40 percent of the paired birds attempt to nest, depending on the amount of flooding. During the rainy season, which begins in November, many cranes leave the area during years of high rainfall, evidently moving to the Magadigadi flats of northern Botswana. In Zambia, near the Kafue Flats, is a small permanent wetland, Busanga, encompassing about 400 square kilometers. This also is a wattled crane nesting area; it is part of Kafue National Park, and is thus protected (Konrad, 1981).

Lastly, the Bangweulu wetlands is a 20,000 square kilometer area composed of a lake and its associated wetlands, and supporting a still unknown number of resident wattled cranes. Konrad (1981) observed 20 cranes there in his 1978–79 census, half of which were paired.

Habitat Requirements and Densities

This is a relatively specialized species of crane, and depends on the presence of shallow wetlands and associated vegetation for its sedge-based vegetarian diet. Foraging is done primarily by probing in a soft substrate, and thus an abundance of aquatic plants that grow in shallow water and can be pulled or dug out, to obtain their roots or tubers, are critical components of the habitat. The birds are also highly territorial during the breeding season, defending an area greater than a square kilometer, which means that breeding densities will always be relatively low. Konrad (1981) estimated that the 6,000 square kilometer area of Kafue Flats might support some 300 breeding pairs, or a breeding range of 20 square kilometers per breeding pair. The other areas he surveyed had appreciably lower estimated breeding densities.

Nonbreeding Range and Habitats

There is little information on the nonbreeding range of this species, although it is clear that in some areas a degree of migration does occur. The most notable example of this is the use of the Magadigadi area of northern Botswana as a wet-season concentration and molting area, but not for breeding. Probably nonbreeding habitats differ little from breeding ones, since the mode of feeding is seemingly the same throughout the year, and thus the environmental conditions probably differ rather little, save for the specific habitat needs associated with nesting sites and other breeding-season activities.

FOODS AND FORAGING BEHAVIOR

According to Walkinshaw (1973), this is primarily a vegetarian and insect-eating species, but at times extends its prey-catching to frogs and snakes. It typically digs in the soil, for plant tubers, insects, and the like. At times it will also eat grain and grass seeds as well, but not to the extent of the other two African cranes.

Konrad's (1981) study of foraging behavior is especially valuable. He noted that the better part of each day is spent in foraging, primarily by digging in a wet substrate. Water lilies (*Nymphaea*) and the underground parts of *Cyperus* and *Eleocharis* sedges are the most commonly consumed foods.

When a food source is located, the bird begins a vigorous probing with its bill, sometimes digging so strongly that the whole body moves with the effort. Most of the digging is done in areas covered by shallow water, and apparently the food is largely found by tactile means. Digging in upland areas is confined to soft soils, such as rain-moistened ones. Of nearly 750 feeding habitat sites observed, 86.5 percent were in shallow water, 10.6 were in uplands, and 2.8 percent were in deep water, where the bird had to submerge its entire head to obtain food. Of nearly 800 feeding activities records, 98.4 percent were by digging, one percent by pecking, and there was a single observation of a crane picking up a snail. Stripping of grass has also been observed in this species (Douthwaite, 1974).

Foods taken by chicks have not yet been studied but presumably are very similar to the predominantly invertebrate foods consumed by other young cranes.

MIGRATIONS AND MOVEMENTS

Although very little is known of the migrations of this species, it is apparent that considerable seasonal movements do occur. These may be opportunistic ones, depending on local water conditions, rather than regular ones associated with seasonal temperature variations, but nonetheless are important to understand in terms of conservation of the species. Thus, the largest single known breeding population, that of the Kafue Flats, apparently regularly moves to Magadigadi during the rainy season. During a normal year, less than 1,000 are present at Magadigadi during high flood, but as the water subsides the population increases and may reach a total of 3,000 birds (Douthwaite, 1974). In different years the total may vary from a few hundred to

2,000 birds, suggesting that this is indeed an opportunistic movement rather than a fixed migratory pattern. There are perhaps also some migratory-like movements between the high and low plateau areas of Mozambique (West, 1976).

Daily movements of this species are still unstudied, although it is reported that the birds are relatively sedentary while on their small wetland nesting territories (Konrad, 1981).

GENERAL BIOLOGY

Sociality

Outside of the breeding season, these birds are moderately gregarious, and at times the flock size may be considerable. West (1963) provides some tabular data on flocks in Natal, indicating flock sizes of up to 89 birds. Of 63 flock counts, 40 percent were up to 10 birds, 19 percent 11 to 20, 6 percent 21 to 30, 5 percent 31 to 40, and 9.5 percent each in the 40s, 50s, and 60s or higher. Konrad (1981) observed nonbreeding birds in groups of from 3 to 43 individuals.

Daily Activities

According to Konrad (1981) most of the daylight activities are foraging activities. Perhaps the specialized foraging behavior of this species requires that a larger part of its available time, be spent in such activities. No specific information is yet available on roosting behavior of the wattled crane.

Interspecific Interactions

Wattled cranes exhibit occasional contacts with crowned cranes, but their habitat needs are considerably different. Thus, Konrad (1981) noted that in the Liuwa area of the Zambezi Basin the crowned cranes were six times more abundant than wattled cranes. This greater abundance was associated with their more upland habitats and greater areas of undisturbed breeding habitat during the rainy season. Crowned cranes typically feed in upland habitats and forage by grazing, pecking, or seed-head-stripping rather than digging.

In nearly all the wetlands studied by Konrad, lechwe antelope (*Kobus leche*) were present in association with wattled cranes. The lechwe and wattled cranes feed on the same plants, with the lechwe consuming the emergent and submerged portions and the cranes eating the tubers and rhizomes, according to Konrad.

Spur-winged geese are also close associates of the wattled crane, but often frequent somewhat deeper waters (Konrad, 1981). They feed on the shoots and seed heads of grasses, the soft parts of aquatic plants such as water lilies, and to a small extent on animal materials.

Thus their foraging niche overlaps somewhat with that of the wattled crane.

No information on important predators of the wattled crane is available, but the large size of adults probably places them out of the reach of most predators. West (1963) mentioned the jackal (*Canis mesomelas*) as a probable predator of one chick, and noted that humans are also an important source of mortality to young birds.

BREEDING BIOLOGY

Age of Maturity and Time of Breeding

In Natal, nesting occurs throughout the year (Cyrus and Robson, 1980). In Zambia also wattled cranes breed throughout the year but with a distinct peak around June (Konrad, 1981). Records from elsewhere indicate breeding in Ethiopia from May to August, in Malawi from May to July and also in October, and in the Transvaal during August (West, 1963).

Although the actual age of maturity in wild wattled cranes is unknown, Konrad (1981) suggests that they mature in their third or fourth year, and at that time form a life-long pair bond. A pair of wattled cranes at the Flamingo Gardens, in England, bred initially when both were eight years old (unpublished survey of Joe Blossom).

Evidently juveniles remain with their parents for their entire first year, since West (1963) observed a yearling with its parents in late April, and by May 19 the pair were again already incubating.

Pair Formation and Courtship

Courtship displays of the wattled crane are still only poorly described. West (1963) described dancing by a breeding pair during late April, just prior to nest-building. Although both birds participated, one danced in a more restrained fashion. During dancing they assumed a weird heraldic attitude, with the wings held high, the beak open, and the legs often lifted from the ground. West did not describe any associated calling, and considered breeding birds to be remarkably silent.

According to Archibald (1975, 1976), the wattled crane's unison call differs from all other species except for the Siberian crane. The female begins the display by quickly lowering her head to the shoulders, then instantly extends the coiled neck to the vertical while holding the head about 30 degrees in front of the vertical. This posture is maintained through the rest of the display, which lasts for from three to seven seconds. The male joins in the display very soon after the female begins her preliminary movements, and his head movements and initial vocalization closely resemble those of the female initially. However, whereas the female utters a series of evenly spaced short calls after her introductory call, the male produces a long and partly broken call, followed by a series of short calls, and ends with another long call. As the final call is uttered he raises his humeri about 20 degrees above the back. The calls of the wattled crane are higher in pitch than those of any other crane except for the Siberian crane.

Copulatory behavior in the wattled crane is still undescribed.

Territoriality and Early Nesting Behavior

According to West (1963), the birds become territorial prior to nest-building; in one case the breeding area was initially occupied in mid-April, the nest site was fixed by late April, and hatching occurred on June 28. The territory seemed to be as large as the birds could see from the nesting vicinity, and was maintained through the rearing period of the chick. The area used exceeded 200 acres (0.8 km^2) all of which was defended and fed over. Even after the chick was able to fly the birds returned to the breeding territory for some lengths of time, and thus it was not totally abandoned, even when the birds were sometimes absent for days or weeks at a time.

West (1963) reported that in 1956 he first saw a pair of cranes at a nest site on April 29, with one of them crouching and apparently stacking bits of grass. They were not seen at the nesting site again until May 15. The nest was not actually visited by West until May 30, and hatching occurred on June 28, indicating that egg-laying and incubation must have begun about the end of May. This would suggest an approximate three-week interval between the initial observed nest-site activity and egg-laying. In large wetland areas the exact timing of nest initiation is probably dependent on local hydrologic factors such as the amount of inflow from local precipitation, the timing of floodwaters from more distant upper basins, and the rate of local outflow. This kind of nest-initiation strategy takes maximum advantage of the large areas of shallow floodplain that "bloom" with new sedge growth after a dormant period during high floods (Konrad, 1981).

The nests are typically built in open grass and sedge marshes that are bordered by drier flat to sloping grassy meadows, with vegetation from knee- to shoulder-high, and water up to a meter in depth. Most nests are large piles of grasses, tossed into a crude heap and gradually packed down. Some are placed on natural mounds, knobs, or old nests of spur-winged geese, while others are built entirely by the cranes themselves. One nest was found on the top of a large submerged rock in the middle of a stream. When the nest is built in a marsh, the area immediately around the nest is stripped of plants for a distance of up to four meters from the nest. The nest itself is often from about 120 to 180 centimeters wide at the water level, and may be in water up to at least 61 centimeters deep (Walkinshaw, 1973).

Egg-laying and Incubation

It is clear that the average clutch size of this species is the smallest of all of the world's cranes (see table 16). Konrad (1981) reported an average clutch of only 1.6 eggs among 95 nests, and suggested that the probability of many of these being incomplete clutches is quite small, since the second egg is laid within 18 hours of the first. It is further possible that many pairs do not attempt to breed every year, but instead breed opportunistically whenever conditions permit. Such breeding occurs in large upland areas when floodwaters recede, increasing the areas of available floodplain for foraging and nesting. In smaller wetland areas nesting occurs when rains provide enough water to provide habitats in the wetland edges and in nearby upland areas.

According to West (1963), during the first week of incubation both birds remained close to the nest and never left the eggs untended. After the end of the first week, the nonincubating member of the pair spent an increasing amount of time away from the nest vicinity, feeding in fields up to a quarter of a mile away from the nest, often in dry cover dominated by tall *Hyparrhenia filipendula*. From about the eighteenth day onward, both birds occasionally were found off the nest simultaneously. However, at the time of hatching, both birds attended the nest once again.

Walkinshaw (1973) noted that during a two-day study, the male incubated at night, while the daylight activities were shared by both birds. The average period of daytime incubation was 157 minutes for the male and 238 minutes for the female. There were four changeover periods during the day, and, in total, the male incubated 35 percent of the daytime hours and the female 59.5 percent of the time, leaving the nest unattended for about 5 percent of the time. The nonincubating bird fed as far as a kilometer away from the nest, and usually walked away to feed.

Incubation periods for this species have been variously reported as 36 days (Crandall, 1945), 38 or 40 days (West, 1963), and 33 days (Sugita and Suzuki, 1980). In any case, this appears to be the longest average incubation period of any crane, and indeed the total breeding season is also one of the longest of all cranes.

Hatching and Postbreeding Biology

Observations by West (1963) are the only available ones for this phase of the reproductive cycle. In 1956, he observed a nest that hatched the first of two eggs on June 28. When West approached the nest the newly hatched chick left the nest and moved about ten feet away. With its parents, the chick slowly retreated from the area. Once in tall vegetation, the two adult birds began to "paddle a circle," lifting their feet high and plunging their beaks into the water. This evidently was done for obtaining food to feed the chick. During the next three weeks the chick was kept close to the nest, and each night the birds would return to roost, with one parent sleeping on the nest with the chick, and the other in the marsh nearby. As the chick grew older, only a single parent tended it as they fed.

In another nest, which hatched in late October of 1955, the parents' behavior was quite different, and both parent birds spread their wings and screeched when approached. In both 1956 and 1957 this display was seen little, if at all, suggesting to West that the birds had become conditioned to this kind of disturbance.

In 1956, when the chick was 80 days old, the parents hid it in tall grass when they went into a nearby maize field to feed. Hiding the chick seems to be typical of the species, and occurs from the moment of leaving the nest until the chick fledges. Hiding the chick usually occurs at the first sign of danger, usually when the intruder is still some hundreds of yards away. However, very young chicks can often be found by their "chirruping" calls, although older ones lie very quietly.

During three different years, West found that fledging occurred at periods of about 103 days, 131 days, and less than 148 days. This is the longest known fledging period of any crane, and places the species at a considerable disadvantage with regard to predators (Konrad, 1981).

In addition to a low initial clutch size, there seems to be little probability of the cranes raising two young even when two-egg clutches are present. Walkinshaw observed twelve groups of two birds, six of three, and three of four, suggesting to him that both young are sometimes raised. However, Konrad (1981) stated that no wattled crane pair has ever been recorded with two chicks. He further noted that only some 10 to 25 percent of the paired birds are successful in raising a chick to fledging; the average of all wetland populations he studied was 13 percent. Further, fledged chicks represented only 4.2 percent of the total populations of these wetlands, and ranged from 3.6 to 9.5 percent. This is the smallest recruitment rate that has yet been reported for wild crane populations. Konrad attributed this to the low initial clutch size, irregularity of breeding attempts, and vulnerability of the young to predation during the unusually long fledging period.

As noted earlier, young birds apparently remain with their parents an entire year, or to the beginning of the next nesting cycle. Rather large numbers of nonbreeding birds often associate in groups of from 3 to about 30 birds, and Konrad (1981) reported a total of 31.5 percent nonbreeding and nonpaired birds among the flocks he surveyed in southern Africa. This is, in fact, a rather low percentage of apparent nonbreeders by comparison with the whooping crane, for example, and may indicate an earlier average age of pairing in the wattled crane than in the whooping crane.

RECRUITMENT RATES, POPULATION STATUS, AND CONSERVATION

As noted earlier, the best estimate of recruitment rate now available is Konrad's (1981) figure of 4.2 percent young among a total of 784 birds. This figure includes 33 young associated with 254 pairs, suggesting that the rate of pair success in wattled cranes is approximately 13 percent. This is appreciably lower than the 45 percent of young whooping cranes relative to the number of known breeding pairs in the 1968 to 1979 whooping crane population (Kuyt, 1981a), and suggests a less efficient degree of nesting and fledging success for the wattled cranes.

There are still no accurate figures for the total population of wattled cranes, but the largest single population unit, in the Kafue Flats area of Zambia, supports about 300 breeding pairs and a maximum total of 3,000 birds at peak populations. Probably most or all of the up to several thousand wattled cranes that sometimes assemble at Magadigadi, in Botswana, are the same birds, and thus cannot be added to the population estimate (Konrad, 1981). If one assumes that these general areas of the upper Zambezi, Okavango, and Luapula rivers support no more than 4,000 wattled cranes in total, then it is apparent that the species' overall African population is probably in the vicinity of 5,000 to 10,000 birds. Some of these probably occur in areas such as the still unstudied Upemba wetland area of nearby southern Zaire, and other breeding populations will likely be found in the Linyanti-Chobe River floodplain area of the Namibia-Botswana border Konrad, 1981). Yet others probably exist in eastern Angola, in addition to the known northern population of Ethiopia and the remnant groups in Malawi, Mozambique, Namibia, and South Africa. The key to the survival of the species clearly lies in the upper Zambezi drainage, and it is extremely unfortunate that the most important of these areas are threatened by various development projects. The damming of the Kafue River about the Kafue Flats to regulate flooding will reduce the floodplain area and stop much of the seasonal flooding on which the wattled crane depends for nesting. The two dams already completed in this project have apparently already had significant effects on breeding success in this area, according to Konrad (1981). Other development projects include the possible damming of the Luapula River, which would convert the Bengweulu basin into a reservoir and destroy its wetland ecology. There are also plans for wetland reclamation in the Okavango, in conjunction with tsetse fly control programs of the Botswana government (Konrad, 1981). All of these possibilities pose serious threats to the future of the wattled crane, which is certainly the most vulnerable of the African cranes.

EVOLUTIONARY RELATIONSHIPS

This species has most frequently been maintained in a monotypic genus (e.g., Sharpe, 1894; Peters, 1934; and Archibald, 1975), presumably largely on the basis of its unique wattle and its distinctive adult plumage pattern. However, Wood (1979) found that in its skeletal characteristics the wattled crane clustered with the Siberian crane, although this clustering did not hold in his analysis of external characteristics. Nonetheless, he suggested that "the two may in the future be considered congeneric," and recent studies of the behavior of the Siberian crane by Archibald (1976) suggested to him that the Siberian crane has closer phyletic relationships with the wattled crane than to the species of *Grus*, with which it traditionally has been allied.

Map of Eurasia, showing most of the localities and political entities mentioned in the text.

Siberian Crane

Bugeranus leucogeranus (Pallas) 1773

Other Vernacular Names. Siberian white crane, Asiatic White Crane; Grue nonne, Grue blanche d'Asie (French); Nonnenkranich, Schnee-Kranich, Weisse indische Kranich (German); Sod egura-zuru (Japanese); Sterch, Belyi zhuravl (Russian); Grulla siberiana, Grulla blanco (Spanish).

Range. Known breeding areas are currently only two. The first is from about the confluence of the Ob and Irtysh rivers north to the region of Berezovo, and the second is from the basin of the Indigirka (from its mouth south to the Moma River) west to the Khroma River and the lower Yana. Other possible breeding areas may extend the second range east to the lower Kolyma and west to the region east of the lower Lena River. Possibly breeding also occurs or once occurred in the valley of the lower Vilyuy and on the Vitim Plateau and, in the west, the swamps north of the Baraba steppe. Breeding was formerly much more extensive, and included the Kirghiz and Siberian steppes, and perhaps from southeastern Transbaikalia to northern Mongolia and northern Manchuria (Vaurie, 1965). Wintering occurs (rarely) in the south Caspian (Iran), and in the Keoladeo Ghana Sanctuary, near Bharatpur, Rajasthan, India. The east Siberian breeding population winters in the Yangtze Basin of eastern China, in the swampy parts of northern Jiangxi Province (Tso-hsin Cheng, in lit.).

Subspecies. None recognized.

Measurements. Wing (chord), males 563-625 mm (average of 8, 607.1 mm); females 538-597 mm (average of 7, 571 mm). Exposed culmen, males 182-199 mm (average of 8, 188.2 mm); females 162-186 mm (average of 7, 178.4 mm). Tarsus, males 241-285 mm (average of 8, 264 mm); females 254-262 mm (average of 7, 258.5 mm). Eggs, average 98.5 mm × 60.9 mm (92.7-107.4 × 54.6-65.7 mm) (Walkinshaw, 1973).

Weights. Four females in summer averaged 5,475 grams (range 4,900-6,000 grams), while eight males in summer averaged 6,387 grams (range 5,100-7,400 grams) (Perfil'ev, 1965). Adult males in winter weighed 7,260 to 8,620 grams, and adult females in winter weighed 5,670 to 7,260 grams (sample sizes not indicated) (Cramp and Simmons, 1980). The estimated egg weight is 202 grams.

Description

Adults of both sexes have the forecrown, forehead, face, and sides of the head (back to the area just posterior to the eyes) bare of most feathers and brick-red, with a few scattered hairlike feathers. The plumage is pure white, except for the primaries, primary coverts, and alula, which are black. The iris is reddish or pale yellow, and the legs and toes are reddish pink.

Juveniles lack a bare face, and instead the entire head and upper neck are somewhat rusty buff, with the future bare area having browner or dingier feathers. The rest of the plumage is buffy, becoming pale on the throat and chin, and deepest on the cheeks, crown, and nape, except for the primaries, greater coverts, and alula, which are blackish (Walkinshaw, 1973).

Immatures from their first autumn to spring have gradually increasing amounts of white on the head, neck, body, and tail coverts, resulting in an adultlike plumage, but the bare skin on the front of the head is still densely feathered. The new feathers on the rest of the head and upper neck are cinnamon, with white bases often visible. The new tertials, larger body feathers, and wing feathers are white, often with a cinnamon wash. Some worn juvenile feathers are retained on the mantle, sides of body, tertials, lesser wing coverts, and back for the first year of life. *Second-year immatures* are like adults, but the head, upper

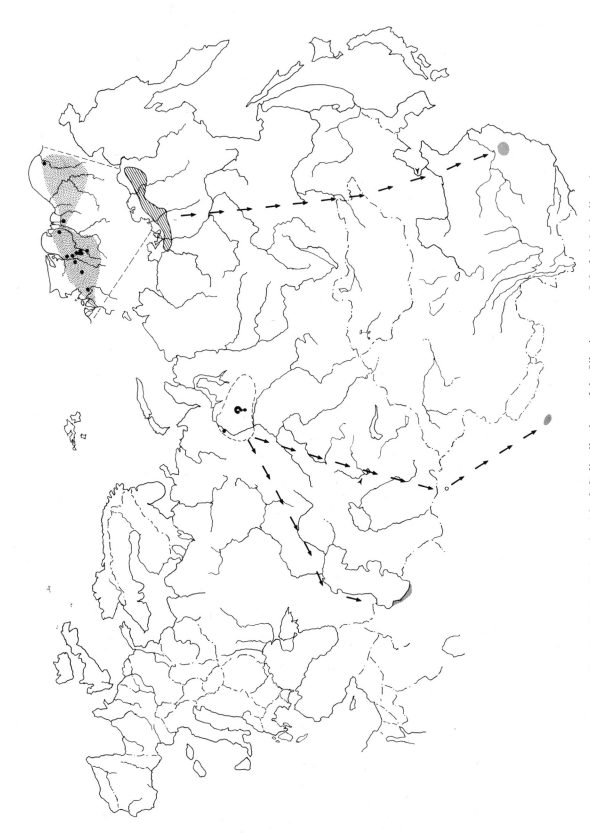

Breeding (hatched) and wintering (shaded) distributions of the Siberian crane. Inked circles indicate known breeding localities, and inset shows probable limits of Yakutia breeding range (after Flint and Kistchinski, 1981). Arrows indicate known migratory routes, with Lake Ab-i-Estada shown as an open circle. Narzum Sanctuary (USSR) and Bei-dai-he Beach (China) are indicated by arrowheads.

• 132 •

neck, and larger body feathers are still tipped with cinnamon, the forehead is only partly bare, and some juvenile flight feathers may remain. *Third-year immatures* are like adults, but may still have some brown on head, hind neck, and back (Cramp and Simmons, 1980).

Downy chicks are dark isabelline (yellowish brown) on the head and neck, with a creamy streak on each shoulder, and the rest of the upperparts are pale chestnut, darker on the middorsal area. The eyes are aqua blue (Ronald Sauey, pers. comm.).

Identification

In the field, this is the only Asian crane that is entirely white except for its black primaries. It differs from the whooping crane in its pink legs and its surprisingly high-pitched and goose-like voice, a whistled *toyoya*. When calling in unison, the male rapidly coils and uncoils his neck, with extreme neck-stretching and bending, and droops his primaries somewhat.

In the hand, the white body plumage and bare face of this species readily identify it. The trachea does not penetrate the keel of the sternum, as it does in the other white-bodied cranes, but instead passes along its anterior edge.

DISTRIBUTION AND HABITATS

Historical Range

According to Flint (1978a) this species was recorded historically during the breeding season in the Urals region, in northern Kazakhstan, in western Siberia, in the Vitim Plateau, on the Lower Vilyuy River, in the Yakutsk region, on the lower Kolyma, and in Transbaikalia. However, no specific breeding locations were verified for these areas. It also was recorded wintering and on migration in the Kura-Araks Lowland (from 1904 to 1914), in northern Iran (until the middle 1800s), and in Japan.

According to Taka-Tsukasa (1967) there are no specific wintering localities known from Japan, but there is a recent Hokkaido record (*Tori* 27:37). There are several known historical wintering localities for Iran (Seitan, Khorasan, Mazandaran, Gilan) (Dementiev and Gladkov, 1968). It historically wintered in northern India, west to northwestern Pakistan, and east occasionally as far as Bihar. The southernmost record is for the Nagpur area in Maharashtra (Ali and Riply, 1969), but the traditional Indian wintering areas were Pyagpur jheel (Uttar Pradesh) and Keoladeo Ghana, Bharatpur (Rajasthan).

In China, the birds apparently have traditionally wintered along the lower Yangtze River, although there is little specific information on this. They also evidently once bred in the Hulungboir Meng area of Mongolia, and at Qiqihar in China's Heilongjiang Province (Cheng, 1981).

The historical status of the Siberian crane in the USSR has been summarized by various authors, including Sludski (1959) and Neufeldt (1974). Sludski reported that the birds were abundant in the southern half of western Siberia during the eighteenth century, were still common in the forest-steppe areas of western Siberia in the nineteenth century, but became rare about the beginning of the twentieth century. In the lake area of northern Kazakhstan the bird seems to have been observed only rarely in the present century, including an occurrence in 1940 near the Smirnovo railroad station, and in earlier decades in the Lake Chagly area before it dried up. In the upper reaches of the Bengapura River in the basin of the Pura River of northern Kazakhstan, nesting may have occurred until about 1960, when the area was settled, and very few cranes were seen after 1970 (Azarov, 1977).

Neufeldt reported that during the time of P. S. Pallas two centuries ago, the species' nesting range consisted of the land between the Urals and the Ob River, as far south as the lower reaches of the Ishim and Tobol rivers in the west, and in the east from the lower reaches of the Yana River to those of the Kolyma. Changes in the past century, especially in drainage and in agricultural development, have brought about major reductions of the range since that time.

Present Range

The known breeding range of the Siberian crane is now limited to two widely disjunctive areas (Neufeldt, 1974; Flint, 1978a). One of these is a small population that inhabits the floodplain of the left bank of the Ob River, in the basin of the Konda and Sossva rivers. In 1981 five nests and a total of eight pairs were observed in the Kunovat River area. Birds from this population have been reported on migration at Naurzum Sanctuary (northern Kazakhstan) and at the Astrakhan Sanctuary on the Volga River delta. During spring from 3 to 20 birds appear at the Astrakhan Sanctuary, while in fall they are present in smaller numbers. The Naurzum population numbers from a few to as many as 50 in the fall (Azarov, 1977; Flint and Kistchinski, 1975). However, on the wintering areas of the south Caspian coast in Iran only 9 to 11 birds were present in the late 1970s (Cramp and Simmons, 1980).

The Yakutia population is known much better, and the western boundary of this population is the lower Yana River, with the right bank of the Alazeya River forming the eastern border. A strip of maritime and arctic tundra forms the northern boundary, and the Kondakovskii Upland and the northernmost belt of taiga forms the southern boundary of the area. The total area within this region is about 130,000 square kilometers, although regular nesting is limited to an area of about 30,000 square kilometers (Flint and Kistchinski, 1975). About 200 to 250 birds, including some 60 territorial pairs, probably occurred in the Yakutia area between 1977 and 1980.

The center of the known breeding ground is between the Khroma and Indigirka rivers, in boggy tundra area bounded roughly by the Berelyakh (Elon), Khroma Lapcha, and Gusinaya rivers, and by the Russko-Ustinskaya arm of the Indigirka River. East of this, the Kondakovskii Upland extends north almost to the sea, compressing the available breeding habitat. Although the habitat widens again farther east, there have been only sporadic sightings there, and Lake Bolshoi Morskoe seems to represent the easternmost extent of sightings, and the southernmost is a group of lakes 120 kilometers northeast of Sredne-Kolymsk (Flint and Kistchinski, 1981).

Apart from the small wintering population on the south coast of the Caspian Sea, the only known present wintering ground is at Keoladeo Ghana Bird Sanctuary, near the city of Bharatpur, in northern India. The numbers of birds wintering here are fairly small, and probably represent about 80 percent of the western or Ob River population. Wintering areas of the Yakutia population, previously believed to occur on the lower Yangtse River, are presently undetermined (Sauey, 1979). Flint and Kistchinski (1981) suggested that the presumed lower Yangtze wintering ground actually referred to other cranes and was never fully established. It is possible that the wintering grounds of the Yakutia population are rather widely dispersed, and perhaps in part they winter in India at the Ghana Bharatpur Sanctuary. However, in 1981, about 100 Siberian cranes were found on the lower Yangtze, at Po-yang Lake, suggesting that earlier ideas on the wintering grounds of this eastern population segment were correct (Fuzhang, Wenning and Ziyu, 1981).

Habitat Requirements, Densities

Flint and Kistchinski (1981) reported that air and ground surveys in 1973 indicate that the average distances between territorial pairs in 1972 and 1973 was 25 kilometers (range 14-30 kilometers), suggesting a density of a territorial pair per 625 square kilometers. They estimated that if territorial pairs comprised 62 percent of the total population, the average breeding-ground density was about 5.1 individuals, or fewer, per 1,000 square kilometers. A second method of censusing provided an estimate of 4.8 individuals per 1,000 square

kilometers in 1971, over a total area of 2,300 square kilometers surveyed. Flint and Kistchinski thus concluded that there are 1-2 territorial pairs per 1,000 square kilometers of total breeding habitat, or about 100 pairs plus 100 additional nonbreeders in the total 30,000 square kilometer area of the eastern population segment.

In Yakutia, the breeding habitat consists of tundra and forest tundra plains having numerous lakes, marshland, and depressions that are filled each spring with water. In western Siberia, the breeding habitat evidently consists of extensive mossy marshland of the northern taiga (Flint, 1978a). Nesting probably occurs on raised moss bogs surrounded by stunted pines.

Flint and Sorokin (1981) stated that the nesting territories of 46 Yakutia pairs were found on tidal flats, and in flat, swampy, grassy depressions, primarily of lake origin. These flats, whose linear dimensions exceeded 2 kilometers, were apparently important because of the unrestricted visibility they provide. The preferred nesting habitat was a damp tidal flat with well-developed vegetative cover made up of typical polygonal swamp associations of sedges and cotton grass (*Eriophorum*) forming sparse, short stands. In two years of late springs, a number of birds nested on drier and more hilly areas of polygonal tundra that evidently were less optimal than the lowland sites.

Perfil'ev (1965) analyzed Yakutia breeding habitats by surveying various habitat types, and found the densest numbers in mossy-lichen tundra with a few *Hypnum*-mossy-grassy bogs (16 birds per 100 kilometers), and similar numbers in lower bogs (14 per 100 km). Much smaller densities (5 per 100 km) occurred in hilly tundra, in tundra with small hillocks, and on higher mossy bogs. Nonbreeders sometimes were found on high hilly banks of rivers and lakes, and in small depressions between large, elongated hills.

Nonbreeding habitats are much more diverse than breeding habitats. They include lakesides and river mouths, steppes near water, open jheels and swamps, but not cultivated fields (Cramp and Simmons, 1980). The best-studied wintering habitat is that of the Keoladeo Bird Sanctuary, and Spitzer (1979) reported that an important habitat component is the presence of aquatic plant roots, especially sedge tubers, growing in water shallow enough for the bird to reach by wading. The birds feed in water from 25 to 68 centimeters deep, or about as deep as their long legs allow them to wade. Competition from the larger sarus crane, which feeds in shallower waters, may have restricted them to foraging in this very restricted ecological zone. However, in any case, it is evident that a critical component of nonbreeding habitat is the availability of aquatic vegetable foods in waters of wading depth.

FOODS AND FORAGING BEHAVIOR

Foods and Foraging Behavior of Adults

Little information is available on the foods of Siberian cranes on their breeding grounds. Dementiev and Gladkov (1968) believed that the serrated bill of the species was adapted for holding live and slippery prey, and that the birds lived chiefly on live animal foods. Uspenskii (1961) reported that four stomachs from birds collected in the USSR during the nesting season suggested a mainly vegetarian but omnivorous diet. In one were the roots of hellebore (*Veratrum misae*), and in a second there were the buds and roots of reed-grass, various grasses, the buds of shave-grass, and seeds of crowberry (*Empetrum nigrum*). A third contained cotton-grass, the buds of grasses, a few seeds and pebbles, and a fourth had the skin and bones of lemmings and voles, shave-grass buds, and pebbles.

Perfil'ev (1965) reported that ten spring and autumn specimens from the USSR had animal foods representing 50 to 60 percent total measured volume, while in four summer specimens the animal materials comprised only 25 percent. Major animal foods of adults consisted of lemmings and voles, and a few earthworms and fish. Voles and lemmings were important only when snow cover made plant foods unavailable. Berries (cloudberries, crowberries, bearberries) were important vegetable foods, as were horsetails, sedges, and grasses.

Sludski (1959) found information on three cranes collected in the USSR in the 1950s. Two that had been obtained during September had been feeding on the roots and stalks of a flowering rush (*Butomus umbellatus*), while a third that was killed in May also had only small pebbles and the roots of flowering rush present. Another bird, collected in March of 1928, had consumed small pebbles, two small plant tubers, and grasses. The presence of a gravelly grit, together with the plant materials, strongly suggests that the birds are vegetarians on the breeding grounds as well as on wintering areas.

Spitzer's (1979) observations in India indicate that the birds forage by wading, and feed mainly on aquatic plant roots 15 centimeters below the marsh bottom, which they cut and extract with their long, knife-like bill. When the bird is feeding, the head and neck may be under water 75 percent of the time, and is often held submerged for about 6 seconds, with a subsequent period of 2 seconds for breathing and surveying the surroundings. Spitzer attributed the absence of feathers on the face to the thrusting of the forehead against the marsh bottom.

Sauey (1976) reported that wintering cranes initially are territorial on their wintering grounds, with pairs or families feeding together and expelling trespassers. The birds would feed where the aquatic vegetation was very thick, and while walking along they would sometimes grab quantities of it with the beak and drag it to the side, thus clearing a small area of surface vegetation. Later in the winter, feeding territories seemed to diminish, but even during that period the birds tend to remain in pairs or families and separated from other such groups at distances of from about 15 to several hundred meters apart (Walkinshaw, 1973).

Foraging behavior on the breeding areas is often similar to that described for wintering birds. They often feed in water 25-30 centimeters deep, immersing the head while standing fairly immobile. Such foraging occurs on flooded bogs. On dry hillocks or grassy tundra the birds move about in a leisurely fashion, evidently seeking animal foods and berries (Flint and Kistchinski, 1981).

Foods and Foraging Behavior of Young

Sauey (1976) stated that chicks tended to do a good deal of foraging on their own in the Keoladeo Ghana Sanctuary, but that their foraging efficiency seemed inferior to that of the adults. At times they would resort to begging foods by uttering a high-pitched whine, which usually resulted in feeding by their parents.

Later (1979), Sauey reported at length of the feeding biology of juvenile Siberian cranes. He found that their begging behavior gradually declined in frequency during the winter, while the incidence of independent foraging increased. Conversely, the efficiency of begging increased, while foraging efficiency remained about the same. He observed two distinct types of foraging in both juveniles and adults. In one, "walk-foraging," the individual walked slowly through the water and picked at small objects on the surface. The second type, "dig-foraging," was more frequent and seemed to be more efficient. This is the typical underwater type of foraging mentioned earlier. Apparently nearly all the foods taken during this type of foraging were the tubers of *Cyperus rotundus*. Sauey believed that the gradual increase in self-foraging by the young birds during winter represents an important stage in gaining parental independence, since shortly after the birds depart from winter quarters the family bonds are broken and the young birds are deserted by their parents.

MIGRATIONS AND MOVEMENTS

According to Perfil'ev (1965), these cranes arrive in their Yakutia breeding grounds during the second half of May, while the tundra is still snow-covered and only some hill summits are free of snow. During four years the birds typically arrived about May 20; the major migration occurred in late May and was over by the first of June. Migrating birds usually flew in groups of 2 to 10 birds, averaging 3.1, and most often were seen in pairs (17 of 44 groups).

The migration from Yakutia begins toward the end of September. During the fall the birds can be observed in central and southeastern Yakutia, in larger groups of from 12 to 15 individuals (Perfil'ev, 1965). According to Neufeldt (1974) the flight to China may be done by one of two routes. They either cross Amurskaya Oblast, Primorskii Krai (Maritime Province) and northeastern China, or fly more directly south across the area east of Lake Baikal, across eastern Mongolia and northeastern China. The latter, more direct route would seem to be the more likely present route, as the birds have recently been reported, albeit rarely, in eastern Mongolia (Bold, 1981). At least during the 1940s the birds were observed in considerable numbers during spring and fall at Pei-tai-Ho (Bei-dai-he) Beach, Hopeh (Hebei) Province, in northeastern China (Hemmingsen and Guildal, 1968; Cheng, 1981). This would suggest that the coast of China may have been an important staging area, at least in the past. Spring records there are from March 17 to March 29, and fall records are for October and November. A total of 984 birds were seen during four years of observation between 1942 and 1945, as compared with more than 170 hooded cranes, 437 Japanese cranes, and about 25,000 Eurasian cranes (Hemmingsen and Guildal, 1968).

The cranes of the Ob population primarily migrate across the Turgaiskaya Lowlands and across Kazakhstan. They stop briefly at an alkaline lake in Afghanistan (Ab-i-Estada) before crossing the Hindu Kush, at the western edge of the Himalayas. Then they continue down into India to winter in the Keoladeo Ghana Sanctuary (Archibald, 1981c). However, a small proportion (about a fifth) of the birds fly in a more westerly direction to the northern coast of the Caspian Sea, and continue south along its shores to winter in northern Iran (Spitzer, 1981).

Birds arrive in northwestern Pakistan between the middle and end of October, and in the more southerly parts of the Indian wintering range by late November or early December. They leave again at the end of March or in early April, but have been seen crossing the Himalayas in Chamba (Himachal Pradesh) as late as May (Ali and Ripley, 1969).

At the Keoladeo Ghana Bird Sanctuary the birds arrive between November and January, and regularly depart in early March. Spitzer (1979) stated that in March it begins to become very hot, and the marshes start to dry out. The birds thus leave the wintering area more than two months before the start of their breeding

season, on a migration route almost 5,000 kilometers long.

Birds crossing the Volga Delta of the northern Caspian Sea have been seen between late March and mid-April. The autumn movement across the delta is smaller, and generally occurs between August and September, but with several records from October to December (A. L. Rak, cited in Cramp and Simmons, 1980).

GENERAL BIOLOGY

Sociality

Most evidence suggests that this is not a very social species. It exhibits a high degree of territoriality during the breeding season and, unlike most cranes, also displays winter feeding territoriality. Flock sizes seem to be relatively small, especially in spring (see Migrations and Movements). Ali and Ripley (1969) state that birds are usually to be found in family groups or in small flocks of 12 to 15 birds. The largest gatherings known are at Keoladeo Ghana Sanctuary, but here they seem to remain in fairly small groups, except perhaps for nocturnal roosting. Walkinshaw (1973) summarized flock sizes of birds leaving night roosts as follows: 1 bird, 2; 2 birds, 6; 3 birds, 9; 4 birds, 2; 5 birds, 2; 6 birds, 1; and 7 birds, 1; averaging 3.1 birds.

Daily Activities

On the wintering grounds at the Keoladeo Ghana Sanctuary, the birds roost in shallow water that may be from one to three kilometers from their feeding territories. While roosting they remain separate from the sarus cranes, which roost on the same ponds, and often are "strung out" in a long line. The water they roost in is up to 15 centimeters (6 inches) deep.

Much of the daylight hours is spent in foraging, which, judging from Spitzer's (1979) description, appears to be arduous and time-consuming. During the late winter months, the birds were observed to spend at least 70 percent of the daylight hours feeding, finding about 0.5 foot item per minute, as compared with more than 1 per minute shortly after they arrived in November.

Interspecific Interactions

On their wintering areas at Keoladeo Ghana Sanctuary, most of the important interactions appear to be with the larger sarus crane. Sarus cranes are common there, and forage in habitats ranging from dry croplands to fairly deep water. However, they rarely forage in water deeper than about 30 centimeters, since to do so would be relatively harder work, and they can easily dominate the shallower areas in contests with Siberian cranes. Thus the latter are forced to forage in relatively deep water. Unlike sarus cranes, which were observed by Spitzer (1979) to occasionally catch and consume water snakes, the Siberian was not observed doing so, and thus is apparently much more specialized in its foraging adaptations.

There seems to be no information available on possible predators, although gulls and jaegers often are serious egg-stealers on the breeding grounds.

BREEDING BIOLOGY

Age of Maturity and Time of Breeding

There is no information on the age of maturity in captive-raised Siberian cranes, since they are not yet bred in captivity.

Various Russian authors have judged that the period of immaturity in this species is very prolonged. Perfil'ev (1965) believed that some yellow (juvenile) feathers are retained up to the age of 3 or 4 years, and likewise Flint and Kistchinski (1981) indicated that the birds do not become fully white until they are at least 4 years old. However, they believed that all pairs holding territories were 3 years old or older, and that sexual maturity is attained at 3 years.

The total range of egg records in the Yakutia population extends from as early as June 7 to as late as July 8. This is a relatively short time, considering an approximate month-long incubation period. However, Flint and Kistchinski (1981) say that the onset of laying depends on the weather conditions at a particular site and might vary considerably.

Pair Formation and Courtship

Doubtless, as in other cranes, the pair bonds in Siberian cranes are permanent, and much "courtship" simply serves to strengthen existing pair bonds or may serve other purposes. Displays have been observed both on wintering areas and on the breeding grounds. Flint and Kistchinski (1981) reported seeing dancing on two occasions in June and July. Perfil'ev (1965) also described dancing behavior, apparently in birds that only recently arrived on the breeding grounds. He said that the birds display in groups of two, three, or four pairs, and that the dances were well known to local people.

Flint and Kistchinski concluded that dancing has no direct connection with the reproductive cycle and is simply a reflection of the bird's excitement. Evidently a crane will dance at any time and with any, or no, partner. The dancing behavior of the Siberian crane resembles that of *Grus* in that leaping occurs. However, the bowing phase is very different from that of other species. In the Siberian crane the head and neck are brought forward from a fully vertical posture (as in the unison call) to a position with the neck and head reaching downward and backward between the legs, as the wings are simultaneously raised to the vertical. This posture is apparently not found in any other crane. The dancing behavior also lacks the "parade step," the throwing of objects into the air, ruffling of the tertials, and squatting on the heels, according to Flint and Kistchinski.

The unison display of the Siberian crane is also highly distinctive. It is of indeterminate length, and is begun by the male rather than the female. He first draws his head and neck back behind the vertical until the neck assumes an S-shape. From this posture he quickly rotates the neck downward, ending with the neck held straight downward and the bill turned up toward the breast. At this point he utters a high-pitched call. Then he raises his humeri and lowers his wrists, so that the primaries are exposed. He then more slowly returns his head until it is extended almost vertically, but moving back and forth over a 30 degree arc, while uttering a series of flute-like calls that continue in regular sequence until the end of the display. The neck gradually assumes a vertical position, with the head lowered between calls and raised during them. The wings remain drooped during this time (Archibald, 1976).

The female typically joins in after the male has begun calling, holding her neck about 70 degrees above the horizontal and moving the head up and down with each call, but to a smaller extent than typical of the male. Her wings are variably drooped during calling. The sexes call alternately, with the female's higher-pitched notes producing the "loo" portion of a "doodle-loo" cadence (Archibald, 1976).

Siberian cranes threaten other pairs by walking and walking around them during the unison call. Sauey (1976) stated that several kinds of nonvocal threats are present, including "threat-walking" and several displays that have been ritualized from maintenance activities such as preening or feeding. This includes a "forage-shoulder-wing threat," which begins with water-swishing and ends with a preening movement on the scapulars while the wing opposite the opponent is lowered. In the "ruffle-bow threat," the bird begins with shaking of the secondaries, follows with a stiff bowing movement of the bill toward the belly, and terminates with a preening movement on the back feathers.

Although Siberian cranes differ in several ways from the wattled crane, Archibald believed that in most of their important behavioral traits, such as in the wing-raising during the unison call and in the initial neck-coiling phase, they more closely resemble this species than any *Grus* forms.

Copulatory behavior in this species is still undescribed.

Territoriality and Early Nesting Behavior

The cranes arrive in their Yakutia nesting areas in late May, while the tundra is still snow-covered. They waste very little time before becoming territorial, and probably in the case of experienced birds simply return to their territories of the previous year. Only a small percent of the available land is actually taken, resulting in a nearly complete lack of direct territorial competition. Flint and Sorokin (1981) report a territorial density of a pair per 290 square kilometers, although the absence of territorial interactions makes the exact size of a defended territory impossible to guess.

The strong tendency to return to the same area each year is indicated by the data of Flint and Sorokin (1981), who found that cranes have been noticed subsequently in 45 percent of the nesting territories known since the initial 1977 census. In 1978 about a third of the nests were located in the same sites as the year before, and in 10 other nesting areas birds without mates remained close by. In 1979 more than 30 percent of the nests were likewise at old sites, and it is possible that at one site the same nesting territory has been occupied over an 8-year period.

The nest is often built at the boggy shore of a large lake, or on a grassy mound in a large depression, surrounded by water about 25 to 60 centimeters deep. The nest may be raised 12 to 15 centimeters above water level, and have a flat top 50 to 80 centimeters across, with a shallow depression in the middle (Perfil'ev, 1965; Flint and Kistchinski, 1981).

Egg-laying and Incubation

According to Flint and Sorokin (1981), eggs may be laid as early as the latter part of May and as late as the middle of June, with the majority of birds laying during the first week of June. This corresponds to the time that the tundra becomes snow-free. The egg-laying interval is not definite, but Flint and Sorokin said that of twelve clutches, the average clutch was 1.75 eggs. Perfil'ev (1965) reported that among ten nests found, one was a single-egg clutch in the early stages of incubation. According to him, incubation begins the moment the second egg is laid, and is performed by the female, with the male remaining close by.

Flint and Kistchinski (1981) state that both birds sit on the nest, although these observers never were able to observe nest-changing behavior. In the nest they watched closely, only the female incubated (which could be recognized by her distinctive plumage features), while the male remained absent and spent his time during the day feeding beyond view and about 2 kilometers away. However, at night he remained only 100-150 meters from the nest, and whenever the female left the nest he joined her immediately.

The hen incubates in a somewhat flattened posture,

holding the head low and constantly watching the surroundings. She rises to turn the eggs about once every two hours. She also occasionally sleeps while incubating. When a person approaches within 2 kilometers she quietly leaves the nest, sneaks away 100-150 meters, then flies off. If a person approaches still closer she may perform a distraction display, walking away while spreading the wings horizontally and bending over slightly. The male may perform the same behavior at a greater distance. According to Perfil'ev (1965) the polar fox (*Alopex*) does not approach the nest, and the Siberian crane is the most formidable of all tundra-nesting birds in its nest defense. However, while the crane is absent from the nest, the eggs provide excellent opportunities for predation by jaegers (*Stercorarius* spp.), glaucous gulls (*Larus hyperboreus*), and herring gulls (*Larus argentatus*). Reindeer do not pose a serious threat to nesting birds (Flint and Sorokin, 1981).

Flint and Sorokin (1981) estimated the incubation period in the wild to be about 27 days. An egg hatched artificially at the International Crane Foundation had a 29-day incubation period (Michael Putnam, pers. comm.). Flint and Sorokin estimated a hatching success of only 33 percent (7 chicks hatching from 21 total eggs).

Hatching and Postbreeding Biology

Perfil'ev (1965) reported that during 1961 and 1962, hatching began at the middle of July, with the first, approximately two-day-old chick seen on July 14. Flint and Sorokin (1981) stated that the majority of chicks hatched during the last five days of June and the first five days of July, with extreme dates of June 26 and July 11 in the years 1977 to 1979. Evidently the close clustering of egg dates within a single year or area reflects the fact that the birds do not attempt to nest at all if conditions are unsuitable during the optimum two-week breeding period.

There is a substantial posthatching mortality of young chicks. Flint and Sorokin (1981) believed that even if both of the eggs should hatch, the weaker of the two chicks dies before fledging as a result of aggressiveness between the two young birds. They suggested that the annual rate of population increase is therefore less than 10 percent.

The fledging period of the Siberian crane is not yet specifically reported, but inasmuch as the fall migration begins during the second half of September, it must require no more than about 80 days. Toward the end of the summer, molt in the adults also occurs. The presences of secondaries and wing coverts near still-unhatched nests indicates that the wing molt may actually begin before hatching (Perfil'ev, 1965). Apparently the primaries are dropped over a period of a few days, while the rest of the molt is greatly prolonged.

Flint and Kistchinski state that the primaries are molted in July, but not simultaneously in all birds. One old male collected by Perfil'ev had fully regrown primaries and secondaries by August 26, and a female obtained on September 6 also had complete new plumage.

RECRUITMENT RATES, POPULATION STATUS, AND CONSERVATION

Recruitment rate data for this species are still rather limited. Walkinshaw (1973) reported that in 1968, among 100 birds at the Keoladeo Sanctuary, there were 15 pairs, each with a single young, or a 15 percent recruitment rate. Spitzer (1979) states that in three of four years for which data are available to him, the percent of immature birds in the wintering flock at Keoladeo was close to 10 percent, while in 1976-77 the recruitment rate was 14 percent. On the breeding grounds the incidence of first-year birds was reported by Flint and Kistchinski to be 7.3 percent. As noted earlier, Flint and Sorokin estimated the fledging success to be in the vicinity of 10 percent or less.

It is thus clear that the Siberian crane has one of the lowest recruitment rates of all cranes, and furthermore has one of the longest and most arduous migratory routes, as well as highly specialized foraging requirements. Flint and Kistchinski state that the two major adverse factors affecting the species in Yakutia are spring hunting and the herding of reindeer. The reindeer herds are often accompanied by dogs, which may find the nest and destroy the eggs. The birds may also lose their eggs to gulls or to jaegers if they are forced off their nest for prolonged periods by reindeer disturbance. Flint and Kistchinski suggested that an establishment of a refuge in the heart of the breeding grounds would do much to help save the species.

Protection of the migratory routes and wintering grounds is equally important. Those birds wintering in India are now well protected, but some mortality occurs en route, especially in Afghanistan. Archibald (1981c) reported that the important stopover point there was recently declared a sanctuary, but recent political upheavals in the country make the fate of the sanctuary most uncertain. Likewise, there is little hope for protection of the remnant flock wintering in northern Iran, and it may soon disappear completely. Spitzer (1981) reported that in 1970 there were 76 cranes at the Keoladeo Sanctuary, down from the 200 birds reported by Walkinshaw in 1964-65. In 1974 Spitzer found only 63, and in 1980 only 33. Archibald (1981c) gave a figure of only 15 birds there in the winter of 1980-81. He estimated the Yakutia population to number about 200

birds during the same period. This is well below earlier estimates summarized by Flint and Kistchinski (1981), who placed the 1971-1973 population at about 300 individuals, including 100 breeding pairs. Only a decade earlier, Perfil'ev (1965) estimated that perhaps as many as 300-350 nesting pairs might be present in this same population. Flint and Kistchinski believe that earlier larger estimates were the result of various errors in calculation, and that the Yakutia population is now relatively stable. Certainly elucidation and protection of the Chinese wintering areas would go a long way toward assuring the preservation of at least this segment of the Siberian crane population.

EVOLUTIONARY RELATIONSHIPS

As noted earlier, Archibald (1976) reported that, on the basis of its unison call characteristics, he believed the Siberian crane to be divergent from *Grus* and more closely related to the wattled crane. He thus suggested that it be classified as *Bugeranus leucogeranus*. He said that its earlier inclusion in *Grus* was based on its whooping crane-like plumage pattern, its short tertials, and the extensive area of bare skin on the head. However, he stated that the bare area ("comb") of the Siberian crane resembles that of the wattled crane except that it lacks wattles. He further pointed out that the uncoiled tracheal condition of the Siberian crane is like that of the wattled crane rather than any of the *Grus* species, all of which have tracheae with sternal coiling.

Later, Wood (1979) found that the Siberian crane indeed resembles the whooping crane in its external characteristics, but in its skeletal features it clusters cladistically with the wattled crane. He too suggested that the similarities with the whooping crane are convergent ones, since no other evidence exists to link these two species taxonomically. He indicated that in the future *leucogeranus* and *carunculatus* might be considered cogeneric.

I find no reason to disagree with these conclusions, and thus have merged *leucogeranus* into the genus *Bugeranus*. However, Ronald Sauey (pers. comm.) informed me that, although the wattled crane may be the Siberian crane's nearest living relative, he does not believe that the two species are actually very close relatives and that perhaps separate genera should be maintained for them. Sauey further informed me (pers. comm.) that Hiroyuki Masatomi, an expert on the behavior of *Grus japonensis*, believes that any conclusion that *leucogeranus* is behaviorally related to *Bugeranus carunculatus* is incorrect.

Australian Crane

Grus rubicundus (Perry) 1810

Other Vernacular Names. Brolga, Native companion (Australia); Grue d'Australie (French); Australischer Kranich (German); Goshu zuru (Japanese); Australiyka zhuravl (Russian); Grulla Australiana (Spanish).

Range. Resident in grassland habitats in lowland New Guinea and northern and eastern Australia, more rarely to southern and southeastern Australia.

Subspecies.

G.r. argentea: Northern Australian Crane. Resident in the north of Western Australia and Northern Territory, intergrading to the east with *rubicundus*.

G.r. rubicundus: Southern Australian Crane. Resident from eastern (Queensland) to southeastern (Victoria and eastern South Australia) Australia, and in lowland New Guinea from Frederik-Hendrik Island to the Fly River-Sepik River basin.

Measurements. Wing (flattened), males 570-595 mm (average of 5, 585-7 mm); females (525-551 mm (average of 5, 538.4 mm) (specimens in American Museum of Natural History). Exposed culmen, males 157-170 mm (average of 10, 164.4 mm); females 145-163 mm (average of 10, 156.1 mm). Tarsus, males 295-317 mm (average of 10, 304.9 mm); females 258-299 mm (average of 10, 278.4 mm). Eggs, average 90.6 × 60.9 mm (85-99.8 × 56.4-67.3 mm) (Walkinshaw, 1973).

Weights. Ten adult males ranged from 6,265.3 to 8,278.2 grams, averaging 6,996.8 grams, and ten adult females ranged from 5,244.7 to 6,350 grams, averaging 5,721 grams (Walkinshaw, 1973). Blackman (1971a) reported that 321 males averaged 6,383 grams (range 4,761-8,729), and 217 females averaged 5,663 grams (range 3,628-7,255). The estimated egg weight is 185 grams. Walkinshaw (1973) states that five eggs averaged 190.9 grams and three chicks 103.2 grams.

Description

Adults of both sexes are alike and have a bare crown covered with greenish gray skin. The face, cheeks, occiput, and pendulous throat pouch are also bare, and are coral red to bright orange up to about the eye. The rest of the face to the bill is covered by fine blackish bristles, and is olive green. The area around the ears is covered by grayish feathers, and the rest of the body plumage is also light bluish gray, with the feathers of the back and wing coverts having light margins. The primaries are blackish; the secondaries are gray, with the inner one somewhat pendant and elongated. The iris is orange, orange yellow, or yellow, the beak is greenish gray to olive green, and the legs and toes are black to dark grayish black.

Juveniles have fully feathered heads that are buffy or gray, dark brown iris coloration, and dark gray legs. The adult iris color is attained in the second to third year of life, when grayish green skin also appears on the crown.

Downy chicks are mostly gray, becoming darker above and lighter below, and buffy on the head and neck. The iris is dark brown, the bill is greenish gray with a pink tip, and the legs are pinkish gray (Walkinshaw, 1973).

Identification

In the field, this is the only crane found in eastern and southern Australia and New Guinea. In northern Australia, it may be separated from the very similar sarus by its dewlap, its blackish rather than reddish legs, and its more silvery gray general appearance. Both species utter similar grating and trumpeting calls, but that of the Australian crane is of much lower pitch.

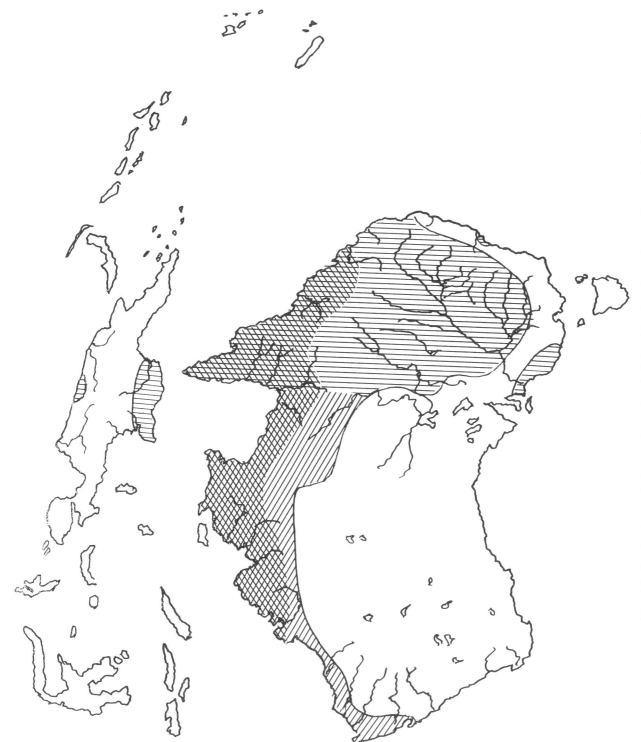

Residential distributions of the southern (vertical hatching) and northern (diagonal hatching) Australian cranes. Areas of greatest abundance are indicated by cross-hatching.

In the hand, the wholly bare head, which is gray to reddish, with a small gray ear patch, and a slight dewlap at the throat, separates this species from all others except the sarus, which has bare skin extending down to the upper neck, is generally more reddish on the cheeks, and also has reddish legs. Hybrids are occasionally found in the area of geographic overlap in northern Australia. In both species the trachea is convoluted within the sternum. At least in the Australian crane, all adult males have two vascularized erectile papillae about 2.5 mm in height just lateral to the opening of the vas deferens. Many 2-year old males (7 of 12 examined) also showed this trait, as did a small number (2 of 9) of yearling males, but no birds of the year exhibited it (Blackman, 1971a). It is thus likely that the trait serves as a useful guide for sexing birds in the hand.

DISTRIBUTION AND HABITATS

Historical and Current Ranges

The present and past ranges of this species are limited to Australia and portions of New Guinea, with some apparent retractions in southern Australia, but no major changes of ranges in recent times except for some expansion in Western Australia.

In New Guinea, the species has long been known to occupy the lowlands of the south, from Frederik-Hendrik Island to Fly River, and a limited area of northern New Guinea, in the middle Sepik River. At least at one time it was apparently common in the Morehead River area near the Dutch border, and on the middle Fly River (north of Timbunke) in the extensive marshes and grass habitats of that area. However, at the time of the Archbold Expedition to southern New Guinea the birds were found only a few times, and in very small numbers near the coast. Some captive birds were also found in the possession of natives, who had apparently hand-reared them, indicating that nesting must have been occurring (Rand and Gilliard, 1968). Little is known of the abundance and present distribution of this population, but in 1980 the birds were observed to be fairly common along the Bensback River from Balam downstream, with some juvenile and immature birds present (*Papua New Guinea Bird Society Newsletter* 171-172, September, October 1980).

In Australia, the species has been known to be widespread and locally common since the early 1800s, when it was initially described from Botany Bay, in New South Wales. It probably has never occurred in the driest interior areas of Australia, and has been absent over much of Western Australia as well. Serventy and Whittell (1967) reported that the brolga was never observed in Western Australia in earlier historical periods, and first appeared there during the 1920s

(apparently near Onslow, on the coast near North West Cape). This general area still represents the approximate limits of the species' Australian range, but the birds have evidently become much more common, particularly after an influx in the early 1950s, and birds have been recorded as far south as Beacon (150 miles northeast of Perth). However, there seems to be no record of breeding south of the Kimberly Division.

Walkinshaw (1973) summarized numerous locality records of brolgas for Western Australia, as well as for Northern Territory and Queensland, where the species is most common. It occurs essentially throughout Queensland, and in all of Northern Territory excepting the driest interior areas. In New South Wales, although the birds are now largely limited to the northern portions of that state, with old nesting records for Maitland and Tumut, there are also more recent records of Yanko Creek, Moree, and Goondublui (Walkinshaw, 1973), which are east-central and south.

In Victoria there are old nesting records for Bendigo, Turkeith, and other areas, but it is uncertain as to whether the species still ever nests in that state. Certainly there is a regular influx of birds into Victoria and adjoining South Australia in the nonbreeding season, and there is at least one early nesting record for South Australia (Teatree Lake) (Walkinshaw, 1973). The species apparently still breeds very locally in the area south of Lake Eyre (*South Australian Ornithologist* 28: 47, 1980), as well as in northern Victoria (*Australian Bird Watcher* 4: 100, 1971; 6: 195, 1976). However the Tropic of Capricorn seems to represent the approximately southern limit of large flocks of brolgas, and only occasionally are flocks of more than ten birds seen to the south of Fitzroy River in Western Australia or Rockhampton in Queensland. Currently, the largest populations, numbering in the thousands of birds, are found only on suitable habitats from "Waverly Plains" near St. Lawrence in Queensland northwards to Rocky River near Princess Charlotte Bay. The densest concentrations, numbering about 12,000 birds, are at Cromarty, about 25 miles south of Townsville (Lavery and Blackman, 1969).

Habitat Requirements and Densities

The general habitat spectrum of brolga primarily includes fresh waters, grasslands, cultivated lands, open forests, and saline areas. The majority of the birds prefer freshwater swamps dominated by bulkuru sedges (*Eleocharis dulcis*). These areas are occupied for most of the year and are used for breeding. This habitat type is also favored by magpie geese (*Anseranas semipalmatus*). However, brolgas are more common in the eastern areas, and magpie geese in Northern Territory. The edges of deep-water lagoons are commonly used only during the months of lower rainfall, when the birds also disperse widely into grasslands, cultivated lands, and sometimes other habitat types. Where sarus and brolgas overlap in Northern Territory the birds usually do not greatly intermingle, since the sarus is largely confined to freshwater areas and cultivated lands. However, they sometimes do forage together and roost together locally (Lavery and Blackman, 1969).

Specific information on breeding densities seems to be lacking. Blackman (1978) provided a map showing the distribution of brolga nests in a small area near Clevedon, of which over 80 percent were associated with freshwater swamp habitats, and most of the rest were in brackish saline swamps, and a very small proportion in saltpan areas. Mangrove and upland habitats did not support any nests. A favored area of approximately three square kilometers of freshwater swamps supported over 40 nests, suggesting a maximum breeding density of roughly 13 nests per square kilometer. However, much nesting is done in inaccessible areas of the swamp, where there is only very limited visibility, and thus it is very difficult if not impossible to accurately survey these habitats.

Nonbreeding Range and Habitats

Nonbreeding habitats are much more diverse and widespread than breeding habitats, and include a variety of wetland and dryland areas, such as pasturelands, croplands including cornfields, brackish and saltwater wetlands, and even relatively dry habitats. Thus, during droughts the species has been reported moving into prickly pear *(Opuntia)* areas to consume the fleshy fruits. However, major concentrations during the dryer periods occur in the bulkuru sedge swamps, where both the brolgas and the magpie geese concentrate, feeding on the tubers of bulkuru. As large portions of the emergent vegetation die back during the drying out of the area, the surface of the swamp becomes a mass of decaying vegetation. This is eventually removed by the cranes and geese, reducing the swamp to open areas of slushy mud. As long as these remain damp the magpie geese continue to feed on the tubers, but as they dry out the geese usually abandon them to move into deeper water. However, the brolgas remain and, by virtue of their sharp, stabbing bills, can excavate holes in the drying swamp to locate bulkuru tubers. This is especially true in areas of alluvial black soils which dry to great hardness, which the magpie geese are unable to penetrate with their rounded bills, but which the cranes can easily deal with. This dry-season habitat association is well established by the end of October, when large flocks of brolgas occur on the drying swamps, whose surfaces are crumbling in the sun (Blackman, 1978).

FOODS AND FORAGING BEHAVIOR

For most of the year, the bulkuru sedge, particularly its tubers, provides the major food of the brolga crane. The area of maximum abundance of this plant is between Darwin and Brisbane, and this corresponds to the area of maximum density of the brolga. Where there are no bulkuru sedges, another sedge (*Cyperus affinis rotundus*) is dug out in a similar fashion (Walkinshaw, 1973).

Besides the sedge tubers, the birds feed on insects that are found in the same habitats, such as grasshoppers, leafhoppers, and the like. In other habitats a wide variety of animal food is consumed, including a wide variety of insects (dragonflies, mantids, beetles, moths), freshwater and saltwater mollusks, crustaceans, spiders, and frogs. Dryland and wetland plants, including corn, are also consumed (Lavery and Blackman, 1969). Walkinshaw (1973) concluded that the birds fed on such crops as corn, wheat, rice, and peanuts, and also consumed at times considerable numbers of animals such as mud skippers (*Periophthalmus*), fiddler crabs (*Uca*), and freshwater crayfish (*Cherax*), when these occurred in waters where brolgas were foraging.

Foods of Young

Little information on foods of young birds is available, but Lavery and Blackman (1969) stated that indirect evidence suggested that downy chicks are fed on insect materials by the parents, who attract the chicks' attention to these items by uttering soft purring calls. As the young become older and move with their parents to the drying swamps, they have difficulty feeding because their bills are not so strongly developed as are those of the adults. At that time they often stand close to their parents, watching them dig and waiting for the adult birds to pass tubers on to them, (Blackman, 1978).

Foraging Behavior

Feeding in the brolga takes much the same form throughout the year, for during both wet and dry seasons it largely feeds on the tubers of sedges (*Eleocharis* and *Cyperus*), with supplemental food in the form of cultivated grains and some animal materials. Its bill is almost identical in shape to that of the sarus crane, and is an ideal digging and stabbing tool, adapting it to animal capture as well as to the consumption of vegetable matter. In some areas, the birds invade croplands of sorghum, and corn, improved pasturelands such as those of *Cynodon*, and other agricultural croplands, especially during the period of grain maturation, which occurs at about the time the birds are dispersing from breeding areas. In those areas some crop damage has been found to occur and control measures are occasionally required (Lavery and Blackman, 1969).

MIGRATIONS AND MOVEMENTS

Apparently all of the movements of the brolga in Australia are related to the timing and severity of the dry season. Nesting mostly occurs during the wet season, which in northern Australia begins in December, when the first heavy winter storms begin. At that time the brolgas range widely over the grasslands in small groups. By the end of February, the extensive flooding of lowlands subsides and all of the swamps and lagoons are full, and the birds have moved on to their nesting territories. Only a small proportion of the birds nest on the large coastal swamps; instead, the birds move into small, isolated freshwater swamps in the coastal hinterlands that allow for large territorial sizes and the relative isolation that is apparently required by the birds (Blackman, 1978).

Throughout June and July there is a slow drying out of the swamps, and it is during this period that the young are being reared. As the small wetlands of the hinterlands gradually dry up, the brolga families begin to move toward the larger coastal swamps, where they join the families that have nested on these areas. Throughout July the brolga population increases on the coastal swamps, and flocking begins. The aggressive behavior typical of the breeding season gradually diminishes, and communal roosting in shallow saltpans begins. The winter flocks of brolgas bring together a large proportion of the breeding population, and consist of family groups, pairs lacking young, and nonbreeders of various age-classes. The amount of water remaining in the swamps by August varies from year to year and depends on the amount of rainfall during the previous wet season (Blackman, 1978). Depending on the severity of the dry season, the brolgas may be forced to move varying distances.

In recent years, various developments have affected the distribution and movements of the brolgas. For example, water impoundments in some areas have increased surface water supplies for the birds, and increased their potential breeding grounds. On the other hand, with destruction of the bulkuru sedge marshes and their conversion to croplands, the birds have been forced to move into cultivated areas for foraging, especially during the drier months. Thus, large flocks previously moved south into Victoria during winter months, where they foraged on croplands and sometimes caused considerable damage. As a result, poisoning campaigns were carried out, and now relatively few birds move this far south in winter (Walkinshaw, 1973).

In recent years, the major dry-season concentrations have occurred in Queensland, in such areas as Townsville, Pallarenda, Cromarty, Giru, and Clevedon, or only as far north as Ingham and as far south as Ayr. In some years when the rains fail to materialize, as was the case in 1968-1969, the birds may remain in the bulkuru sedge areas, but very few attempt to nest there. At such times the birds may do considerable damage to crops such as rice, sorghum, and corn, especially when these croplands are close to bulkuru sedge swamps (Walkinshaw, 1973).

During the dry season the birds are also often forced to fly some distances for daily water too. At times, hundreds will drink and roost at small dams, making the water supply so dirty that it can't be used by livestock. Many such dams, created to provide water supplies for cattle, occur throughout Queensland and Northern Territory, and probably allow for greater inland migration during the dry season than was true before the establishment of these small reservoirs.

Daily Movements

Like the other cranes, brolgas typically spend the nonbreeding season in flocks, roosting communally in shallow water whenever possible, and feeding during the daylight hours. There is much foraging during the daylight hours, with intensive searching until midmorning and extensive searching during late afternoon (Lavery and Blackman, 1969). Walkinshaw (1973) observed that during October to December, near Pallarenda, the birds flew from tidal flat roosting areas to bulkuru sedge marsh regions about a quarter mile away, beginning as early as about 5:00 a.m.; all had left the roost by 5:50 a.m. On another day the birds left between 5:00 and shortly after 6:00 a.m. Some of the birds flew as far as three to seven miles away to obtain fresh water at dams or ponds.

In the evening, the birds generally moved into a nearby feeding region that was located about a half mile from the roost during the afternoon. Sunset was at 6:00, and by 5:50 the first birds began moving into the tidal salt flats or the muddy areas beside it. By 7:02 p.m. it was nearly completely dark, and only a few birds were arriving. The peak numbers of more than 700 arrived between 40 and 50 minutes after sunset.

At a small freshwater lake about a mile from a saline roosting site, Walkinshaw observed that the first cranes arrived to drink at 9:01 a.m., or almost four hours after sunrise (5:33 a.m.). A total of 447 arrivals were counted, most of which remained until 10:35 a.m., when they began to depart.

GENERAL BIOLOGY

Sociality

Walkinshaw (1973) made various counts of social groups of brolgas as they arrived at and left roosting sites. Counts on October 21 and November 6 indicated the following breakdown of over 200 group sizes flying into or out of roosts: singles, 4 percent; pairs, 35 percent; triples, 25 percent; groups of four, 15 percent; larger groups, 21 percent.

These data suggest that even during the nonbreeding season the commonest social groupings are of from two to four birds, presumably primarily representing pairs and families with one or two dependent young. Certainly many, if not most, of the larger groups also represent assemblages of such social units as well.

While roosting or feeding, each bird in a family group stands or feeds about 5 to 7 feet from the others, and each family group in turn forages or roosts about 7 to 25 feet from their nearest neighbors (Walkinshaw, 1973).

Daily Activities

As described under "Daily Movements," this species is highly diurnal, and spends much of the daylight hours during the nonbreeding season in foraging. Photographs of nonbreeding birds suggest that they do not maintain separate foraging territories during that time of year, but instead move about in rather closely associated groups, only a few feet apart from one another. During the dry season the birds also drink water frequently. Walkinshaw (1973) stated that he occasionally saw roosting birds on tidal flats sip saline water, but not often. Instead, during the hottest days and during the driest periods there was a constant stream of birds moving from feeding areas to watering sites between midday and about 5:00 p.m. After drinking, the birds would return to forage again, until it was nearly dark.

Interspecific Interactions

Lavery and Blackman (1969) reported that the native dingos (*Canis dingo*) and introduced foxes (*Vulpes vulpes*) both prey on young birds, and that red-backed sea eagles (*Haliastur indus*) prey on eggs.

In northern Australia there is now a limited amount of contact between the self-introduced sarus crane and the native Australian crane, and hybridization between the two species has been discovered (Archibald, 1981b). He suggested that since the sarus is a larger species and thus tends to dominate the native birds, it could well displace them from their primary nesting habitat. However, the sarus tends to occupy the more upland and agriculturally associated areas of northern Australia, while the brolgas are more associated with the coastal marshes, at least during the nonbreeding season. Should the sarus crane begin to occupy the sedge marsh habitats of the brolga for its major breeding areas, serious interactions between these two species could well result.

BREEDING BIOLOGY

Age of Maturity and Time of Breeding

Little specific information on the age of maturity in captivity is available, but Blackman (1978) states that male brolgas do not breed until their fourth or fifth year, while females probably breed their third year of life.

Throughout Australia as a whole, the breeding season is rather distinctly concentrated in the wet season, but some records extend into the dry season as well. Walkinshaw (1973) reported that 27 records from Queensland range from September to June, with a peak in February and March. Nine nest records from Northern Territory range from January to June, with a peak in March. There is a February nest record from Western Australia, four October and November records from New South Wales, and Victoria records extending from August to November (Walkinshaw, 1973).

Pair Formation and Courtship

Pair formation in this species apparently occurs in wintering flocks, in which dance-like displays are common and a conspicuous aspect of these flocks. Many such displays are intitiated by young, unpaired males in search of mates, according to Blackman (1978). Their displays are sometimes misdirected toward other males or toward females of established pairs, but eventually become directed toward a receptive female and the displays are reciprocated. Such activities are the start of casual attachments, which may or may not lead to permanent pair bonding. However, an important point is that these activities occur at a time when the food is normally abundant, when there is maximum contact with prospective mates, and when the young birds can direct much of their energy toward pair formation.

There do not seem to be any specific descriptions of copulatory behavior in this species, but the unison call is performed in a manner very similar to that of the sarus crane. According to Archibald (1975, 1976) the associated call is also very much like that of the sarus, but is of a much lower pitch. This low pitch is perhaps associated with the large gular sac of the male, which is inflated during the display and quite possibly helps to resonate low-frequency sounds. The final calls at the end of the display, when the gular sac is inflated, are particularly long, broken, and low-pitched. Sometimes the males raise and lower the humeri in synchrony with the call, while at other times the humeri are stiffly raised and the wrists similarly lowered throughout the entire display sequence. As with the sarus crane and the white-naped crane, the dark primaries are at that time especially conspicuous, and at times the male's raised wings actually touch the female's back. The female remains with her neck held near the vertical throughout the display sequence, but does not raise her humeri or expose the primaries. Typically the two birds stand nearly side by side and motionless during the display, rather than walking about as do Japanese cranes and whooping cranes for example.

According to Walkinshaw (1973) the call of the male during the unison display is one in which the second note is much the loudest, and thereafter the call gradually tapers off: *kawee-kreee-kurr-kurr-kurr-kurr*. The female similarly utters an extended series of *kuk* notes immediately following each syllable of the male's call.

According also to Walkinshaw, dancing in this species occurs most commonly during the onset of the wet season, and is similar to that of the sarus crane in that both birds in a dancing pair sometimes bring their throats close together. He also observed tossing behavior during dancing, and noted that dancing occurred in a variety of situations, as for example when he approached a flock or went to a nest.

Territoriality and Early Nesting Behavior

With the onset of the wet season, a series of ecological changes begin to occur in the swamp. As storms become more frequent, the male cranes became more antagonistic and hostility becomes more evident within the flock. Young birds of the previous year are among the first birds to be affected, and are driven away. Such young birds soon begin to associate and form small flocks, which spend the breeding season outside the nesting areas as outcasts.

As the established pairs move into the nesting areas, they select territories that offer food, nest sites, and areas of very dense vegetation that can hide the young. The nests are located in such a way as to provide a panoramic view of the environment.

Nest construction usually begins with the birds pulling up plant materials and throwing them backwards. Materials are gathered from an area about three meters in diameter and are heaped into a mound. Nests are often constructed from grasses, especially saltwater couchgrass (*Sporobolus*), on the moist ground of an island in the swamp. Nests that are built on moist ground sites are composed of grasses and earth clods, with a shallow cup in the center. However, such nests do not float, and thus may be flooded with the heavy rains. Early-nesting birds benefit by constructing floating nests of the stems of sedges, sometimes in water up to 300 millimeters deep. Such nests are able to accommodate to minor increases in water levels during periods of flooding (Blackman, 1978).

Various other nests described by Walkinshaw (1973) were constructed of para grass (*Brachiaria*), *Cyperus*, and even water hyacinth (*Eichornia*); seven nests averaged 86 centimeters across at the base, but ranged from 57 to 142 centimeters. Lavery and Blackman described the nests as averaging about four feet in diameter, with little or no lining of feathers.

According to Blackman (1978), nearly all the nest sites in the large coastal swamps are ones that have been used previously. Additionally, several unused nests are sometimes apparent in the vicinity of an active nest. It would thus appear that birds tend to return to the same territory year after year, or perhaps there are certain habitat features that tend to attract cranes to a particular nesting site.

Egg-laying and Incubation

Within a few days of the completion of the nest, the first egg is laid. Normally two eggs constitute the clutch; Walkinshaw (1973) reported that 20 or 27 clutches contained two eggs, and a single nest contained three. Both sexes incubate, and while one bird is on the nest the other frequently flies some distance away to forage. During changeovers in incubation the birds typically utter a bugling unison call, which Blackman attributes to the establishment and maintenance of dominance in the nesting territory.

The responses to intrusion into their nesting territories are quite variable. Blackman noted that the nests are often located in inaccessible parts of the swamp, with searches requiring tedious wading through heavy vegetation, and thus it is unlikely that many nests would be disturbed either by humans or by dingos. Large intruders, however, are either driven off, or attempts are made to lure them away by the use of broken-wing displays and loud alarm calls. When the intruder leaves the area the birds return, examine the nest, and then call in duet to signify their regaining of territorial control. Only seldom do the birds abandon their nests because of such intrusions, in Blackman's experience.

The eggs are incubated for 28 to 30 days, according to Blackman, while most records of cranes hatched in captivity indicate an incubation period of from 32 to 36 days. Perhaps the tropical environment in which the birds breed results in somewhat faster development than occurs in temperate climates where periodic cooling might occur.

Hatching and Postbreeding Biology

Blackman (1978) reported that the chicks hatch by using a well-developed egg-tooth, and emerge from the egg within 36 hours of pipping. The adults offer bits of food to the chicks during the first 24 hours, but it is probable that such feeding is not important at that stage, while the yolk sac is being resorbed. By the third day after hatching the young chicks are moving away from the nest to hide in nearby cover whenever disturbance occurs. At that time the surrounding cover is extremely dense, and offers great protection for hiding birds. It is probable that the birds remain in the wet swamps for as long as enough water remains to provide protection and easy foraging. Finally, however, the drying ponds force the birds to move to more coastal areas. The young cranes continue to be fed by their parents for as long as an entire year, but begin to supplement their diet of insects, spiders, mollusks, and vegetable materials with independent foraging almost from hatching.

As the chicks grow, the nesting territory becomes a home range that progressively expands in size and eventually is vacated completely. Birds nesting in brackish areas have larger territories and home ranges than do those nesting in the freshwater swamps, and also vacate their areas earlier. As the birds become more mobile they tend to encounter the home ranges of other pairs and families, but there is usually little conflict during this stage of the nesting cycle. The first contour feathers appear at 4 to 5 weeks, and fledging occurs when the young birds are about 14 weeks old (Lavery and Blackman, 1969).

Presumably during the time that the young birds are being reared, the adults also undergo their general body molt, but there does not seem to be any specific information on this. Most probably it occurs before the birds leave their heavy swamp cover, where they can fairly safely spend their flightless period.

Lavery and Blackman (1969) reported that the young birds remain with their parents into the third year of their life, although they are of course evicted from the nesting territory during the breeding season. Predation causes some losses of young, in which case the parent birds renest. Second renestings have also been reported, in which case only a single egg is laid.

RECRUITMENT RATES, POPULATION STATUS, AND CONSERVATION

There is still surprisingly little information available on recruitment rates for this species. Blackman (1971a) reported that young birds comprised 17 percent of the birds in flocks observed between 1968 and 1970, although sample sizes were not indicated. This is a relatively high recruitment rate, and might be related to the opportunities for renesting during the relatively long potential breeding season in northern Australia. The cranes are protected in Queensland, but dead cranes are often encountered during the dry season. The majority of these are young of the year, suggesting that juveniles associated with family groups that remain together have an increased probability of survival (Blackman, 1978).

The population of the Australian crane is impossible to estimate with any degree of certainty at the present time; no census figures have yet been published. Some crop depredation problems involving cranes on agricultural lands have generated poisoning efforts. However, most of the Queensland birds are still distributed in a few large and relatively remote swamps, and furthermore the construction of water impoundments in the drier areas is actually increasing potential breeding habitat in some parts of the Australian continent. Further, the increase in grain crops in some areas serves as a food supply in times of drought, although of course this sometimes leads to conflicts between agricultural interests and those of conservationists.

At present, the Australian crane is still quite secure, at least as compared to most of the temperate-zone Asian cranes.

EVOLUTIONARY RELATIONSHIPS

On the basis of both the unison call and general social behavior (Archibald, 1975, 1976) and its general and skeletal anatomy (Wood, 1979), the Australian crane and sarus crane can be confidently called very close relatives, a fact that is further indicated by natural hybridization occurring between them in an area of recent secondary contact in northern Australia, and by the fertility of the resulting hybrids.

Sarus Crane

Grus antigone (Linnaeus) 1758

Other Vernacular Names. Sharpe's crane; Khur-sang, Korchan (Assam); Grue antigone tropicale, Grue à collier (French); Sarus-kranich, Halsband-kranich (German); Saras, Sirhans (Hindi); O-O zuru (Japanese); Belyi zhuravl (Russian); Grulla blanco cuello (Spanish).

Range. Resident in northern India, east to Burma, on the Malay Peninsula, and in Indo-Chinese countries, and in northern Australia. Probably extirpated from the Philippine Islands, and perhaps also from Burma, Thailand, and Malaysia.

Subspecies.

G.a. antigone: Indian Sarus Crane. Resident in northern India from western Assam west to the Indus in Pakistan, and south to the Bombay area on the west and to the Godavari River on the east.

G.a. sharpei: Burmese Sarus Crane. Resident or former resident in Assam, Burma, the Malay Peninsula, Cambodia (Kampuchea), southern Laos, southern Vietnam, and northern Australia (Kununurra to Atherton). Formerly occurred in Thailand (at least to 1964) and also (perhaps still) on Luzon.

Measurements (both subspecies, *antigone* averaging slightly larger than *sharpei*). Wing (chord), males 514-675 mm (average of 16, 619.3 mm); females 557-671 mm (average of 11, 612.5 mm). Exposed culmen, males 156-187 mm (average of 16, 169.3 mm); females 155-169 mm (average of 11, 161.4 mm). Tarsus, males 269-352 mm (average of 16, 323.1 mm); females 272-350 mm (average of 11, 304.1 mm). Eggs, average 104.4 × 64.3 mm (93.2-113.2 × 53.8-69.8 mm) (Walkinshaw, 1973).

Weights. Five adult males (presumably of *sharpei*) averaged 8.4 kilograms (Archibald, 1981b). Specimens of *antigone* from India range from about 6,800 to 8,000 grams (Ali and Ripley, 1969). Estimated egg weight, 238 grams. Ten fresh *antigone* eggs averaged 212.56 grams (Walkinshaw, 1973).

Description

Adults of both sexes have the head, throat, and upper neck bare of feathers. The crown skin is smooth and pale ashy green, while the remaining bare areas are orange red and covered with coarse granulations, becoming brighter during the breeding season. The upper throat and some of the neck are covered with long, hairlike bristles, and a small area of grayish white feathers surrounds the ears. In *antigone* a ring of white feathers occurs between the bare neck and the gray neck feathering below, and the inner secondaries are also white, while in *sharpei* this white neck area is lacking and the body and wing feathers are generally darker, especially on the secondaries. The primaries, primary coverts, and alula are dark gray or blackish, and the innermost secondaries are lengthened and pointed. The other secondaries are darker on the outer webs and lighter on the inner ones. The remainder of the plumage is rather uniformly gray to bluish gray. The iris is yellowish brown to orange, the bill is greenish, with a darker tip, and the legs and toes are red, fleshy red, or bluish pink.

Juveniles have entirely feathered heads and necks, which are buffy in color. The feathers of juveniles are edged with brownish gray, and those of the upperparts are cinnamon brown, often with downy tips adhering.

Downy chicks are pale isabelline (yellowish brown) on the head, neck, and throat, becoming darker on the lower neck, the sides of the breast, the thighs, and the vent, and white on the center of the breast and on the belly. Two broad lines of dark brown extend from the base of the neck to the rump, enclosing a paler brown median stripe, and a large buffy white spot is near the base of each wing (Walkinshaw, 1973).

Residential distributions of the Indian (diagonal hatching) and Burmese (vertical hatching) sarus cranes. Areas of light stippling indicate regions of prior or uncertain occurrence.

Identification

In the field, this is the only resident crane in southeastern Asia south of the Himalayas, and the only crane of Asia that has both a generally grayish plumage and the upper neck and head bare of feathers and mostly reddish, except for a gray crown and a gray, feathered ear patch. Where the Australian crane might also occur (in northern Australia), the reddish legs of the sarus provide a good basis for the separation, as well as its absence of a dewlap at the throat, its bare, red head skin extending to its upper neck, and a whiter ear patch and inner secondaries.

In the hand, the very large size of this crane (wing usually over 600 mm) separates it from most other cranes, but the very similar Australian crane is nearly as large. The latter species lacks reddish legs, has less elongated and decurved inner secondaries, and the bare area of the head does not extend down to include the upper neck. The trachea of the sarus is coiled within the keel of the sternum.

DISTRIBUTION AND HABITATS

Historical Range

The historical distribution of the sarus crane is probably less different from its current distribution in India than in any other area. Ali and Ripley (1969) described it as extending through the northern parts of the Indian subcontinent south of the Himalayas (including the Tarai Lowlands of southwestern Nepal) from Sind and Punjab in Pakistan eastward through Uttar Pradesh, Bihar, and northern Bengal to western Assam in India. It apparently occurs fairly regularly at altitudes to about 1,650 meters, and rarely reaches as high as 1,700 meters (Kashmir Valley). It becomes more common below Dharmsala, Himachal Pradesh, and extends south through eastern Rajasthan, Gujarat, and northern Madhya Pradesh, reaching its limits at about a line extending from Surat on the west to the Godavari Delta on the east. According to Ali and Ripley, it is most numerous in Gujarat, eastern Rajasthan, and on the Gangetic Plain. In northeastern India (Assam) there are early breeding records for Dibrugarh and Chotta Bheel, Cacher (Walkinshaw, 1973).

Its western historical limits are in Pakistan, where breeding was recorded as far west as Hardoi, Northwest Frontier Province, in 1901 (Walkinshaw, 1973).

In Nepal the sarus crane has been collected at about 300 meters at Dhangarhi, which is near the Uttar Pradesh boundary of westernmost Nepal (Walkinshaw,

1973). Probably nearly all of Nepal is too high or arid to provide suitable breeding habitat, except for the "tarais" of the southwestern border.

Historically, the sarus crane in Burma was evidently fairly common over much of the country, but most common in central Burma and the Shan states, with breeding records known from Myitkyina in Kachin State, the Shweli River in Mongmit, and in the Shan Hills (Smithies, 1953). Walkinshaw (1973) reported eggs from Pegu, Martaban, and "lower Burma."

Farther south and east, the Burmese race of the sarus crane at least once bred in Thailand, with a nesting record from Muang Fang (Walkinshaw, 1973). King and Dickinson (1975) described its range as including central and peninsular Thailand, Cambodia, Cochin-China and southern Annam provinces in Vietnam, and southern and central Laos.

Although the sarus crane once occurred locally on the Malay Peninsula, extending south to Perak, there are apparently no breeding records for the peninsula (Medway and Wells, 1976).

Evidently the sarus was once fairly common in some areas of Luzon, the Philippines. Thus, it was reportedly once abundant in Cabanatuan of Nueva Ecija Province, and bred in open swampy areas of that province. It was also observed in the Candaba Swamp of south-central Luzon near Manila, and in Cagayan and Isabela provinces of northern Luzon (Madsen, 1981).

Prior to the 1960s, the sarus crane was not known to occur in Australia (Gills, 1969).

Current Range

According to Archibald et al. (1981) the sarus crane is now thriving in India, for the Indians have considered it a sacred bird since the early days of Hinduism, and it is strictly protected. The birds have lost their fear of man and prosper over much of northern India.

In Nepal, the sarus is now occasional in the damp, cultivated fields of the western tarai, and scarce in the central tarai (Fleming, Fleming, and Bangdel, 1976).

The crane's status in Burma is quite uncertain. King and Dickinson (1975) listed it as "resident" on the plains of Burma, but Archibald et al. (1981) considered it almost if not totally extirpated from Burma and Thailand, and of undetermined status in Laos, Cambodia, and Vietnam. Medway and Wells (1976) stated that there have been no recent reports of the species in the Malay Peninsula.

Madsen (1981) searched unsuccessfully for the sarus crane on Luzon in 1979, where she believes that although perhaps a few individuals may still exist, a sizable crane population is unlikely. There have been sightings of a single pair as recently as 1979 at Tabuk, Kalinga-Apayao Province, and other sightings in the 1960s for the municipalities of Jone, Ilagan, and

Cauayan, all in the Cagayan River valley. The Philippines government is currently interested in starting a restocking program, using hand-reared birds of Australian stock (Archibald et al., 1981).

In Australia, the sarus crane was first identified in September of 1964, at Hasties and Willet's swamps on the Atherton Tableland in northeastern Queensland (Archibald, 1981b). Later in that same year, about 15 were reported at Normanton (Gills, 1969), and in 1967 a total of 23 individuals were counted among a flock of brolgas (Lavery and Blackman, 1969). Blackman (1971b) reported seeing the crane at more than thirty localities in 1969, including one flock of 75 birds at Willet's Swamp. By 1972 at least 200 sarus cranes were present on the Atherton Tableland. The birds are apparently increasing and are also expanding their range, since they seem to be able to out-compete the slightly smaller brolga crane (Archibald, 1981b).

Habitat Requirements and Densities

Nesting habitats in India have been described by Walkinshaw (1973). The Keoladeo Ghana Bird Sanctuary area, where the birds nest commonly, is in a forestry region where many trees such as babul (*Acacia arabica*), kandi (*Prosopis spicigera*), and keli kadamb (*Stephegyne parvifolia*) occur in higher elevations and on the impoundments. Some dead trees also occur on the flooded marsh. The entire area is pastured by cattle and water buffalo, and during the rainy season no vegetation protrudes above the water for a time. However, soon after the rains begin, there is an extensive plant growth. The total annual rainfall is about 27 inches, mostly coming during the monsoon period. Nesting is tied to the wet period, and in years where nesting areas remain unflooded the birds may not nest at all, even though they may remain on the territory.

Walkinshaw found the pH of the water of Keoladeo Ghana to be about 9.0, while in another area (Baroda in Gujarat) where he found a nest in a sewer pond the pH was 7.2. Some of the plants growing in the vicinity of this pond included various grasses (*Oyrxa, Fatua, Paspalum, Echinochloa*), sedges (*Scirpus maritimus*), water lilies (*Nymphaea lotus* and *Limnanthemum indicus*), pulse (*Aeschyomene indica*), blue-green algae (*Lyngliya*), and other vegetation (*Limnophylla heterophylla, Melochia corchoriflora*).

The total area of the Keoladeo Ghana Sanctuary is 2,900 hectares, of which about 2,200 hectares are wet during the monsoon season. However, the water is seldom more than 1.5 meters deep anywhere in the sanctuary, and usually is from 0.6 to 1.0 meter deep (Sauey, 1976). Walkinshaw (1973) reported that he saw an average of 171 birds per day there in February of 1969, and a maximum of 308, while during September he saw as many as 103 birds in a single day. Since

September represents the breeding season, it might be judged that the breeding season density on the sanctuary is roughly one bird per 30 total hectares, or one per 20 hectares of wet areas. Nonbreeding densities may be about twice as great. In September Walkinshaw found three active nests, as well as others not yet ready for eggs, indicating that a bare minimum breeding density would be in the range of a pair per 400 hectares of water area. He states that after the start of the monsoon period and the onset of breeding behavior, he found no more than 27 pairs within the limits of the sanctuary, indicating a possible maximum breeding density of a pair per 80 hectares of water area. This would tally with his estimate of individual territories ranging from no less than 40 hectares to about 61 hectares at maximum.

In Burma, the sarus crane seems to occur in more isolated swamps and marshes than is true in India, while in its newly acquired range of Australia the species occurs much in the same habitats as does the Australian crane, although the two species tend to remain separated from one another (Walkinshaw, 1973). Lavery and Blackman (1969) state that the sarus feeds in freshwaters and cultivations, while the Australian crane occurs in these areas but also in grasslands, open forests, and saline areas. Vegetation of favored freshwater swamps of the sarus, such as Willet's Swamp, consists of sedges (*Rhynchospora, Cladium*), grasses (*Schoenus*), and herbs (*Eriocaulon, Melastoma, Philydrum*).

Nonbreeding habitats are evidently the same as breeding habitats, since the species appears to be essentially sedentary.

FOODS AND FORAGING BEHAVIOR

Foods of Adults

Most evidence indicates that this species is highly omnivorous. Plant materials that are eaten include grain from stubblefields, the tubers and corms of aquatic and marsh plants, the green shoots of grasses and cereal crops, the pods of groundnuts (*Arachis*), and the like (Ali and Ripley, 1969). Walkinshaw (1973) stated that during the harvest season the birds feed on waste wheat and gram (*Cicer arietinum*) and also strip ripened rice (*Oryza*) from the stalks. In Australia sarus cranes sometimes feed in cornfields, and also consume native grasses (Lavery and Blackman, 1969).

Insects, especially grasshoppers, are also commonly consumed. Walkinshaw (1973) stated that the cranes fed at times in very dry areas of the Keoladeo Ghana Bird Sanctuary where there are few seeds, and apparently ate grasshoppers and other insects. Likewise in northern Australia he observed them feeding on short-grass plains where grasshoppers were very abundant. Walkinshaw believed that aquatic snails may sometimes be eaten by sarus cranes.

Vertebrates are also consumed fairly regularly by sarus cranes. Walkinshaw (1973) observed an adult male killing a two-foot water snake (*Natrix piscator*) and feeding it to a youngster, then later the same bird caught a second snake of the same size and offered it to a smaller chick, which was unable to swallow it. The male then swallowed the snake, tail first. Spitzer (1979) also saw sarus cranes killing and consuming water snakes on several occasions, and once saw a crane kill a large frog but later drop it and lose interest in it. Fish have also been reported as a minor food source for sarus cranes (Law, 1930).

Foods of Young

As noted above, the chicks are fed by the adults for a prolonged period; the chick that Walkinshaw saw being fed a large water snake was about two-thirds grown, and probably was four or five months old. No other specifics as to the foods or foraging behavior of young in the wild seem to be available.

Foraging Behavior

According to Spitzer (1979), the sarus crane feeds at the Keoladeo Ghana Sanctuary in water no deeper than about 30.5 centimeters, probably because wading is relatively hard work, and sarus crane's dominance over smaller cranes such as the Siberian allows the sarus easier foraging opportunities elsewhere. At the upland edge of its foraging habitat in India the sarus crane also encounters the Eurasian crane. This latter species primarily feeds in cultivated fields and, furthermore, is somewhat smaller than the sarus, so it certainly poses no serious competitive threat to it. Although sarus cranes also sometimes field-feed, they do not do so in the large flocks that are characteristic of Eurasian cranes, but instead tend to forage in scattered pairs. Baker (1929) stated that the birds regularly feed in cultivated fields and open plains, as well as in water up to about 18 inches (45 centimeters) deep.

MIGRATIONS AND MOVEMENTS

Seasonal Movements

There are few, if any, seasonal movements of sarus cranes in India, where the birds are forced to migrate only in times of extreme drought (Walkinshaw, 1973). However, in Thailand there are apparently some seasonal movements, as Deignan (1945) stated that at Chiang Mai, the birds appear only during the colder nonbreeding period between December and March.

Certainly there must be occasional movements of vagrant birds; otherwise, one could not explain the development of an isolated population on Luzon Island, at least 700 miles from the nearest possible mainland range. More surprising is the recent establishment of a population in northern Australia, at least 3,000 miles from the species' probable present range limits in southeastern Asia. In spite of their large size and relatively heavy weight, the cranes are fully capable of extended soaring (Ali and Ripley, 1969), and so such occasional long-distance movements are certainly within the limits of possibility.

Daily Movements

According to Ali and Ripley (1969), short "commuting" flights are normally made each day between foraging areas and midday roosting places at the edges of rivers or jheels, with the birds flying only at about treetop height.

Walkinshaw (1973) reported that there are daily flights to and from roosting sites every morning and evening at Keoladeo Sanctuary. During the nonbreeding season some birds remained on the roosting ponds all day, while others flew out to nearby meadows, fields, and grain fields, although Walkinshaw did not estimate the flight distances involved.

GENERAL BIOLOGY

Sociality

The sarus crane seems to be relatively nonsocial. Although large flocks have on rare occasions been mentioned, such as groups of as many as 200 birds, this appears to be distinctly unusual (Walkinshaw, 1973). Rather, families and pairs seem to make up the social groupings of sarus cranes, even during the winter period. Walkinshaw reported on group sizes moving to and from roosting areas at the Keoladeo Sanctuary in September, just about at the start of nesting. Of 503 total groups, the most prevalent group size was of 2 birds (87 percent), while the next most common unit was of single birds (8.5 percent). The largest group he observed was of 9 birds, and the average group size was 2.02 birds. Only 13 of the groups (2 percent) were of 3 or 4 birds, suggesting that by this time of the year nearly all of the family groups had already broken up. Walkinshaw stated that the young birds remain with their parents for at least ten months, but after the breeding season begins they begin to assemble and roam the vicinity in groups.

Only a few days after Walkinshaw made the group counts summarized above, the monsoons began and the pairs dispersed for breeding. Before that time, he noted that foraging territories of the birds were well defined, with pairs occupying areas separated by as little as 100 feet and as much as 1,200 feet or more, averaging about 467 feet (142 meters). This would suggest an average foraging territory of about 1.6 hectares. Alternatively, 45 groups of cranes occupied an area of some 450 acres, providing a potential of about 10 acres (4 hectares) per foraging territory. As noted earlier, during the nesting season the breeding territories are much larger than this.

Daily Activities

Sarus cranes leave their nocturnal roosts shortly after daylight (Walkinshaw, 1973). On one occasion, when sunrise was at 7:07, the first of the birds to leave their roost departed at 6:49 and the last to leave departed at 7:50. About 80 percent of the birds that left the roost did so before sunrise. Walkinshaw noted that the birds left their roosts earlier than did the Siberian cranes and also began to call at a much earlier hour. However, when flying from the roost the birds tend to be silent. In the evening, after returning to the roost, sarus cranes once again become very noisy, as they also are in early morning hours.

During initial phases of roosting, pairs or individuals typically are dispersed from 3 to 100 meters away from other birds, but as darkness increases, they tend to move together toward an area of shallow water. After their early morning flights out for foraging, many of the birds return to the roosting area after about 10:00 a.m. for drinking. They then later return again to their foraging areas (Walkinshaw, 1973). In Australia, both the sarus and the Australian cranes feed periodically throughout the day, with intensive foraging occurring until midmorning, and again during late afternoon (Lavery and Blackman, 1969).

Interspecific Interactions

Walkinshaw (1973) reported finding the decapitated body of a young crane in an area where the day before he had seen a jackal (Canis aureus). He suggested that the presence of such predators is probably the major reason the birds normally roost in shallow water. In Australia the dingo (Canis dingo) and foxes (Vulpes vulpes) are known to feed on young birds, and red-backed sea eagles (Haliastur indus) are egg-predators (Lavery and Blackman, 1969).

As the largest of cranes, the sarus is easily able to dominate the much smaller Siberian crane, and it also dominates the Eurasian crane. Spitzer (1979) recounts seeing a pair of sarus cranes put to flight a flock of about 75 Eurasian cranes that landed within the feeding territory of the sarus pair; the sarus cranes drove off the Eurasian cranes simply by taking a few stiff-legged steps in their direction. However, Eurasian cranes and sarus cranes were sometimes observed roosting together.

These birds were occasionally even joined by a few Siberian cranes, suggesting that "safety in numbers" during roosting might outweigh any possible disadvantages of social interactions at that period.

Because of its very large size, the sarus probably dominates all other birds, and is unlikely to be a significant target of predation once the young are fledged. However, the Indian and southeast Asian population lives in close contact with humans and associated animals such as dogs, and probably these human-related influences are the greatest threat to the species.

BREEDING BIOLOGY

Age of Maturity and Time of Breeding

Walkinshaw (1973) reported that egg dates in India range from June to March. He found two records for India in June, probably six for July, eight for August, twelve for September, one for October, five for December, one for January, five for February, and three for March. There are Burmese records for March (one), August (two), and September (two), and a July record for Thailand. Walkinshaw also found a nest in northern Australia in January. In all areas, nesting is apparently stimulated by the onset of the wet season, with associated flooding and environmental changes that favor nesting at this period.

Among captive breedings, one pair of sarus bred initially when both members of the pair were 7 years old, while another pair bred initially when both members were at least 5 years old (private survey of Joe Blossom, pers. comm.). A pair of birds obtained by the Lesna u Gottwaldova Zoo of Czechoslovakia nested initially in 1966, when both members were 6 years old (Klika, 1974).

Pair Formation and Courtship

Dancing has been observed in the sarus crane both during the winter months and also during the breeding season. According to Walkinshaw (1973) dancing follows the typical pattern of the Australian crane, and lasts only a few minutes. The birds do not seem to whirl about when jumping. Instead, they tend to bound and bow directly up and down, although while on the ground they often run about in circles. In all cranes the functions of dancing are varied and often obscure. Dancing thus sometimes occurs as a displacement activity when the nest, eggs, or young are threatened.

Archibald (1975, 1976) states that this species resembles the Australian and white-naped cranes behaviorially. In all, the female begins the call, and during the introductory phase there is a short continuous call that is followed by a pause and then an extended series of sexually distinct calls. In the Indian race of the sarus crane the introductory note of the female is followed by a rapid series of short notes that transpose gradually into her regular series of calls, which average about two to three notes per note of the male. In the eastern race the female's calls are more highly pitched, and her notes are not given in synchrony with the regularly spaced notes of the male. In the males of both races, the introductory note is followed by an extended series of pulsed notes that average about a half-second in length, with the total duration of the display dependent upon the intensity of stimulation. Walkinshaw (1973) describes the female's unison call as a series of "tuk" notes, while that of the male is a loud, trumpeting *krrr* or *garrrooa*.

Posturing during the unison call consists of the female elevating her beak to or beyond the vertical between the horizontal and about 60 degrees above the horizontal for the remainder of the call, with her wings remaining folded and her neck extended vertically. The male extends his head and neck about 45 degrees beyond the vertical during the introductory note, and then elevates his humeri and lowers the wrists, exposing most of the wing to view. He remains in this posture for the rest of the display. The pair typically remains stationary and side by side for the entire display, with the male's raised wings sometimes touching the female's back (Archibald, 1975, 1976).

Walkinshaw (1973) observed copulation in a pair of sarus cranes about a week after the onset of their nest initiation but two days before he observed dancing in that pair. Initially, the birds were feeding about 300 yards apart and some 500 feet from their nest. The birds began to walk toward each other, then the female suddenly stopped, turned her back toward the male, and raised her head and neck, while pointing her bill forward and upward. The male hurried toward her, and as soon as he arrived, he stepped on her lowered back. Copulation lasted about 30 seconds, with the male slowly wing-beating during treading. He then hopped forward over the female's head.

Territoriality and Early Nesting Behavior

Walkinshaw's (1973) observations at the Keoladeo Ghana Sanctuary indicate that nesting may begin within a week after the start of the rainy season. He noted that the day after his arrival, September 1, the rains began, and 19 inches of rain occurred during the next three days. By September 7 the roosting marsh was flooded with 7 to 12 feet of water, and on September 8 the first territorial battles and nest-building were observed. He studied four separate pairs, each of which established territories ranging from 40.47 hectares (100 acres) to 60.7 hectares (150 acres) in area. In pair A, the first to begin nesting, the female worked adjacent to the

nest site, taking wads of debris and vegetation out of the water and piling them on the nest site with a lateral movement. The male stood about 15 feet from the nest, also extracting material from the water, and dropping it near the nest just beyond the female's reach. She initially worked 33 minutes on the nest, and her mate 25 minutes. Then they were interrupted by territorial invasion from a second pair. When the two pairs were only about 7 or 8 feet apart the males began false-preening furiously, with their respective mates immediately behind them and also preening. Then a third pair arrived, and was immediately attacked by the resident male. The situation returned to normal about 20 minutes later.

Two days later the nest was a huge pile of vegetation in the shallowest part of the marsh, where the water was about 12 to 18 inches deep. Both birds continued to pile material onto the nest, and the female twice sat down on it. This time they were interrupted by a fourth pair, which they met about 50 feet from their nest site. When the two pairs were about 9 feet apart, another intensive bout of "false preening" ensued. Pair A retreated to their nest, and were followed by the intruding pair. The latter actually climbed up on A's nest, and the female intruder began to tear it to pieces. This activity continued for about 75 minutes, during which time the male of the intruding pair stood guard, and the resident pair stood silently nearby. After the intruding pair returned to their own territory about 600 feet away, the resident female returned to her nest and began repairing the damage.

Judging from the size of one nest, Walkinshaw estimated that it must have been in use for years. It readily supported the weight of the bird, but nevertheless floated in the water of a sewer pond. Most nests that Walkinshaw saw rested on the mud beneath the water, while some were placed on higher sites where the water was quite shallow, and still others were among groups of dead stumps, adding support. The birds continued to add materials to the nest as long as the water levels rose. The average height above water to the nest rim was 17.36 centimeters (3.0 to 25.4), and the average water depth adjacent to the nests was 33.4 centimeters. Nine nests averaged 150.7 × 167.7 centimeters across at water level, and were narrower toward the top. They were constructed of available materials, including vegetation and various debris such as cattle dung.

Egg-laying and Incubation

Nearly always two eggs are laid, and according to some remarkably detailed observations on the species by the Mogul emperor Jahangir (reigning A.D. 1607-1627), the interval between the laying of the two eggs is 48 hours (Ali, 1927). The same authority gave the incubation period as 34 days, which agrees well with modern estimates of 31 to 36 days (Archibald, 1974).

Walkinshaw (1973) was able to find only four records of single-egg clutches and two for three-egg clutches among a total of 132 sets. Thus, the sarus seems to be remarkably consistent in laying two-egg clutches.

Although incubation is performed by both sexes, most incubation is done by the female, while the male tends to assume watch duties. Walkinshaw studied one pair in which the female remained on the nest all of one night, while the male roosted very near the nest in shallow water. The male went to the nest only five minutes after sunrise and a nest exchange occurred. About three hours later the female returned to the nest, while the male went off to feed. The female again left for feeding later in the morning and returned to incubate in early afternoon. Less than an hour later the male took over once again and incubated until nearly 4:00 p.m. The female then took over and remained on the nest through the night. In all, the male incubated for a total of about 7.5 hours during the 24-hour span, including three separate attentive periods.

Walkinshaw observed no distraction behavior at two areas where he watched incubation. However, while on a train he did observe the behavior of a nesting pair when men approached an active nest and picked up one of the eggs. Both members of the pair ran with outspread wings directly away from the men, although neither bird called. As the men returned to the train and it started away, the birds quickly returned to their nest.

In captive breeding attempts described by Klika (1974), the eggs of three different clutches were invariably laid about 70 hours apart, and in each of several years the nest was constructed in the same place. During two years of observation, the nest exchanges were performed very punctually. They typically occurred six times a day, between about 5:00 or 6:00 a.m. and late afternoon. The last one usually occurred about 7:00 p.m., and the female always brooded overnight, with the male standing several meters away.

Hatching and Postbreeding Biology

At the time of hatching the chicks are very weak, and may remain in the nest for as long as two days. However, even before they can readily walk they are good swimmers. By two days of age, they can walk well and swim very well. Both parents guard them continuously, feeding them and accompanying them. At the call of their parents, the young birds "freeze," and do not move again until the parents call once more. Within a few days the young are obtaining much of their own food. Walkinshaw believes that the birds seldom raise more than one young under natural conditions, although Kiracofe (1964) found that the young cranes that he raised in captivity were not aggressive toward one another.

Ali (1958) described how a newly hatched chick continued to fidget and cheep after a brooding adult sounded an alert call, a short, subdued, and staccato *kor-r-r* note. The adult then stalked back to the nest, gently pecked the chick, and repeated the note. At this the chick became silent and immobile. In another case, a pair leading another set of chicks uttered the same call and the chicks seemed to disappear as if by magic. One of the chicks was later discovered lying half submerged in a puddle at the base of a grass tussock, while the parents performed "broken-wing" distraction displays and alternated exciting trumpeting and the commanding *kor-r-r* notes.

Klika (1974) reported that during the first few days after hatching both parents held out food for their single chick, although by the second day the chick could feed independently. Its food consisted of a variety of insects, spiders, and worms that were offered by the adults. After the third day following hatching the duration of parental feeding lasted about 20 minutes.

There is no good detailed information on the timing of the molts in the species, although it is known that a flightless period does occur (Blaauw, 1897; Moody, 1932). In the pair of cranes studied by Klika, both members began to molt 9 days after the death of their 13-day-old chick, or about three weeks after its hatching date.

The fledging period of sarus cranes was estimated by Rothschild (1930) to be about three months. Walkinshaw (1973) believed that the young birds remained with their parents for at least ten months, or until the parents began breeding again.

RECRUITMENT RATES, POPULATION STATUS, AND CONSERVATION

Surprisingly little information is available on recruitment rates. Among a flock of 137 birds observed in Australia, 16.7 percent were young birds, suggesting a relatively high recruitment rate, approximately the same as that observed in Australian cranes (Blackman, 1971a). The apparent absence of migration, the prolonged breeding period, and the very large size of the adults and the associated effectiveness of parental protection perhaps all contribute to a seemingly rather high reproductive potential in this species.

EVOLUTIONARY RELATIONSHIPS

As indicated in the section on the Australian crane, the sarus and Australian cranes are very close relatives and probably can be considered to constitute a superspecies.

White-naped Crane
Grus vipio Pallas 1811

Other Vernacular Names. Japanese white-necked crane; Ts-ang-kua (Chinese); Grue à cour blanc (French); Weissnacken-Kranich (German); Mana-zuru (Japanese); Dachkai zhuravl (Russian); Grulla de cuelle blanco (Spanish).

Range. Breeds on the Transbaikalian steppes probably from the Onon and Argun rivers eastward through northwestern and central Manchuria to the southern Ussuri Valley, the basin of Lake Khanka, and in southwestern Ussuriland. Known recent breeding areas (Yamashina, 1978) include the marshlands around the central part of the Primorskiy Kraj (Maritime Territory), the middle drainage of the Amur River (from the upper Zeya to the Bureya and the Archara), and in northwestern Manchuria (Jaranton). Also breeds in eastern Mongolia to headwaters of the Kerulin River (Bold, 1981). Migratory, wintering in Korea, in southern Japan (Arasaki, Kyushu), and (formerly) on the lower Hwang and Yangtze rivers of eastern China, with vagrants sometimes reaching Fukien and Taiwan.

Subspecies. None recognized.

Measurements. Wing, males 510-585 mm (average of 9, 562.9 mm); females 521-560 mm (average of 6, 546.8 mm). Exposed culmen, males 128-155 mm (average of 9, 145.1 mm); females 128-148 mm (average of 6, 137.8 mm). Tarsus, 242-262 mm (average of 9, 253.7 mm); females 230-263 mm (average of 6, 242.3 mm). Eggs, average 99.3 × 61.5 mm (92.7-103.0 × 58.5-62.7 mm) (Walkinshaw, 1973).

Weights. Adults of both sexes range from 4,750 to 6,500 grams (Tso-hsin Cheng, pers. comm.). Four hand-reared young averaged 3,294 grams at 70 days of age (Archibald and Viess, 1979), and five hand-reared birds averaged 3,405 grams at 73-78 days (Christine Sheppard, pers. comm.). The estimated average egg weight is 207 grams.

Description

Adults of both sexes are alike, with the face and forehead mostly bare of feathers to about 25-30 mm behind the eye, and reddish, with dark bristly hairlike feathers scattered on the cheeks and forehead, and with a small oval-shaped area of light gray feathers around the ear opening. The rear portion of the head, the entire hindneck, and the throat are white. The front of the neck is dark grayish, the grayish area extending up the sides of the neck and terminating in a point close to the bare facial patch. The primaries are black, with white shafts, and the basal portions of the inner webs are also white. The secondaries are blackish, with whitish bases that are mottled from about the fourth secondary inward, while the innermost secondaries are white, decurved, lengthened, and pointed. The wing coverts are light gray, and the greater coverts are white terminally. The lower portion of the body and the breast are dark slaty gray and continuous with the dark gray of the neck. The tail is dark gray, tipped with black. The iris is orange yellow, the bill is greenish yellow, and the legs and toes are pinkish.

Juveniles have the head entirely covered with cinnamon brown feathers, which also occur on the neck. The throat is yellowish white, and the breast and underparts are gray, the feathers with slightly yellowish margins. The tail and wings are blackish gray.

Downy chicks are tawny yellow, becoming somewhat white below and more brownish above, with darker spots on the upper parts of the wings, the rump, and the lower back (Walkinshaw, 1973).

Identification

In the field, the dark grayish body, becoming silvery gray on the wings and wing coverts, and the white

Breeding (hatched) and wintering (dark shading) distributions of the white-naped crane. Broken lines enclose regions of possible but unproven breeding, and arrows indicate known migration routes. Light stippling indicates region of prior or uncertain wintering. Insets show locations of breeding season occurrence in the Amur Valley (above), and wintering localities in Korea and Kyushu, Japan (below).

hindneck and nape, surrounding an extensively reddish face patch, serve to identify this species, which is the only crane with pinkish legs and a dark gray and white striped neck. Its calls are loud, and during the unison call the male strongly raises his wings while letting the primaries droop.

In the hand, the combination of pinkish legs and a neck that is vertically striped with dark gray and white serves to identify this species. The trachea is coiled within the keel of the sternum.

DISTRIBUTION AND HABITATS

Historical and Current Breeding Ranges

The exact limits of the past and current breeding ranges of this rare species are still extremely uncertain. Probably it was more extensive in the past, although summer records west of Lake Baikal are likely to have resulted from nonbreeding birds summering outside the known breeding range.

The western limits of the current breeding range may be in the Zabakalskiy area south of Lake Baikal, in the valley of the Selenga River, and the eastern limits are around Lake Khanka, Maritime Territory, where breeding occurred as recently as the early 1960s. Apart from this latter area, known recent breeding areas are very few. They include the middle courses of the River Amur and its northern tributaries (the Zeya, the Bureya, and the Archara), and the vicinity of Jaranton in northwestern Manchuria (Yamashina, 1978). However, the major part of the nesting range probably occurs in northeastern Mongolia, in the basin of the Kerulen River, and especially in the Uldz and Onon River valleys (Flint, 1978b, Kucheruk, unpublished ms).

In Mongolia, the white-naped crane is a common but not numerous nesting species throughout the forest-steppe zone of eastern Mongolia, from the Halhin River to the headwaters of the Kerulen (Bold, 1981). Kucheruk (unpublished ms) found that in Mongolia its breeding range is confined to a narrow strip of forest-steppe of the southeastern Hetiy foothills, but does not include the steppe plains and the eastern Gobi Desert. Isolated encounters with the bird in the basin of the Halhin River and to the north of Tsitsikhar (Ch'ich'ihaerh) in the region of Haerhpin (Harbin) in Manchuria suggest that its range stretches in a narrow band of forest-steppe along the western and eastern foothills of the Greater Khingan Range and the northern edge of the Central Manchurian Plain, northward into the lowlands of the Zeya and Bureya river basins, and eastward to Lake Khanka. The range configuration seems to coincide with that of the Daurian and Manchurian mole-rats (*Myospalix* spp.), according to Kucheruk.

In the upper and middle reaches of the Uldz River and west to the vicinity of Hentiyn Nuruu, the species is fairly common in the breeding season. Kucheruk observed 35 cranes in five areas along a 530 kilometer route through this region. Two pairs with three juveniles were seen in the valley of the Dzharkai-Bulka River, 15 kilometers south of the Uldz. This river is a tributary to the Uldz, and flows into it 30 kilometers west of Dash-Balbar. A group of 15 was observed feeding in the Uldz Valley, near Norovlin, and a pair was seen where the Shasyn River flows into the Onon. Six more were seen along the lower reaches of the Dund-Bayan, which enters the Uldz about 50 kilometers from the mouth of that river. Finally, two pairs were seen in the wide, swampy valley of the Barunburt River about 20 to 25 kilometers northeast of Omnodelger.

The other major apparent breeding area of the white-naped crane is in the middle Amur River drainage, especially between the Bureya and Uril Rivers, and possibly extending to the middle reaches of the Zeya River and into the valley of the Urkanka. About ten pairs nest in the Amur region at present (USSR Crane Working Group Information Bulletin No. 2, 1981). In 1970 four pairs were known to be nesting in an area of 300 square kilometers of the Amur Basin (Dymin and Pankin, 1975). In the same year, an estimated two to four pairs nested on an area 50-300 square kilometers between the mouth of the Bureya River and the Bureinskii Range, according to Kucheruk, and perhaps referring to the same observations. Yamashina (1978) has plotted breeding records and other areas of occurrence during the breeding season for this region; the map inset is based on his compilation. The birds have been seen summering in the Jewish Autonomous Region (Yevreysk A.O.), and in the Bikin River basin of northern Primorskiy Kraj, and possibly have nested there too (Flint, 1978b). No nests have been found in the Upper Amur basin, but pairs have been encountered along the Zeya and its tributary streams (Dymin and Pankin, 1975). It is possible that at present no more than about twenty pairs exist within the USSR, with the remainder of the population presumably breeding in Mongolia and Manchuria (King, 1979).

In the Ussuri River valley, white-naped cranes were fairly common when studied by Prezhwalsky (1877), nesting on the Prihanka plain. Vorobiev (1954) observed the birds to be present in the Lake Khanka region in late spring of 1945, but was unable to confirm that they still nested there. Shibaev (1975) found no information on nesting there after Prezhwalsky's studies (1877) except for a report of nesting in the middle reaches of the Bolshaya (Greater) Ussurka River, in 1938-39. However, he stated that as recently as the 1960s an amateur observer reported white-naped cranes nesting in the Bikin River area. As recently as 1961-1964 four or five pairs still nested at Lake Khanka, and in 1980 four or five pairs were counted there at the mouth of the Ilistay River (USSR Crane Working Group, Information Bulletin No. 2, 1981).

Habitat Requirements, Densities

Flint (1978a) characterized the breeding habitat as level, marshy, and unforested areas within forest-steppe habitats. He also describes it (1978b) as consisting of grassy moors or herbaceous swamps, and flooded meadows, in wide river valleys and lake hollows in steppe or forest-steppe. These are essentially the same conditions required by Japanese cranes, and such habitats are frequently the ones affected by drainage and subsequent cultivation or used as hayfields and pastures. Kucheruk stated that the species nests only in wide, dish-shaped boggy and unwooded valleys in the upper reaches of small rivers, and believed that in such areas of the Onon and Uldz river valleys the breeding density is in the vicinity of about a pair per 30-50 square miles. As noted earlier, a nesting density of about four pairs in 300 square kilometers (a pair per 75 square kilometers, or 29 square miles) was estimated for the Amur Valley.

Nonbreeding Range and Habitats

The historic wintering range of this species included Korea, southern Japan (Kyushu), and eastern China (the lower Yangtze), according to Vaurie (1965) and Walkinshaw (1973). Records indicate that in China the major wintering area is the Yangtze River, although a few may also winter in the southern park of the Maritime Province on the Suyfun River south of Lake Khanka. Cheng (1981) lists the white-naped crane among the species of cranes currently wintering in China, and stated that some birds also occasionally winter in Fukien and Taiwan provinces. However, King (1979) indicates that there are no recent records of white-naped cranes wintering on the Lower Yangtze River. The species used to winter in large numbers in Korea, prior to the Korean war, and still occurs in fair numbers there. However, its major current wintering area is now probably in Kyushu, Japan. It was also collected once on Bonin Island well to the south of Japan, (Walkinshaw, 1973).

In Korea, the species once wintered throughout the entire country, but now is found primarily in North and South Chungchong provinces, with the Han River Estuary of the Demilitarized Zone an important staging area. The species was designated a Natural Monument in 1968 in South Korea, and the Han River staging area has been named a provisional Natural Monument, as well (King, 1979). The wintering status of the birds there has been recently summarized by Kyu and Oesting (1981), Won (1981), and Archibald (1981a). The white-naped cranes arrive in Korea in early October, and

concentrate in October and November on the Han River Estuary. Several hundred also gather along the Sachon River, which passes through the center of the DMZ, and a group of 15 to 20 winters in the Cholewon Basin of the central highlands, some 75 kilometers east of the Han River estuary. The Sachon River and Cholewon Basin populations are stable through the winter, but about half of the Han River population migrates south in late November, and is presumably the flock that winters in Kyushu, near Izumi.

The wintering population of the white-naped cranes in Japan is concentrated in the vicinity of Izumi, Arasaki, and Sendai City, Kagoshima Prefecture. Nishida (1981) has summarized the recent numerical data on this flock, which is summarized in table 32. Walkinshaw (1973) has described the wintering activities around Arasaki, as has Archibald (1973). Inasmuch as this group seems to be simply a subcomponent of the Korean flock, total numbers wintering in Kyushu in any given year may not reflect actual population changes so much as changes in local weather or feeding conditions in Korea. Thus, the increases in numbers of birds in the late 1970s were much larger than could have occurred by reproduction alone.

Wintering habitats in Korea are mostly brackish marshlands and rice paddies, with roosting occurring on salt marshes and mudflats. Those cranes wintering along the Sachon River sometimes are forced by bad weather to roost on open water and sandbars of a sheltered lake near Panmunjom (Archibald, 1981a).

FOODS AND FORAGING BEHAVIOR

Foods of Adults

In the Korean wintering areas, the white-naped cranes are primarily vegetarians, and in the salt marshes of the Han River estuary the birds feed on sedge tubers of *Scirpus maritimus* and seeds of various grasses. In rice paddies they feed mainly on gleanings of grain. They prefer to forage in the recently wetted area of the Han marsh, usually along tidal channels where there is moist mud where they can easily dig for tubers. Where the soil isn't covered by water at high tide, the birds often walk slowly about, apparently searching for seeds or small animals on the surface. When feeding on tubers, the birds are primarily diggers, rarely moving much, and often exhibit feeding territoriality, but when feeding on seeds they are wandering searchers, and usually are nonterritorial (Archibald, 1981a).

In Kyushu, white-naped cranes feed in company with hooded cranes, and their fecal droppings have been analyzed by Nishida (1981). He reported that rice hulls comprised the most common food residue, occurring in 73.2 percent of the droppings. Wheat or barley husks were in 35.7 percent of the droppings, grass fragments were in 26.8 percent, and other edible materials (seeds, shell fragments, and insects) occurred in less than 4 percent. Grit was also found in nearly 20 percent of the droppings. Probably the majority of these droppings were those of hooded cranes, rather than white-naped cranes, since the former are much more common in the area. Walkinshaw (1973) stated that in early years the birds of the Arasaki area fed largely on bulbous roots, grain, and foods given them by local residents, but more recently feed almost entirely on wheat and carp fed them by a local crane warden and his helpers.

On the breeding grounds, the foods of this species are essentially unknown.

Foods of Young

No specific information is available on the foods of young cranes in the wild.

Foraging Behavior

Walkinshaw (1973) stated that while on their wintering areas of Japan, the cranes are no longer distinctly territorial, but instead feed side by side for some time, day after day, and are usually strung out in a long line. However, small territories are maintained around each family and even around each individual, with the male being more obvious in his territorial behavior than the female. Nishida (1981) also reported winter foraging territories in white-naped and hooded cranes in Kyushu. He stated that territories in rye, wheat, or rape fields during winter range from 20 to 300 square meters, and average about 100 square meters. The size of a particular territory seems to be influenced by population size or the area of standing crops available. Nishida did not specify differences in territorial behavior of the two species studied. As noted earlier, Archibald (1981a) found that white-naped cranes feeding in salt marshes on sedge tubers are often territorial, while those foraging on surface seeds are usually nonterritorial.

MIGRATIONS AND MOVEMENTS

Seasonal Movements

According to Dementiev and Gladkov (1969), initial arrival of these cranes on their breeding grounds in Maritime Territory occurs during the second half of March, with a major movement in mid-April. They begin to depart in September and October, remaining in southern Maritime Territory until the end of November. The fall migration mainly occurs during the second half of October and early November. By the middle of October the birds are in the vicinity of Lake Khanka and the mouth of the Tumannaya River. By the last third of October they are appearing in central Korea; presumably these not only include Maritime Territory birds, but also those from farther west, in Mongolia and Manchuria. However, in the spring the cranes are not seen in the Ussuri area until about two weeks later than the time they leave the Korean peninsula, suggesting that the first birds to leave Japanese and Korean wintering grounds are those that are headed for the more western areas, while those nesting in the Ussuri Basin leave the wintering grounds later.

Archibald (1981a) reported that the first fall arrivals of white-naped cranes reach Korea in early October, and increase to about 2,000 by mid-November. Kyu and Oesting (1981) stated that the white-naped is the first of the cranes to arrive in Korea in autumn, appearing in late October and November in Kangwon Do Province of North Korea.

Arrival in Japan seems to be associated with yearly weather variations. Some of the white-napes wintering there arrive in mid-October, while others do not appear until January. Many begin departing shortly after the middle of February, and all are usually gone by the first of March (Walkinshaw, 1973). Walkinshaw reported on the departure of one large group of birds on the morning of February 21, 1969, after eight days of rainy weather. In late morning, after a period of feeding, preening, drinking, and loafing, the birds left during conditions of a light northeasterly wind and a clear sky. In the DMZ area of Korea, the white-naped cranes remain in the area until mid-March (Won, 1981). Shibaev (1975) reported arrival in the Lake Khanka area at about the end of March.

Daily Movements

At least on the wintering grounds, daily movements of white-naped cranes seem to consist of flights from nocturnal roosting sites to daytime feeding sites, and back again. In the Izumi area of Kyushu, all of the wintering cranes, white-naped and hooded, numbering about 1,000 or more, roost in a common location, although the two species remain separate. Archibald (1981a) stated that in Korea the families leading young are usually the first to leave the roosting flock at dawn. Some of the families and pairs establish feeding territories that roughly include an area of 10 to 20 meters in diameter from their prime foraging spot, while the rest of the cranes usually feed at or near their roosting site and do not evidence territorial behavior. This flock is surrounded by the family groups holding territories. Sometimes small groups leave the main flock and fly elsewhere in the estuary to forage, but they usually return at dusk to roost with the large flock. During very cold weather, the birds abandon their feeding territories, flock together, and sometimes circle high in the sky, as if to migrate further south. During such cold weather they may also remain on their roosts until early afternoon, fly out to wetlands for a few hours to feed, and then return again to their roosts. As the weather becomes mild again in spring, the birds leave their roosts early in the morning, but instead of visiting rice paddies, they move to freshwater wetlands and probably begin foraging on aquatic animal life prior to departing in mid-March.

GENERAL BIOLOGY

Sociality

At least on the wintering grounds, the social structure of white-naped cranes seems to consist of two subunits: a large group of nonbreeders, plus a smaller component of breeding pairs leading young (Archibald, 1981a). Nishida (1981) stated that in a sample (size unstated) of white-naped cranes in Kyushu, the ratio of cranes leading two young to those leading a single young was 27:73, suggesting that about one in three families are able to raise both young successfully, and that brood size averaged 1.27 young in this case.

In Korea, wintering white-naped cranes often associate with Japanese cranes, often feeding together in rice paddies, where the slightly larger Japanese cranes dominate the white-napes. The two species roosted in adjacent areas. In one area where they were being fed corn, a pair of white-napes supplanted several pairs of Japanese cranes that attempted to land there, but on the other hand territorial pairs and families of Japanese cranes, even though they were dominant, did not attack intruding white-napes (Archibald, 1981a). In general, the white-naped crane is more of a vegetarian than is the Japanese crane, and thus competition is not likely to be severe between these two species.

Daily Activities

According to Walkinshaw (1973), white-naped cranes on their wintering grounds of Kyushu would feed for hours, more or less, during the early morning hours, at times during midday, and again about 4:00 p.m. When it was nearly dark, they would return by family groups to their roosting field, which in the case described by Walkinshaw was an old rice field covered by shallow water. In the mornings the birds did not leave their roosts until all or nearly all of the hooded cranes had departed, and then the white-naped cranes departed as a single flock at about sunrise. While on their foraging grounds, family groups tended to become separated from larger groups, but the members of each family remained in fairly close proximity to each other.

Interspecific Interactions

As noted above, associations with Japanese cranes are common in Korea. Likewise, in Kyushu, Japan, association with the smaller hooded cranes is frequent, although the two species roost separately. In Korea,

they also feed in company with bean geese (*Anser fabalis*), white-fronted geese (*Anser albifrons*), and mallards (*Anas platyrhynchos*). Although both white-tailed sea eagles (*Haliaeetus albicilla*) and golden eagles (*Aquila chrysaetos*) prey on these waterfowl, Archibald (1981a) noted that the cranes paid little attention to these particular predators.

The species has been studied too little on the breeding grounds for any significant predators to be identified there.

BREEDING BIOLOGY

Age of Maturity and Time of Breeding

There are only a limited number of egg records for this species (see table 14), but these suggest that the egg-laying period begins in April, with most records for May and a small number extending into June. Dementiev and Gladkov (1968) indicate that egg-laying occurs from the end of April until the end of May. In the Ussuri Valley and Lake Khanka area the earliest reported broods are for May 30 and June 1, according to these authors, although Prezhwalsky (1877) reported that young were collected at Lake Khanka on May 19, while Grote (1943) stated that hatching occurs toward the end of May.

In the Amur River valley, a full clutch of eggs was reported on April 19 (Dymin and Pankin, 1975), or about a month after spring arrival.

The age of maturity and initial breeding is not known for wild birds, but is presumably similar to that of other large *Grus* species. At Flamingo Gardens in England a pair of white-naped cranes initially nested when the male was 12 years old and the female the same age (unpublished survey of Joe Blossom pers. comm.).

Pair Formation and Courtship

According to Archibald (1975, 1976), the white-naped crane is part of a species group that also includes the sarus and brolga. In all of these, the female begins the unison call, and the vocal patterns during the introductory phase of the unison display are similar in both sexes, with a short continuous call that is followed by a pause and then by a series of sexually distinct calls. During the introductory portion of her call, the female white-naped crane extends her head and neck farther back behind the vertical than do female sarus or brolga cranes. She then utters a rapid series of short calls that grade into her more pulsed and broken calls, which are uttered with the neck vertically outstretched, the bill pointed upward, and the wings held against the body. Following his introductory call, the male likewise begins a series of pulsed calls, which are longer and lower in pitch than the female calls, and with each call the male raises his humeri and drops his wrists, while between calls the humeri are lowered and the wrists folded. The neck is thrown back well behind the vertical, and this movement is accentuated by the contrasting neck and nape patterning. The light gray tertials and wing coverts likewise contrast with the darker gray flight feathers, emphasizing the wing movements. The male remains in this conspicuous posture for the rest of the display. The pair remains stationary and side by side throughout the entire display.

Walkinshaw (1973) reported that dancing occurs both in adult and in young birds. He observed that adults jumped, catapulted, spread their wings, and sometimes called while dancing. They also picked up objects with their bills, and sometimes had synchronized dancing. He noted that the unison call was uttered throughout the winter in Japan, and under zoo conditions he observed it once when the pair was exchanging places at the nest and on another occasion when they were attacking a pair of sarus cranes.

Threat displays of the white-naped crane appear to be identical to those of other *Grus* species. Walkinshaw observed that on two occasions, attack was preceded by "false-preening" displays, and on two other occasions, by laying down in front of other birds, the "squat-threat" display. The usual aggressive sequence observed by Walkinshaw was the false-preening display, followed by arching the neck, and pointing the bill groundward, and finally by overt attack. At times, a "fluffed feather" display occurred after the false preening; presumably this corresponds to the "ruffle" display described in Chapter 2.

Territoriality and Early Nesting Behavior

As noted earlier, territorial behavior is evident during winter as well as during the breeding season, particularly among birds that are tending young. Walkinshaw (1973) states that the birds are to some extent territorial during the fall period too, and probably are especially so during spring.

Wintering territories are relatively small, as noted earlier, but there is no good information on the size of breeding territories in the wild. There are also rather few descriptions of nesting sites of wild birds. Blaauw (1897) reported that the nest is placed in the marshy parts of steppes. The birds use an islet that is elevated a few inches above the surrounding marsh, and build a nest of dead, dry grasses. The nest is flat, with a depression in the middle. Dymin and Pankin (1975) likewise reported that the nest is placed in the middle of a grassy marsh, and is a mound of dry leaves of sedges and grasses, with some additional mosses and aquatic plant stems. The diameter on one nest was 90 centimeters, the height was 20 centimeters, the diameter of the depressed area was 50 centimeters, and its depth was 2 centimeters.

In zoos, white-naped cranes typically build their nests on dry ground. Walkinshaw (1951) reported on four nests built by a pair of cranes at the Detroit Zoological Park during successive years. The first two nests were in nearly the same location, and about 46 meters from the small lake in the enclosure. The nest was even farther from the water the third year, but in 1948 it was on an "island" almost surrounded by water and well up on a ridge. In that year, the birds were released into the area in mid-April, and both eggs hatched on June 1, suggesting that nest-building must have begun almost immediately and the first egg must have been laid about April 30.

Egg-laying and Incubation

The normal clutch size is two eggs, although there are relatively few data available on clutch sizes in the wild. Koga (1975) reported that in captivity white-naped cranes lay up to eight clutches (16 to 17 eggs) in a single season when the eggs are taken from their nests, suggesting that two eggs are the normal clutch, and that rarely three may be laid. His data suggest that the eggs are usually laid two or three days apart, with gaps of about ten days between successive laying cycles.

Walkinshaw (1951) provides considerable information on incubation behavior in a pair of white-naped cranes obtained during two days of observation. During these two days, the female was on the nest a total minimum of 536 minutes (probably over 1,200 minutes, including the preceding night), and was off feeding 13 times for a total of 197 minutes. Her incubation periods ranged in length from 55 minutes to more than 12 hours (one night). The male incubated for a total of 1,373 minutes, and was off feeding 8 times for a total of 117 minutes. His incubation periods ranged from 65 minutes to more than 16 hours (including one night). During a total of 32 hours of observation, the eggs were being incubated by one or the other bird for all but about ten minutes. When not incubating, the birds were either feeding on provided grain, probing in the earth (apparently for earthworms), drinking, bathing, or preening.

While incubating, the female rose from the eggs to turn them or adjust the nest on an average of once every 28 minutes, ranging from 1 to 114 minutes. The male did so on an average of once every 80.5 minutes, ranging from 41 to 139 minutes.

The incubation period is 30 to 33 days, averaging 31 days, under conditions of zoo incubation (Walkinshaw 1973).

Nest defense displays and distraction behavior are evidently performed by either sex. Walkinshaw (1951) stated that whichever crane was not incubating always watched the other zoo animals. It would chase away Dorcas gazelles and attack other cranes, such as white-naped, Eurasian, blue, sarus, crowned, and demoiselle. The larger sarus cranes were usually given more "respect" than the other cranes, and once a male sarus attacked the female white-naped. On occasion the incubating male rushed from his nest and both birds attacked the sarus, chasing it to the far corner of the island. Other large birds, such as vultures, peafowl, pelicans, storks, flamingos, and geese were also attacked when they approached the vicinity of the nest, but the cranes paid little attention to the smaller birds.

Hatching and Postbreeding Biology

Walkinshaw (1951, 1973) observed that the parent birds fed a chick the day following its hatching. In only a few more days it was picking up objects by itself, although the parents continued to feed it periodically, even into the following winter. When it was 10.5 months old, it was evicted from its parents' vicinity, by the male repeatedly driving it away when it approached the female. However, Walkinshaw noted that during the winter months in Japan, when the young birds were probably approaching 10 months old, they were still with their parents in late February, and departed with them.

The fledging period has not yet been accurately determined for this species, but it is apparently in excess of 70 days (Archibald and Viess, 1979). The distinctive nape marking is present in young white-naped cranes but the cheeks are still feathered. Judging from migration records, it is likely that fledging has occurred by about this time. By the spring after hatching, the cheeks become bare but are not as red as in the adults, and the iris has changed from dark brown to yellowish as in adults (Walkinshaw, 1973).

There is no detailed information on molting cycles in the adults.

RECRUITMENT RATES, POPULATION STATUS, AND CONSERVATION

The best information on recruitment rates in this species is that of Nishida (1981), who reported an overall 16.0 percent juvenile component in a sample of 1,826 wintering cranes between 1968 and 1972. However, individual samples ranged from as little as 4.7 percent to 27.8 percent, suggesting that the sampling error might be substantial. Quite possibly the proportions of

young in the wintering flocks in Korea are different from those in Japan, although Archibald (1981a) stated that in Korea the proportion of juveniles is about 15 percent, or close to that of the Japanese estimate. These figures would suggest that the white-naped is somewhat more successful in breeding than most other Northern Hemisphere cranes. Additional information on family size and on the percentage of wintering birds leading young would be very valuable. Nishida (1981) stated that the ratio of families leading single young to those with two young was 73:27 in a 1980 count, but did not provide an indication of actual sample size.

The information on wintering populations in Japan (table 32) is certainly suggestive of a favorable trend, although it must be remembered that Korea is the primary wintering area and that the numbers in Japan are largely a reflection of how many birds continue on to there from Korea. Both wintering areas are crucial to the continuing survival of the white-naped crane, especially as there is no definite indication that the Chinese wintering areas are still being used. Given the very limited known breeding range of the species, it seems unlikely that China would support a significant number of wintering birds at present. Thus, continued monitoring of the Korean and Japanese populations is especially important. The problems caused by large numbers of cranes in the Izumi area of Kyushu, with attendant problems of crop damage, sightseers, and the like must also be solved if the birds are to continue to thrive there (Nishida, 1981).

White-naped cranes breed very well in captivity, and such efforts as those of Koga (1975) prove that substantial success is possible in developing captive populations of this species through avicultural techniques.

EVOLUTIONARY RELATIONSHIPS

There is some evidence that the sarus and brolga are the closest relatives of the white-naped crane, as Archibald (1975, 1976) has concluded on the basis of behavioral studies. However, Wood (1979) determined that, except for one analysis, the Eurasian, hooded, and white-naped clustered in the same cladistic group, so the problems of relationships of the white-naped crane are perhaps not fully settled.

Sandhill Crane

Grus canadensis (Linnaeus) 1758

Other Vernacular Names. Canadian crane, Little brown crane; Grue du Canada (French); Kanadischer Kranich (German); Kanada-zuru (Japanese): Kanadaski zhuravl (Russian); Grulla del Canada (Spanish).

Range. Breeds in extreme northeastern Siberia and in North America from Alaska to Baffin Island, south to northeastern Colorado, Minnesota, Wisconsin, and Michigan. Additional nonmigratory populations exist in Georgia, Florida, Mississippi, Cuba, and the Isle of Pines. The migratory races winter from California and Baja California eastward to New Mexico, Texas, and Florida. The breeding range was formerly much more extensive in the United States, extending south to Nebraska, Indiana, and Ohio.

Subspecies.

G.c. canadensis: Lesser sandhill crane. Breeds in northeastern Siberia along the lower Anadyr River and its tributaries, and recorded from the Chukotski Peninsula, Wrangel Island, and the arctic USSR coastline west to the Indigirka River. Breeds on St. Lawrence Island and in North America from northern Alaska to Baffin Island, probably south to Cook Inlet in Alaska, and to central or southern Mackenzie, southern Keewatin, and Southampton Island. Intergrades with *rowani* to the south, making range limits uncertain. Winters in central California, and from eastern New Mexico and northwestern Texas south to Chihuahua and rarely to central Mexico.

G.c. rowani: Canadian sandhill crane. Breeds in central Canada, probably from eastern British Columbia through the northern portions of Alberta, Saskatchewan, and Manitoba, and probably also northern Ontario. The limits of this form's range are extremely uncertain. Migratory, wintering in eastern Texas, less frequently in western Loui-

siana, western Texas, and eastern New Mexico (Aldrich, 1979). A transitional race, essentially linking *canadensis* with *tabida*, and considered by Tacha (1981) as questionably distinct.

G.c tabida: Greater sandhill crane. Breeds in the United States and southern Canada south of *rowani*, from southwestern British Columbia south to northern California and northern Nevada, in the Rocky Mountain region south from Montana to northern Colorado, in the central plains and Great Lakes region from southern Manitoba and northern Minnesota to central Wisconsin and southern Michigan, and also southeastern Ontario. The range possibly also extends to northern Ontario, but this area's birds are probably closer to *rowani* (Walkinshaw, 1973). Migratory, with the Great Lakes population wintering in Florida, those in the Rocky Mountain population wintering along the Rio Grande in New Mexico and in northern Chihuahua, and the westernmost breeding populations wintering in California, including the Central and Imperial Valleys.

G.c. pratensis: Florida sandhill crane. Resident in southern Georgia, from the Okefenokee Swamp (Charlton and Ware counties) to Florida, and in Florida mostly from Alachua and Putnam counties south to the Everglades. Cranes reported from southern Alabama may be of this form or of *pulla*.

G.c. pulla: Mississippi sandhill crane. Resident in southeastern Mississippi (Jackson County), and probably formerly also in southern Louisiana.

G.c. nesiotes: Cuban sandhill crane. Resident on the Isle of Pines and western Cuba, with the latter population now nearly extirpated.

Measurements. Wings of male *canadensis* average 469.9 mm (range 418-510 mm), those of *tabida* 539.7 mm (460-598 mm), of *pratensis* 501.1 mm (460-533 mm), and of *nesiotes* 480.5 mm (460-533 mm).

Females of *canadensis* average 447.6 mm (420-500 mm), of *tabida* 485 mm (467-510mm), of *pratensis* 477.9 (445-517 mm), and of *nesiotes* 440.8 mm (425-460 mm). Exposed culmens of male *canadensis* average 92.6 mm (69-110 mm), those of *tabida* 138.6 mm (116-159 mm), of *pratensis* 127.7 mm (113-144 mm), and of *nesiotes* 116.6 mm (115-118 mm). Females of *canadensis* average 91.8 mm (80-103 mm), of *tabida* 131.2 mm (113-147 mm), of *pratensis* 123.3 mm (110-142 mm), and of *nesiotes* 110.4 mm (100-122 mm). Tarsi of male *canadensis* average 189.3 mm (156-228 mm), of *tabida* 244.2 mm (225-265 mm), of *pratensis* 244.6 mm (223-264 mm), and of *nesiotes* 216.3 mm (206-232 mm). Those of female *canadensis* average 181.8 mm (162-212 mm), of *tabida* 231.4 mm (222-240 mm), of *pratensis* 236.3 mm (220-257 mm), and of *nesiotes* 200.0 mm (187-218 mm) (Walkinshaw, 1949). Aldrich (1979) provided comparable data for *rowani*. Wings of males average 497.3 mm (482-525 mm); females 474.25 mm (456-492 mm). Exposed culmens of males average 118.6 mm (109-127 mm); females 103 mm (93-114 mm). Tarsi of males average 226.8 mm (203-240 mm); females 212.25 mm (210-215 mm). Eggs of *canadensis* average 90.45 × 57.32 mm; of *tabida* 96.24 × 61.00 mm, of *pratensis* 92.46 × 59.33 mm, of *pulla* 95.96 × 58.55 mm, of *nesiotes* 87.94 × 57.13 mm, and of *rowani* 91.69 × 59.27 mm (Walkinshaw, 1973).

Weights. A sample of 15 adult males and 19 adult females of *rowani* averaged 4,079 and 3,775 grams respectively, while 27 adult males and 25 adult females of *canadensis* averaged 3,746 and 3,355 grams (Lewis, 1979a). The average weight of 46 adult males of *canadensis* shot during winter in New Mexico was 3,515 grams, and that of 50 adult females was 3,203 grams (Boeker, Aldrich, and Huey, 1961). Six males of *tabida* averaged 5,385 grams (range 4,762-5,895 grams) and four females averaged 4,308 grams (range 3,628-4,988 grams). One female of *pratensis* weighed 3,741 grams, and two males weighed 4,081 and 4,988 grams (Walkinshaw, 1973). Adult males of *rowani* range from 3.5 to 5.2 kilograms, and adult females from 3.4 to 4.5 kilograms (Tebbel and Ankney, 1979). Hand-reared birds at 70 days of age averaged 2,823 grams in *rowani*, 2,982 grams in *canadensis*, 3,086 grams in *pratensis*, and 3,268 grams in *tabida* (Archibald and Viess, 1979). The estimated egg weights are 158 grams (*nesiotes*), 164 grams (*canadensis*), 178 grams (*rowani*), 180 grams (*pratensis*), 189 grams (*pulla*) and 204 grams (*tabida*). Egg weights of *canadensis* averaged 138.3 grams, of *rowani* 173 grams, of *pulla* 147.9 grams, of *pratensis* 164.4 grams, of *nesiotes* 133.2 grams, and of *tabida* 196.19 grams; of these only the weights of *tabida* are specifically of fresh eggs. Weights of chicks include six *pratensis* and *pulla*, averaging 101.1 grams, 4 probable *rowani*, averaging 107.7 grams, and 58 *tabida*, averaging 115.1 grams (Walkinshaw, 1973).

Description

Adults of both sexes are alike, with a bare reddish forehead, lores, and crown to just below the eyes, with sparse blackish bristles. The cheeks, ear coverts, chin, and upper throat are white to pale gray. The nape is pale gray to whitish, and the mantle, scapulars, upper wing coverts, tertials, and tail are pale slate gray, the feathers darker toward their tips. The back, rump, tail coverts, and underparts are pale ashy gray to brownish gray, the feathers broadly fringed with pale ashy gray. The wing feathers are ashy gray to dark slate, the latter color including the primaries, greater primary coverts, and alula. Especially in summer, much of the plumage is often heavily stained with rusty, except on the head and underwing. The iris is reddish to brownish, the bill is dull gray to olive gray, and the legs and toes are blackish.

Juveniles and *immatures* during the first autumn and early winter are similar to adults, but many of the body and wing feathers are washed with ocher or tawny toward their tips, and the head and upper neck area are pinkish to cinnamon. The crown, occiput, and nape are covered with tawny feathers, and there are short gray feathers on the forehead. The tertials are shorter than in adults but are molted by early winter, and from autumn onward the new plumage of the neck and head are essentially grayish, with cinnamon tips. The iris is gray brown to reddish brown. Immatures in late winter and early spring have partially to mostly bare foreheads, and the rest of the plumage is also adultlike, with only scattered brownish juvenile feathers on the wings and body. By this time there has been a complete molt except for the primaries, secondaries, some wing coverts, and the rectrices. Rust-stained feathers of adults may resemble the partially tawny wing coverts of juveniles, but the staining of adults lacks patterning, while that of juveniles often forms distinct patterns (Lewis, 1979d). *Second-year immatures* from autumn to spring resemble adults, but have some old brown feathers retained on the body and upper wing surface, and may also retain some juvenile flight feathers (Cramp and Simmon, 1980; Lewis, 1979d).

Downy chicks are generally tawny, becoming burnt sienna on the occiput and light buffy white or light gray on the sides of the face and the forehead, with a darker line beneath the eye, enlarging to a spot on the lores. A dark brownish area extends from the occiput to the rump. The throat is white, and the breast and underwings are dull grayish white. The bill is dull flesh, and the legs and toes are initially flesh-colored, while the iris is brown. By about 50 days, the bill is pinkish buff, with a vinaceous cinnamon base, and the legs and toes are a darker pinkish buff (Walkinshaw, 1973). Fledging occurs at about 70 days in the greater sandhill crane (Walkinshaw, 1949), and probably in not less than 60 days in the lesser (Boise, 1976).

Identification

In the field, this is the common wild crane of North America, and is almost uniformly light gray, with a reddish crown patch and black legs, and whitish cheeks. Its calls are rattling, and fairly high-pitched in the lesser sandhill, but louder and more resonating in the larger races.

In the hand, this is the only uniformly gray-bodied crane that is totally feathered on the head except for the crown. Its trachea is coiled inside the sternum.

DISTRIBUTION AND HABITATS

Historic Breeding Range

Walkinshaw (1949) has summarized the historical status of the major sandhill crane populations of North America. Little can be said of the lesser sandhill crane's historic range, since Walkinshaw was able to find only a handful of breeding records prior to 1920 (ranging from the tip of the Chukotski Peninsula of the USSR to eastern Baffin Island), which collectively would suggest that there have been no major range changes since that time. The breeding range is now known to extend considerably farther west in the USSR than is indicated by Walkinshaw's map, but this is possibly the result of improved information rather than actual range changes. According to him (1973) the subspecies' known breeding range extends from Wrangell Island and extreme northeastern Siberia, across much of western Alaska, some of the Aleutians, south possibly to northern Kamchatka and Cook Inlet, Alaska, and east across Canada to Banks, Victoria, and Southampton Islands, and south to southern Mackenzie, Keewatin, western Hudson Bay, and possibly to the Hudson Bay drainage of western and northern Ontario. Most of these areas represent arctic tundra habitats.

At the time of Walkinshaw's monograph on the sandhill cranes, the Canadian sandhill crane was still undescribed, and his later (1973) description of this race assigned the birds of intermediate size between lesser and greater sandhill cranes to this race, most of which in his opinion probably breed in central Saskatchewan, central Alberta, or central Manitoba, and possibly also nest in eastern British Columbia or northern Ontario. The indefinite morphological limits of this subspecies

make it impossible to judge its previous or current range limits. Aldrich (1979) reviewed over 400 specimens and concluded that the form's known range occurs in aspen parklands and boreal forests from central southern Mackenzie District and central Alberta eastward through northern and central Saskatchewan, central Manitoba, and northern Ontario to James Bay. The limits may also extend farther to the northwest than available records indicate.

Walkinshaw (1949) reported that the greater sandhill crane was formerly found throughout southern British Columbia, central and southern Alberta, Saskatchewan, northern Manitoba, southwestern Ontario, and Michigan south to northeastern California, northern Nevada, Arizona, northern Utah, northwestern Colorado, Nebraska, Iowa, Illinois, Indiana, and central Ohio. It disappeared from many of these areas in the late 1800s and early 1900s, disappearing as breeding birds from Nebraska in the 1880s and from Arizona about 1910. They also became extirpated as nesting birds from South Dakota (1910), Iowa (1905), Illinois (1890), Indiana (1929), and Ohio (1926), and virtually disappeared from North Dakota, where single pairs have been observed breeding at rare intervals. It is not known when they disappeared from southwestern Ontario, where they were apparently rare nesters even in early days (Walkinshaw, 1949), and have evidently recently reinvaded.

The Florida sandhill crane formerly bred as far west as southern Louisiana. The birds were probably never common in Alabama, where they were last reported nesting in 1911, and once occurred northward to southern Georgia, from Okefenokee Swamp to Wakulla County. The crane population of the Okefenokee Swamp dwindled until the area was made into a refuge in 1936, and thereafter began a slow increase (Walkinshaw, 1949).

Nothing is known of the historical range of the Mississippi sandhill crane, which was not formally described until 1972. It is possible that the birds breeding in southern Louisiana were of this species, and even more probably the population of southern Alabama may have belonged to this subspecies. Cranes with chicks were seen in southern Louisiana as late as 1918. They were found nesting in Mississippi in 1938, but it was not until the 1960s that the birds were suspected to be a distinct subspecies. By that time the total population was believed to number less than 50 birds, and the entire breeding range was determined to be limited to the area between the Pascagoula River and the Harrison-Jackson county line (Walkinshaw, 1973; Valentine and Noble, 1970).

The historical status of the Cuban sandhill crane is also extremely obscure. However, all of the available nesting records are from the Isle of Pines (Walkinshaw, 1973). It also probably was a resident of the provinces of

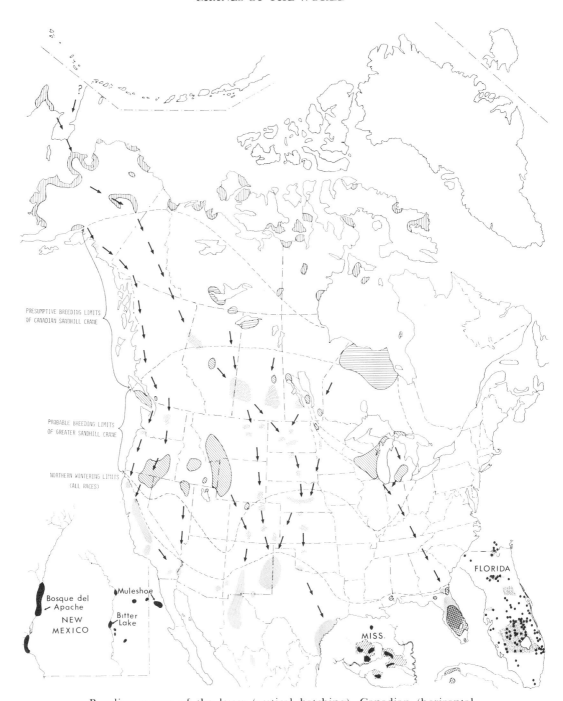

Breeding ranges of the lesser (vertical hatching), Canadian (horizontal hatching), and greater (diagonal hatching) sandhill cranes, and residential distributions of Mississippi, Florida, and Cuban sandhill cranes (cross-hatching). Fine shading indicates major wintering areas of migratory races, and coarse stippling indicates migratory staging areas. Insets show locality records and concentration areas (stippled) of Florida sandhill cranes, breeding areas (and associated refuge limits) of Mississippi sandhill cranes, and wintering concentration areas in New Mexico.

Pinar del Rio, Habana, Matanzas, Santa Clara, and western Camaguey (Walkinshaw, 1949).

Current Breeding Range

Presently it is believed that the lesser sandhill crane still nests over most or all of its historical range in North America, from western Alaska to the Hudson Bay area of Canada. The Siberian breeding population has recently been found to be considerably larger than had been generally appreciated. As early as 1909 the birds were observed in pairs during summer as far west as Kilyuchin Bay, and in the early 1970s were found to be a common nester in that general area (Krechmar, Andreev and Kondrat'ev, 1978). It is not yet known to be a definite nester on Wrangel Island (Portenko, 1981), although pairs or individuals have been observed summering as far west as the Indigirka River. The total Soviet population probably now numbers about 20,000 individuals and may still be dispersing westward (USSR Crane Working Group Information Bulletin No. 2, 1981). Its eastern breeding limits in North America are apparently on Baffin Island, where it is rare, and in the vicinity of Churchill, Manitoba (Walkinshaw, 1981a).

The current known range of the Canadian sandhill crane was described in the previous section.

Walkinshaw (1981a) has summarized the present known breeding range and status of the greater sandhill crane. Little is known of the British Columbia segment, but a few are known to nest at Pitt Meadows. In Oregon the birds nest in Malheur, Harney, Lake, Grant, Baker, Union, Deschutes, and Klamath counties, and in California in Modoc, Lassen, Siskiyou, Sierra, Plumas, and Shasta counties. This population winters in California and consists of some 3,000 to 3,200 birds, exclusive of any from British Columbia and Washington (Littlefield and Thompson, 1979).

The Nevada breeding population is centered in Elko County, and the birds winter along the Colorado River near Poston, Arizona (Drewien, Oakleaf, and Mullins, 1976). This population probably consists of more than 1,000 birds.

The major Rocky Mountain population nests from northeastern Utah northward along the Idaho-Wyoming border to southwestern Montana, and in the early 1970s was estimated to consist of some 10,000 to 15,000 birds (Drewien, 1973). A small extension of this population, of about 250 birds, also occurs in northwestern Montana in Routt, Moffat, and Jackson counties (Beiniasz, 1979).

There was a single breeding record of sandhill cranes in North Dakota in 1973 (Johnson, 1976), but this state must still be considered extralimital for sandhill crane breeding. In Minnesota there were about 70 pairs plus nearly 150 nonbreeders in 1977, scattered over Anoka,

Aitkin, Beltrami, Chisago, Kanabec, Lake of the Woods, Mahnomen, Marshall, Mille Lacs, Morrison, Kittson, Pine, Sherbourne, Penington, Polk, and Roseau counties (Grewe, 1977).

The current status of the sandhill crane in Wisconsin has improved from a situation of perhaps as few as 25 pairs present in 1936 to an estimated 1,000 birds in 1973, including 250 pairs in 32 counties (Hunt and Gleusing, 1976). In the late 1970s nesting was reported from northeastern Illinois for the first time in this century (Walkinshaw, 1981b).

The Michigan population now includes an Upper Peninsula segment of about 130 pairs occurring over some 218 square miles of the eastern part of the peninsula (Tayler, 1977). Walkinshaw (1978) recorded crane nests from Alger, Baraga, Chippewa, Delta, Luce, Mackinac, and Schoolcraft counties, and observed a general trend of population increase and spread in recent years. The birds have also recently moved into adjacent Ontario, where they are again nesting (Tebbel and Ankney, 1979), and have spread south into the Lower Peninsula, breeding as far as Cheboygan County and possibly to Mason County (Walkinshaw, 1981b). Elsewhere on the Lower Peninsula, Walkinshaw (1981b) reported cranes nesting since 1930 in Mason, Clinton, Shiawassee, Barry, Eaton, Ingham, Livingston, Kalamazoo, Calhoun, Jackson, Washtenaw, St. Joseph and Branch counties, and during the past few years nests have also been found in the southern tier of Michigan counties.

Evidence of the great increase in greater sandhill populations in the eastern states comes from surveys of fall populations at the Jasper-Pulaski Game Area, in northwestern Indiana, where the birds increased from 35 in 1935 to about 14,000 by the fall of 1979. This area is the only known major fall staging ground for the eastern population, and probably includes birds from breeding areas in Michigan, Wisconsin, Minnesota, Ontario, and perhaps Manitoba (Shroufe, 1976).

The population of the Florida sandhill cranes has recently benefited from improved protection, and probably numbers at least 5,000 birds. Many of these are in large refuges, including Okefenokee National Wildlife Refuge, in Georgia, and Payne's Prairie (Alachua County), Three-lakes Wildlife Area (Osceola County), Avon Park Wildlife Area (Polk and Highland counties), Fish-eating Creek Wildlife Management Area (Glades County), and Loxahatchee National Wildlife Refuge (Palm Beach County). However, the other old breeding areas are disappearing as a result of human use, and thus the situation is a mixed one (Walkinshaw, 1981b).

In Mississippi, the crane population continues to remain at a low but stable level of about 40 to 50 birds, but has been helped by the establishment of the Mississippi Sandhill Crane National Wildlife Refuge in 1974. Twenty nesting territories have been located since 1965, but at least nine have apparently been deserted (Valentine, 1979).

No new information on the status of the Cuban sandhill crane is available, but Walkinshaw believed that in the early 1950s there were probably 100 birds on the Isle of Pines, with the greatest concentration near Los Indios. The mainland population was then probably much lower, but has more recently begun to increase or at least has remained stable (Walkinshaw, 1981a).

Breeding Habitat Requirements and Densities

Breeding habitats of the lesser sandhill crane are lowland tundra and associated marshes, shorelines of rivers, lakes, and coastal areas, and grassy slopes up to about 1000 meters elevation. In some areas, such as on southern Banks Island, in arctic Canada, the birds nest on grass-covered sand dunes, and they also often nest in muskeg areas where there are open, sedge or moss-covered areas surrounded by spruces and with scattered bushes present (Walkinshaw, 1973). On the Yukon-Kuskokwim Delta the birds were found nesting on two general habitat types, heath-marsh mosaic tundra areas and sedge-grass meadows. Most nesting occurs in wet marshes of the mosaic tundra areas and in the sedge-grass meadows, but extends onto dry heath tundra. Nesting density was found to range from 0.54 to 0.74 nests per square kilometer during two years of study, with aerial surveys suggesting a minimum density of 1.5 birds per square kilometer over a 1,250 square kilometer area (Boise, 1977).

The Canadian sandhill crane nests in inaccessible bulrush marshes or muskeg areas vegetated with dwarf birches (*Betula pumila*) and tamaracks (*Larix laricina*). In Mackenzie District the birds appear to prefer extensive bulrush cover and associated shallow marshes, while in the James Bay area of Ontario they have been observed nesting in sphagnum bogs, among tamaracks and associated heather vegetation. This general sort of vegetation is scattered but widespread across western and central Canada, allowing for a dispersed but fairly substantial total population (Aldrich, 1979). Carlisle (1982) has described the sedge-marsh nesting habitats of sandhill cranes in central Alberta, which may be referable to this race.

The greater sandhill crane's breeding habitats in the western states consist of open mountain parks in coniferous forests, willow-dotted streams in sagebrush areas, extensive shallow freshwater marshes in sagebrush or arid grasslands, beaver ponds and associated wetland habitats, and other similar habitats. Their densest known concentrations occur at Gray's Lake, Idaho, where about 200 pairs nest within an area of about 10,000 hectares, and territory sizes average only about 17

hectares (Drewien, 1973). By comparison, territories at Malheur National Wildlife Refuge in Oregon were estimated to average about 25 hectares (62 acres), according to Littlefield and Ryder (1968).

Walkinshaw (1973) judged that in Michigan the territories he studied on the Lower Peninsula have averaged about 53 hectares (132 acres) and those on the Upper Peninsula about 85 hectares (210 acres). He believed that an essential territorial component is fresh water (pH 5.0-7.6), with preferred depths of from a few inches to two or three feet near the nesting site. The plant cover usually consists of sedges (*Carex*), grasses, cattails (*Typha*), rushes (*Scirpus*), and reeds (*Phragmites*), at least in southern Michigan and Wisconsin. However, in northern Michigan the typical breeding habitat consists of bogs, with associated heath vegetation (*Ledum, Kalmia, Andromeda*) and such trees as tamaracks, pines, and black spruce (*Picea mariana*). Generally nesting densities are quite low; Taylor's (1977) estimate of 130 pairs in 56,486 hectares suggests an overall density of a pair per 434 hectares over large areas. Walkinshaw (1981a) stated that although cranes in Michigan only used larger (324-810 hectare) marshes during the early years of his studies, they recently have begun to move into smaller marshes, including some less than 5 hectares in area.

The Florida sandhill crane nests in pond areas associated with prairies dominated by saw palmettos (*Serenoa repens*) and scattered wooded hammocks that support cabbage palms (*Sabal palmetto*), pines, oaks, and wetland trees such as magnolias and cypress (*Taxodium distichum*). Most nesting apparently occurs on shallow-water ponds grown up thickly to emergent vegetation such as pickerelweed (*Pontedaria*), bog-button (*Lachnoculon*), pipewort (*Ericaulon*), goldies (*Xyris*), rushes (*Juncus*), arrowleaf (*Sagittaria*), maiden-cane (*Panicum*), saw-grass (*Cladium*), cattail (*Typha*), and spike rush (*Eleocharis*). The average pond size of nests studied by Walkinshaw was 3.9 hectares, ranging from 0.2 to 18.2 hectares. However, at the Loxahatchee Wildlife Refuge the birds nest mainly in an area where the wet prairie "tree island" zone is located within a surrounding wet prairie matrix of sawgrass and slough communities (Walkinshaw, 1973). In the central area of Florida the nesting population of cranes was estimated by Walkinshaw (1976) to consist of from 96 to 107 pairs of birds on 123,000 hectares in 14 different sites, suggesting a general density of about a pair per 1,200 hectares. Excluding land that does not provide suitable crane habitat, the actual density was probably about twice that great, and the pairs tended to be separated by average distances of about 1.6 kilometers.

Studies of the Mississippi sandhill crane by Valentine (1979; 1981) indicate that about 20 territories (some of which have been abandoned) occur on 11 general areas in Jackson County. Nesting habitats consist of swamps and prairie-like savannas surrounded by natural pine forests or pine plantations. The planting of trees on most of the native savanna has restricted the breeding range recently, as has natural succession of brush, bald-cypress, and pines, which tend to close over the swamp savanna vegetation. Density estimates are not available, but one swampy area of about 324 hectares supported three nests in one year, and another area of 364 hectares supported two nests in one year. One small savanna only about 4 hectares in area, surrounded by swamp and pine forests, also supported a nest territory one year (Valentine, 1981). Generally the habitats and territorial requirements of this form would seem to be very much like those of the Florida race.

In Cuba, the birds nest in relatively dry habitats that are typically parklike and sparingly grown to shrubs and trees, although some open prairie habitat does occur. Nests have been found on dry ground, as in bottle palm (*Colpothrinax*) flats along grass-covered arroyos, or in dry and sandy lowland situations, with an abundance of dead grasses and scattered trees such as tropical pines, palmettos, (*Acoelorraphe*) and various shrubs (Walkinshaw, 1973). In one area Walkinshaw found eight pairs in an area of 3,108 hectares (a pair per 388 hectares), while in another he found three pairs in an area of two square miles (a pair per 173 hectares). No other comparable concentrations were found by him.

Wintering Range and Habitats

Walkinshaw (1949) described the wintering range of the lesser sandhill crane as extending from central California, central New Mexico, and the panhandle of Texas south at least into Baja California, San Luis Potosi, and Jalisco, and perhaps as far south as the Central Valley of Mexico. About 20,000 to 23,000 currently winter in the Central Valley of California, especially in San Joaquin County (Littlefield and Thompson, 1979). The largest numbers of sandhill cranes wintering in Mexico are probably found in Chihuahua (Lewis, 1977), and no significant numbers are known to winter in northeastern Mexico to the south of their known wintering areas in southern Texas (Aldrich, 1979). However, the major concentration areas for many decades have been Bitter Lake National Wildlife Refuge, in Chaves County, New Mexico, and Muleshoe National Wildlife Refuge, in Bailey County, Texas. The wintering flock at Bitter Lake dates back at least to the 1940s, when about 11,000 birds were known to winter there. Similar numbers of 8,000 to 15,000 were also present during the same period at Muleshoe Refuge, while smaller numbers wintered along the Texas coast, including about 1,500 in the Aransas area (including unknown numbers of Canadian and greater sandhill cranes).

Recent studies of the birds wintering on the coast of Texas indicate that lesser and Canadian sandhill cranes winter all along the Texas coast from the Mexican border to Houston, while the greater sandhill winters mainly from Aransas County eastward. The total wintering population in the early 1970s was estimated to be approximately 4,350 lessers, 15,550 Canadian, and 2,000 greaters (Guthery and Lewis, 1979). It is thus apparent that the majority of the lesser sandhill cranes winter in interior Texas and adjacent New Mexico.

Buller (1979) summarized late fall population survey data of sandhill cranes in eastern New Mexico and western Texas taken from 1960 to 1976 and indicating peak concentrations in these two states that usually ranged between 110,000 and 340,000 birds, with very large year-to-year differences. Some of the areas in New Mexico where the birds roost during winter in addition to the Bitter Lake area include Lewiston Lake, Salt Lake, Bottomless Lakes, Dexter Slough, and the Ft. Sumner area of Pecos River. Major wintering areas in western Texas besides Muleshoe Refuge include Rich Lake, Mound Lake, Double Lakes, Cedar Lake, Coyote Lake, and Baileyboro Lake (Boeker et al., 1961). Nearly all of these winter roosting areas are shallow, alkaline lakes with grain sorghum fields nearby in which the birds forage. A substantial number of sandhill cranes also winter in the Central Highlands of Mexico; Buller (1982) reported from 5,745 to 33,315 birds in 1977-1981 surveys.

It is likely that a substantial percentage of the cranes currently assigned to the Canadian race winter along the Gulf Coast of Texas, since, as mentioned earlier, an estimated 15,550 of the cranes studied in the Gulf Coast area by Guthery and Lewis (1979) were judged to be of the Canadian race, or about 70 percent of the total wintering population. Populations of at least 1,000 birds were reported from Fort Brent, Colorado, Wharton, Matagorda, Lavaca, Jackson, Calhoun, Karnes, Arkansas, Kellberg, Hidalgo, and Cameron counties. While wintering in coastal Texas the birds concentrate in coastal areas and a short distance inland, feeding in such habitats as ephemeral ponds and marshes, coastal scrub oak, and post oak savanna. They also forage in agricultural fields of rice, sorghum, and a few other crops, but the most important energy sources for the birds are native plants, especially nutgrasses (*Cyperus*), with rice and sorghum of secondary importance (Guthery, 1976). Favored wintering habitats in southern Texas typically consist of large and fairly inaccessible bodies of water, broad tracts of land in native vegetation, and nearby fields under intensive crop production (Aldrich, 1979).

Wintering areas of the greater sandhill crane are widely scattered. The Central Valley of California supports about 3,000 birds, in an area extending from about 10 miles southwest of Chico, Butte County, south and east to near Delano, Tulare County. The largest numbers winter just south of Thornton, in San Joaquin County, with Butte County supporting the next largest concentrations. Progressively smaller numbers winter in Stanislaus, Merced, and Tulare counties (Littlefield and Thompson, 1979).

Eastward, the central Rio Grande Valley, particularly the vicinity of Bosque del Apache National Wildlife Refuge in New Mexico, is a major wintering area for birds of the Rocky Mountain population (Drewien, 1973; Drewien and Bizeau, 1974). Few, if any, of the cranes wintering in the eastern counties of New Mexico and the western counties of Texas are of the greater subspecies (Boeker et al., 1961). However, a few greater sandhill cranes winter along the eastern coast of Texas, especially from Aransas County eastward, where perhaps 2,000 birds of these races were judged present in the early 1970s (Guthery and Lewis, 1979). There is also a small wintering flock of sandhill cranes in coastal Louisiana (Smith, 1979), although their subspecific identity is not yet known.

Greater sandhill crane wintering areas in Florida have recently been studied by use of radio-tracking methods (Toepler and Crete, 1979), and 22 use areas supporting over 4,000 cranes have thereby been located in that state. All these roosts were shallow freshwater wetlands within 9.6 kilometers of wetland and upland foraging areas, and they extend from Baker and Lafayette counties in the north to Indian River and Highland counties in the south. Among the most heavily used sites were Emeralda Marsh, Lake County; Church Lake Prairie, Marion County; Rhodes Dairy, Lake County; and James Hill Farm, Highland County, all of which supported in excess of 300 birds during the period of study. Probably the most important single wintering area is Payne's Prairie, Alachua County (Williams and Phillips, 1972).

FOODS AND FORAGING BEHAVIOR

Foods of Adults

Some information on the seasonal foods of sandhill cranes may be found in table 7; this table includes immature birds as well as adults, and includes birds representing the greater (Idaho), lesser (Nebraska), and Canadian (Texas) races. There is little reason to believe that any significant differences exist in the races as to preferred foods, and it is evident that sandhill cranes tend to be able to adjust their diets to the local sources of abundant vegetable foods, especially grain crops when they are available. It is clear that, for example, corn provides the single most important source of food energy among lesser sandhill cranes during their spring stopover in Nebraska, and probably contributed about 96 percent of the total daily food intake per bird during this important period of their spring migration (Reinecke and Krapu, 1979). Since corn contains only about 10 percent protein, the birds apparently supplement their protein intake somewhat by foraging on various invertebrates, which comprise nearly all of the remaining food materials that the birds consume during this period, according to Reinecke and Krapu. Lewis's (1979a) studies in the same area indicate a similarly high (89 percent) proportion of corn among the dietary components, and he noted that corn has a high net energy value, as much as 80 percent nitrogen-free extract, and it is an excellent food for fattening poultry. Lewis suggested that this high corn diet in spring may be an important factor in the substantial weight gain that the birds put on while in the Platte Valley, and Iverson, Tacha, and Vohs (1982) also suggest that the high energy values of cereal grains are an important aspect of crane survival strategies in winter and spring.

Food of Young

No special studies of the foods of young sandhill cranes have been undertaken, but by the time the young are migrating during the fall they appear to be eating essentially the same foods as the adult birds. None of the several food-analysis studies done on migrating or wintering sandhill cranes has reported any age-associated food intake variations. Walkinshaw (1949) described the food of a chick that he raised as including earthworms and beetles by the time it was three weeks old. It also ate mosquitos, spiders, grubs, moths, millers, and some houseflies. By about a month of age it was very fond of earthworms and would eat as many as 400 in a single day. At this time it was also eating crickets, katydids, and short-horned grasshoppers on an everyday basis, as well as other foods.

When over three months old it began to eat sweet corn, and within a week was eating an ear per day. Later in the fall it consumed mainly scratch food such as wheat and cracked corn, but it also consumed fruit and vegetables such as carrots, lettuce, and celery. Walkinshaw summarized information on the food of dependent young wild cranes, suggesting that earthworms are probably an important source of food under natural conditions, and that grasshoppers and other insects are also probably eaten regularly.

Foraging Behavior

Sandhill cranes forage primarily on land, and do a great deal of digging with their bills when necessary to extract materials from under the soil. More often, they feed on visible food from the soil's surface. Large pieces of food, including live prey, are broken into smaller bits by piercing them or threshing them against the ground. Smaller pieces of food are delicately picked up from the ground with the tip of the bill, then tossed into the air and caught farther back in the bill, where they can be more readily handled and swallowed (Walkinshaw, 1949; 1973).

MIGRATIONS AND MOVEMENTS

Seasonal Movements

Walkinshaw (1949, 1973) described the migratory patterns of both greater and lesser sandhill cranes in great detail, and rather little needs to be added to update his very complete summaries. The migration of the lesser sandhill crane from Siberia and the northernmost portions of Canada begins in late August, reaches a peak during the third week of August, and after the middle of September begins to decline, until the last birds leave after mid-October (Stephen, 1967). At about the same time large numbers of birds build up in North Dakota, especially in Kidder, Stutsman, and McLean counties, with smaller numbers in various areas of eastern Montana (Bowdoin, Medicine Lake, and C.M. Russell National Wildlife Refuges). The birds move southward across eastern Wyoming and the western parts of South Dakota and Nebraska to eastern Colorado and central Kansas, with birds arriving in the Arkansas Valley by mid-September to mid-October and in various refuges of Kansas (Kirwin, Quivira) between mid-October and late November. A few areas in Oklahoma (Salt Plains and Washita National Wildlife Refuges, as well as the Red River bottoms) are usually stopping points before the birds arrive in the New Mexico, Texas, and Chihuahua wintering areas (Buller, 1967).

The spring migration takes a rather different form, with the vast majority if not virtually all of the lesser sandhills wintering east of the Rocky Mountains stopping in the Platte Valley of Nebraska for approximately six weeks, from late February or early March until the second week of April (Frith, 1974, 1976). During that period perhaps all but the approximately 20,000 or so lessers wintering in California, or at least 90 percent of the entire lesser sandhill crane population, are concentrated into a relatively few river miles (U.S. Fish and Wildlife Service, 1981). Spring surveys along the Platte River between 1959 and 1978 indicate peak populations of from about 80,000 to 225,000 birds, averaging nearly 160,000, although a few larger estimates of the mid-continental sandhill crane population have been made, such as Lewis (1979b), who believed that the number of birds in the entire Central Flyway area approached 400,000 in 1976, which would include both lesser and Canadian sandhill cranes. In any case, after the birds leave Nebraska in the first half of April they begin to spread out, and there is no comparable staging area farther north during the spring migration.

The migration routes of the Canadian race are still only very poorly understood, but it is believed that virtually all these birds also have their spring staging area in Nebraska as well (Krapu, 1979). Lewis (1979a) judged that the Canadian race is more abundant at the eastern end (Overton to Grand Island area) of the central Platte Valley, while the lessers are more common to the west. A few greater sandhill cranes may also stop along the Platte Valley between Wood River and Chapman, perhaps from the population nesting in Manitoba and wintering in eastern Texas and Oklahoma. Most of the birds that stop in the Platte Valley must still fly anywhere from 1,280 to 5,440 kilometers (795-3,380 miles) to reach their nesting areas, and thus the fattening process that they undergo there may be of particular importance to their physical condition at the critical time of reproduction (Lewis 1949a).

Three major migratory routes are known for the greater sandhill cranes. One leads from nesting areas in Oregon and California to relatively nearby wintering areas in California (Littlefield and Thompson, 1979). A second extends from the northern Rocky Mountain breeding population concentrated in Idaho, Montana, and Wyoming to wintering areas in the central Rio Grande Valley of New Mexico, with a stopover in the San Luis Valley of southern Colorado (Drewien and Bizeau, 1974). The third route, probably followed by all of the greater sandhill cranes nesting from Minnesota to Michigan and adjoining areas, funnels initially into the Jasper-Pulaski Fish and Wildlife area near Medaryville, Indiana (Shroufe, 1976), and then continues more or less directly southeastward across Kentucky, Tennessee, Georgia, and on into Florida (Toepler and Crete, 1979; Nesbitt and Williams, 1979). The return route in spring is probably very similar to the fall route (Williams and Phillips, 1972), although less extensive use of the Jasper-Pulaski area occurs at that time of year.

The remaining populations, the Florida, Mississippi, and Cuban sandhill cranes, are all believed to be essentially sedentary.

Daily Movements

Studies by Toepler and Crete (1979) on radio-tagged greater sandhill cranes indicated that at least five birds flew some 584 kilometers in 9.5 hours (from Chattanooga, Tennessee, to Impassible Bay, Florida) without stopping. During spring migration, one pair of birds migrated 850 kilometers in 55 hours, and made two overnight stops en route from the Jasper-Pulaski area to its breeding marsh in central Minnesota. The birds seemed generally to migrate during clear to partly cloudy weather, flew from 272 to 484 kilometers per day, and landed before sundown. Only a few birds migrated into headwinds or crosswinds, and most apparently migrated at altitudes of from 50 to 1000 meters. Melvin and Temple (1982) stated that most migration occurs within 1,600 meters of the ground, and that daily flights of 48 to 740 kilometers have been documented.

GENERAL BIOLOGY

Sociality

Information on relative sociality in sandhill cranes can be extracted from average flock sizes under various conditions. Walkinshaw (1949) reported flock sizes of lesser sandhill cranes leaving and arriving at winter roosts in eastern New Mexico and Texas. His data would suggest that flocks leaving roosts at dawn average from 16 to 20 birds, while similar counts made during return flights to roosts in evening indicate average flock sizes of about 35 birds. These sizes are, of course, highly variable, and it is probable that in part they reflect relative security; the largest flock sizes seem to be those associated with wintering birds in refuge areas. By comparison, Bliese (1976) reported daytime flock sizes in spring during the birds' stopover period in the Platte Valley. These counts, made of standing and flying birds in field-feeding situations, indicate a much smaller flock size, with over 77 percent of the flocks having 50 or fewer birds, and 84 percent having no more than 100. The most common social units reported by Bliese were groups of two birds (11.7 percent of the total) and three birds (9.6 percent), supporting the general idea that the pair and family group are probably the nuclear units of crane flocks.

Daily Activities

In sandhill cranes the daily flights to and from roosts are closely tied to light levels. Walkinshaw's (1949) data on morning and evening flights at the Bitter Lake National Wildlife Refuge, for example, suggest that most birds left the roost shortly after sunrise, and there was a massive evening return immediately around the period of sunset. Almost certainly light levels, rather than sunrise or sunset per se, are the critical factor, for in the Platte River area the cranes always begin returning to the river before sunset on cloudy days, but often wait until a half hour or later beyond sunset on sunny days with extended periods of twilight.

When foraging, the birds tend to form generally linear flock shapes, although this is quite variable, and many other flock conformations also occur (Bliese, 1976).

Interspecific Interactions

Walkinshaw (1949) judged that only a few predators probably affect nesting success of lesser sandhill cranes, including such types as wolves, foxes, dogs, jaegers, hawks, eagles, and owls. He believed that jaegers (*Stercorarius* spp.) might be the most significant avian egg predator of the lesser sandhill crane, and that crows and ravens might also be significant predators, at least for greater sandhill cranes. Among Florida sandhill cranes, raccoons are probably the most common predator of nesting birds, although various snakes and crocodiles might perhaps also pose a danger. There are no wild mammalian predators such as wolves or foxes in Cuban sandhill habitats, and very few dogs; Walkinshaw pointed out that it is under such conditions that the birds can nest successfully in dry areas, apparently requiring water only for drinking.

BREEDING BIOLOGY

Age of Maturity and Time of Breeding

The normal age of maturity in the wild is still uncertain, but semen has been obtained from hand-reared male birds that were only three years old (Archibald and Viess, 1979). A pair of sandhill cranes at Flamingo Gardens, in England, initially bred when the male was eight years old and the female six. Johnson (1979) assumed that both sexes of sandhill cranes begin to breed in the wild at four years of age, but this remains to be proven. It is quite possible that a small proportion, particularly males, may be able to breed at four or even three years, but several more years may be needed before all of the birds are successful at mating and establishing territories.

A substantial amount of information is available on the timing of breeding in the various races of sandhill cranes (see table 14), and not surprisingly there is a marked relationship between latitude and the onset as well as the duration of the nesting period, based on available egg records. The more southern populations of sandhill cranes not only begin nesting earlier but also have a much more prolonged egg-laying period. This perhaps reflects a considerable incidence of renesting behavior, although the incidence of renesting in these races is still undetermined. Walkinshaw (1965a) reported that in Michigan he located 82 nests in April, 37 in May, and one each in June and July. He judged that nests found in late May were second nesting efforts; three nests were listed as being found after May 20. Including the two June and July records, this would suggest that under 5 percent of the nests located were likely to have resulted from renesting. Limited studies of the lesser sandhill crane, however, have offered no firm evidence of renesting behavior in that race (Boise, 1977). Three probable cases of renesting have been reported in the Mississippi race (Valentine, 1982).

Pair Formation and Courtship

Walkinshaw (1965a) reported that little is known of the process of pair formation in cranes, but he judged that it occurred when the birds were about three years old. Thereafter the newly mated pairs probably spend a summer or more on their territories, usually in marshes unoccupied by resident birds. The sandhill cranes return to Michigan in pairs, and these immediately disperse to breeding territories after their spring arrival. Thus, pair-bonding must occur on wintering areas or during the rather brief spring migration.

Current evidence suggests that pair-bonding in this species is similar to that of other cranes, with the unison-call ceremony playing a vital role in the establishment and maintenance of pairs. Archibald's (1975,1976) descriptions indicate that the behavior in this species is significantly different from that of other *Grus* species to warrant its placement in a separate "species-group." In the sandhill crane, both sexes keep their wings completely folded during the display, and the only significant movements are the vertical head movements of the male, performed each time he utters a call-note. Typically the female begins the display with a long, pulsed call sounding something like machine-gun fire, and followed by a prolonged series of short calls uttered in synchrony with slightly longer calls by the male. Occasionally a male will raise his back feathers and also his inner wing feathers while calling during high-intensity threat situations. Both birds typically remain stationary during the entire ceremony.

Copulation in the sandhill crane takes the typical form found in other *Grus* species. Walkinshaw (1973) has observed copulation on several occasions, and noted that it is typically performed on the birds' breeding territories, and in all of five cases it occurred during morning hours. In every case the female approached the male with her head held low and assumed a receptive posture, with her neck extended forward at a 45-degree angle and her wings somewhat extended. The male swiftly approached, and copulated with his wings beating slowly. Littlefield and Ryder (1968) observed copulation on 25 occasions, and noted that it occurred at various times throughout the daytime period. On only two occasions was any dancing behavior associated with copulation, one occurring both before and after, and once only after.

Territoriality and Early Nesting Behavior

Walkinshaw (1965b) studied the territoriality of the greater sandhill crane in Michigan, and reported that the average territorial size of 76 breeding territories in the Lower Peninsula has been 132 acres, while 13 Upper Peninsula territories averaged 210 acres. By comparison, 7 territories of the Florida sandhill crane averaged about 103 acres, and 4 territories of greater sandhill cranes in Idaho averaged 161 acres. In a dense concentration of birds at Michigan's Phyllis Haehnle Memorial Sanctuary, 7 pairs usually nest each year in an area of only about 260 acres of actual marsh, and the average territory size over a five-year period was estimated by Walkinshaw to be about 43.5 acres. This is somewhat similar to the fairly dense territories reported by Drewein (1973) in the Gray's Lake area of Idaho, where 10 territories averaged 17 hectares (about 42 acres). Such territorial sizes probably approach the minimum generally acceptable to greater sandhill cranes, although Walkinshaw did estimate that some birds occupied territories as small as 8 acres. In the Phyllis Haehnle Sanctuary, the birds not only defended the wet marsh area but also used adjacent dry marsh areas after their young were hatched. When these dry areas are included in the estimates, 71 territories (counting the territories of each pair every year separately) averaged 39.62 acres, and ranged from 8 to 90 acres (Walkinshaw, 1973). Littlefield and Ryder (1968) estimated that the smallest territory in their study area in Oregon was 3 acres, and the largest was 168 acres, with 8 averaging 62 acres.

Walkinshaw (1965a) found that all of 120 greater sandhill crane nests he studied on Michigan's Lower Peninsula plus one in the Upper Peninsula were built in shallow-water marshes, typically among cattails and sedges. Twelve of 13 nests in the Upper Peninsula were built in bogs, usually of sticks and clumps of mosses. In that area, the period of nest construction requires approximately a week, and the nest is constructed by both birds working a few hours each day. Of 26 nests of the lesser sandhill crane studied by Boise (1977), most were on slightly raised mounds in wet marshes. However, the sites used ranged from shallow-water ones to some on dry tundra, and were generally in drier situations than those typical of greater, Florida, and Mississippi sandhill cranes. Relatively dry nest sites were also reported by Walkinshaw (1973) as seemingly typical of the Cuban sandhill crane. Over half of 49 nests in Michigan's Upper Peninsula analyzed by Walkinshaw (1981b) had no standing water beside them, but all were surrounded by water, and all were well isolated from humans. Nests in the Upper Peninsula bogs tend to be smaller than those built in marshes, and some nests built on dry land tend to be very small indeed. The size of the nest is evidently largely a reflection of the amount of water and associated vegetation immediately around the nest, and this is highly variable. Walkinshaw (1965c) noted that one lesser sandhill crane nest he observed on Banks Island merely consisted of a few pieces of willow torn from nearby plants, situated on the highest tundra mound in the vicinity. This nest contained the remnants of egg shells apparently from the year before, indicating that sandhill cranes sometimes use the same nest site in subsequent years.

Egg-laying and Incubation

In his Michigan studies, Walkinshaw (1965a) found that the eggs were laid from two to three days apart. As soon as the first egg is laid, incubation begins, and is performed alternately by both members of the pair. The attentive period of the cranes is to some extent regulated by the behavior of the nonincubating bird, since the incubating bird seldom leaves the nest until it is relieved by its mate. Walkinshaw found that male attentive periods averaged 215 minutes for 41 periods, and females averaged 195 minutes for 33 periods. The eggs were always found to be incubated during the night, and in four observed cases this was being performed by the male. The average nighttime attentiveness period for the five nests was 938 minutes. During the daytime hours the nests were found to be incubated for 97.6 percent of the observed time, and slightly over half of this daytime incubation was observed to be performed by the male. Daytime changeovers in incubation duties were found to range from once to seven times, and during 29 observation days the average number of changeovers was 3.6 times. There are evidently no changeovers during the nightime hours (Walkinshaw, 1965d, 1973).

Loss of clutches prior to hatching have been studied in various crane populations (table 35). In Walkinshaw's (1965a) Michigan studies, he noted that 73.8 percent of 107 nests were successful, and that 68.1 percent of 201 associated eggs hatched. If deserted nests are discounted, young hatched in 78 (81.2 percent) of 96 nests, and 134 eggs (74.4 percent) of a total of 180 hatched. In Michigan, raccoons were found to be the most serious predators of eggs. Raccoons were also reported to be serious egg predators in Oregon by Littlefield (1976), where coyotes are also present and were found to be minor egg predators but serious sources of mortality of young birds. Coyotes were also reported by Drewien (1973) to be significant predators in the Gray's Lake area of Idaho. Boise (1977) estimated that predators were responsible for the loss of 27.3 percent of the eggs of lesser sandhill cranes in western Alaska, where overall nesting success was estimated at 66.7 percent and hatching success was 63.6 percent. Gulls, jaegers, foxes, and Eskimos were considered probable nest predators in that area.

The incubation of greater sandhill cranes has been found to average 30 days under natural conditions, with a range of 28 to 32 days (Walkinshaw, 1981a). There is no evidence of significant variations in incubation among the various subspecies.

Hatching and Postbreeding Biology

Typically, a single day separates the time of hatching of the young in two-egg clutches. Newly hatched young are usually fed the eggshells from which they have hatched by the parent attending the nest, who breaks it up into very small pieces and feeds it to the young bill-to-bill. However, very little if any food is usually fed them on the first day. Yet, by the time they are about six hours old they often leave the nest a short distance, sometimes even swimming short distances. By the day after hatching the young are eating small items, and if the two eggs hatch on separate days the older chick often follows one of its parents away from the nest while the second one is being brooded. After both chicks are fairly strong they are generally taken away from the nest site by their parents, often into dry fields or drier marshy areas where insect foods are abundant (Walkinshaw, 1973).

TABLE 35

Sources of Nesting Losses in Greater Sandhill Cranes

	Idaho[1]	Oregon[2]	Michigan[3]	Michigan[4]
Total Failed Nests	71	255	45	31
Lost to:				
Predation:	47.9%	92.1%	31.1%	7%
Desertion	8.5%	7.1%	24.4%	10%
Eggs addled or infertile	18.3%	.4%	31.1%	72%
Flooding or weather loss	2.8%	.4%	6.7%	—
Unknown causes	22.5%	—	4.4%	11%

[1] Drewien, 1973.
[2] Littlefield, 1976.
[3] Walkinshaw, 1981a.
[4] Hoffman, 1979 (percentages are of egg losses rather than nest losses).

Fledging in the greater sandhill crane occurs at about three months of age. The exact time of fledging in lesser sandhill cranes is still unreported, but it is evidently longer than 60 days (Boise, 1976, 1977). In general, there is a relationship between the rate of development of young and the geographical distribution of the races, at least under captive rearing conditions (Baldwin, 1977a, b).

The rate of survival of young birds until autumn is probably fairly high in most cases. Walkinshaw (1981a) reported that 284 birds fledged out of 294 hatched young among Lower Peninsula nests, again suggesting a very high (96.5 percent) fledging rate. By comparison, Boise (1977) reported that 57 percent of the lesser sandhill crane chicks she observed in 1975 survived to fledging, while in 1976 the figure was 71 percent.

RECRUITMENT RATES, POPULATION STATUS, AND CONSERVATION

Based on studies from 1952 to 1973, Walkinshaw (1981a) noted that during late summer the greater sandhill crane population in Michigan consisted of about 55 percent adult breeders, 16.6 percent fledged young, and 51 percent nonbreeders. This would mean that, on average, each breeding pair raised an average of 0.6 young to fledging during those years. This is a considerably smaller productivity rate than is indicated by hatching and rearing success rates estimated by him for the same area, suggesting that these rates are probably not representative for the Michigan crane population as a whole. Instead, a collective success rate of approximately 40 to 60 percent of the total eggs laid resulting in fledged young would seem to be typical of sandhill cranes, assuming that all of the paired birds lay two eggs, and that paired birds make up approximately half of the nonjuvenile population. This in turn would mean that the incidence of juveniles in the fall populations would be approximately 10 to 15 percent, or close to what seems to be fairly typical of sandhill cranes. Data summarized in table 8 indicate that the fall recruitment rates of sandhill cranes seem to range from about 8 percent to as high as 15.6 percent, averaging about 11 percent.

Walkinshaw (1981a) has attempted to provide a recent population estimate of the greater sandhill crane population, which he judged to be about 35,000. Of these, somewhat over half are associated with the West Coast and Rocky Mountain population, and about 11,000 are of the Great Lakes population.

The Canadian sandhill crane population perhaps numbers about 54,000 (Aldrich, 1979), although its actual size is difficult to determine because of intergradation with the lesser sandhill crane. A more realistic estimate is one based on the total of the Pacific coast population of lesser sandhill cranes wintering in California (about 20,000 birds) plus the midcontinent population that winters primarily in Texas and New Mexico and stages in the Platte Valley. Estimates in the Platte Valley would suggest that this population is probably in the neighborhood of 250,000 birds. Assuming that no more than 50,000 of these are Canadian sandhills, then the total North American population of lesser sandhills might number about 200,000. This is considerably less than Johnson's population estimate of 250,000 to 400,000 lesser and Canadian sandhill cranes in the Central Flyway, on which he based his population modeling base. Clearly more reliable estimates of lesser and Canadian sandhill crane populations must be made before convincing judgments of the effects of present or possible future levels of sport hunting can be made.

The Florida sandhill crane is currently fully protected, and its population as of 1980 was approximately 5,000 birds. It has recently been receiving better protection, and is at least stable, although increased human population in southern Florida could eventually affect the crane population adversely (Walkinshaw, 1981a).

The Mississippi sandhill crane is at an extremely low population of about 40 to 50 birds, but also is essentially stable (Valentine, 1979, 1981). Valentine (1981) stated that the continued survival and increase of this population depend on an improvement of the habitat conditions within the existing refuge lands and an enlarged captive propagation and release program.

The status of the Cuban sandhill crane remains uncertain, but the most recent reports are that the birds on the mainland are now beginning to increase in numbers, or are at least stable. No information is available on the Isle of Pines population, which is probably the larger of the two components (Walkinshaw, 1981a).

EVOLUTIONARY RELATIONSHIPS

Although obviously a part of the *Grus*, the sandhill has no strong behavioral similarities to other members of the genus (Archibald, 1975, 1976). Wood (1979) reported that morphologically the species seems to cluster in a loose group of *Grus* species that also includes the Eurasian crane, the hooded crane, and the white-naped crane, but no clear evidence for its nearest relatives emerged from his analysis.

Whooping Crane

Grus americana (Linnaeus) 1758

Other Vernacular Names. Whooper; Big white crane; Grue de Amerique, Grue blanche Americaine (French); Schreikranich, Trompeterkranich (German); Amerikanishiy krikpivy zhuravl (Russian); Grulla griteria, Grulla blanca (Spanish).

Range. Breeds in Wood Buffalo National Park, Northwest Territories. Migatory, wintering at Aransas National Wildlife Refuge, coastal Texas. Formerly much more widespread, breeding south to North Dakota, Minnesota, Iowa, and Illinois, and reported from as far west as Utah, east to Cape May New Jersey, and south to coastal Louisiana. Birds hatched from eggs recently transported to Grays Lake, southeastern Idaho, have been reared by greater sandhill cranes and now winter with them in the Rio Grande area of south-central New Mexico.

Subspecies. None recognized.

Measurements. Wing, males 550-630 mm (average of 15, 601.7 mm); females 535-610 mm (average of 7, 597.9 mm). Exposed culmen, males 129-147 mm (average of 15, 138.5 mm); females 117-148 mm (average of 7, 136.7 mm). Tarsus, males 265-301 mm (average of 15, 276.5 mm); females 260-295 mm (average of 7, 281.4 mm) (Ridgway, 1941). Eggs, average 98.4 × 62.4 mm) (87-108 × 50.2-76.5 mm) (Walkinshaw, 1973).

Weights. Six immatures (250 days old) weighed 5,700 to 6,700 grams (Stephenson, 1971). Adults range from 15 lb. 12 oz. to 17 lb. 5 oz. (7,142-7,851 grams) (Roberts, 1932). Erickson (1976) reports the average adult male weight as 7,300 grams, and that of adult females as 6,400 grams. The estimated egg weight is 212 grams.

Description

Adults of both sexes have the crown and anterior portion of the occiput covered with warty, carmine reddish skin that is sparsely covered by black hairlike feathers, especially on the crown. The lores and malar region, including a narrow strip extending down the throat, are also naked, carmine, and similarly bristled. There is an elongated postoccipital patch of blackish feathers, but the rest of the body and the wings are pure white except for the primaries, their greater coverts, and the alula, which are slate black. The bill is wax yellow, tipped with dull greenish or yellowish, the iris is yellow, and the legs and toes are black.

Juveniles have entirely feathered heads, and the feathers on the areas that become bare are short and rather dusky. The rest of the plumage, excepting the primaries, their greater upper coverts, and the alula, is whitish, heavily washed, mottled, and blotched with cinnamon or brownish. The upperparts of the body and the wings are heavily mixed with white and cinnamon buff feathers, with the cinnamon ones more numerous on the scapulars, interscapulars, and back. The primaries are dull blackish, the alula and greater upper coverts are dull blackish tinged with buffy, and the bill is as in the adults, but darker (Ridgway, 1941). The development of the juvenile plumage requires about 100 days, and the molt to the adult or all-white plumage is completed at 450 days in hand-reared birds (Stephenson, 1971). Fledging occurs at about 90 days, and by the second autumn young birds are not easily distinguished from adult-plumaged birds (Erickson, 1976).

Downy chicks are generally dull cinnamon to brownish on the upperparts, becoming deeper brown to russet on the rump, paler and grayer on the neck, and still paler behind the wings. The underparts are pale dull grayish buffy or dull brownish white, tipped or suffused with pale cinnamon. The bill is pale buffy brown with a flesh color basally and a small whitish spot on the upper mandible, and the legs and toes are light

Breeding (hatched) and wintering (inked) ranges of the whooping crane, together with major migratory routes (arrows), primary migratory staging areas (cross-hatching), regular migratory stopover points (arrowheads), and total current migratory corridors (stippling). Probable historic breeding and wintering areas are shown by broken lines, and Gray's Lake National Wildlife Refuge and Aransas National Wildlife Refuge, which are intensively used by whooping cranes, are shown in insets.

brownish (Ridgway, 1941). The downy stage lasts about six weeks (Stephenson, 1971).

Identification

In the field, this is the only North American crane that is pure white, except for black primaries, and it is the largest crane in North America. Its calls are loud and penetrating, and when calling in unison both sexes tend to droop their primaries somewhat, but males do so more strongly.

In the hand, this extremely large crane (wings at least 550 mm.) is readily identified by its white plumage with black legs and primaries. Even juveniles are much whiter than are juvenile sandhill cranes. The trachea in the whooping crane is much more extensively coiled within the sternum than is that of the sandhill crane.

DISTRIBUTION AND HABITATS

Historical Breeding Range

According to Allen (1952), the whooping crane's historical summering range consisted of four separate regions of known use. These included two separate nesting areas, a large area in western Canada and the north-central United States and a small area in Louisiana, and two summering areas used by nonbreeding birds, one area in the northern United States (primarily North Dakota) and the other in the Gulf Coast. The major nesting area in the north included portions of seven states and provinces, as well as the Mackenzie District of Canada's Northwest Territories. Records obtained between 1748 and 1922 indicate that seven nesting sites were known from Saskatchewan, five from Manitoba, four each from Alberta and Ontario, and two from Mackenzie. In the northern United States twelve nesting sites were reported from Iowa, three from Minnesota, two from North Dakota, and one from Illinois. The last known nesting of this migratory population south of Canada occurred in Minnesota in 1889, and the last Canadian record prior to the discovery of the breeding area in Wood Buffalo National Park in 1955 was one at Muddy Lake, Saskatchewan, in 1922. There was also a resident breeding colony in the marshes above White Lake in southwestern Louisiana. Although specific information is lacking, there was certainly a fairly extensive colony in the area that centered in the *Panicum* marshes of White Lake and extended as far west as Mallard Bay, the northeastern arm of Grand Lake. The colony evidently declined rapidly after 1900, and there is no exact information on its size until it was studied in the late 1930s. In 1938, only 11 birds were present in this colony (table 29). No

nesting is known to have occurred in Louisiana after the late 1930s, and the population was totally eliminated by 1950.

A tabulation of 74 historical occurrences of the birds in Canada between 1748 and 1922 indicated that 47 percent were in aspen parklands, 15 percent were in transitional (plains to parklands) communities, 13 percent were in northern coniferous forest types, and the remaining 25 percent were in a variety of community types. Fourteen of the 18 Canadian nesting sites were in aspen or transitional communities, and all of the northern U.S. nesting sites and summer occurrence records were in prairie habitats (Allen, 1952).

Allen believed that the Iowa area may have represented the optimum breeding habitat of the species, namely tallgrass prairie marshes. However, there is little real information on the distribution of whooping cranes in northern prairie areas, for these areas were abandoned by the birds for nesting soon after white settlement. Indeed, all of the Iowa nesting records are for the period 1868-1894, during the major homesteading era. During that same period the whooping crane was apparently still abundant on the similar tallgrass prairies of Louisiana, in the parishes of Calcasieu, Jeff Davis, Allen, Evangeline, and Acadia. In all, there may have been close to two million acres of tallgrass prairie in southwestern Louisiana before the advent of rice culture, and clearly this area could have supported a potentially large whooping crane population. It was not until the late 1920s, when the U.S. Army Engineers extended the Intracoastal Waterway to Grand Lake, that the *Panicum* marshes in the White Lake area became easily accessible to humans and the center of the whooping crane's Louisiana habitat thus became threatened. In 1940 the population was reduced from 13 to only 6 individuals, effectively destroying that population and making the fate of the species dependent on the highly vulnerable migratory population, which was then known to winter largely if not entirely in the Aransas area of coastal Texas and to breed somewhere in northwestern Canada.

Current Breeding Range

The discovery of the whooping crane's northern breeding grounds in 1955 represents one of the most famous detective stories in American ornithological history, and has been fully recounted by Allen (1956), the man most responsible for its ultimate success. With the observation of a small group of whooping cranes by a mammalogist doing a survey in Wood Buffalo National Park in June of 1954, the stage was set for Allen's survey of the area in 1955, and the sighting of several pairs with young. Rather remarkably, the birds were nesting in an area already designated as a national park, in the middle of a wilderness area covering about

17,300 square miles. The actual region where the birds were found to be nesting was a pothole area of about 500 to 600 square miles, between the extreme headwaters of the Nyarling, Klewi, and Sass rivers, and the Little Buffalo River. This is an area of mostly small ponds and small lakes, varying from about an acre to up to 50 or 60 acres in area, nearly all extremely shallow and separated from one another by low ridges that support dense thickets of dwarf birch, willows, black spruce, and tamaracks. Many of the ponds have border growths of bullrushes (*Scirpus validus*) and cattails (*Typha*), which occasionally cover entire bays and arms of the larger lakes. Additionally, sedges (*Carex*), spike rush (*Eleocharis*), musk grass (*Chara*), bent-grass (*Calamo-grostis*), arrow grass (*Trilochin*), and other marsh plants are present. In general, the area lies at the northern edge of the Boreal Forest region in the Hay River Forest Section, and just west of the limits of the Canadian Shield. Because of glacial action, a high proportion of the surface drift material is calcareous, with associated leaching of the limestone soils (Kuyt, 1981a).

Nesting associates of the whooping cranes in these ponds include the sora (*Porzana carolina*), the red-winged blackbird (*Agelaius phoeniceus*), the arctic loon (*Gavia arctica*), and various ducks. Mammals include the red fox (*Vulpes vulpes*), moose (*Alces americana*), black bear (*Ursus americanus*), and wood bison (*Bison bison*). Lynx (*Lynx canadensis*) and wolves (*Canis lupus*) also occur in the general region (Allen, 1956).

The water conditions of the Wood Buffalo nesting area are rather variable in pH, and the cranes apparently use only those areas with water of pH of 7.6 to 8.3, whereas the water in adjacent potholes that are not used is approximately 7.2 to 7.3. Additionally, only those potholes are used that are shallow enough to all for feeding by wading. The dominant vegetation in the potholes occupied by the cranes is bulrush, which also forms a major component of their nests. Cattails and sedges, although common in the area, are associated with deeper sloughs that are usually not used by the birds (Novakowski, 1966). However, Kuyt (1981a) reported that all these plants are used as nesting materials.

Historical Wintering Range

Allen (1952) believed that wintering of the whooping crane occurred in five major habitat types. The first of these consisted of coastal lagoons and maritime beaches that extended from the Brazos River to the Willacy County line, in Texas. The second, and perhaps the most important, consisted of interior tallgrass prairies of southwestern Louisiana; these prairies also extended to eastern Texas. Sea-rim and brackish marshes, extending from southwestern Louisiana west to the Brazos River, Texas, constituted the third habitat type. The fourth consisted of fresh swales and prairie marshes of southwestern Louisiana, which are characterized by intermittent ponds and areas of permanent fresh water, which may have been used more by nesting than by wintering birds. The last and most widespread habitat was the interior grassland plateaus of Texas and north-central Mexico. These upland grasslands are still the major wintering areas of sandhill cranes, and probably whooping cranes intermingled with these smaller cranes to a limited extent, judging from available records.

There are also scattered historical records of migrant or wintering birds extending as far east as the Atlantic Coast, which may have represented a wintering area for birds breeding in the prairie areas of Iowa and Illinois, and as far west as Great Salt Lake. However, by the early 1950s Allen (1952) was able to state with certainty that the species then wintered only on the Aransas National Wildlife Refuge of Texas and on nearby Matagorda and St. Joseph Islands.

Current Wintering Range

Apart from a recent development of limited wintering in the Rio Grande area of central New Mexico, the wintering areas used by whooping cranes are exactly the same at the present time as they were when Allen (1952) summarized the species' status. That is, the Aransas National Wildlife Refuge of coastal Texas is still the wintering area of the entire breeding population of whooping cranes (Labuda and Butts, 1979). Regular wintering still occurs only on Aransas, Matagorda Island, St. Joseph Island, and portions of the Lamar Peninsula and an area on the eastern side of San Antonio Bay called Welder Point. Altogether, about 20,000 acres of salt flats on the refuge and these adjacent islands comprise the species' principal wintering grounds (Derrickson, 1980).

Since 1950, intensive studies on habitat use in the refuge have been carried out, and four areas have been found to be of major value to cranes during that period. Sundown Bay, covering about 372 hectares and averaging less than a meter in depth, has accounted for about 45 and 53 percent of the adult and juvenile use-days between 1950 and 1978. The Dunham Bay Area, of 1,502 hectares, has accounted for 14.3 and 11.4 percent of the adult and juvenile use-days during the same period. South Matagorda Island averaged 13.2 and 11.8 percent of adult and juvenile use, and an area composed of Mustang Lake, Redfish Slough, Mustang Slough, and surrounding tidal flats and encompassing 697 hectares has accounted for 12.3 and 22.6 percent use by adults and juveniles respectively. A large number of other areas have been used to a minor degree.

Generally, all of these areas may be characterized as having a flat, estuarine topography, with salt flats that vary under differing tidal conditions from dry sandy flats to pools of salt water up to a meter in depth. Characteristic plants include such salt-adapted forms as *Distichlis, Monanthorchloe, Spartina, Borrichia, Salicornia,* and *Lycium* (Labuda and Butts, 1979).

The reasons for the highly localized distribution of the birds in Aransas are still unknown, but it is unlikely that major differences in local food supplies account for these patterns. Labuda and Butts (1979) suggested that perhaps site preferences are associated with traditional use patterns. All of the most heavily used areas are close to the heavily used Gulf Intracoastal Waterway, indicating that human use is not a significant factor in determining crane distribution, at least under conditions of protection from disturbance.

Breeding Habitat Requirements and Densities

Allen (1956) noted that 60 percent of the total whooping crane population known to exist in 1956 was found on a single survey flight within an area of some 12 square miles, but he did not attempt to judge the basis for this extreme degree of population localization. He judged that four successful pairs nested in the Sass River area that year, and at least two additional families were probably present in the Klewi River area, with additional unsuccessful or nonbreeding adults also present in the same general area.

Kuyt (1976b) reported that pairs return annually to the same general vicinity, and in the Sass River area there are six nesting sites to which the birds have returned almost annually since at least as far back as 1966. By mapping circles around all of the nests built by a single pair over their years of known occupancy, Kuyt judged that the radius of nesting territories varied from 0.6 to 1.3 kilometers, with an average of 0.9 kilometer. Only rarely has he found active nests of adjoining pairs closer than 1.3 kilometers apart. Thus, in spite of a tendency for clustering of nests into the same general area, there is also a definite tendency toward dispersion within that area.

Because of the inaccessibility of the area, and the danger that human disturbance might affect reproductive success, there are few detailed studies on the flora and fauna of the area. Annual precipitation in the nesting area averages only 13 inches, but higher than normal rainfall early in the season causes delayed nesting, nest flooding, and lowered success. When the weather is unusually dry the nesting proceeds normally, but adults and young have to travel farther from the nest site to feed. However, there are enough potholes of varying depths in the general area to assure foraging sources regardless of these weather conditions. Areas around the nests tend to dry up each summer, and may remain dry until the following spring. This might explain why nest sites tend to be abandoned and not

used in the following year. Kuyt (1976b) observed birds nesting in the same marsh or on the same island in subsequent years, but never on the exact nesting mound. Novakowski (1966) stated that nests are rarely used more than four years.

Novakowski investigated food supplies in the nesting area, and questioned whether local variations in these were responsible for nesting locations. He was unable to confirm Allen's (1956) view that the fat and protein content of the mud at the bottom of the ponds was unusually high and thus would provide unusual food value for the bird. The major insect and crustacean life of the ponds likely to be important foods for the cranes are mostly naiads of dragon-flies, larvae of caddisflies, mayflies, and chironomids, and some amphipods (*Hyalella*). However, the occurrence of all of these forms is sporadic, and may account for the tendency of individual families to forage in so many different potholes during a single summer. Although numerous, small mollusks such as snails (*Physa, Stagnicola*) and pill clams (*Pisidium*) probably provide little organic matter for food. Terrestrial food supplies, such as berries, are probably also very secondary as food sources for young cranes.

It is clear that there are no specific aspects of the habitat that clearly make this small region different from all others, or that can be selected out as critical habitat components for nesting. The general isolation of the area, and the more local isolation as provided by the numerous small potholes visually isolated from others by intervening woods and scrub, may provide the spatial separation from one another required by these highly territorial birds. Further, a low incidence of human disturbance is also apparently needed. Food supplies are obviously not unusually high, and the length of the breeding season is marginal at best, considering the long periods required for incubation and fledging of the young. It seems likely, in fact, that Wood Buffalo National Park actually represents only marginally acceptable breeding habitat, the birds having long been evicted from more favorable and more productive habitats farther to the south.

Breeding densities are difficult to judge with any degree of accuracy, because of the problems of estimating territory and home-range sizes for the species. Kuyt (1981a) reported that 18 whooping crane territories averaged about 710 hectares, but it is clear from his maps (e.g. 1976b, 1981a) that substantial areas of apparently unused territory often exist between adjoining nesting territories.

Wintering Habitats and Requirements

Allen's (1952) early studies on Aransas Refuge brought out the fact that winter territoriality is an important aspect of the whooping crane's biology, and that about

400 acres of salt flats, including water areas, are needed for each family or pair of birds. He believed that killifishes (*Fundulus*) and decapod crustaceans, especially blue crabs (*Callinectes sapidus*), probably represent the key food forms for whooping cranes. He also believed that the most important mortality factors on the wintering grounds were probably illegal shooting and periodic failures of the natural food supply. Disturbance by cattle was considered to be a negligible factor in the crane's welfare.

More recent studies by Blankinship (1976) indicate that blue crabs and several genera of clams (*Tagellus, Ensis, Rangia, Phacoides, Barnea*) are the preferred and most important food items of wintering whooping cranes, and that water levels influence the particular species that are consumed. He estimated an average territorial size for 10 territories of 176 hectares (as compared with Allen's estimate of 400 acres, or 162 hectares, for 14 territories), but also found that some pairs and family groups shared territories in some areas. He observed considerable variation in the degree of territorial defense and interactions between pairs and families, and in one case found an area of about 77 hectares being shared between a family and a neighboring pair. He believed that the most important threat to whooping cranes on their wintering grounds is the possibility of an oil and chemical spill from barges in the Intracoastal Waterway. He noted that during times of low crab populations, clams seem to offer an important alternative food supply and that cranes are very efficient at capturing both crabs and clams. Besides blue crabs and clams, cranes have been observed feeding on fiddler crabs (*Uca*), mud shrimp (*Callianassa*), white shrimp (*Penaeus*), eels, snakes (*Natrix, Thamnophis*), and crayfish (*Cambarus*), as well as on acorns and the fruit of the salt-flat cranberry (*Lycium*). Various of these foods have been examined for chemical contaminants and these have all been found to be quite low.

FOODS AND FORAGING BEHAVIOR

Foods of Adults

The early studies of Allen (1952) summarized what was known at that time about the foods of the whooping crane. Using early published and unpublished records, he concluded that the animal foods of the whooping crane included crayfish, blue crabs, aquatic insects, and freshwater minnows. Plant foods included marsh onions (*Crinum*), prairie lily (*Nothoscordum*), roots of three-square (*Scirpus olneyi*) and *Spartina*, and also such crops as sweet potatoes and sprouting corn. Later observations indicated that shellfish and fish also are consumed, but it was not until the detailed studies of

Allen and Francis Uhler at Aransas that any real information on feeding behavior and foods began to emerge. By observing foraging birds, collecting droppings, and inspecting areas where the cranes had been feeding, Allen was able to establish that at least 28 types of animal materials and 17 kinds of plants are consumed on the wintering grounds. The seven major foods were determined to be a polychaete worm (*Laeonereis*), pistol shrimp (*Cragnon*), mud shrimp (*Callianassa*), blue crabs (*Callinectes sapidus*), crayfish (*Cambarus hedgpethi*), short razor clams (*Tagellus gibbus*), and green razor clams (*Solen*). Of these, blue crabs, mud shrimps, and other decapods are taken first and by preference, as they are abundant and tend to be easily obtained. Fish, insects, and reptiles are apparently chance prey, as are probably frogs and birds, at least at Aransas. However, on migration the birds evidently fed on the egg masses of frogs and toads, on various insects, and perhaps on a variety of freshwater fishes. Blankinship's (1976) recent studies at Aransas indicate that adult cranes are very efficient at capturing both crabs and clams, in spite of the latter's burrowing abilities. A female was observed to capture 32 clams in 30 minutes, and similar rates were observed on various occasions. Clams and smaller blue crabs are swallowed whole, while large crabs are carried to shore, where the claws are broken off and the body then swallowed, followed by the claws. Clams at least 10 centimeters long and 4 centimeters in diameter are also swallowed whole.

Foods of Young

Little is known of the food of juveniles on the breeding grounds, but it presumably consists of insects and aquatic invertebrates. One crane that was captured on the breeding grounds in 1964 excreted berries in its feces, suggesting that older juveniles may use berries for a supplemental food source to these animal materials (Novakowski, 1966).

On the wintering ground the young birds feed within their parents' territories, and are regularly fed by them. Usually the young bird remains within a few yards of its mother and utters a series of soft but penetrating calls, especially when the female has captured a food item and the juvenile begins begging. About half of the food caught by the female is passed on to the young, at least during fall and winter months. As spring approaches the young birds show more independence, and sometimes move up to 90 meters away from her, periodically returning to her. Males occasionally also feed the young, but this task is seemingly done primarily by the female. Males have also been observed to bite a begging juvenile. One crane, evicted by his mother's new mate, was observed to capture and consume nine blue crabs in only ten minutes, suggesting a considerable degree of foraging independence (Blankinship, 1976).

Foraging Behavior

On the wintering areas, daily activity is divided between active foraging and defense of the foraging territory. The adult male is the defender of the territory, as well as a general guardian. Females and young remain together throughout much of the daylight hours in their foraging activities. The birds generally also drink the brackish water in their own foraging ponds.

When foraging, the birds wade in water 5 to 10 inches deep, lowering their heads at intervals, They evidently probe in the holes of clams and burrowing crustaceans such as mud shrimps, presumably usually capturing these animals at the mouths of their burrows, rather than digging them out. However, most of the clams taken are burrowing species, and thus the long bill must be used as a digging tool on occasion.

MIGRATIONS AND MOVEMENTS

Seasonal Movements

Allen (1952) analyzed the migrations of this species in great detail, and Derrickson (1980) supplemented these early records with more recent ones. The material in table 2 summarizes the timing of the spring and fall migrations by state and province, and also provides information on average flock sizes for these two time periods.

In general, the migration follows a narrow and direct corridor between Wood Buffalo National Park and Aransas National Wildlife Refuge. The corridor is widest in the Canadian provinces and North Dakota, and generally narrowest in the area from the Platte Valley of Nebraska southward. Nebraska provides the largest number of historical records of migrating cranes, primarily because the Platte River was apparently their most important spring and fall staging area. Like the sandhill cranes using the same general area, the whooping crane also roosted on the river bars at night and came to buffalo wallows early in the morning, where they fed on various aquatic life. The birds also foraged on the prairie uplands, often turning over cattle chips and feeding on the beetles below them. An analysis of the migrations of whooping cranes through Nebraska was provided by Swenk (1933), which up until the establishment of the Aransas refuge was the major source of information on whooping crane populations. Swenk's acceptance of many unverified records proved to be a near disaster for the cranes, whose status by the

1930s was much more precarious than Swenk estimated (Johnsgard, 1982), but nevertheless a good deal of useful information was assembled by Swenk. A more recent summary of whooping crane migrations in Nebraska was provided by Johnsgard and Redfield (1978).

Derrickson (1980) has summarized the general migratory picture for this species. According to him, spring departure from Aransas usually falls between April 1 and April 15, with the last birds leaving by May 1, but with occasional stragglers remaining until mid-May, and rarely staying all summer. Spring departure from Aransas may extend over a period of as long as 44 days, or as short a period as 13 days. Allen (1952) estimated the spring migration to require from 9 to 23 days, averaging about 15-16 days. The first birds generally arrive on the Wood Buffalo National Park breeding grounds in late April.

The southward migration from Wood Buffalo falls between September 12 and September 26, and normally all the birds have arrived at Aransas by mid-November. Nonbreeding birds evidently migrate earlier or faster than do breeders, since the earliest arrivals rarely have any immatures with them. Some stragglers arrive as late as the latter part of December (Derrickson, 1980). The normal fall migration, from late September to early November, is a more protected movement than is the spring migration.

Daily Movements

Daily movements are so far rather little studied, but by using radio-telemetric methods biologists were able to track one whooping crane family all the way from Wood Buffalo National Park to Aransas in 1981. The family left the park on October 4 and flew 175 miles to the Ft. McMurray area of Alberta, where they remained for five days. On October 9 the birds flew 270 miles to Reward, Saskatchewan, and there they spent 11 days. On October 20, as snow was falling, the birds flew 175 miles to Swift Current, Saskatchewan. On the next day they flew 150 miles to Plentywood, Montana, and 470 miles the day thereafter to Valentine, Nebraska. On October 23 they flew about 125 miles to Kearney, Nebraska, and on October 24 some 190 miles to Rush Center, Kansas. On October 25 they covered 120 miles, to Waynoka, Oklahoma, and on the next day they flew 140 miles to Lawton, Oklahoma. On October 27 the birds flew an additional 30 miles to the Red River, near Byers, Texas. They remained along the Red River until November 1, when they flew 230 miles to Rosebud, Texas. The next day they flew 178 miles to Tivoli, Texas, only 18 miles from Aransas. The next morning they flew on to Aransas, completing a 2,271 mile journey (*American Birds* 36:196, 1982).

GENERAL BIOLOGY

Sociality

Information on average flock sizes during spring and fall migration periods is presented in table 2, where it may be seen that whooping cranes tend to migrate in very small groups. Part of this is of course a reflection of the overall rarity of the species, but there is little evidence of large flocks even during historical times. In the fall as well as in the spring, single birds, pairs with or without young, and other small groups are the typical social units. The largest group reported in Derrickson's (1980) summary of confirmed sightings, which updated Allen's earlier report, is of a group of 12 birds observed during March in Oklahoma. The next largest unit is of 9 birds, observed during April in Nebraska, and a group of the same size observed in North Dakota in November.

Daily Activities

Like the other cranes, the whooping crane is diurnal, and while on migration it roosts in shallow water at night. In Nebraska, whooping cranes traditionally have used the same areas of the Platte River as do the sandhill cranes, and spend the daylight hours foraging in the same manner, but apparently covering a good deal more ground. According to early observers, they also apparently left the Platte Valley in the middle of the day, rising and circling on air currents under favorable weather conditions (Allen, 1952).

Besides foraging and roosting, some time is spent on migration and wintering areas in such social interactions as fighting and dancing. Dancing occurs throughout the time that the birds are in the Aransas area, but the greatest amount of activity is observed just after fall arrival and again prior to departure in the spring (Blankinship, 1976).

Interspecific Interactions

There is relatively little information on whooping crane predators, but presumably predation on adult birds is extremely rare, because of their large size. However, one cross-fostered juvenile bird was observed to be attacked and killed by a golden eagle (*Aquila chrysaetos*) during its first fall migration south between Idaho and New Mexico.

As noted earlier, potential predators in the breeding grounds include lynx, black bear, and wolves, but it is unlikely that any of the species pose regular serious threats to young cranes or crane eggs. Kuyt (1981a) mentioned that one young crane was killed by a wolf about a week before it had attained fledging. He also noted (1981b) an instance of an egg having apparently been taken by a black bear. Most evidence indicates that it is the juvenile segment of the population that is most susceptible to mortality, especially during their first spring migration, when they become isolated from their parents and must face long migration routes, food changes, and imperfectly known obstacles (Novakowski, 1966). Mortality rates appear to be very high in the first year of life, at least as compared to that of adults (Johnsgard, 1982), but probably many of the postfledging losses can be attributed to accidents, illegal hunting mortality, and similar factors independent of predation.

The sandhill crane is theoretically a competitor of the whooping crane, but besides being much smaller it is clearly adapted to a much more vegetarian and land-based form of foraging. Thus, at least at the present time, there does not seem to be a significant degree of competitive interaction between these two species.

A considerable number of threats to the wintering habitat at Aransas exist, including the possibility of oil spills, chemical contamination of foods, disturbance by humans, accidental kills by waterfowl hunters, and possible housing developments along St. Charles Bay. All of these human-caused interactions might pose serious problems for whooping cranes in the future.

BREEDING BIOLOGY

Age of Maturity and Time of Breeding

Derrickson (1980) noted that plumage and behavioral evidence suggest that whooping cranes probably become sexually mature when from four to six years old. Males raised in captivity have produced viable semen when between three and four years old, and one female laid eggs in her fifth year. Apparent pair-bonding behavior has been observed in two- and three-year-old birds (Bishop and Blankinship, 1981).

Historical whooping crane records (table 14) indicate that about two-thirds of the available egg dates are for May, and nearly all of the remainder are for June. Recent observations in Wood Buffalo National Park indicate that eggs are normally laid in late April or early May, and hatching occurs a month later at the end of May or in early June (Derrickson, 1980). Old observations from the White Lake marsh area of Louisiana also indicate that most eggs there were found in May or early June, although newly hatched young were also reported in April and well-grown young in May, suggesting a considerably earlier onset of the nesting season there than in Canada. In a nesting effort by semicaptive birds at Aransas in 1949 the birds apparently laid their eggs on April 29 and May 1 (Allen, 1952).

Pair Formation and Courtship

Allen's (1952) early accounts of whooping crane courtship are still among the most detailed available.

He observed "solo" dancing by a male as early as mid-December, and dancing by a pair in late January. He noted that dancing became more frequent as the spring migratory departure approached, and that it could be set off, for example, by the pair encountering a group of ducks. Blankinship (1976) also observed that dancing is common while the birds are at Aransas, but that it is not limited to a courtship role, and sometimes occurred as part of antagonistic behavior between males of two pairs. Interestingly, Blankinship observed that in January of 1973 one of the parents (probably a male) of a family was lost to unknown cause. The remaining bird and its offspring stayed in the same area without obvious change in behavior, but only three weeks later the surviving bird took a new mate. This was evidently done rather rapidly, and Blankinship made no mention of the process other than that the new male would not tolerate the juvenile and repeatedly drove it away. Thus, pair bonds can evidently be formed fairly rapidly in whooping cranes, in spite of the permanent pair-bonding typical of all cranes. Maroldo (1980) also provides an interesting history of the famous whooping crane Crip, the male that was involved in the 1950 nesting attempt at Aransas, and which had first been observed as a cripple at Aransas in the winter of 1945 or 1946. Crip also was the male of the pair that nested in the mid-1950s at the Audubon Park Zoo, in New Orleans (Conway, 1957). During his lifetime of at least 35 years (he was of unknown age but in adult plumage when first noticed), Crip had a total of five different mates, three of which were provided him under captive conditions.

After his first wild mate was shot in March of 1948, he was observed with a new mate within a month, indicating that mate replacement under wild conditions can occur fairly rapidly.

The unison call ceremony of the whooping crane places it in the same behavioral category as that of the Japanese, Eurasian, and hooded cranes (Archibald, 1975, 1976). The female's voice resembles that of the hooded crane; she usually utters one long call, followed by a short call, for each male call, but sometimes also utters two or three short calls for each male call. The female does not usually lower her wrists during the unison call ceremony, but the male strongly lowers his, exposing the black primary feathers. The curved tertial feathers are held upward, forming a distinct plume, in both sexes.

Copulatory behavior in the whooping crane is apparently still undescribed, but is probably very similar to that of the Japanese crane and Eurasian crane, which are both well studied in this regard.

Territoriality and Early Nesting Behavior

Nesting studies at Wood Buffalo National Park have been carried out since 1966, and especially since 1970. Kuyt (1981a) has summarized much of the resulting information on territoriality and nest use. He noted that of 192 nest sites studied, at no time have the birds used the same nest in successive years, although they often nested in the same marsh. Territorial defense occurs in these areas, but the breeding range is lightly populated, and there are contacts with only a few other birds each year. Since the birds are both very long-lived and have a high fidelity to old territories, there is probably only a small amount of territorial interacting each year. Kuyt noted that resident birds attacked and chased off both single and paired cranes. He believed that the territorial bond is sufficiently strong for a bird to return to its territory even in the event of the death of its mate. Thus territories are likely to be reused for many years, and may become vacant only in the event that both adults die during the same year. The composite nesting areas in the Sass River and Klewi River vicinity range from 1.3 to 11.2 square kilometers, averaging (in 15 cases) 3.9 square kilometers each. Two territories in the Nyarling River area averaged 34.8 square kilometers, and one in Alberta only 0.4 square kilometer. The grand average from all areas is 7.2 square kilometers. These generally large areas include some habitats not used for nesting, although much of the area becomes used by the pairs or families during foraging or other daily activities. The present low density of the breeding population probably is responsible for the large breeding territories and the extensive areas between active territories which cranes rarely used, according to Kuyt.

Most historical records of crane nests indicate that they are located along lake margins or among rushes or sedges in marshes, with the water anywhere from 8 to 10 inches to as much as about 18 inches deep. The nest studied by Allen (1952) at Aransas was constructed in cattails, in water apparently initially about a foot deep. However, falling water levels eventually made this level much less. The nests often are between 2 and 5 feet in diameter, and range in height from about 8 to 18 inches above the surrounding water level. Nesting has also been reported on muskrat houses and on damp prairie sites.

Egg-laying and Incubation

Judging from various accounts, it is likely that the eggs are normally laid two days apart, and that in most cases two eggs are laid. Kuyt (1981b) reported that of 203 clutches observed between 1966 and 1980, 90.6 percent of them contained two eggs, 7.9 percent had a single egg, and 1.5 percent had three eggs. He also reported two apparent cases of renesting in wild birds. One nest with a single egg was found abandoned on May 1, 1976, but a new nest about a kilometer away in the same territory was found on May 6 with two eggs. In 1980, a nest with two eggs was found abandoned on May 14, but on June 3 a new nest was found 700 meters away from the abandoned one.

Both sexes incubate, and Allen (1952) provided detailed observations on incubation behavior and nest-relief activities. He noted that the male spent more time on the nest than did the female, and that there was an average of 7.6 nest exchanges per day. Toward the end of the incubation period the female began to spend more time on the eggs and to relieve the male more frequently. Walkinshaw (1973), studying the same birds for seven days, made similar observations. He found that the female did more nighttime incubation than did the male, but that the male did 52.9 percent of the daytime incubation. During the entire seven-day period the eggs were incubated 92.7 percent of the time. Conway (1957) watched the same pair some years later when they nested in the Audubon Park Zoo, and found that on that occasion the male did most of the nighttime incubation and the female undertook most of the daytime responsibility.

Whichever bird does the incubating, the other one serves as a "guard." In particular, Allen found the male to be intolerant of intruders such as herons, egrets, and spoonbills, particularly the herons and egrets. Vultures and deer were also sometimes challenged by the cranes. Walkinshaw observed cranes chasing herons, egrets, pelicans, ducks, and even swallows. Historical accounts by egg collectors indicate that injury-feigning, with wings drooping and spread and the head lowered, is a common response to human intrusion near the nest.

The incubation period is probably 33 to 34 days under wild conditions, but has been found to be 30 to 31 days at the Patuxent Wildlife Research Center. Conway (1957) reported that the second chick hatched three days after the first one, and the second-hatched bird did not feed until some 30 hours after hatching.

Hatching and Postbreeding Biology

Conway (1957) reported that the newly hatched chicks at the New Orleans Zoo were fed earthworms, dragonflies, and grasshoppers by their parents, and that the young birds were offered food almost constantly. Rusty, a chick hatched at Aransas Refuge in 1950, was quite active within 24 hours after hatching and by the fourth day was being brooded more than 100 yards from the nest.

During the first 20 days after hatching, the families generally remain within 1.8 kilometers of the nesting site, with daily movements averaging about 0.8 kilometer (Derrickson, 1980). The young birds fledge when they are about 80 to 90 days old. Until that time they are vulnerable to large predators such as wolves, and Kuyt (1981b) reported at least one case and perhaps two of unfledged young being killed by wolves.

Kuyt's (1981b) data suggest that chick and juvenile losses tend to occur throughout the summer, rather than being concentrated during the first two weeks after hatching. He suggested that relatively dry conditions during recent summers in the breeding grounds may have made the older young more vulnerable to large predators than is the case when water supplies are adequate.

Whooping crane juveniles continue to be fed by their parents, especially the female, for an extended time during their first fall and winter of life, and probably do not become truly independent until they are gradually abandoned by their parents the following spring. However, the young birds often do follow their parents northward in the spring, and it is likely that they are not forcefully separated from them until their arrival on the breeding grounds.

RECRUITMENT RATES, POPULATION STATUS, AND CONSERVATION

A great deal of information is now available on recruitment rates in the whooping crane, owing to the opportunities for a complete yearly census of the entire wintering population at Aransas Refuge (table 29). Absolute mortality rates as well as natality rates and rates of population increase can also be easily calculated (Johnsgard, 1982; also table 8). It is apparent that since 1938 the age ratios, and thus gross recruitment rates, have declined considerably, but there has also been a decline in mortality rates, presumably reflecting a higher level of protection from poaching and other losses caused by humans. However, the actual annual rates of population increase are currently at an all-time low (Johnsgard, 1982), and in recent years the Canadian and American conservation agencies have made innovative efforts in trying to protect the whooping crane population by cross-fostering efforts with greater sandhill cranes. These efforts, discussed more fully in chapter 9, are not yet far enough along to predict with certainty their success or failure. So far, none of the cross-fostered birds have successfully paired and bred. However, they have drawn a good deal of attention to the plight of the whooping crane, and have virtually made it the universal symbol of wildlife conservation in North America. It can only be sincerely hoped that such efforts will succeed in preserving the most spectacular of all wild birds in North America for future generations to see and admire.

EVOLUTIONARY RELATIONSHIPS

There can be little doubt that the nearest living relative of the whooping crane is the Japanese crane, as is indicated by their behavior (Archibald, 1975, 1976) and also by their anatomy (Wood, 1979). The two might well be regarded as a superspecies, judging from their great morphological and behavioral similarities.

Japanese Crane

Grus japonensis (Müller) 1776

Other Vernacular Names. Manchurian crane, Red-crowned crane; Tan-ting ho, Hsien-ho (Chinese); Grue de Mandchourie (French); Mandschuren-Kranich (German): Tancho, Tozuro (Japanese); Manshuskiy zhuravl, Ussuriskii zhuravl (Russian); Grulla blanc (Spanish).

Range. Breeds in northeastern Mongolia on the border of Manchuria (Hahlin Basin) and eastwards through northern and central Manchuria to Lake Khanka and along the Ussuri to its mouth, and in the middle Amur Valley west to the Bureya or Gorin River. An essentially resident population also occurs in northeastern Hokkaido, Japan. The continental population is migratory, wintering in Korea and in eastern China (north of the Gulf of Chihli, and occasionally also the lower Yangtze and sometimes on Taiwan), with vagrants reaching Sakhalin (Vaurie, 1965; Yamashina, 1978). There is apparently also a small resident population near Pyongyang, North Korea (King, 1979).

Subspecies. None recognized. Archibald (1975) has suggested that the mainland population should perhaps be distinguished (as *punmunjomii*) from the Japanese population on the basis of vocal differences, although evidence so far does not indicate any morphological differences between these groups, and no formal description of *punmunjomii* has appeared.

Measurements. Wing (chord), males 560-670 mm (average of 8, 618.6 mm); females 557-635 mm (average of 11, 609 mm). Exposed culmen, males 151-167 mm (average of 8, 159 mm); females 135-167 mm (average of 11, 150.9 mm). Tarsus, males 267-301 mm (average of 8, 285.7 mm), females 255-297 mm (average of 11, 271.9 mm). Eggs average 101.2×64.9 mm (94.8-108.0 × 61.2-68.8 mm) (Walkinshaw, 1973).

Weights. Dementiev and Gladkov (1968) report questionable weights of 9,000 to 10,500 grams, even to 15,000 grams. Cheng (1964) indicates adult weights of 7,000 to 9,000 grams, with a year-old female weighing 5,250 grams. Heinroth (1922) indicates adult weights of 6,000 to 7,000 grams. The estimated egg weight is 235 grams; the actual weight of 16 eggs averaged 239.4 grams (Ma, 1981).

Description

Adults of both sexes are nearly alike, but the cheeks, throat, and neck are ashy black in males and pearly gray in females. The forehead and crown are without feathers and red, becoming brighter during breeding, and covered with black hairlike bristles down nearly to the eyes. Starting below and behind the eyes, a white band extends from the ear coverts and occiput down the hindneck to meet with the blackish lower neck in a sharp point. The rest of the body and wings are white except for the secondaries, which are black. The innermost secondaries are somewhat pendent and pointed. The bill is olive green to greenish horn, the legs are slaty to grayish black, and the iris is dark brown.

Juveniles are a combination of white, partly tawny, cinnamon brown, and rusty or grayish. The neck collar is grayish to coffee brown, the secondaries are dull black and brown, and the crown and forehead are covered with gray and tawny feathers. The primaries are white, tipped with black, as are the upper primary coverts. The legs and bill are similar to those of adults, but lighter in color.

Immatures in their first winter show an indefinite brownish rather than sharply defined black or grayish neck area, and also have dark-tipped primaries and primary coverts (Masatomi and Kitagawa, 1975). Scattered dark feathers also occur on the upper and lower wing surfaces.

Breeding (hatched) and wintering (dark shading) ranges of the Japanese crane, and residential range of the species in Japan (inked). Known migratory routes are indicated by arrows, and previous or uncertain wintering areas are shown by light stippling. Insets show summer occurrences in the Amur and Ussuri valleys (above), and local residential distribution on Hokkaido, Japan (below).

One-year-old birds lack brown on the upper wing or back, but have a dark brown upper neck band and black tips on the outer primaries. During their second year this neck band gradually attains the adult black color. *Two-year-old* birds are essentially like adults, but may show black tips on some of the outer primary coverts.

Downy chicks are tawny brown to cinnamon brown, becoming darker on the shoulders and rump, and tawnier on the head and neck. The cheeks are light gray and tawny, and a white spot is present at the base of the wing. The bill is flesh-colored, with a more yellowish base, the iris is dark brown, and the legs are initially bluish, becoming flesh-colored a day or two after hatching. The toes and tibio-tarsal joint are bluish, tinged with yellowish flesh color (Walkinshaw, 1973). By two months of age the down is shed and most of the juvenile feathers are grown.

Identification

In the field, the Japanese crane appears white-bodied except for black inner secondaries and a black neck that passes forward under a white nape and eye patch. Except for the much broader white area behind the eye and on the nape, this crane is somewhat similar to the black-necked crane, but the latter has a darker and more ashy-gray body color. The calls of the Japanese crane are loud and resounding, and while calling in unison both sexes often raise the wings and droop the primaries.

In the hand, the combination of a pale grayish white body, a black neck, and a white patch that extends to the nape serves to identify this species. The trachea is coiled inside the keel of the sternum.

DISTRIBUTION AND HABITATS

Historical Range

The historical range of this species is only very poorly known, for although the Japanese crane was described over two centuries ago, its breeding grounds remained undiscovered by scientists for another century. Prezhwalsky was the first naturalist to provide any information on the summer occurrence and biology of this species, and in 1870 found it common in the area of Lake Khanka. Quite probably it once bred in marshes around Lake Khanka, along the Prihanka plain and throughout the valley of the Ussuri River. Around Lake Khanka itself, the birds nested on the swampy plains to the east of the lake and on the marshy areas of the lower Lefu River to the south. Shulpin found a nest on the lower Lefu in 1928, and the birds were also then apparently common along the lower Mo River and the Sugatch River in the same area. Little if any other

historical evidence on the original breeding areas exists for the mainland. Dementiev and Gladkov (1968) suggested that the species might have bred beyond the Ussuri River to the lower Amur River, as well as in the valleys of central and western Manchuria, and in the valley of the Sungari River (a Manchurian tributary to the Amur).

There is no evidence that the birds bred in Korea, although wintering was regular in Korea during the late 1800s and early 1900s. Indeed, even after the birds became rare as winter visitors in eastern China, they continued to be common in Korea during winter, where they have probably been trapped for sale in Japan and China for hundreds of years.

The historical distribution in Japan was certainly more widespread than at present. Probably the species was not uncommon in eastern and northern Honshu during winter, and nested not only in eastern Hokkaido but also in southwestern parts of that island. Until the latter part of the nineteenth century, some might have wintered in central Japan. However, after the Meizi Restoration the birds rapidly declined, and were rarely seen on Honshu after the early 1900s. Indeed, some ornithologists believed that they might have been extirpated from Japan about that time, but they were found nesting at Kushiro in 1924, when about 20 birds were believed to be present in the Kushiro Marsh. Thereafter, the population increased very little until the 1950s, when artificial feeding in winter was begun (Masatomi, 1981a).

Current Range

Apparently, the area around Lake Khanka still represents the center of this species' mainland breeding range. However, there are now known to be several nesting areas in the USSR. In addition to the nesting area on the eastern shore of Lake Khanka, the crane also nests along the lower Amur River (the basin of Lake Bolon and the Evron-Chukchagir lowlands), the middle Amur (the Arkharinsk lowlands and the area of the confluence of the Bureya and Amur Rivers), and the Zeya River (along the Ulma and Tom Rivers, which are tributaries to the Zeya). However, all told, there may have been no more than 25 or 30 breeding pairs in the entire USSR in the late 1970s (Flint, 1978a). The breeding range also extends into northern China a considerable distance along the Sungari River, and west into the drainage of the Nun River, a tributary of the Sungari. There the breeding density is greatest in reed swamps in the lower reaches of the Wu Yu-erh and the Du-lu rivers, and in the Qu-xing River basin (Ma, 1981). The total population of this area is not known, but on the Sung-nun plains 233 cranes were observed in 283 hours of field observation, and on the San-jian plains 98 cranes were observed in 115 hours. Undoubtedly these numbers represent many repeated observations, but they nonetheless suggest that the Chinese population is appreciably larger than that of the USSR.

Lake Bolon, on the western side of the lower Amur River in Khabarvsk Territory, USSR, was discovered to be a nesting area of the species in 1975, when it was estimated that 13 to 15 pairs nested in the Lake Bolon basin. In 1980, 6 territorial pairs were found in this basin (USSR Crane Working Group Information Bulletin No. 2, 1981).

In the upper Amur River basin, along the lower Bureya River, this species has been observed during summer since 1956, and chicks were found in 1965 (Dymin and Pankin, 1975). In 1981, 8 pairs nested between the Bureya and Kingan rivers. In 1977, a survey was made of the upper Zeya River, northwest of the Bureya, and 4 nests were found, as well as 4 additional pairs and 2 lone birds. Nesting apparently also occurred in 1978 and 1979 in the upper Zeya Basin, but no cranes were observed there in 1980 (USSR Crane Working Group, Information Bulletin No. 2, 1981).

The Lake Khanka area of Maritime Territory is still believed to be the major nesting area for Japanese cranes in the USSR. In 1980 nesting was observed along the Ilistay River, on the marshy plain to the northeast of Lake Khanka, and in the Sungach River basin (upper reaches of the Chertov, and Chertov Marsh). At the end of August 116 individuals were counted there, including 18 young birds. During the spring of 1981 there were 70 to 74 birds in these areas. Finally, in the summer of 1981 a new nesting area was discovered in the Bikin River basin to the northeast of Lake Khanka (USSR Crane Working Group Information Bulletin No. 2, 1981).

The present distribution of the species in Japan is limited to southeastern Hokkaido, and consists of the marshes near the Otsu River mouth (Takochi District), the Kushiro Marsh and adjoining lowlands along the Bekanbeushi River, the Kiritappu Marsh (Kushiro District), the marshes of Nemuro Peninsula, Lake Furen, and Nishibetsu and Shibetsu rivers and the lowlands between them (Nemuro District). The major wintering grounds in Japan are generally restricted to several areas of Kushiro District (Masatomi, 1981a)

Since the Korean War the wintering flocks in South Korea have steadily declined, and there are few recent records except for the area of the demilitarized zone. Archibald (1981a) reported that a group of about 15 winters on the mudflats and rice paddies just north of the west coastal city of Incheon, another group of about 40 winters in Panmunjom Valley along the Sachon River, and a third flock of 80 to 100 winters in the Cholewon Basin.

Breeding Habitat Requirements and Densities

In the USSR, the typical breeding habitat of this species consists of wide sedge-cottongrass (*Carex-Erio-*

phorum) marshes and sedge-smallreed (*Carex-Calamogrostris*) wet meadows. Such habitats are usually located near rivers and lakes, and often are interspersed with larch (*Larix*) and birch (*Betula*) growths. Waterlogged meadows and extensive tussocky marshlands provide the tall grassy cover favored by these birds for nest sites, and the birds build their nests in those areas where the previous year's growth is still standing. In the USSR prime nesting habitats are being degraded because of land reclamation, soil cultivation, cattle grazing, and fires (Flint, 1978).

In Hokkaido, the habitat requirements for breeding have been analyzed by Masatomi and Kitagawa (1974). They reported that breeding territories must provide for the range of all daily activities, including foraging, nesting, and roosting. They must also provide a safe nesting site, usually reeds in watery surroundings, and also a brood-rearing location. Generally, nesting occurs in one of three habitat types: loose forests or groves, low moor covered with dense and tall grass, and relatively open lowlands. Of these, the first is less preferred than the others, the second is more favored. Open high moor, such as *Sphagnum-Empetrum* habitats, is apparently not utilized.

Even in the favored habitats, breeding densities are quite low. Flint (1978a) reported that in the USSR neighboring nests may be up to several kilometers apart. Masatomi and Kitagawa (1974) reported that 13 pairs observed during the breeding season had maximum home ranges of from 1 to 7 square kilometers, averaging about 2.8 square kilometers. The breeding area of Kushiro Marsh apparently consists of about 2,700 hectares, and in the early 1970s supported about 10 breeding pairs each year, suggesting a density of roughly a pair per 270 hectares (2.7 square kilometers). This is probably a maximum density estimate, and it is undoubtedly much higher than most other breeding areas. However, Cheng (1981) reported a breeding density of about 120 cranes in a sanctuary of 169.5 square kilometers, representing a similar maximum density of about 2.8 square kilometers per pair (assuming all the birds present were paired). Viniter (1981) estimated that in the central Amur region of the USSR the territorial sizes ranged from 4.0 to 12.3 square kilometers, and that up to 8 pairs nested in an area of 162 square kilometers, a breeding density of 20 square kilometers per pair.

Nonbreeding Range and Habitats

The wintering habitats of this species in Korea primarily consist of paddy fields and grassy tidal flats or mudflats. The mudflats and tidal channel areas are generally used in early fall, when the birds feed on earthworms, small crabs, other small aquatic invertebrates, and some plant seeds. When the cold weather arrives the birds usually move to nearby paddy fields, where they feed on rice gleanings (Won, 1981).

In Japan, most of the birds of Hokkaido leave their breeding areas in late autumn, and form flocks at various wintering sites where artificial feeding stations have been developed for them. At such times, flocks of up to 80 birds will sometimes approach farms to obtain food, including grain. However, some pairs or families never leave their breeding habitats, and maintain their territories throughout the year. Such pairs occur now in Takkobu, in Shimochanbetsu in Kushiro District, in Tofutsu in Abashiri District, and possibly also in Nemuro District (Masatomi, 1981a).

FOODS AND FORAGING BEHAVIOR

Foods of Adults

Rather little is known of natural foods of this species. Masatomi and Kitagawa (1974) stated that in Japan the natural plant foods so far known include parsely, some water plants, carrot, pasture plants, the young buds of reed, the inflorescence of *Potamogeton*, acorns and buckwheat. Animal foods reported by various authors include loaches, crucian fish, snakes (*Radix japonica*), sticklebacks, tadpoles, and frogs. Additional animal materials found as foods by these two authors included mud snails, dragonflies, lampreys (*Entosphenus*), carp (*Cyrinus carpio*), goldfish (*Carassius auratus*), frogs (*Rana chensinensis*), mallard duckling, juveniles of reed-warbler (*Acrocephalus*), and small mammals (mole or mouse). Nothing in detail is known of the proportions of these foods taken by the birds.

However, in winter, Japanese cranes are now largely dependent on corn in Hokkaido. Nonetheless, they seem to prefer animal foods when available.

In Korea, the birds also seem to be relatively carnivorous during winter months, although they also feed on rice gleanings during that season. When foraging around the Sachon River and around unfrozen springs, the birds probe for aquatic animals, especially amphipods, snails, and small eels (Archibald, 1981a). Won (1981) stated that earthworms, small crabs, and various plant seeds (*Salsola*, *Suaeda*) are consumed in tidal mudflat areas before cold weather forces the birds into rice paddies for the rest of the winter.

Foods of the Young

Feeding of the young chick begins soon after hatching, and observations by Masatomi (1970, 1972) indicate that initially the chick is fed little tidbits from the ground, such as *Anisogammarus*. There is a record of a chick being fed a small fish (probably *Pungitius pungitius*) only three days after hatching. Other foods include *Moroco percnurus*, Salmonidae, and Gobidae.

Later on, aquatic animals are consumed as staple items. Within 20 days of leaving the nest the chicks feed heavily on dragonflies (Odonata), such as *Libellula*. As the young grow the parents feed them larger fish. The parents have also been observed feeding them frogs (*Rana chensinensis*). By 12 weeks of age, the young are being fed from two to five times per hour, and the foods include fishes such as *Barbatula*, *Misgurnus*, *Cyprinus*, and *Carassius*.

Foraging Behavior

Little specific information on foraging patterns is available for the species. Masatomi and Kitagawa (1975) reported that food-searching behavior takes two forms, including walking about slowly while searching for food with the head variably lowered and the bill directed downwards, and probing in mud or the ground surface, often inserting the bill into the mud repeatedly at the same place. Small food items such as corn are held by the tip of the bill and then swallowed by tossing the head upward a little. When the bird catches a small fish or similar agile animal it performs a heronlike thrust. Although larger fish or small mammals are sometimes swallowed directly, the bird more often tears the food into pieces by grasping it in the bill and shaking the head, and then swallowing each piece separately. Foraging is often performed at wet grasslands, on cultivated fields, along shallow rivers, and on lakeshores. Probing into the ground, under the water, and obtaining items from the ground surface are all commonly performed.

Viniter (1981) also described foraging behavior in this species and noted that during the breeding season the foraging areas were located from 600 to 1,500 meters from the nest, and coincided with the deepest portions of the nesting marsh. Foraging birds would walk slowly for several hundred meters and, having caught something, would often rinse the catch in water, before swallowing it. At times a bird would catch flying horseflies or other flies by rapid lunging movements.

MIGRATIONS AND MOVEMENTS

Seasonal Movements

Since the Japanese population is now essentially sedentary, only the mainland population needs to be dealt with in any detail as to migration. Masatomi (1981a) reported that most of the Hokkaido population moves less than 150 kilometers between breeding and wintering areas, and some families never leave their breeding territories all year. Those birds that do migrate leave their summer habitats during October and November, and the movement is generally ended by mid-December. In late February they begin to leave their wintering areas, and by early April they have established their individual breeding territories. This period generally corresponds to the time of disappearance of snow in Hokkaido. The birds leave their wintering areas in pairs or small flocks of nonbreeders, and typically return in the fall as pairs or family groups.

In Korea, where the birds are only migrants, they arrive in fall, from mid-November until early December, somewhat later than do white-naped cranes, and remain until March (Archibald, 1981a).

In China, fall migration extends from late October to mid-November and the return flight northward occurs in March, judging from historical records. Observations at Bei-dai-he Beach, Hebei (Hopei) Province, in the early 1940s, suggest that the species was the fourth most common migrant crane (after Eurasian, Siberian, and hooded) in that area. Ma (1981) reported that the birds arrive on the Chinese breeding grounds in early or mid-March, with nest-building beginning as early as the end of March. Fall migration begins in early to mid-October.

In the USSR, the cranes begin to return to the southern parts of the Maritime Territory during the first third of March, or about a month before the marshes begin to thaw. At about the end of March or the beginning of April the birds move into the lowlands around Lake Khanka and to their nesting areas along the Ussuri and Amur rivers. About the same time they usually arrive in Lake Bolon area and also in the vicinity of the Zeya and Bureya rivers of the upper Amur. Since eggs have been found by late April, nesting must get underway soon after arrival. Most birds leave these areas in October, with a few late fall records extending into early November.

Daily Movements

Nothing specific has been reported on daily movements in this species.

GENERAL BIOLOGY

Sociality

Flock sizes are bound to be limited in this very rare species, and furthermore the species' relatively carnivorous foraging habits are likely to cause group dispersion except under artificial feeding conditions. Archibald (1981a) reported that in Korea the wintering birds around Panmunjom spend part of the day foraging as family groups, pairs, and single individuals, but roost together in flocks. Pairs and family groups tend to forage in the same region for much of the winter. The nonbreeders, on the other hand, will forage in a single area for several days, and then without apparent reason will move to a different region.

In Hokkaido, where winter feeding is regular, the birds gradually begin to associate during the late fall months. Pairs and families that initially remain rather scattered and occupy separate feeding territories gradually concentrate in areas centering around the feeding stations. Thus, two or three large flocks of 40 to 80 cranes, and several smaller ones, are formed annually in December. The activity range of each flock, including its roosts and feeding areas, has a diameter of a few kilometers. Most of the birds roost communally in shallow unfrozen rivers, but some families remain to themselves in separate roosting areas. In February the paired birds begin to leave the area, leaving their last-year's young and the subadults behind (Masatomi and Kitagawa, 1974).

Daily Activities

As in most other cranes, roosting is performed in relatively safe locations, and normally the birds leave the roost site at dawn, returning again at dusk. During unusually cold weather, the birds may remain on their roosts until early afternoon, flying out to foraging areas for a few hours, and then returning to their roost sites (Archibald, 1981a).

Interspecific Interactions

Studies by Viniter (1981) in the central Amur area of the USSR indicate that the birds are indifferent to most other nearby nesting birds while on their breeding territory, including some raptors. Thus, falcons (*Erythropus amurensis*), buzzards (*Buteo buteo*), and owls (*Asio otus* and *A. flammeus*) would sometimes hunt above an incubating crane, and a harrier (*Circus melanoleucus*) was observed to land in sedge cover as close as 50 meters from the nest. However, when a harrier (*C. aeruginosus*) appeared above a nest when a crane chick was present, the parents uttered unison and warning calls. When crows (*Corvus corone*) came too close, they would be chased for some distance. The strongest responses were found toward spotted eagles (*Aquila clanga*), which in one case nested some 300 meters from a crane nest. Such birds would be watched intently by the breeding birds, and Viniter saw several aggressive encounters. In all cases, one of the cranes remained on the nest while the other pursued the enemy.

One encounter with a wolf was also observed by Viniter. When the male crane observed a wolf about 600 meters away, it flew over and landed within 10 to 15 meters of the animal. Then, standing very erect, it approached to within 6 or 8 meters. For about 30 minutes the crane followed the wolf until they came to the edge of woods, after which the crane flew back to its mate on the nest. Similarly, when a large dog was released near a pair of cranes with chicks, the birds swiftly ran at the dog from both sides, chasing it for about 200 meters, and attempting to peck at its flanks. Likewise smaller carnivores, such as foxes, badgers, raccoon-dogs (*Nyctereutes*), and similar mammals are regularly chased by the adult birds without hesitation.

Masatomi and Kitagawa (1974) likewise reported that most birds are ignored by breeding cranes, but that carrion crows (*Corvus corone*) and jungle-crows (*Corvus macrorhynchos*) frequently take eggs and chicks. Occasionally the black kite (*Milvus migrans*), buzzards (*Buteo buteo*), and marsh harriers (*Circus aeruginosus*) do the same, but the adult birds can readily drive away these species. The breeding birds pay particular attention to white-tailed sea eagles (*Haliaeetus albicilla*), but attacks by this species have not been observed.

Competition between the white-naped crane and the Japanese crane is perhaps of some local significance, but the former is much more a vegetarian than is the Japanese crane, and thus the levels of foraging competition are probably reduced. Archibald (1981a) found that when an artificial breeding station was established in Korea, a pair of white-naped cranes attacked and supplanted several Japanese cranes that attempted to feed there. On the other hand, territorial pairs of Japanese cranes were dominant over the white-naped, but did not attack them when they were present on their feeding area.

BREEDING BIOLOGY

Age of Maturity and Time of Breeding

Few records on the age of maturity of the Japanese crane are available. A female at the Cologne Zoo bred for the first time when she was approaching 6 years old, and Archibald and Viess (1979) reported that semen was obtained from males in their third year of life. Masatomi and Kitagawa (1974) believed that maturity probably occurs at 3 to 4 years of age.

The time of breeding in this species is quite restricted (see table 14), and is largely centered in April. Masatomi and Kitagawa (1974) reported egg-laying as early as the start of April and extending to the latter part of May in Hokkaido. Ma (1981) likewise stated that in northern China the egg-laying period begins in April and ends in late May. In the Central Amur valley egg-laying occurs in the second half of April (Viniter, 1979).

Pair Formation and Courtship

In their analysis of the social/reproductive behavior of this species, Masatomi and Kitagawa (1975) divided the components into duetting, dancing, copulatory behavior, nest-building, and incubation behavior. Duetting display is normally only performed by pairs, in a variety of situations such as after copulation, in winter-

ing flocks, and when there are territorial intruders. Thus the unison call has manifold functions, including formation and maintenance of the pair bond, as well as territorial advertisement and agonistic signaling. As described by Archibald (1975, 1976) and other authors, the display begins with the birds standing 1 to 3 meters apart. Either sex can initiate the call, but this is usually done by the female. Both sexes raise their humeri and expose their primaries during the calling, and these are usually moved in a rhythmic manner during the calling. The male's wings are usually raised higher than those of the female during display. Both birds call in an antiphonal manner. For each male call, which is typically monosyllabic, the female utters two (mainland population) or three or four (Japanese population) calls. Unison calling often provokes the same display from other nearby pairs, sometimes resulting in a synchronous chorus of calling.

In addition to the unison call, several other social vocal signals occur among paired birds, and Viniter (1981) reported a total of six call types among adults. Many of these are associated with alarm, threat, or communication between members of a pair.

Like the unison call, dancing is a complex behavior having several probable functions, of which pair maintenance is perhaps a minor one. The movements associated with dancing were described by Masatomi and Kitagawa (1975), who recognized eight distinct postures and four types of movements. These movement categories are pumping (of the head and neck), bouncing, pursuing movements (as in chasing and fleeing behavior), and throwing movements. Dancing often occurs in winter flocks at feeding places, and also solitary dancing sometimes occurs, as when a bird has left the nest after being relieved of incubation. Dancing behavior toward other species, including both other cranes and such birds as crows, has also been reported, further suggesting multiple functions of this behavior. Perhaps dancing is best considered simply a general signal of excitement, and this can include intraspecific agonistic and sexual excitement, as well as a variety of other interspecific responses.

Copulatory behavior has been described in detail by Masatomi and Kitagawa (1975). It apparently differs little at all from the pattern described earlier for cranes in general. It can be initiated by either sex, by a bill-raising display that stimulates the mate to follow. The receptive female turns her back to the mate, and sometimes begins to spread her wings. The male then approaches, uttering a series of *kotz* sounds, which gradually become louder and increase in pitch. As he steps upon the female the calls become even higher in pitch, and while mounted the male calls continuously. As treading is completed the male stops calling abruptly, and slides down forward over the female's head. The pair then invariably performs bowing, and sometimes assumes an arching posture, with the bills raised vertically and the heads turned at right angles to the body.

Territoriality and Early Nesting Behavior

Shortly after their return to the breeding areas, paired cranes establish territories, or reclaim those of the previous year. Masatomi and Kitagawa (1974) estimated that territories in this species range from 1 to 7 square kilometers, an area coequal with their reported home range estimate, since all activities occur within the territorial boundaries. Viniter (1981) similarly estimated that the territories of three pairs ranged from about 4 to 12 square kilometers, and consisted of tussocky cotton-sedge marshes mixed with oak-birch islands, these also containing a sparse undergrowth of shrubs and saplings. Four of the eight territories studied by Viniter were in marshes that ranged from about 1 to 2 square kilometers in area, and a fifth was in a marsh of about 0.1 square kilometer. Distances between neighboring nests ranged from 2.7 to 4.0 kilometers, and the nearest settlements were 8 to 10 kilometers away. Ma's (1981) study of breeding birds in China indicated a territorial size of 45 and 130 hectares for two pairs, and a minimum distance between nests of 800 to 1,000 meters.

Of 13 territorial pairs studied by Masatomi and Kitagawa (1974), nearly all could be characterized as low moor habitats, ranging from reed communities to reed-sedge or reed-grass communities, or sparsely wooded and alder-dotted habitats. Probably the presence of tall grassy vegetation from the previous year is an important territorial component, insofar as well hidden nest sites seem to be critical. In the central Amur it was found that pairs chose nest sites in flooded sedge marshes that had not been burned the previous year and provided cover from 30 to 80 centimeters in height (Viniter, 1981). Of twenty nest sites in China, ten were well hidden, and only two were unconcealed. Of these nests, thirteen were constructed almost entirely (90 percent) of reeds. Viniter stated that the five nests he studied were raised above water level 15-30 centimeters and were oval platforms about 100 centimeters in diameter. Likewise, the Chinese nests observed by Ma had average outer nest diameters of about 135 × 165 centimeters and were from 10 to 39 centimeters high.

Masatomi (1970-1972) believes that the female probably chooses the nesting site, but both sexes help build the nest, with the male primarily cutting the materials and the female placing them on the nest. It requires from two to three days at minimum to construct a nest, depending on weather and other disturbances. There is no good information on the frequency with which old nest sites are reused, but one pair observed by Viniter built their nest 600 meters away from the previous year's site.

As the nest is constructed, an open area around it is formed because of the cutting or pulling of reeds and grass. The diameter of this open space may be about 4 to 5 meters, and several paths often radiate from the area out into the reeds, reflecting the birds' movements. Sometimes nestlike platforms are found near the nests and apparently serve as nocturnal roosting sites. These structures are also used for roosting during the brooding period by the young (Ma, 1981).

Egg-laying and Incubation

Typically, egg-laying occurs during morning hours, often between 6:00 and 10:00. During the four years of observation at Tsuru Park, the first eggs were laid between March 18 and April 4, and about a month after the first copulations were observed. Eggs are laid from 2 to 4 days apart. It is believed that incubation begins with the first egg laid (Viniter, 1981). Of 20 nests studied by Ma (1981), 13 contained 2 eggs, 1 had 3 eggs, and 4 (possibly incomplete) nests had only a single egg. Five nests in the Amur River area had either 2 eggs (4 nests) or a single egg (1 nest). These data, together with those of Walkinshaw (see table 16), suggest that 2-egg clutches are normal in this species.

Most observers have found that incubation required from 29 to 31 days under wild conditions (Viniter, 1981; Ma, 1981), although Masatomi (1970-1972) reported durations in the wild of 31 to 34 days, and 31 to 36 days in Kushiro Park. Incubation is by both sexes, but females tend to spend more time on the nest than do males, especially during the nighttime hours (Viniter, 1981). Masatomi (1970-1972) reported that during the daytime hours, however, the male tends to incubate for a greater proportion of the time than does the female, with a particular tendency to incubate during the middle portion of the day. The eggs are usually turned when the birds exchange incubation duties, and in general the male tends to do more shifting of the eggs than does the female. In captivity, there are usually 2 to 6 shifts in incubation per day, but sometimes as many as 12.

The male takes the primary role in defending the nest against possible danger, and whichever parent is off the nest keeps a sharp lookout for possible intruders. Other Japanese cranes that enter the territory are immediately chased away, and white-naped cranes have also been observed being evicted.

Hatching and Postbreeding Biology

A few days prior to hatching, weak cries can be heard from the chicks inside their eggs, and shortly thereafter pipping begins. Although there is considerable variation, about 30 hours often elapse from the time the egg shell is initially pierced until the chick is completely out. The second egg often pips the second day after the hatching of the first chick, although at times the second chick may emerge as soon as a day after the first chick. As soon as the chick has emerged from its shell, the parent crushes the shell and throws it from the nest (Ma, 1981).

Viniter (1981) reported that if food was plentiful near the nest, the brood remained on the pair's feeding territory for 1 to 2 weeks, but should they be disturbed the birds would move to the most distant areas of the marsh on the day after hatching. Ma (1981) found that birds moved about 20 meters from the nest on the day of hatching, and up to about 100 meters by the second day. Masatomi (1970-1972) found that the chicks may remain in the nest for 3 to 5 days. He noted that within 2 days of hatching parental feeding was noted only once, but 10 times on the third day, 5 times on the eighth day, and 93 times by the twenty-fifth day. Both parents feed the young, with no obvious tendency for one sex to do this more than the other. By the time the young are 10 weeks old, the chicks are being fed about twice an hour, and by 12 weeks from 2 to 5 times per hour. Generally the female pays more attention to the chicks than does the male, probably because the chicks tend to follow the female. By 3 months after hatching, the young are easily able to keep up with their parents, and fledging occurs at about this time. In China, fledging occurs in August, and by mid-September the young are able to fly for considerable distances. At this time they begin to move out into nearby uplands and cornfields, and within a month they begin their fall migration (Ma, 1981).

RECRUITMENT RATES, POPULATION STATUS, AND CONSERVATION

Age-ratio data for this species (tables 8 and 30) suggest that the annual recruitment rate is probably between 12.8 and 15.2 percent for the Japanese population, which is essentially fully protected. There seems to be no good information on age ratios for the population wintering in Korea. Of these, the majority probably come from the Manchurian portion of China, and at least part of that population is protected by the Jalong Natural Reserve, in the lower portion of the Wu Yu-erh

River, southeast of Chichihar, in the Nun River basin. In the middle Amur Valley of the USSR the birds are so far subject to limited human disturbance, and a provincial refuge has been established there that may help to secure future nesting. However, the development of the Amur and Bureya floodplains by drainage activities and increased use by cattle has had a negative effect on crane populations (Dymin and Pankin, 1975). Similarly, the Lake Khanka area has suffered from intensive land development, and the white-naped crane no longer nests in that area at all, while the Japanese crane nests only in quite small numbers. In the Lake Bolon area of the lower Amur, some 13 to 15 pairs of Japanese cranes are known to be nesting, and part of this basin has been recommended as a preserve.

It is apparent that international efforts of the USSR, China, Japan, and Korea will be required to save the Japanese crane from extinction. Although the Hokkaido population is relatively secure because of its sedentary nature, its size is evidently close to a saturation point, as it has remained at about 200 birds since the late 1960s. Very little unoccupied marshland now exists in eastern Hokkaido, so it seems unlikely that the population will be able to increase very significantly from its present level. Indeed, only a section of the Kishiro Marsh and the Kiritappu marshes have been designated as a natural monument and are fully protected. Additionally, several wildlife protection areas and prefectural parks include some summer habitats. Nevertheless, reclamation of marshlands, primarily by drainage, threatens parts of the Kushiro Marsh, and several other summer habitats are in danger of land development programs (Masatomi and Kitagawa, 1974.)

EVOLUTIONARY RELATIONSHIPS

Archibald (1975, 1976) concluded that the closest relationships of the Japanese crane are with the hooded, Eurasian, and whooping cranes, based on unison call characteristics. However, Wood (1979) found that the hooded and Eurasian crane tended to cluster with the white-naped cladistically, so it seems likely that the nearest relative of the Japanese crane is the whooping crane.

Hooded Crane

Grus monachus Temminck 1835

Other Vernacular Names. None in general English use; Huan-has (Chinese); Grue-moine (French); Mönch-skranich (German); Nabe-zuru (Japanese); Chernyi zhuravl (Russian); Grulla capachina (Spanish).

Range. Breeding range not well known, but currently known to breed only in a few isolated areas of the USSR, including the Ussuri River and the lower Amur, in the basin of the middle reaches of the Vilyuy, and in the Olekma-Chara uplands. Breeding probably also occurs in the upper Nizhnaya Tunguska River and its tributary the Nyepa, along the Chona River, in the lower Amur along the In and Mukhen rivers, in the basin of the Evur River and Lake Evonon, in the upper part of the Gorin River, and in central Sakhalin. Possibly also breeds in northwestern Manchuria (Hai-la-erh) and the middle Sungari. Migratory, wintering in Korea (irregularly) and Japan (Kyushu and Honshu, Kagoshima and Yamaguchi prefectures, and formerly Hokkaido). Also winters in unknown numbers in the lower Yangtze Valley of China (Cheng, 1981), and has been seen rarely in India.

Subspecies. None recognized.

Measurements. Wing (chord), males 479-525 mm (average of 7, 506 mm); females 453-560 mm (average of 9, 487.9 mm). Exposed culmen, males 99-107 mm (average of 7, 103.7 mm); females 89-101 mm (average of 9, 95.4 mm). Tarsus, males 194-222 mm (average of 7, 209.3 mm); females 199-223 mm (average of 9, 208.8 mm). Eggs, average 91.25 × 58.97 mm (86.0-97.4 × 55.7-59.7 mm) (Walkinshaw, 1973).

Weights. Seven adult males at the International Crane Foundation averaged 3,930 grams (range 3,284-4,870 grams), and four adult females averaged 3,540 grams (range 3,397-3,737 grams). Two breeding-grounds females weighed 3,110 and 3,550 grams (Andreev, 1974). The estimated egg weight is 173 grams, but four fresh eggs averaged 149.6 grams (Christine Sheppard, pers. comm.).

Description

Adults of both sexes are alike, with the forepart of the crown unfeathered, red, and covered with black hairlike bristles. The upper eyelid is also bare and is horn-colored. The rest of the head and neck are white, sometimes tinged with gray. The white extends down the neck, about half way down the front side and almost to the shoulders posteriorly, sometimes abruptly changing to the blackish gray of the back and breast. The body is otherwise slaty gray, with some brownish or grayish tinge above and with the feathers tipped with grayish. The primaries, secondaries, tail, and tail coverts are black, and the inner secondaries are elongated, pointed, and drooping. The iris is hazel yellow to orange brown, usually with yellowish present, the bill is yellowish horn, and the legs and toes are nearly black.

Juveniles have the crown covered with black and white feathers during their first year, and exhibit some brownish or grayish wash on their feathers, especially on the head and neck.

Downy chicks are rusty ochre, darker on the shoulders and back, and noticeably lighter on the belly and the rump. Each down feather is lighter at its tip; the basal third is dark brown with a cinnamon tinge, while the tips of the feathers have a golden tinge. The beak is yellow at the base, gradually shading to light flesh color, and getting darker only at the very tip. The eyelids are yellow, and the iris is dark cinnamon. The toes, tarsus, and bare portions of the tibia are initially yellow, but by the time the chick is 24 hours old they have taken on a brownish tone. The beak begins to darken by the end of the third day (Pukinskii and Ilynskii, 1977).

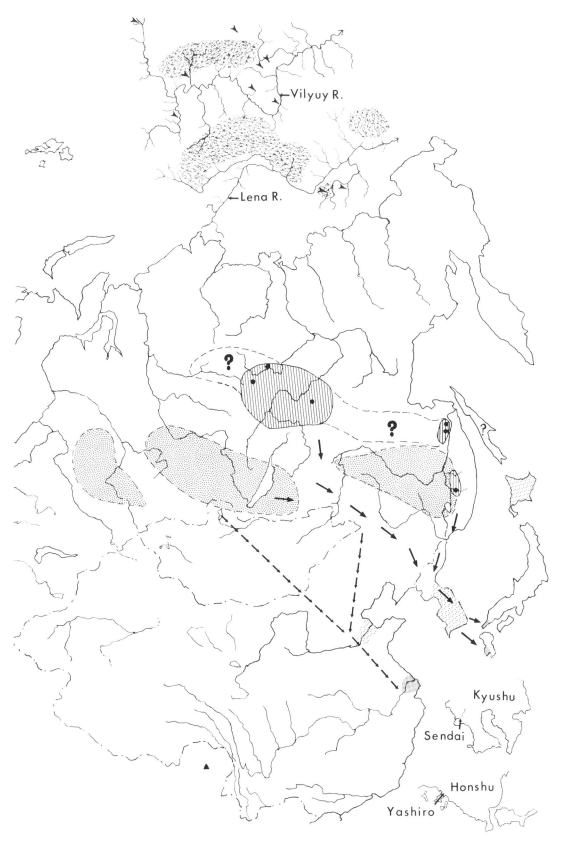

Breeding (hatched) and wintering (dark shading) ranges of the hooded crane. Areas of nonbreeding summer occurrence are indicated by coarse stippling, and prior wintering areas are shown by light stippling. Arrows indicate known (large arrows) or probable (small arrows) migratory routes, and inked circles indicate breeding records. The small triangle indicates an extralimital winter record. Upper inset indicates summer occurrences in Vilyuy and Lena basins, and distribution of bog forest habitats (overlay). Lower inset shows locations of major wintering vicinities on Kyushu and Honshu islands, Japan.

Identification

In the field, this is the only crane that has a medium-gray body color that contrasts with the pure white neck and head, with a small reddish "hood" provided by the bare crown skin. In flight, the birds appear uniformly dark above and below on the body and wings. The call is relatively high-pitched, but is very similar to that of the common Eurasian crane.

In the hand, the distinctive white neck and head but otherwise gray body serve to identify this species immediately. Apart from the absence of black on the neck and head, the hooded crane is very similar in general color to the Eurasian crane. As in the Eurasian crane, the trachea is coiled within the keel of the sternum. The hooded crane is generally a darker tone of gray on the body than is the Eurasian crane, and has smaller but overlapping body measurements. Wild hybrids between these species sometimes occur.

DISTRIBUTION AND HABITATS

Historical Range

The breeding range of this rare species has only begun to be identified in the past few decades. Dementiev and Gladkov (1968) considered the breeding area to be "unclarified," since at the time of their writing only a single hooded crane nest had ever been reported, and this was found about 40 kilometers west of Kainsk (Kuibyshev) in 1908 or 1909. This record was later found to be erroneous, as was the record of an egg obtained in the vicinity of Tomsk and wrongly identified as that of a hooded crane. Indeed, it was not until 140 years after the species was initially described that the first nest of the hooded crane was found, in 1974. As a result, almost nothing can be said about the historical breeding range with any degree of certainty. Certainly, many of the earlier summer records of birds in the vicinity of Tomsk, Minusinsk, and the Lake Baikal region generally believed to be nesting birds were obviously only those of nonbreeders summering in these areas (Neufeldt, 1977).

It was not until Vorbiev (1963) discovered a nesting area in larch-peat bogs of southwestern Yakutia that the actual nesting grounds of this species began to become apparent, and it is now clear that their major nesting habitats are the wide, mossy taiga bogs, interspersed with stunted larch trees and bushes, of that area. For example, Vorobiev provided an account of a man who observed a family of hooded cranes in August of 1961, at the mouth of the Nezhnyeye Dzhegye (above the mouth of the Tyana River), and quoted several other accounts of paired birds seen in the general area of the Olekmo-Charskoye uplands during the 1950s. Later nesting was verified in the Bekin River area by Pukinskii and Ilyinskii (1977).

Current Breeding Range

It is now apparent that the hooded crane nests over much of the southern part of the Yakut Autonomous Republic, generally between Lake Baikal and the Amur River, in the Amur Region of Khabavorsk Territory, and in the Maritime Territory. Its patchy distribution is a reflection of the discontinuous occurrence of its favored breeding habitat, namely raised mossy bogs in central and southern taiga country where stunted trees, especially larches, occur.

Studies by Andreev (1974) in the Vilyuy Basin have confirmed the fact that hooded cranes nest regularly over this rather broad area. From the Vilyuy's tributary river the Appaiya and the town of Kuomaryka (approximately 117° east longitude) the range extends to the north as far as the middle reaches of the Posporin River (about 60° north latitude), and the upper reaches of the Morkoka River. Andreev reported that old hunters had regularly met cranes with fledged young in the area of Annar (along the Kukuhungda River, a tributary to the Oylenck River), and also nesting in the lower Vilyuy in the vicinity of Kobyayski. Andreev judged the breeding range in this area to be at least 3,000 square kilometers, associated with thin, middle-aged taiga on basaltic landscapes. Within this area, nesting habitats are marshy forests with peat areas and wetter open-water bogs with cottongrass and sedges. Nesting in the Vilyuy Basin has been confirmed on the River Chona (near Tuai Khaya), in the bases of the Akhtaranda and Syuldyukar rivers, and near the village of Vilyuchan. In the last-named area mixed pairs of hooded and Eurasian cranes have been observed (Neufeldt, 1981a). The lower reaches of the Vilyuy, as in the vicinity of Yakutska, where adult specimens have been collected in May, is perhaps also a nesting area, but so far this remains unproven. In the Vilyuy Basin the Eurasian crane is somewhat separated ecologically from the hooded crane, with the former preferring wide, flat valleys with reed and sedge meadows and drier areas with birches, while the hooded prefers mossy hammocks or damp moors in boggy larch forests, at altitudes of 500 to 700 meters. In the Bikin River valley the birds nest at similar altitudes of 200 to 600 meters.

The second area of hooded crane nesting to have been discovered recently is in the Bikin River area of the Ussuri Basin, in Maritime Territory. This breeding area was discovered by Yuri Pukinskii in 1974, near the settlement of Barkhatnoya. The habitat in that region is a depressed mossy swamp, enclosed by hills, and with floodplain woods along one edge. Most of the swamp is covered by scattered and stunted larches (*Larix dahurica*) and in some places there is an undergrowth of birch (*Betula fructiosa*). The most recent observations in this area (in 1980) suggest that about 50 pairs may summer in this area presently, of which about two-thirds apparently nest. The population density there is about a pair per 20 to 25 square kilometers (USSR Crane Working Group Information Bulletin No 2, 1981). Areas of probable breeding in the lower Ussuri River include some 6,000 square kilometers of area, from the Nizhni Pereval to the Ulunga, where 14 to 16 nesting pairs were recorded in the early 1970s. At lower population densities the birds might reach the middle parts of the Khor Ri River (a Ussuri tributary), and its lower reaches near Sukpai Village. They also occur during the breeding season northeast of Birobidzhan city, at the mouth of the Simmi River, close to Evoron Lake, in the Evur River basin, in the In River basin, and along the Mukhen and Gorin rivers (Neufeldt, 1981a). Lone birds, pairs, and small groups have been observed in late spring in the In River basin of the Jewish Autonomous Republic (Yevreysk A.O) in typical peat bogs among larch and shrub habitats, and distraction displays have been observed as well, strongly suggesting nesting there. Birds performing distraction behavior have also been observed along the Mukhen River, a tributary to the Neptu, which flows into the Amur River below Khabavorsk (Neufeldt and Wunderlich, 1978).

Besides these areas, the Vilyuy Basin and the adjoining Olekmo-Charskoye uplands, and the Bikin area of the Ussuri Basin, there are but few definite records of breeding. In 1980 nesting was found to occur along the Uda River and at Lake Bolon, and in the mossy larch bogs at Lake Udyl, in the lower Amur Valley, Khabavorsk Territory (USSR Crane Working Group Information Bulletin No. 2, 1981). Beyond that, it is possible that the birds are nesting in the upper reaches of the lower Tunguska River, in the upper Zeya River, and in the upper parts of the Selemdsha and its tributary river, the Nora, since the same kinds of habitat are to be found in these regions (Neufeldt and Wunderlich, 1978). Similar habitat occurs on Sakhalin Island, and elsewhere in eastern Siberia.

Additionally, there are a considerable number of areas where nonbreeding birds gather, both in wooded steppes and in open steppe habitats. Of these, two are especially important. The first consists of open, swampy lowlands in forest-steppes and steppes of southern, middle, and western Siberia, westward to Barabinsk steppe, in the Ob Basin. The second important area is the treeless steppes of southern Transbaikalia (Dauria), including the Torei Lakes and Borzya Lakes. This area seems to have been the most important concentration area of hooded cranes in the past, from June to August. At various times as many as hundreds of birds have been seen there in earlier times, but recent increased agri-

cultural activities, livestock grazing, and hunting have caused a reduction of use. At the present, most hooded cranes occurring on these summering grounds are in small groups, often in company with Eurasian cranes (Neufeldt, 1981a).

Apart from these areas, there may be a very limited amount of breeding in China, in the lower Sungari River area of extreme northeastern China in the middle Amur basin and in the Hai-lao-erh area of northwestern Manchuria, near the Soviet and Mongolian borders (Cheng, 1973). There is no definite evidence of nesting in Sakhalin, and Cheng (1981) reported that there are no recent reports of Chinese nesting for this species.

Thus, it is clear that virtually the entire breeding population of this species is confined to the USSR, and is not confined to any single critical area. In general, its nesting habitats are relatively remote and in areas having little human influence, except perhaps for lumbering. Such activities may increase the nesting habitat by making it more open, and thus the total nesting range may be increasing rather than declining.

Habitat Requirements and Densities

Studies by Yuri Pukinskii in the Maritime Territory provide the best information about breeding habitats. Nesting there occurs in wet, swampy areas dominated by heathers such as Labrador tea (*Ledum palustre*), and leatherleaf (*Chamaedaphene calyculata*), as well as bog whortleberry (*Vaccinium uliginosum*) and cranberry (*Oxycoccus quadripetalus*). In some areas iris (*Iris laevigata, I. kaempferi*) grow, as do various sedges (*Carex* spp.), reeds (*Phragmites*), buckbean (*Menyanthes trifoliata*), and cottongrass (*Eriophorum vaginatum*). The ground cover is mostly of mosses (*Sphagnum, Polytrichum, Aulacomnium*). In the nesting marsh that was studied there was no open water except for two brooklets and a pond area of about 10×100 meters. Under the moss cover, there was also water, which oozed up to the surface along animal trails. On one side of this boggy area larch growth was present, and much of the bog was covered by scattered, low-growing larches.

In the Vilyuysk Basin, where breeding was reported by Andreev (1974), the breeding habitats appear to be very similar bogs that either lack open water or have open stretches, and are covered on their banks by cottongrass and various sedges. Nesting occurs in boggy, burned-out patches of habitat near the higher marshes of the drier or "tumara" type. Wetter marshes of the "eeii" type are apparently used for brood-rearing. In early fall, as the young are fledging, the birds use meadows with grassy areas along the small taiga rivers.

Nesting densities appear to be extremely low. In the Bikin River area, covering about 6,000 square kilometers, only about 7 to 12 percent of the land represents possible nesting habitat, in which 14 to 16 nesting pairs were recorded (Neufeldt, 1981a). This would represent a breeding density of about a pair per 25 to 50 square kilometers of suitable habitat. The local distribution of the birds seems to be closely associated with the distribution of bogs of the type described earlier. On one section of the Bikin River (between Verkhnyeye Oerevalo to Ulunga) there are 6 or 7 bogs, and a pair of hooded cranes was reported associated with each. These mossy bogs probably provide only limited visual and acoustic separation from other pairs of hooded cranes and may set territorial limits according to the size limits of the bogs. Pukinskii and Ilyinskii (1977) stated that the nesting territory may be 4 to 6 square kilometers, or even ten times larger, depending on the size of the bog occupied by the pair.

Nonbreeding Range and Habitats

As mentioned above, some of the steppes and wooded steppes of central Asia that were once believed to be breeding habitats are actually only summering habitats of nonbreeding birds. One such area, in the upper Ob Basin, stretches from Verkhny Uimon Village on the Altai northward to the Ket River, and from Bateni Village along the Yenisei River in Tuva to the edges of the steppe marshes in the basin of Tes-Khen River and Tere-Khol Lake. This area is used by both nomadic hooded cranes and Eurasian cranes, mainly from May to July, but sometimes into September or even October (Neufeldt, 1981a).

The other summering area, the Daurian steppes, is still used to a limited extent by hooded cranes in summer, and extends southward into neighboring regions of eastern Mongolia and China (Neufeldt, 1981a).

The wintering area of the hooded crane is now apparently almost entirely limited to Japan; current wintering in eastern China is not well documented but is believed to take place in the lower Yangtze Valley (Cheng, 1981). There is no convincing evidence that the species ever wintered in significant numbers in Assam or Manipur.

Fortunately, the hooded crane's status in Japan has been well documented, and this provides an excellent opportunity to monitor the species' overall status (table 31). Two major wintering areas occur in Japan, at Arasaki, Kagoshima Prefecture, and in Yashiro in Yamaguchi Prefecture. The population at Yashiro has been reported on by Kawamura (1981) and Koga (1981), and that at Arasaki by Nishida (1981). Only a relatively few hooded cranes winter at Yashiro, generally less than 100, while sometimes as many as 3,000 have been reported at Arasaki (Sendai City). The birds forage in grain fields, and at Yashiro have been found to feed mainly on rice from late October to early December, and

later on wheat and barley. Roosting is done in shallow water paddies associated with rice culture. Some of the major roost locations are at Yashiro (Kumage Town), Nakasu (Tokuyama City), and Nakayama (Shuto Town). Feeding is done in areas ranging from 2 to 26 hectares, which usually are located near their roosts, and which typically are harvested rice paddies, where the birds forage on waste rice. Some of the Yashiro roosts are known to have been used annually since 1960, and the number of birds using them has varied from only a few to as many as nearly 50 (Kawamura, 1981). At Izumi almost all the cranes, more than 1,000, roost in a single location, but hooded cranes and white-naped cranes remain separated (Nishida, 1981).

FOODS AND FORAGING BEHAVIOR

Foods of Adults

Very little is known of the foods of adults on the breeding grounds. Andreev (1974) reported that the birds eat large quantities of mountain cranberries and especially bog bilberries. In a stomach that he examined he found seven mosquito larvae (Platytipula), and large numbers of threadlike aquatic plants. Local residents told him that the birds capture and eat hynobiids, which they obtain by digging in the mossy bogs. Besides insects, some frogs (Rana cruenta) and salamanders (Hynobius keyserlingi) may also be consumed in summer, but apparently plant food predominates even during the breeding season (Neufeldt and Wunderlich, 1978; Pukinskii and Ilyinskii, 1977).

Foods on the wintering areas consist of cultivated grains such as rice, wheat, and barley, particularly rice (Nishida, 1981). Mixed samples of crane droppings from hooded and white-naped cranes exhibited a high occurrence of rice hulls in them, with smaller amounts of wheat or barley husks, and very small quantities of other seeds, grass fragments, shell fragments, and insects. There is no indication that animal materials play a significant role in the diets of these birds, at least during winter months.

Foods of Young

Nothing specific has been written on this subject.

MIGRATIONS AND MOVEMENTS

Seasonal Movements

The migratory movements of this species have been discussed by Neufeldt (1981a), who believes that the Yakutia birds of the Vilyuy Basin migrate over the northern part of the Irkutskaya Oblast and Trans-baikalia in a generally southwestern direction, where they merge with local summer resident birds and those migrating almost directly east out of the summering area in eastern Siberia. This route crosses over the Torei lakes, where flocks of 80 to 100 birds are still encountered. Then the birds fly through northeastern Mongolia and Barga, cut through Inner Mongolia (Dalai-Nur and Kalgan), Hopei (Hebei) Province of China, over Korea, and cross especially the Tsushima Straits to reach their wintering areas in southern Japan. It is possible that some of the birds of the Siberian population, together with cranes from unknown nesting areas north of Amurland, pass over the Zeya Basin and farther south through the middle Amur plains, where they join migrants from the lower Amur Basin.

The migration through the Maritime Territory is less obvious, but evidently passes southward along the Ussuri River valley past Lake Khanka, and south into Korea. However, apparently only small migrations take place in southern Maritime Territory, and probably many of the birds breeding in the Bikin area and north on the lower Amur fly up the Sungari River basin over Liaoning Province of northeastern China, and then southward to China or Japan.

At least in earlier years there was moderate migration of birds during both spring and fall over Hopei (Hebei) Province of northeastern China (Hemmingsen and Guildal, 1968; Cheng, 1981), during which most of the migrant birds coming out of western Siberia on their way south to wintering areas of the lower Yangtze River, where it has long been believed that the species occurred. Yet, there is no specific information on the numbers of birds now wintering there, although Cheng reported (1981) that spring and fall migrations still occur along the lower Wu Yu-erh River near Qiqihar in Heilongjiang Province.

In earlier years, substantial numbers of hooded cranes remained in Korea over the winter, arriving in late November or early December and departing in March. However, since the Korean War very few have been observed, so the birds must now largely overfly Korea on their way to Japan and back. In the Yashiro area, the cranes usually arrive in late October (range of 10 years, October 23 to November 7), and leave in March (latest dates range from 28 February to 16 March over 9 years) (Nishida, 1981). Kawamura (1981) reported that the birds begin leaving in spring when the maximum daily temperatures exceed 10° C, typically departing on the morning of a nice day when the atmospheric pressure is high. Sometimes the birds all depart during a single day, while at other times several days may be required.

The hooded cranes arrive on their breeding areas of the lower Amur at about the beginning of April, and in the Vilyuy Basin they were reported by Andreev (1974) to arrive at about the beginning of May, with the largest flocks (up to 26 birds) seen on May 19. However, eggs have been reported there as early as mid-May. The movement out of that area begins in mid-August, according to Andreev.

Daily Movements

On the wintering areas, the daily activities of the hooded cranes appear to be very much like those of other species. They forage during daylight hours, and begin returning to the roost at dusk. They often leave their feeding grounds before dark, land at a point near their roost and remain there until almost dark, and then fly into the roost. Or, they may remain in the feeding area until dark, and then fly directly to the roost. In either case, it is as dark as 0-50 luxes when they fly into their roosting areas. After landing, they drink, utter unison calls, or walk around a bit before settling in for the night. While roosting they maintain moderate distances between one another, probably to avoid wing contact should they have to take flight rapidly.

Studies by Nishida (1981) indicate that cranes are very sensitive to light intensity, and that light between 0 and 20 luxes tends to stimulate movement to and away from the roost at dusk and dawn.

Observations by Kawamura (1975) indicate that the roosts tend to be located from 0.75 to 10.2 kilometers from feeding areas, and the majority (15 of 19) studied were in wet paddies. The roosts ranged in area from 40 to 1,250 square meters, and in water depth from 1.0 to 7.5 centimeters, with 5.0 centimeters representing an ideal water depth. Mud depth ranged from 4.5 to 10.5 centimeters.

Interspecific Interactions

Very little is known of the possible predators of this species on the breeding grounds, but it is moderately large and probably safe from most if not all avian predators. In the Bikin River breeding area, both the pied harrier (*Circus melanoleucus*) and the crested honey buzzard (*Pernis ptilorhynchus*) occur regularly, and black storks (*Ciconia nigra*) also occur. Some of these species might represent threats to eggs or young birds. The Manchurian wapiti (*Cervus elaphus*) also is common, and indeed nests of hooded cranes are often placed at intersections of paths made by these large animals, which might well trample nests. It seems likely, however, as with the sandhill cranes, that the adult cranes are able to chase those ungulates away from their nesting territories.

As noted earlier, Eurasian cranes nest in some of the same areas as do hooded cranes, as for example the Vilyuy Basin. Although the two species tend to be ecologically separated, they often associate during migration, and mixed pairing has been observed on the breeding area. Thus, in 1865 a pair in which the male was a Eurasian crane and the female a hooded crane was observed during May (Andreev, 1974), which was the same combination as a mixed pair observed at Izumi, Japan, during seven winters (1968-1975). During this period the birds had seven hybrid offspring (Nishida, 1981).

BREEDING BIOLOGY

Age of Maturity and Time of Breeding

Hooded cranes have so far been bred in captivity only once (Katz, 1979), and no information is available on age of maturity under captive conditions. Presumably maturity is not attained before the third year, and possibly requires longer than that.

There are extremely few records of eggs in the wild. Eggs have been found on the Bikin River in the latter part of May; these proved to be well incubated, suggesting that incubation may have started in late April. In the Vilyuy Basin a hunter reported seeing eggs about the middle of May, and both downy young and large flightless young in late June. Flightless young have also been seen there as late as the end of July. All of this would suggest that most egg-laying probably occurs in late April and early May, and hatching probably occurs about the beginning of June.

Pair Formation and Courtship

The best descriptions of social behavior in the hooded crane come from Archibald (1975, 1976), who described the unison call behavior. He placed the species in the group also containing the Eurasian, whooping, and Japanese cranes, but noted that unlike these other three species the hooded crane does not usually lower its wrists during high intensity threat posturing. The female usually utters a long call and a short call for every male call. Male calls tend to be disyllabic. During the unison call the tertial feathers are raised to form a conspicuous plume in both sexes, and the head and neck are variably extended upward and backward.

In its posturing and calls the hooded crane closely resembles the Eurasian crane, and as noted earlier mixed pairing has been observed under wild conditions. Likewise, the two species often associate on migration.

Although dancing behavior and behavior associated with copulation have not been described in detail, at least the dancing behavior does not seem to differ significantly from that of other *Grus* species. Katz (1979) observed two pairs and two additional females of hooded cranes in captivity during 1977, and reported that sexual displays of the species included the unison call, the contact call, dancing, copulatory behavior, and nesting behavior. Males consistently performed more breeding displays than did females, and one of the extra females participated in unison calls and precopulatory behavior with a male Eurasian crane in the same pen.

Territoriality and Early Nesting Behavior

The observations of Pukinskii and Ilyinskii (1977) are essentially the only ones available on early nesting behavior of these birds. In spring, when it is still easy to see across the nesting marsh, it is still difficult to observe hooded cranes, for the birds are surprisingly well camouflaged. The slate-gray body color and the white head and neck blend well among the branches of birch and larch, and after the trees and undergrowth have leafed out the cranes are impossible to see more than about 50 meters away. The birds nest on those parts of the marsh that are nearly devoid of trees or brush, but otherwise they prefer to keep to the birch thickets.

It is probable that the birds return to the same territory and may even nest in the same site year after year, for Pukinskii and Ilyinskii found fragments of old eggshells in one active nest, and in a second nest remnants judged to be three years old were also found.

Not a single nest of the four that were located was placed on hummocks of cottongrass and sedges, which were abundant in the bog. Instead they were all placed in paths or path intersections of Manchurian wapitis, or on those areas where the natural ground cover had been flattened or suppressed. Perhaps the hummocky areas are not sufficiently stable for nest sites. Most nest bases are dense heaps of damp sphagnum moss, with chunks of peat and sedge rhizomes added. The upper part of the nest is made of the stalks and leaves of sedges, along with sedge rhizomes, some branches of birch, and occasionally also larch branches. The cup of the nest is lined with sedges. Since all of the materials are gathered in the immediate vicinity, a small moat develops around the nest. One nest was about 20 centimeters high, with a basal diameter of 75×80 centimeters and a platform of 40×45 centimeters.

Egg-laying and Incubation

Nothing is known of the egg-laying behavior of this species in the wild, but it is probably identical to that of the Eurasian crane. The few available records would suggest that two eggs constitute the normal clutch. The clutches of hooded cranes are very similar to those of the Eurasian crane, averaging about 93×54 mm in the case of those found in the Bikin River area.

While incubating, the birds are remarkably secretive and quiet, calling only for a short time at dawn and again at dusk. When disturbed on the nest, they would sometimes fly for about 500 meters, or about twice the distance typical of Eurasian cranes. Normally, however, they tried to leave the nest without being observed, by skulking away through the bushes while keeping close to the ground. They also returned silently and stealthily, according to Pukinskii and Ilyinskii (1977).

Various observers have reported seeing distraction behavior in hooded cranes, which is typical of birds leading newly hatched young or of birds frightened from their nest.

Pukinskii and Ilyinskii (1977) found that the female did the majority of the incubation, with the male taking over for brief periods of 40 minutes to an hour during the morning and evening hours. The role of the male increased considerably during the week prior to hatching, when he spent almost as much time on the nest as did the female during the daylight hours. The female continued to incubate at night, however.

These authors reported that hatching in the nest they observed required about 24 hours, with the shell of the first egg pipping one morning, the chick completing hatching that night, and the second egg hatching in the same manner a day later. In the nest where they were making regular observations the first chick hatched on the night of 20-21 May.

Hatching and Postbreeding Biology

Pukinskii and Ilyinskii (1977) reported that a newly hatched chick weighed 93.5 grams shortly after hatching, while the second chick in the clutch weighed 85 grams. At the age of only a day or two the chicks were producing two special sound signals. One of them, first observed when the chick was still in the shell, is a vibratory, ringing peeping indicating distress. The other is a possible location call, and is a louder, clear, rhythmically repeated peep. The second call is present until the chick is a year old, and is the major means of communication used by young birds, according to these authors.

By three days after hatching the older chick was making expeditions away from the nest, up to as far as 20 meters. There the father would brood the chick, while the mother brooded the chick that was still in the nest. By the fifth day the chicks were moving along animal trails 250 meters from the nest, and on the seventh day the two chicks moved in company with their parents about 2 kilometers to a small peaty lake at the opposite end of the nesting bog. Thereafter the family remained in this bog, feeding throughout its 6 square-kilometer area, until at least mid-August.

Very little information is available on the molting patterns of hooded cranes in the wild. Andreev (1974) reported that he observed extensive body molt occurring in a crane that he collected in early June, but that the flight and tail feathers had not yet been molted.

Apparently after hatching has occurred, the parents move their young to damp bogs of the "eeii" type, which have areas of open water and bankside vegetation of cottongrass and sedges. Later, the well-grown fledglings move to meadows with grassy knolls along the small taiga rivers. Migration out of the area begins in mid-August, probably not long after the young have fledged. At least in captivity, about 75 days are required for fledging (Michael Putnam, pers. comm.).

Pukinskii and Ilyinskii (1977) reported that they found an abundance of fallen contour feathers in the nesting area during the latter part of the breeding season, especially in July. However, they did not find any tail feathers or wing feathers that would indicate the timing of a flightless period. Most of the feathers were found on the relatively open parts of the bog that were used by the birds after hatching.

From mid-August until the end of September the hooded cranes depart from their breeding areas in the Maritime Territory, leaving in small groups. They typically rise in spirals up to about 300 meters and, selecting a course, fly out in echelon formation over the peaks.

RECRUITMENT RATES, POPULATION STATUS, AND CONSERVATION

Only a few data are available on recruitment rates. Jahn (1942) observed a 13 percent incidence of juveniles in Yashiro, during February of 1939, which compares very closely to a 13.5 percent juvenile incidence among more than 3,000 birds counted by Nishida (1981). Nishida also noted that 48 percent of the families he observed in 1966-67 were leading two young, which represents a surprisingly high incidence of successful "twinning"; by comparison, Jahn did not observe any pairs with more than a single offspring.

Counts in Japan would indicate that the world population of hooded cranes was approaching 3,000 birds in the late 1970s, and they clearly have shown a consistent increase from earlier decades (see table 31). The widely dispersed nesting areas of the species, and their fairly remote locations help to provide further security for the birds. Indeed, the cranes may be increasing in both abundance and breeding range because of protection in both the USSR and Japan and because of the feeding program that has developed in Japan. Limited timbering in some parts of the breeding range causes little if any damage to the habitat, and perhaps even improves it to some degree by making it more open. Flint (1978a) suggested that additional attention and protection for the birds be provided in the Bikin River area, the Vilyuy Basin, and the Olekmo-Charskoye uplands as well as in the summer aggregation areas on the Torei Lakes.

EVOLUTIONARY RELATIONSHIPS

Archibald (1976) included the hooded crane in a species group that also contained the Eurasian, whooping, and Japanese cranes, although he noted that the hooded crane was behaviorally distinct in its lack of wrist-lowering during high-intensity threat. Wood (1979) found that anatomically the hooded crane is similar to the sandhill crane in external characteristics, but not consistently so otherwise. I believe that the Eurasian crane is perhaps the hooded crane's nearest living relative, in part because of the occasional occurrence of wild hybrids between these two species, but also because of general behavioral similarities.

Black-necked Crane

Grus nigricollis Prezhwalsky 1876

Other Vernacular Names. None in general English use; Grue à cour noir (French); Schwarzhals Kranich (German); Cheniozheuleu zhuravl (Russian); Grulla de cuello negro (Spanish).

Range. Breeds from Ladakh east through Tibet (Xizang Zizhiqu) to the Koko Nor Region in eastern Tsinghai (Qinghai), probably mostly between 4,300 and 4,600 meters elevation. Migratory, and reported on migration or during winter from central and eastern Sikang, Yunnan, and Tonkin (Vaurie, 1965). Also winters in small numbers in the southern Himalayas (Bhutan and Frontier Division of Subansiri Pradesh) at elevations of 1,500-3,000 meters (Ali, 1976).

Subspecies. None recognized.

Measurements. Wing, males 569-677 mm (average of 8, 623 mm); females 585-628 mm (average of 7, 606.5 mm). Exposed culmen, males 110-129 mm (average of 8, 120.5 mm); females 111-124 mm (average of 7, 116.4 mm). Tarsus, males 226-262 mm (average of 8, 247.4 mm); females 214-252 mm (average of 7, 231.7 mm). Eggs, average 102.6 × 62.8 mm (96.4-105.3 × 59.6-69.1 mm) (Walkinshaw, 1973).

Weights. Cheng (pers. comm.) reported a female weighing 6,000 grams. The estimated egg weight is 222 grams. Lu, Yao, and Liao (1980) reported that 17 eggs averaged 217.7 grams, and ranged from 200 to 245 grams.

Description

Adults of both sexes are alike, with a nearly bare red crown and lores, sparsely covered by black hairlike feathers, primarily on the lores. The rest of the head and the upper part of the neck are black, except for a small white or light gray spot extending backward from the rear and lower edges of each eye and sometimes extending as a narrow line above the eye. Otherwise the body is ashy gray, becoming almost whitish on the underparts. The tail is black, and the upper tail coverts are grayish. The primaries and innermost elongated secondaries are black, and the outer secondaries are black on the inner webs, as are many of the secondary coverts and the tips of some scapulars. The smaller wing coverts are pale gray. The iris is yellow. The bill is greenish horn to grayish horn, with a yellowish tip. The legs and toes are black.

Juveniles at 70 to 90 days have yellow brown feathers on the crown, and a gray abdomen. The primaries and secondaries are black, the feathers of the back are grayish yellow, and black and white feathers alternate on the neck. By eight months the iris color is yellow brown, and one-third of the neck is grayish black, with some yellowish brown feathers remaining on the back. By one year of age the bird resembles the adult (Lu, Yao, and Liao, 1980).

Downy chicks are covered by a brownish down, and have a bill that is flesh red, becoming whitish at the tip. The feet are reddish, with a touch of gray. When the chick is 20 days old the color of the head and tail becomes darker, and at 4 weeks the toes become grayish brown, the primary quills begin to emerge, and the top of the head becomes pale yellow (Lu, Yao, and Liao, 1980).

Identification

In the field, the limited Himalayan range of this species makes it unlikely that any other crane would be confused with it. It is the only grayish crane with black flight feathers and a black neck that extends forward to include the nape. Its calls are loud and high-pitched trumpeting notes, similar to those of the sarus.

Breeding (hatched) and wintering (shaded) ranges of the black-necked crane. Inked circles indicate breeding records, and insets show breeding-season occurrences in Tsinghai (Qinghai) Province, China (above), and location of known breeding pairs in Ladakh (below). The small arrow indicates the location of the Sea of Grass, Kweichow (Guizhow) Province, China.

In the hand, this species may be readily recognized by the entirely black head and neck, except for the bare red crown and face patch and a small white area behind the eyes. The trachea is coiled inside the sternum.

DISTRIBUTION AND HABITATS

Historical and Current Breeding Ranges

Of all the cranes, this species is the least known in every respect. Indeed, it was the last of the cranes to be discovered and described (in 1876). Walkinshaw (1973) described its summer range as consisting of the higher mountain valleys of the Himalayas and their neighboring ranges, and occurring between longitudes 78° and 101° east and between latitudes 28° and 37° north, with the northern limits around Lake Koko Nor, Chinghai (Qinghai) Province, China.

In an excellent review, Archibald and Oesting (1981) summarized the information on the historical distribution of this species, and the present account is a brief summary of their findings. They suggested that the species breeds in Ladakh, in the vicinity of the upper reaches of the Indus River in southwestern Tibet, in areas bordering the Brahmaputra River in southern Tibet, and in Szechwan (Sichuan) and Chinghai provinces of China. There are no specific breeding records for the Tibetan Plateau area between Ladakh and Koko Nor, but inasmuch as large migrating flocks have been at Jalung in south-central Tibet and near Seshu (north-western Szechwan) there are almost certainly some still-unknown breeding areas in the Central Plateau of Tibet. Archibald and Oesting found only 9 definite nesting localities, 8 areas where pairs have been presumed to be breeding, 6 areas where migration has been reported, and 9 wintering sites. The accompanying range map is largely based on the one produced by these authors, with some additional information as provided by Lu, Yao, and Liao (1980).

The western part of the species' range is a somewhat crescent-shaped series of breeding and wintering grounds from Ladakh on the west to eastern Tibet, skirting the northern parts of the Himalayas. Some of these populations may be almost sedentary, since Walton (1946) reported that both breeding and wintering occur near Lhasa, Tibet.

The eastern part of the species' range extends from Lake Koko Nor of Chinghai Province in the north, south through western Szechwan, and southward into wintering areas of Yunnan and the Vietnam lowlands near Hanoi. The breeding range in Chinghai (Qinghai) Province has recently been more fully described by Lu, Yao, and Liao (1980). They reported that the species is widely distributed across this province, in marshes, along lakeshores, and on rivers. The areas of breeding

season concentration include Zeku (Tse-k'u), in Huang-nanzhou (Huan-nan-chou Tibetan District), an area about 100 miles south of Xining (Hsi-ning), the Honan Mongolian Autonomous County (an area about 30 miles south of Zeku), Gongo (Kung-ho), Guide (Kuei-te), and Qinghai Lake (Koko Nor) in Hainanzhou (Hai-nan-chou) (a large region stretching to the south from Lake Koko Nor). Birds also occur at Gangcha (Kang-ch'a), Qilian (Ch'ilien), and Menyuan (Men-yüan) in Haibeizhou (Hai-pei-chou) (a large region extending to the north of Koko Nor).

Concentrations also occur at Dulan (Tu-lan), Niaolan (Niao-lan), Goermu (Ko-erh-mu), and Tianjun (T'ien-chun) in Haixizhou (Hai-hsi- chou Mongol-Tibetan Autonomous District) (a large region stretching to the west from Koko Nor). Other areas include Yushu (Yü-shu), Qumalai (Chu-ma-lai), Zhiduo (Chih-to), and Chengduo (Ch'eng-to) in Yushuzhou (Yu-shu-chou Tibetan Autonomous District) (a large region in central Chinghai Province). Birds also occur at Maduo (Ma-to), Jiuzhi (Chiu-chih), and Magin (Ma-ch'in) in Guoluozhou (Kuo-lo-chou) (a large region in south-eastern Chinghai Province). The major areas of breeding are Longbaotan in Yushu (Chich-ku) County, at Lake Shalin (Cha-ling) near Maduo (Mato), Nuomu-hong near Dulan (Tulan), Muli near Gangcha (Kang-cha), Shule (Shu-le) near Qilian (Ch'i-lie), and the Zha (Cha) River and Kouquian (K'ou-ch'ien) River near Zhiduo (Chito), all in northern Chinghai Province.

Breeding Habitat Requirements and Densities

Archibald and Oesting (1981) reported that the nesting areas of the species are from 3,962 to 4,571 meters above sea level (13,000 to 15,000 feet), and consist of tundralike marshes and bogs around the margins and on islands of lakes in the Tibetan steppes. Lu, Yao, and Liao (1980) reported that the breeding areas of Chinghai Province in China have a moist climate, fertile soil, plentiful vegetation, and abundant aquatic life. Among the plants present are *Phragmites, Carex,* and *Eleocharis.* The primary nesting areas seem to be marshy areas, such as reed marshes of Nuomuhon and the grassy marshes of Longbaotan. The latter area lies 4,200 meters above sea level, with an average temperature of about 5° C, and temperatures ranging from -12° to 19° during May and June. The ponds of the area contain grass mounds that are formed into small islands, some of which are relatively soft and are seemingly floating on the water surface. The water depth varies, to a maximum of 2 meters, and the bottom of the lake is covered by a deep layer of silt.

In a breeding area in Ladakh, near Chusul, the elevation is 4,328 meters, and a freshwater lake is surrounded by a broad stretch of marshland in a vast, sandy plain through which occur scattered streams,

CRANES OF THE WORLD

brackish pools, extensive belts of caragana, and salt beds. The lake itself has some tiny islands, on which a nest was discovered (Gole, 1981).

The only information on breeding densities is that of Lu, Yao, and Liao (1980), who reported that during the first ten days of May, when the birds are establishing their nesting territories, the density was as high as 1.45 birds per square kilometer. In June, after the carrying capacity has been established, the density was 0.76 birds per square kilometer, or 0.38 pairs.

Nonbreeding Range and Habitats

Large winter flocks have been reported in south-central Tibet (Walton, 1946), and in southwestern Szechwan and northwestern Yunnan (Schäfer, 1938; Dolan, 1939; Archibald and Oesting, 1981). Small numbers also traditionally wintered in Bhutan and the Frontier Division of Subansiri Pradesh (Ali, 1976). In earlier years there were records of a few birds wintering on the Plain of Hanoi and in the province of Hadong, Vietnam.

Reports by Schäfer (1938) and Dolan (1939) indicate a major historic wintering area in western Szechwan, on the Plain of Litang. To what extent this area may still be used by the birds is unknown. However, in 1979 a major wintering habitat was discovered by Zhou, Ding, and Wang (1980) in the Sea of Grass in Weining County, in the eastern part of the Yun Kwei Plateau. This area in Guizhou (Kweichow) Province, is at an elevation of 2,200 meters above sea level, and is located at 104'14" east longitude, 26' 51" north latitude. The lake, which was once 45 square kilometers in area, is now only 1.2 square kilometers of open water, and some 20 to 50 centimeters deep. Surrounding the lake are vast marshes, and stretching out from these to the original limits of the lake is an area that has been put under cultivation. Both the Eurasian and black-necked cranes winter here, with the latter's population much the smaller. On 11 December 1979, 46 cranes in a flock of 600 were black-necked, while on the next day 52 were counted in what was apparently the same group of 600 birds in a separate part of the marshes. About 20 to 30 or more were in scattered flocks of both species that numbered about 200 to 300 in all. Altogether, perhaps 70 to 80 black-necked cranes and some 800 to 900 Eurasian cranes were wintering in the area that year.

FOODS AND FORAGING BEHAVIOR

Foods and Foraging Behavior of Adults

While on their breeding grounds in Chinghai Province, the birds apparently feed from dawn until dusk. They forage both from the ground and in water, and when flock-feeding the individuals tend to remain within a set area. Mated birds tend to feed side by side.

One female dissected in June was found to have consumed green plant materials, while a male that was examined during May was found to have eaten *Potentilla anseriana*, as well as stones and pebbles.

In Ladakh, a pair of territorial cranes was observed feeding in a muddy area that contained a species of coarse grass, but no tubers. The birds also fed in freshwater streams that contained a species of carp, some mollusks, algae (*Nostoc*), moss, and submerged aquatic plants (mainly *Hydrilla*) (Gole, 1981). Gole believed that the birds were mainly feeding on grass.

In their wintering area of Bhutan, the cranes feed in stubblefields, gleaning waste grain. They are also attracted to boggy areas bordering grainfields, and seem to prefer them for feeding. There they dig up small round bulbs. The soil of these areas also contained large numbers of earthworms and hibernating frogs, which perhaps also are eaten (Khacher, 1981). In general, the species appears to be less aquatic in its winter foraging behavior than is the sarus crane or the highly aquatic Siberian crane, and Khacher suggested that the black-necked crane is perhaps thus less susceptible to habitat changes than at least the latter species. However, on the Sea of Grass area, the black-necked crane was observed in six of eight observations of Eurasian and/or black-necked cranes feeding in marshes, but on none of the four occasions where cranes were observed feeding on cultivated lands, suggesting a preference for marshes and wetlands (Zhou, Ding, and Wang, 1980).

Gole reported that when a pair was feeding, one member of the pair normally would be alert. At times, when there was no apparent danger, both birds would forage simultaneously. When feeding in water, the birds would often splash water with sideways sweeps of their beaks, as if they were removing mud from their bodies. At times they would immerse their entire head in the water and splash it on their bodies, as if bathing.

Foods and Foraging Behavior of Young

No specific information is available on foods or foraging for wild birds of this species. Young hand-reared cranes a month old are able to catch flies (*Musca*), *Lucilia*, and small insects. By the time they are two months old they like to eat cooked rice, green vegetables, and egg yolks. Later, they were fed a diet consisting of about 80 to 90 percent animal materials, and thereafter the birds did not like to eat vegetable matter (Lu, Yao, and Liao, 1980).

MIGRATIONS AND MOVEMENTS

Seasonal Movements

Archibald and Oesting (1981) have summarized what little is known of the migrations of this species. They suggested that observations by Schäfer (1938) of migrating cranes at Jalung in south-central Tibet and near Seshu in northwestern Szechwan were probably of birds moving between southern wintering grounds and unknown breeding areas on the central plateau of Tibet. They also suggested that there may be both migratory and relatively sedentary populations in western Szechwan, with the birds of the Koko Nor region and northern Szechwan migrating through this area and continuing on to wintering grounds of Yunnan and North Vietnam, while others remain in Szechwan. They also suggested that some of the birds breeding near Lhasa, in Tibet, may be migratory, and that perhaps the birds breeding in the eastern part of the species' range may be either sedentary or longitudinal and altitudinal migrants, while those from the western areas may be either sedentary or latitudinally migratory. They also proposed that the many hot springs that occur on the Tibetan Plateau serve as wintering areas for some cranes.

The cranes return to their breeding areas in Chinghai Province in March, and large flocks are seen well into April. One "relatively large" flock of 36 birds was seen on April 16 (Lu, Yao, and Liao, 1980). Likewise, large spring flocks have been observed in mid- to late April in northwestern Kansu Province (Meise, Schönwetter, and Stresemann, 1938). The fall migration out of the Chinghai region occurs in October (Lu, Yao, and Liao, 1980).

Wintering arrival times in Bhutan and Assam do not seem to be well established, but the birds leave these areas at the end of February or in early March (Gole, 1981; Khacher, 1981). In the Sea of Grass area of Kweichow Province, China, the birds typically arrive in October and leave in March (Zhou, Ding, and Wang, 1980).

Daily Movements

On their wintering areas of the Sea of Grass, these birds fly daily from roosting areas to other areas of the marsh for foraging. However, actual distances involved were not indicated.

GENERAL BIOLOGY

Sociality

Little information is available on flock sizes. Of the wintering birds observed at the Sea of Grass, a group of about 50 birds comprised one flock that in turn associated with about 550 Eurasian cranes. However, each species tended to remain separated within this larger flock. Several smaller mixed flocks of the two species also occurred, ranging in size from about a dozen to a hundred or so birds. Within these smaller flocks the black-necked cranes maintained a similar proportion (Zhou, Ding, and Wang, 1980).

On their breeding grounds during spring arrival in March, the birds are in groups of 5 or 6 to as many as 20, and occasionally to as many as 36. Flock behavior persisted through April and until mid-May, especially during periods of bad weather. After the start of the reproductive period there was no longer any flocking except for a group of about 10 cranes that moved through the area from mid-April until the end of May. It was believed from the appearance of one of these birds that probably the entire group was composed of immatures (Lu, Yao, and Liao, 1980).

Daily Activities

On the Sea of Grass wintering area, the daily behavior pattern of the black-necked crane is similar to that of the Eurasian crane. When dawn is breaking, about 7:00, the first birds begin to call. This gradually builds up to a mass chorus that can be heard for miles. At 7:20 the birds would take to flight, and by 7:40 the sky would be full of cranes. The birds then alight and begin foraging. At this time they may be spread out over an area of a thousand meters or more, or clustered into a smaller group. The major morning foraging is between 8:00 and 10:00, and is marked by much aggressive behavior. From about noon to 2:00 p.m. the birds rest. From 3:00 to 4:00 the birds again begin feeding, reaching a climax at 5:00 p.m. Sunset is shortly after 6:00 and by 7:00 the flock quiets down and it is completely dark (Zhou, Ding, and Wang, 1980).

Interspecific Interactions

Foraging interactions with the Eurasian crane have already been mentioned, and in general it would appear that these two species are quite tolerant of one another, with the Eurasian crane perhaps slightly more adapted to terrestrial grazing in cultivated fields (Zhou, Ding, and Wang, 1980).

On its breeding grounds in Ladakh, Gole (1981) observed no predators and perhaps as a result the eggs were sometimes left unattended for as long as a half an hour. Three pairs of ruddy shelducks (Tadorna ferruginea) nesting in the area were extremely alert, and raised a warning cry at the first sign of disturbance. The cranes evidently used the ducks as a kind of lookout, and would return to their foraging field to feed whenever they saw the ducks doing the same.

This same species of duck is an associate of black-necked cranes in the Chinghai area of China, as are also the bar-headed goose (Anser indicus), the common tern (Sterna hirundo), the redshank (Tringa totanus), and the coot (Fulica atra). Possible enemies of the black-necked crane in that area are the common buzzard (Buteo buteo) and the tawny eagle (Aquila rapax). The latter was observed to circle low over a nest, and a common buzzard was attacked and chased away by a nesting crane when it landed within 30 meters of the nest.

BREEDING BIOLOGY

Age of Maturity and Time of Breeding

The small number of egg records (see table 10) suggest that laying begins in May, peaks in June, and a few egg records continue on into July. Gole (1981) found a nest on May 26 in the Chusul area of Ladakh. In the Longbaotan area of Chinghai Province, China, the egg-laying period in 1979 extended from May 1 to June 8 (Lu, Yao, and Liao, 1980). Schäfer (1938) believed that in western China the eggs were first laid in late May, with the chief breeding season occurring between June and August.

There is no information on the age of maturity in this species, which has never been bred in captivity.

Pair Formation and Courtship

Archibald (1975, 1976) was unable to include this species in his comparative behavior study, and thus detailed information on the unison display and associated behavior is still lacking. Dancing behavior was observed by Gole (1981), who stated that as he approached a pair they engaged in dancing behavior, with the male moving around the female with outstretched wings, and trying to lead her. He also observed an apparent courtship dance once. After the pair had alighted, the male began waving his neck up and down, tiptoed several paces ahead, turned, and while spreading his wings came dancing back toward the female, As the male came nearer, the female responded with a similar movement of her neck. The male uttered a short call as he had begun his display, and he responded to the female's neck-waving by standing beside her, still waving his neck. The female did not respond any further. Dancing behavior has also been reported by Ali (1946), Schäfer 1938), and Ludlow (1928), and Schäfer reported a threat display in which the male flapped its wings, bent its neck so that its head nearly touched the ground, and ran around in a circle with its toes pointed inward.

One account of mating is available for the species. Lu, Yao, and Liao (1980) reported that on April 20 they observed a female uttering a low *gu—gu—* mating call. At the same time, both members of the pair pointed their bills and necks upward and began a mating dance with their wings outstretched. The male then quickly mounted the female, and copulation occurred. The male flapped his wings during treading, which lasted up to 20 seconds. After mating, the male jumped off, and both birds uttered a loud clear *guoguo—guoguo* call. The last day that they observed soliciting behavior by a female was on May 16, or about two weeks before the first nest containing eggs was found.

Territoriality and Early Nesting Behavior

In the Chinghai area of China, breeding birds moved into their nesting territories in mid-April and early May, when competition for suitable areas evidently occurs and the population temporarily exceeds its carrying capacity. By the final attainment of breeding density in June, the number of birds on the area was approximately half of the original number, perhaps owing to the exclusion of immature nonbreeders. In their 1978 studies, Lu, Yao, and Liao (1980) found only three nests, but in 1979 they found seven more, plus an abandoned nest having a single old egg. The nests were contructed in marshy areas out of reach of man and domesticated animals, and were usually on grass mounds or dirt "islands." Such mounds may rise only a little above water, be on somewhat higher ground, or have relatively thick grass and some dead grass present. The nests were round to elliptical, and were produced by piling up *Carex*, *Eleocharis*, and grasses found in the immediate vicintiy. Some of the nests were simple and crude, others were "tightly" constructed. The external diameter of 11 nests averaged about 80 centimeters, ranging from 46 to 124, and the average height was 10.6 centimeters, ranging from 4.5 to 16. The depth of the depression averaged 4.5 centimeters, and its diameter about 40 centimeters. Nest-building continued beyond the egg-laying period right up to the middle of the incubation period.

The nest that Gole (1981) found in Ladakh was in a shallow, marshy pool, about 30 meters from the shore and in water about 0.3 meters deep. The nest was built of aquatic vegetation, entirely composed of *Hydrilla*, and was about 25 centimeters high and about 60 to 150 centimeters in length and width. Other nests from Tibet and elsewhere seem either to consist of this rather large and typical crane type, with a pile of vegetation pulled from the vicinity and piled up on a marsh border in a shallow marsh, or to be very small and on an island having little or no vegetation. In this latter situation, mud may be piled up, or short, dead grass as is available may be used (Schäfer, 1938; Ludlow, 1926; Ali, 1946). Evidently the size and construction of the nest vary greatly under these different environmental conditions (Walkinshaw, 1973).

Egg-laying and Incubation

Nests in the Chinghai study area varied from about 500 to 2,000 meters apart, and each of the nests had one or two eggs. A total of 17 eggs was reported for ten active nests, suggesting an average clutch of 1.7 eggs. The egg-laying interval was found to range from one to three days (Lu, Yao, and Liao, 1980).

Incubation begins with the first egg, with one bird of the pair feeding while the other incubates. The nonincubating bird forages in an area extending out some 200 to 300 meters from the nest. In a nest studied in 1978, the female bird was on the nest 61.8 percent of the time, and the male for 38.2 percent. In 1979, the daytime incubating activity of the female also exceeded that of the male in one nest studied. The number of nest exchanges per day ranged from as few as two or three to as many as seven or eight (Lu, Yao, and Liao, 1980).

In the nest studied by Gole (1981), both sexes incubated about an equal amount of time. In one 24-hour period, the male incubated for nearly 10 hours, the female for somewhat over 10 hours, and the nest was left unattended for nearly 4 hours. Normally, each bird would incubate for 1 to 1.5 hours between changeovers, which would be done silently. During nighttime hours, the bird sat on the nest for longer periods, with the nonincubating bird resting within 3 meters of the nest. Evidently the male did most if not all of the nighttime incubation. During the day, the incubating bird would normally sit facing the sun, with the bill resting on its chest and the nape touching the back.

According to Lu, Yao, and Liao (1980) the incubation period lasts from 31 to 33 days. In two years of study, no cases of unhatched eggs were found.

Hatching and Postbreeding Biology

Based on two years of observations, Lu, Yao, and Liao (1980) reported that it requires about one day from the time that pipping begins until the young chick hatches. On the day before hatching, a small hole is made in the egg, and a vocalization can be heard. The newly hatched chick has a flesh-red bill, becoming almost white at the tip, and the reddish feet have a touch of gray. By the second day, the chick is able to stand, and moves about close to the nest. By the third day, it begins to eat. As the chick begins to eat, the parents lead it around the grassy and sandy areas near the nest. The chick imitates the food-searching behavior of the parents, and they sometimes place food in front of its head so that it can peck at it. About a week later, the young cranes were taken to an area where there was plentiful food. If the birds are frightened during the hatching period, the adults will lead their young away the second day after hatching, and not return again to the nest. At least among the chicks raised by hand, considerable fighting among the chicks occurs from the first or second day after hatching, and they must be kept separated thereafter.

In the case of hand-raised chicks, body weight increased for the first 180 days after hatching, reaching a maximum of about 6,750 grams. Thereafter, it declined some, and stabilized at about 5,500 grams. The flight feathers are fully grown at 90 days after hatching, so fledging must occur somewhat before this age.

Apparently the young birds remain with their parents during the first winter, with parents and young all feeding in a single group (Ludlow, cited in Walkinshaw, 1973).

RECRUITMENT RATES, POPULATION STATUS, AND CONSERVATION

There is no good information on recruitment rates for this species, nor is there any convincing information on its population status. Cheng (1981) reported that in September of 1973 a flock of 300 to 400 birds was seen at the Tangra Range Pass in Chinghai (Qinghai) Province, and also that in the fall of 1979 a flock of at least 600 was observed in Muomubong, in the Tsaidam Basin of Chaimadu Pendi. These observations would suggest that northern Tibet might support a substantial population of black-necked cranes, the exact breeding distribution of which remains completely unknown.

Archibald and Oesting (1981) summarized available information on the black-necked crane's distribution and population size, and suggested that at least in fairly recent decades as many as thousands of birds might winter in the Kyi-tschu Valley around Lhasa, and in the Brahamaputra Valley between Samyea and Yalong Podrang. At least until the Chinese influence became strong in the 1950s, the Tibetans considered all living things sacred, and thus the birds were fully protected and relatively tame.

Information gathered by Archibald and Oesting, as well as that of Khacher (1981), suggests that the birds no longer winter in the Apa Tani Valley of Aranuchal Pradesh, India. However, perhaps as many as 200 winter in eastern Bhutan, in the narrow river valleys from Punakha east to Bumthong and Tashigan. They probably still also winter in north Burma, in the western area and the Triangle area of Kachin Hills, between the Mali Hka and the Nam Tamai valleys, as well as in the Tarun Hka Basin, the major headwaters of the Chindwin River of northwestern Burma. Although the birds did not winter in North Vietnam during the period of bombing, they have since returned to the vicinity of Hanoi and elsewhere in the Babco Delta (Archibald and Oesting, 1981).

The number of black-necked cranes in China is not possible to guess, but one crane sanctuary has already been established at Longbaotan in Qinghai (Chinghai) Province (Cheng, 1981). The species is now receiving the highest level of protection in China, and is the subject of detailed biological study there (Lu, Yao, and Liao, 1980). The director of the Peking Zoological Gardens (letter of June 12, 1981) informed me that black-necked cranes have been kept there since 1965, and are now being exhibited or have been exhibited at five Chinese zoos. They have not yet bred at any zoo, but such captive birds might provide a means of learning more of the basic biological requirements of this little-studied species.

EVOLUTIONARY RELATIONSHIPS

Wood (1979) was unable to include the black-necked crane in his phenetic study of the Gruidae, nor was Archibald (1975, 1976) able to study the species' vocalizations. In the Peters (1934) taxonomy the black-necked crane is placed sequentially between *grus* and *monachus*, and Archibald evidently accepted this general idea (cf. Wood, 1979). In the absence of any new data on its anatomy or behavior, it is necessary to accept these ideas for the present time. Recently Archibald was able to observe several captive specimens of this species, and on that basis was able to judge that the black-necked crane is in the same evolutionary group as the whooping, Japanese, and Eurasian cranes (*Brolga Bugle*, 6(1):3-4, 1980).

Eurasian Crane

Grus grus (Linnaeus) 1758

Other Vernacular Names. Common crane, Crane; Hui-ho (Chinese); Grue cendree (French); Kranich (German); Kuro-zuru, Kurotsuru (Japanese); Seryi zhuravl (Russian); Grulla comun (Spanish).

Range. Breeds in northern Eurasia from Scandinavia east to at least the Indigirka River, and probably to the Kolyma, and south to northern Germany, the Ukraine, the Kirghiz Steppes, Russian and Chinese Turkestan, Mongolia, and northern Manchuria, with isolated colonies in the Dobrogea, Turkey, and Transcaucasia. Migratory, wintering in the Mediterranean region to northwestern and northeastern Africa, the Persian Gulf region, peninsular India, and from southern China to northern Indo-China, Burma, and Assam (Vaurie, 1965).

Subspecies (after Vaurie, 1965).

G. g. grus: Western Eurasian Crane. Breeds west of *lilfordi,* with the limits uncertain and probably intergrading with that form, but at least including the central parts of the Kola Peninsula, Solovetskie Islands, and gouvernement of Archangel north to the forested tundra and the Pesh River, and east to the middle Pechora and Ust Usa. Winters in the southern and eastern parts of the Iberian Peninsula, northwestern Africa, southern Italy, Turkey, Iraq, southwestern Iran, Egypt, Sudan, and Ethiopia.

G. g. lilfordi: Eastern Eurasian Crane. Breeds in Russia and Siberia east of *grus,* and in western Chinese Turkestan, Tannu Tuva, western Mongolia, Transbaikalia, northwestern Manchuria, and perhaps northern Manchuria. Also breeds in isolated colonies in Turkey, Transcaucasia, and Armenia. Winters in Turkey, eastern Transcaucasia, Iran, southeastern Afghanistan, southern Baluchistan (perhaps), India, China, Burma, and Assam. Vagrants have reached Korea, Japan, and North America.

Measurements (both subspecies). Wing, males 507-608 mm (average of 20, 547.8 mm); females 529-550 mm (average of 10, 533.9 mm). Tarsus, males 202-252 mm (average of 20, 229.3 mm); females 201-242 mm (average of 10, 221.1 mm). Exposed culmen, males 95-116 mm (average of 20, 105.6 mm); females 201-242 mm (average of 10, 220.1 mm). Eggs, average 95.34 × 60.05 mm (84.9-109.4 × 56.1-65.4 mm) (Walkinshaw, 1973).

Weights. Three males of *grus* ranged from 5,095 to 6,100 grams; four females ranged from 4,500 to 5,895 grams. Six winter adults of *lilfordi* ranged from 3,000 to 5,500 grams, averaging 4,583 grams (Cramp and Simmons, 1980). Eggs average 183.0 grams (range of 40, 144-211 grams) (Walkinshaw, 1973). The estimated weight of fresh eggs is 188.7 grams. The average of 8 eggs of *lilfordi* was 175 grams (Dementiev and Gladkov, 1968). Three newly hatched young averaged 105.3 grams (Walkinshaw, 1973).

Description

Adults of both sexes have the forehead and lores blackish, covered with black, hairlike feathers, and the crown likewise nearly bare of feathers but red. The nape is slate gray, and the chin, throat, and anterior portion of the neck are blackish or very dark gray. A white stripe extends from behind the eyes through the ear coverts around and behind the nape, and then down the neck to the upper back. The rest of the body plumage is slaty gray, being darkest on the back and rump and lighter on the breast and wings. The back is often tinged with brownish in breeding birds. The primaries, the tips of secondaries, the alula, the tip of the tail, and the edges of upper tail coverts are black, while the bases of the rectrices are slaty gray. The inner secondaries may be lighter than the rest of the plumage (*lilfordi*), or about

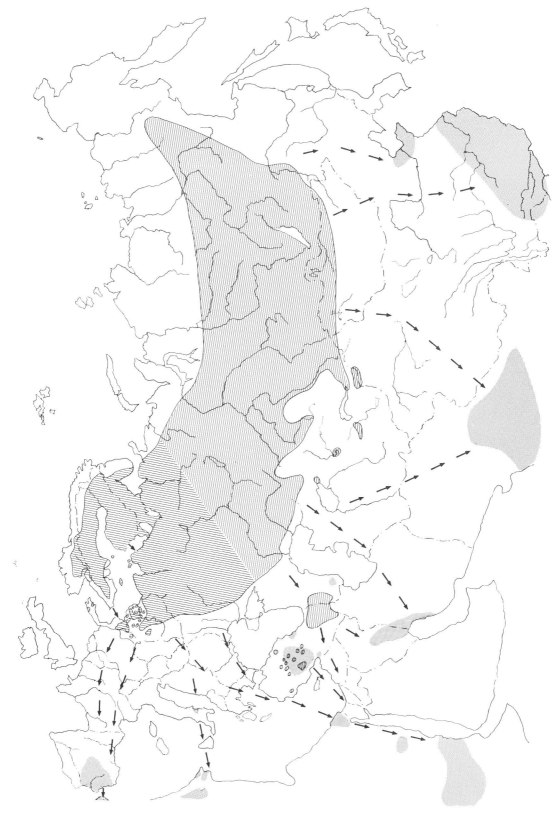

Breeding ranges of the western (vertical hatching) and eastern (horizontal hatching) Eurasian crane, and wintering ranges of both races (shading). Major migratory routes are indicated by arrows.

the same color as the other wing and body feathers (*grus*). The innermost greater coverts are greatly elongated and drooping. The legs and toes are black, and the iris varies from yellow to reddish brown or crimson.

Juveniles have pale yellowish brown edges on their body feathers, and the crown is covered by feathers; there also are no drooping inner wing feathers. From the first autumn, the new feathers of the head and neck are gray, tipped with cinnamon.

Immatures in their first spring have the crown and forehead partly bare, covered only by some bristle-like feathers. The remaining plumage is adultlike, with scattered worn juvenile feathers. The flight feathers and most tertials are still juvenile, and are narrower and browner than in adults. *Second-year immatures* are like adults, but retain some old brown feathers on the body and upperparts, and some flight feathers may still be immature (Cramp and Simmons, 1980).

Downy young are deep chestnut dorsally, being darkest on the back of the neck, along the middorsal line, over the back of the wings, on the rump, and down the sides to below the wings. Similar dark lines extend from the base of the bill below and behind the eyes and up over the crown, where they join. The head is lighter chestnut, and the underside is even lighter, sometimes almost white. There is a small area of white on the anterior base of each wing. The iris is brown, and the bill and legs are initially flesh-colored but soon darken and become grayish with a bluish tinge. There is a yellowish tinge at the base of the upper mandible, and the tibio-tarsal joint remains flesh-colored for a few days (Walkinshaw, 1973). Older chicks have a second coat of down that is more brownish gray (Fjeldså, 1977).

Identification

In the field, this is the common crane of Europe and much of Asia. It appears to have a rather uniformly gray body, with darker flight feathers. The neck is strongly contrasting, with black in front and white on the sides, with a long black nape stripe. The calls are loud and trumpeting, and are often uttered with wing-drooping during unison calling.

In the hand, the combination of a black-and-white striped neck and an otherwise gray body serve to identify this species. Unlike the similar hooded crane, black is present on the nape and upper hindneck, and unlike the black-necked crane extensive white is also present on the face and nape. The trachea of the Eurasian crane is extensively coiled within the keel of the sternum.

DISTRIBUTION AND HABITATS

Historical Breeding Range

The largest changes in the breeding range of this species in historical times have been in Western Europe, as summarized by Cramp and Simmons (1980). According to them the Eurasian crane may have bred in Ireland until the fourteenth century, and nested in East Anglia of England until about 1600. In Spain it bred in the central area during the fourteenth century, in the southern marismas of Guadalquivir until the end of the nineteenth century, and in the Cadiz area until 1954. It bred in several areas of Hungary in the nineteenth century, and was last known to breed there in 1952. It also formerly bred in northern Italy, with some birds nesting annually around Venice in the late 1800s. It also probably bred in Czechoslovakia during the nineteenth century, and in Austria breeding persisted in the Burgenland area until about 1900. In Germany the species was once much more widespread, but there is no proof of reported breeding in Bavaria during the mid-nineteenth century.

Current Breeding Range

Nesting in the southern parts of Europe is now irregular at best, judging from the recent summary of Cramp and Simmons (1980). In Greece the species bred in the Evros Delta as recently as 1965, and perhaps nested elsewhere in earlier years. In Yugoslavia it now nests only irregularly, with 1965 the last known breeding record. In Romania there may be sporadic nesting in the Danube Delta, but this is not fully confirmed. In Denmark, where the species was extirpated early in the nineteenth century, it has again been breeding in small numbers since about 1925. In East Germany there may be 350 to 450 pairs altogether, with some local decreases but no certain trends. In West Germany there has been a decline in the breeding range in northern areas during the present century, and only 16 to 19 pairs were present in 1974. In Finland, there has been a slight expansion to the north, and perhaps as many as 8,000 pairs in the 1950s. In Norway there may be 2,000 pairs present, including nonbreeding birds, while in Sweden there are an estimated 11,000 pairs, representing a slight increase since the period 1920-1930 but a slight decline since the previous century. There is also a small breeding population in Estonia, which numbered about 100 birds in 1971. A few pairs still breed in Austria as well (Glutz, 1973). Finally, Turkey supports a relatively isolated breeding population that perhaps numbers between 300 and 500 pairs.

The heart of the species' breeding range is in the USSR, for which relatively little detailed information is available. Perhaps 60,000 to 100,000 cranes occur there, based on circumstantial evidence, and over most of the USSR the numbers appear to be declining as a result of drainage of marshy areas and disturbance of major breeding habitats. In northwestern Manchuria the Eurasian crane occurs in the lakes and marshes south of Tsitshar (Vaurie, 1965). It breeds in Hulungboir Meng of the Mongolian Autonomous Region, and also in the Xinjiang Autonomous Region around Tianshan in China (Cheng, 1981). Thus, virtually all of the Asian breeding population of the species is apparently confined to the USSR.

Dementiev and Gladkov (1968) described the USSR breeding range as extending from the Kola Peninsula north to 68° north latitude, and east of this north to 66-67 north latitude, including the lower reaches of the Ob, and the Lower Tunguska, Vilyuy, Lena, and Indigirka rivers, possibly to as far east as the Kolyma River. In the west, the species extends from the Baltic south to the central Ukraine, with the southern boundaries to the regions of Kiev, the central Dnepropetrovsk, the lower Volga (to 47° north latitude), the middle reaches of the Ural and Emba rivers, the northeast shore of the Aral Sea, the lower Syr-Darya, the Sary-Su, Chu, and Ili rivers, Lakes Issyk-Kul and Zaisan, the Altai Mountains, Transbaikalia, and Dauria. Isolated colonies also exist in Sivashe and Prisivash'e, but no nesting occurs in the Crimea. The extreme eastern breeding limits of this crane are very uncertain, but it was not reported from the Chukotski Peninsula by Portenko (1981). Dementiev and Gladkov (1968) stated that some nesting occurs on the Kolyma River, but no positive information on nesting is available from Anadyr Territory, Kamchatka, Koryak Land, or the Okhotsk coast. There is no nesting of this species in either the Maritime Territory or the Amur Territory.

The western boundary of *lilfordi* is extremely ill-defined, and probably this race intergrades with *grus* over a broad zone. The form breeding in the European portion of the Molotov Oblast may be *lilfordi*, but the differences between the two supposed subspecies are marginal and it is questionable whether they should indeed even be separated at all. In general, birds breeding east of the Ob River are believed to belong to *lilfordi*, while *grus* is believed to breed east to the Pechora and Volga rivers.

Details on current breeding distributions in Norway, Sweden, and Finland are provided by Walkinshaw (1973). He also summarized the recent breeding localities known to him from East and West Germany, Scandinavia, and elsewhere in Europe. Glutz (1973) has provided a highly detailed distribution map of recent breeding areas in Germany, Poland, and adjoining areas of eastern Europe. An inclusive European breeding distribution map is that of Cramp and Simmons (1980), which is more detailed than the one prepared for this book.

Breeding Habitat Requirements and Densities

According to the summary of Cramp and Simmons (1980), in the western Palearctic this species now breeds largely in upper middle latitudes between the arctic tundra and steppe regions, specifically in boreal and temperate taiga and deciduous forests, from lowlands to as high as 2,200 meters. At higher altitudes breeding occurs on treeless moors, on bogs, or on dwarf heather habitats, usually where small lakes or pools are also found. In Sweden, as well as in other areas, breeding habitats are typically small swampy openings in dense pine forests, while in East Germany reedy wetlands are used. In Spain, nesting formerly occurred in reedbeds from 1 to 2 meters high, and in water 20 to 40 centimeters deep, with the nests raised high enough to permit the bird to see out over the tops of the reeds. In the USSR a similar array of nesting habitats is used, including some in steppe or even semidesert areas provided that water is locally present. Everywhere in its range the most important criterion for nesting habitat seems to be an inaccessible nest site (Glutz, 1973; Cramp and Simmons, 1980). Vaurie (1965) described the breeding habitats as wooded swamps, morasses with or without scattered trees, bogs and fens, open marsh or meadows, and reed beds along rivers or lakes. Van der Ven (1981) stated that cranes need a safe, quiet place for nesting, with an area of several hectares around the site, and at least 0.5 meter of water depth is also necessary.

Breeding densities appear to be very low even in the better parts of the species' range. Merikallio (1958) estimated Finland densities to range from 1 to 18 pairs per 100 kilometers over broad areas of that country. In the area of Mecklenburg, East Germany, estimated breeding densities also range from 1.32 to 5.02 breeding pairs per 100 square kilometers, while in Norway an estimated density was 9 to 13 pairs in an area of 585 square kilometers, or 1.5 to 2.2 pairs per 100 square kilometers (Glutz, 1973). Nilsson (1982) reported that two areas in southern and central Sweden had breeding densities of 1.5 and 1.7 pairs per 100 square kilometers, with the higher density associated with a more southerly area having a higher amount of fen habitat. All of these estimates would suggest that densities of more than 5 pairs per 100 square kilometers must be quite unusual.

Nonbreeding Range and Habitats

After the breeding season, this species moves to floodland, shallow sheltered bays, and swampy meadows. During the flightless period there is a need for shallow waters or high reed cover for concealment. Later, after the migration period, the birds winter in open country, often on cultivated lands and sometimes also in savannalike areas, as for example on the Iberian Peninsula (Cramp and Simmons, 1980).

There are a large number of rather widely separated

wintering areas for this species. The most westerly of these is in Portugal and especially in southern Spain (Extremadura and Andalucia), with the major winter concentrations near Badajoz and Cordoba (Fernandez-Cruz, 1979-1980). A few of the birds from this population, which is derived from birds breeding in the south Baltic countries, part of the Scandinavian population, and perhaps some birds from the USSR, continue south to winter in Morocco. The total size of the Iberian wintering population is in the vicinity of 10,000 to 15,000 birds (Cramp and Simmons, 1980); Fernandez-Cruz (1979-80) reported a maximum 1979-1980 count of 14,721 birds.

Birds that breed in Finland and Russia, as well as part of the Swedish population, take a more direct southerly migration route, with some entering Tunisia but others wintering farther east in Turkey, northern Israel, Iraq and parts of Iran. However, the majority winter in the river valleys of Sudan (south at least to Malakal), and in Ethiopia, where they occupy both the high plateau country as well as the Eritrean lowlands (Cramp and Simmons, 1980). The population wintering in Tunisia occurs in two major areas. Thousands of birds winter north of Tunis, roosting in a few lakes, and others still roost on the dry bed of Lake Kelbia west of Sousse, where they drink at small wells in the area (van der Ven, 1981).

The third major wintering area is on the Indian subcontinent and presumably represents the western portion of the *lilfordi* population. Ali and Ripley (1969) stated that the birds are most abundant in the northwestern parts of the subcontinent, including Sind, Rajasthan, Gujarat, Punjab, Uttar Pradesh, and extending eastward to Behar, Orissa, and West Bengal, and southward through Madjya Pradesh and northern Andhra. No estimates of population size are available for this region.

Some wintering also occurs in Burma, Vietnam, and Thailand, and perhaps also in Bangladesh and Cambodia (Walkinshaw, 1973; Archibald et al., 1981), although most of these would appear at present to represent rather marginal wintering areas. King (1979) reports the species as occurring only in west, northeast, and east Burma, and in Vietnam (north and central Annam, plus Tonkin).

The last remaining major wintering area is in China. Cheng (1981) reported that the Eurasian crane is the most common of all the Chinese cranes, and cited as evidence the migration figures of Hemmingsen and Guildal (1968), who reported a total of more than 4,000 birds counted during three springs, and more than 20,000 observed during four autumn migration periods in Hebei (Hopei) Province. The birds evidently winter over a fairly broad area in China, from the Yangtze Valley south to Hainan. Wintering also occurs as far as the Sea of Grass in western Kweichow Province, where

this species outnumbers the black-necked crane by a ratio of about ten to one (Zhou, Ding, and Wang, 1980).

Outside of China, Eurasian cranes sometimes straggle to Korea (where formerly they were regular in winter), and rarely reach Japan (Honshu and Kyushu). Even more rarely they have reached western and central North America during winter, typically in association with sandhill cranes.

FOODS AND FORAGING BEHAVIOR

Foods of Adults and Young, Breeding and Nonbreeding

The Eurasian crane appears to be rather similar to the sandhill crane in its food consumption, with plant material making up the majority of the volume, including roots, rhizomes, tubers, stems, leaves, fruits, and seeds. The most commonly consumed plant items are the shoots of green grasses, the leaves of herbs (chickweed, clover, nettle, brassicas) and crop plants, grains of cereal crops (wheat, barley, oats, rye, corn, rice), pondweeds, berries of heaths (*Empetrum, Vaccinium*), peas, potatoes, olives, acorns, cedarnuts, and the pods of peanuts and *Cajanus*. The rhizomes and leafy parts of *Phragmites* are a favored food. In Spain, wintering birds live largely on cereal grains until mid-November, then consume acorns (*Quercus ilex*) until late December and germinating cereals and legumes from January until their March departure. Stomachs of three individuals taken in spring in Sweden contained only barley (*Hordeum*) grains and wheatgrass (*Agropyron*). The above summary is based on information in Glutz (1973) and Cramp and Simmons (1980).

Animal foods are taken more frequently in summer months, and at times may even predominate over vegetable materials at that time of year. The animal foods are mainly of such invertebrates as insects (Coleoptera, Orthoptera, Odonata, Diptera, Dictoptera, and larval Lepidoptera), snails, earthworms, and occasionally millipedes, spiders, and woodlice. Vertebrates that have been found to be consumed include frogs, slow-worms, lizards, and snakes, as well as some small mammals (rodents and shrews). Less frequently fish and the eggs and young of small birds are eaten, and the remains of a single adult warbler (*Acrocephalus paludicola*) has been found in one case (Cramp and Simmons, 1980).

Foraging Behavior

Foraging is done on dry land or while standing in water, with materials being taken from the ground surface or by probing with the bill to extract plant and animal materials underneath the surface (Cramp and Simmons, 1980). Acorns are sometimes eaten in quantity, presumably by gathering them from the ground, and one bird in Tunisia was found to have 272 olive seeds in its stomach (Walkinshaw, 1973). In the fall months the birds often concentrate in grainfields, and may cause damage locally. In the Castile area of Spain, cranes have been found to have from 200 to 500 partially germinated kernels of grain present in their digestive tracts. Probably most damage occurs in fields where the grain crops are still ripening and unharvested; Eurasian cranes, like the sandhill cranes, doubtless also consume a good deal of waste grain from previously harvested fields, thus actually benefiting the farmers.

As in other cranes, feeding is done in pairs or family groups, and foraging is alternated with drinking and roosting activities. In India, the birds fly out daily to newly planted and ripening crops, especially those of wheat and gram. They also are said to be especially fond of the young pods of arhar dal (*Cajanus indicus*) and peanuts, the latter being dug out of the soil with the bill. The birds sometimes also cause damage to watermelons by jabbing into them with their bills (Ali and Ripley, 1969).

MIGRATIONS AND MOVEMENTS

Seasonal Movements

Like other cranes, this species may be characterized as having a highly traditional pattern of wintering and staging areas, the latter being stopover points between breeding and wintering grounds where the birds remain for varying lengths of time to forage and sometimes also to wait for favorable weather for crossing long areas of water. The areas used in fall are often different from those used during spring.

The most important fall staging areas in northern Europe are the shallow parts of the Baltic Sea in the German Democratic Republic (GDR), particularly in the vicinity of Rügen and MüritzSee. Until about 20 years ago over 20,000 cranes visited the Müritz area every fall, but then suddenly the birds stopped using this area and moved to Rügen. Still more recently they have begun roosting around Bock and Zingst, evidently because of recent high water levels in the Baltic. In 1980 the fall crane population there reached 18,000, and there have been local problems of crop damage to unharvested fields or newly seeded fields (van der Ven, 1981). Other important fall staging areas for the European population include Öland Island of Sweden, Matsalu Bay in Estonia, and the Oder Valley near Szczecin, Poland (Cramp and Simmons, 1980). In Hungary the most important fall roosting areas are in the Puszta Hortobagy, near Kardoskut in the Danube Valley, and sometimes near Biharugra. In Romania an important staging area is the east coast of the Dobrogea (van der Ven, 1981). During September

and October thousands of cranes gather in Turkey, supplementing the resident breeding birds. The most important staging areas in eastern Turkey are near Mus, near Bulanik, east of Ercis, and southeast of Van. There are perhaps two flyways for Turkish birds. One of these follows the Murat Nehri, with the birds then probably migrating over Cyprus. The other passes east of Van over Cavustepe and goes south from Urfa. The major movement over Cyprus occurs in September and October (van der Ven, 1981). Some of the birds winter in Turkey, while others do so in northern Israel, and yet others in Iraq and Iran. However, the majority cross the Sinai to enter the Nile Valley south of Cairo. The majority of the population reaches Ethiopia later than does the demoiselle crane, and Eurasian cranes are present in their African wintering grounds mainly from October to March (Cramp and Simmons, 1980).

For those flocks that fly southwesterly from the Baltic to winter on the Iberian peninsula, the birds move southwest in a corridor some 200 to 300 kilometers wide over the southeastern Netherlands and Belgium to west-central France. In France the most important staging areas are Lac du Der-Chantecoq and the southwestern parts of Gascogne (van der Ven, 1981). The birds then move south to the Pyrenees and on into Spain, where the majority winter.

The migration and wintering ecology of the Eurasian crane in Spain has been under intensive study (Fernandez-Cruz, 1979-1980), and some of the best available population data for the species are available as a result of this study. Groups of fall migrating flocks averaged about 50 birds, while those in spring averaged slightly more than 100 individuals. The estimated percentage of juvenile birds, based on a sample of 17,240 birds, was 11.42 percent, and the average winter brood size was 1.17 per successful pair.

The return flight north for this population is similar to the fall pattern. At this time the birds also assemble in northern GDR to roost at Rügen Island and mainland areas immediately south and southwest of Rügen. This spring migration in the Baltic area has been studied by radar (Alerstam and Bauer, 1973; Alerstam, 1975; Pennycuick, Alerstam, and Larsson, 1979). In early April the birds fly across the Baltic to southern Sweden, typically leaving in midmorning, reaching a peak migration in early afternoon, and using a combination of soaring flight and flapping flight. Overland flight is often aided by use of thermal soaring, while oversea flights are done by flapping. The maximum height observed on this flight by Pennycuick et al. (1979) was slightly above 2,000 meters, but the birds flew low in bad weather and with flapping rather than soaring.

There is also one important spring staging area in Scandinavia, the marsh Hornborgasjön, which is in Skaraborg and 120 kilometers east-northeast of Gothenburg, Sweden. Since perhaps the entire Scandinavian population stops here, it provides a means of estimating total population size. Numbers in 1967 and 1968 were 5,500 and 5,700, while in 1973 and 1974 there were 4,500 and 4,700 birds respectively. On the other hand, Alerstam and Bauer (1973) estimated that the numbers of birds crossing the Baltic Sea in the spring of 1972 was from 24,000 to 48,000, which they thought to represent the Scandinavian population. This is far greater than the collective estimates of birds for Norway and Sweden, so perhaps some Finland birds also cross the Baltic as well. However, it is believed that the Finland population migrates east of the Baltic. In the fall, about half of the crane population of Sweden normally uses the island Öland (east of Kalmar) as a staging area, and in 1968 some 4,170 birds were found there, with a corrected total estimate of about 6,000 (Swanberg, 1981). Use of Hornborgasjön has greatly declined in recent years, since potatoes are no longer grown in that vicinity (Karlsson, 1980).

The migratory pathways of the eastern race *lilfordi* are much more poorly known, but there is an important migration route around the Caspian Sea presumably used primarily by birds wintering in Iran and Iraq. The Eurasian crane is the most common crane wintering in Iran, and total numbers of estimated birds in the early to middle 1970s ranged from about 2,000 to 3,000. The birds arrive in late September or early October and depart in March and early April. The major areas used are arable lands and wetlands in southern Iran, along the Karkheh, Dez, and Karun rivers in Khuzestan, in central Fars, and in Seistan. A substantial but unknown number probably continues to winter in Iraq. The breeding origin of these birds is unknown; there are no recent records of nesting in Iran (Scott, 1981).

Birds wintering on the Indian subcontinent arrive in northwestern Pakistan in August and September, by directly overflying the Safed Koh Range of Afghanistan (elevation about 3,800 meters), rather than its lower western shoulder. The earliest dates for migrants arriving over the Salt Range in Rawalpini District was August 15, and the average was August 25. Between the third week of February and the end of March large departing migrating flocks overfly the Kurram Valley, and from mid-March also overfly the Great Rann of Kutch. This is done when thermals are available near the middle of the day. Northwardly migrating flocks have also been reported moving through Baluchistan and over Lahore. Spring migration continues through April and at least until mid-May, when the birds are found over Dharmsala and the Dhola Dhar Range (about 4,600 meters elevation) (Ali and Ripley, 1969).

In the USSR the fall migration of *grus* begins in late July or early August, as the families begin to merge and move away from nesting regions. Large-scale movements continue during September, with a few birds lingering into late October. However, there is a surprisingly early departure even from southern areas such as the Ukraine. Likewise, the *lilfordi* migration begins in

Yakutia in late August or early September. On the other hand, there are substantial variations in spring arrival times, not only in eastern and western Siberia but also in various parts of Soviet Central Asia and Kazakhstan, apparently resulting from the wide dispersion of the wintering areas and the often long migration routes. Birds breeding at Lake Sevan in Armenia arrive as early as mid-April, while those reaching Verkhoyansk, the Indigirka, and the mouth of the Moma River do not arrive there earlier than May (Dementiev and Gladkov, 1968).

Daily Movements

There seem to be few specific studies on daily movements in this species. However, Alerstam (1975) used radar to track single-day flights of cranes across the Baltic Sea. They found that the birds usually made this crossing during daylight hours when there was 2/8 to 5/8 cumulus cloud cover, which favors the development of thermals and thus greatly facilitates overland migration. Cranes leaving Rügen Island before 10:00 or 11:00 a.m. were judged to be able to reach Hornborgasjön Lake (about 400 kilometers north) by sunset the same day, while those waiting until early afternoon to leave are probably unable to get there before dark, and arrive the following morning. The true airspeed of migrating birds over land was calculated to be 70 kph in flapping flight between thermals, 44 kph when flying in thermals, and 67 kph in flapping flight over sea. Most migrating birds did not fly above 1,000 meters, and when climbing in thermals they gained no more than 500 meters of elevation. Over land the birds appeared to be able to compensate for wind drift, but they did not completely compensate for this factor when over sea.

When not actively migrating, it is not unusual for birds to travel as far as 12 or 14 kilometers between their roosting and foraging grounds, or even up to as much as 20 kilometers (Glutz, 1973).

GENERAL BIOLOGY

Sociality

The Eurasian crane is relatively gregarious during the nonbreeding season, and in particular tends to migrate in fairly large flocks. However, these large flocks are probably associated with needs for safe roosting and foraging areas, causing considerable numbers to concentrate. On migration, flocks sometimes contain as many as 400 birds, and flocks tend to keep in sight of one another (Cramp and Simmons, 1980). However, the flocks are not stable social units, and their numbers are easily affected by such things as disturbance and the presence of thermals. Pennycuick et al. (1979)

reported that 17 radar tracks of migrating cranes crossing the Baltic Sea ranged from 2 to 31 individuals.

According to Swanberg (1981), nonbreeding birds and adults without young are the first cranes to arrive in the Hornborgasjön area of Sweden in early fall. The percentage of young birds then gradually rises until late September, suggesting that perhaps the adults that have raised young must wait for them to fledge before leaving their breeding grounds, or perhaps their own molt patterns require a later departure than that of nonbreeding birds. Such conditions probably affect the social structure of fall flocks.

Daily Activities

Judging from the account of Zhou, Ding, and Wang (1980), the daily winter activity patterns of the black-necked crane and the Eurasian crane are similar to one another and to that of other cranes. This daily activity pattern was summarized in the account of the black-necked crane and need not be repeated in detail here. In general, the birds leave their nighttime roosts about a half-hour before sunrise, forage actively in early morning and during the afternoon, sometimes returning to the roost at midday to drink and rest. The birds return again to their roost area after sunset. As the breeding season begins the birds become more solitary, but early in the breeding season the pair may roost together, outside of their nesting territory.

As noted earlier, migration in the Eurasian crane is begun during daylight hours, typically during the middle or latter part of the morning, which maximizes the amount of time that the birds can use thermal updrafts associated with the warmer afternoon hours.

Eurasian cranes prefer to roost by standing in shallow water, as do other cranes, but in unusual circumstances the birds will accept waterless areas for roosting if they are familiar with the area and its safety (van der Ven, 1981). Where roosting sites are limited, the numbers of cranes using an area sometimes become very high. One of the largest reported congregations of cranes is a molting group of 3,500 flightless birds on Lake Selety-Tengis, in Kazakhstan, in May 1962 (Stresemann and Stresemann, 1967).

Interspecific Interactions

Few predators are likely to be serious threats to adult cranes, but the white-tailed sea eagle (*Haliaeetus albicilla*) has been seen to attack standing birds. In these cases the crane may leap up into the air and strike with its bill, or try to fend off the eagle with its legs (Moll, 1963). Sea eagles may also try to attack flying birds, in which case the cranes may counterattack. Large mammals such as wild boars, red deer, and foxes are also

sometimes threatened and hissed at (Glutz, 1973). Thus, even large predators tend to avoid nesting birds. On the other hand, carrion crows (*Corvus corone*) have been observed to steal eggs successfully in the presence of adult birds (England, 1963).

On their African wintering areas, Eurasian cranes sometimes associate with the smaller demoiselle cranes, while in India and Asia they are often seen with such species as demoiselles and also with the larger *Grus* species. There is no information on any possible significance of such interactions. While on migration the birds sometimes also associate with white-fronted geese (*Anser albifrons*) and bean geese (*Anser fabilis*) (van der Ven, 1981).

BREEDING BIOLOGY

Age of Maturity and Time of Breeding

As indicated in table 14, most egg records for the Eurasian crane occur in May, with a smaller number in April and a still smaller total in June. However, in Germany there are some records of eggs as early as the end of March, for example March 27 in the Oberlausitz, March 29 in Schleswig-Holstein, and March 31 in Mark Brandenburg. In the last-named area newly hatched young have been reported as early as April 22, indicating clutch completion by no later than the third week of March (Glutz, 1973).

The age of sexual maturity in the wild is not known with certainty, but it probably normally occurs at five years, but possibly at four and perhaps as late as six (Glutz, 1973). Semen has been obtained from captive males only three years old (Archibald and Viess, 1979). There do not seem to be any records of initial captive breeding by known-aged birds. It is very unlikely that breeding ever occurs as early as the second year of life as suggested by Dementiev and Gladkov (1968). A hand-raised male described by Sieber (1932; translated and reprinted in Walkinshaw, 1973) acquired a wild mate for the first time when he was five years old. Over a period of (apparently) seven years he had a total of three different wild mates.

Pair Formation and Courtship

Like the other cranes, this species exhibits indefinite monogamous pair bonds. This is supported by the observation of known pairs on the same breeding area over several years (Makatsch, 1970). Nevertheless, courtship begins annually at the time of arrival on the breeding grounds and continues until the start of incubation. However, if a breeding partner is lost, courtship of a new mate may begin. For example, a bird that had lost its mate in late July in Schleswig-Holstein was observed with a new partner only two weeks later (Glutz, 1973).

Dancing behavior can be observed in sexually immature birds during summer and fall, and dancing can be seen frequently in winter quarters before the northward migration (Moll, 1963; Glutz, 1973). Dancing behavior in this species has been described and illustrated by many authors, including the accounts in Moll (1963), Glutz (1973), Cramp and Simmons (1980), and Makatsch (1970). As in the other *Grus* species, dancing includes a variety of bobs, bows, pirouettes, and stops, interspersed with leaps into the air and the tossing of vegetation above the head. An aggressive "parade march" posturing is also an important part of the repertoire, and often immediately precedes attack. A common form of threat is dorsal-preening, with the wings held slightly away from the body and the inner wing feathers strongly ruffled. The bare red crown may also be directed toward the opponent, or may be less specifically expanded and exhibited during agonistic display, as for example during the parade-marching behavior.

The period of pair formation is apparently a prolonged one. Seiber (1932, in Walkinshaw, 1973) believed that its initial stages consist of the male marching continuously behind the courted female, in a distinctive "stalking" or marchlike manner, with the thighs pressed outwards, the legs lifted high, and the ornamental tertials erect. This stalking behavior may go on for hours or even days, and is sometimes interrupted by display preening. Thus, the behavior associated with initial pair formation is seemingly little if at all different from agonistic encounters between birds of the same sex.

The unison call of this species places it in a group of species that also includes the hooded, whooping, and Japanese cranes. In members of this group, either sex may initiate the call, but this is usually done by the female. Her calls begin with a long scream, which is followed by several shorter calls that then give way to a series of regularly spaced notes, performed with the tertial feathers raised maximally and the head gradually moving forward from its initial position behind the vertical. The male begins his calling in a similar posture, but utters a single long call, lasting almost a second, for every three short calls uttered by the female (Archibald, 1975, 1976). During high degrees of threat both sexes raise their humeri about twenty degrees above the back and lower their wrists, exposing the dark primary feathers, but this is more likely to occur in males than in females. Sometimes the sexes call in an antiphonal fashion, and there are also other variants of the unison call notes (Cramp and Simmons, 1980).

The copulation-invitation call of the species is a repeated note, apparently uttered by the female. The male may also utter rather loud notes as he approaches to mount her. As in other *Grus* species, the posturing associated with copulation is distinctive (see figure 9, which is based on drawings in Glutz, 1973). The female assumes a solicitation posture with the wings open and drooping and the neck and head extended almost vertically upward. The male approaches rapidly in an erect "parade march" posture, uttering a series of notes that rise in pitch. He then leaps on the back of the female, which tilts forward to the horizontal to accommodate him. Balancing on his tarsi, the male flaps his wings to maintain his position, and completes the copulation in four or five seconds. The male then leaps over the head of the female, uttering a low growling sound that terminates with a louder call. He then runs forward several feet, while beating his wings, and both birds utter the unison call and begin to shake and preen. They may also throw vegetation into the air, or even crouch on the ground. Reversed mounting, during which the female leaps on the back of the male, has also been observed (Glutz, 1973; Cramp and Simmons, 1980; Moll, 1963, 1967).

Territoriality and Early Nesting Behavior

Territories of the Eurasian crane are normally very large, but their exact size depends largely on the habitat. In open areas, such as bogs with sparse scrub cover, they may vary in size from 50 to 500 hectares. Frequently the nests of adjacent pairs may be 5 or 6 kilometers apart, and nests are rarely closer than 2 or 3 kilometers apart (Dementiev and Gladkov, 1968). However, in one area three to five pairs were found to occupy a 40-hectare moor of bog and thick reedy heather, producing a density of about 20 to 25 acres per pair (Sieber, 1932, in Walkinshaw, 1973). These unusual situations evidently occurred because the habitat was subdivided into several solid and well isolated areas of marshy fen by vast reed thickets, so that the birds were able to visit foraging areas without crossing other pairs' territories. Very often foraging occurs outside of the defended territory, and courtship or copulation may occur 1,500 meters from the nest site (Moll, 1963).

In common with the sandhill crane, adults of this species often "paint" their upper body and wing covert plumage reddish brown with mud or decaying vegetation (Berg, 1930; Glutz, 1973). These are the only two species of cranes known to perform this behavior, and both are essentially medium gray in color. It seems likely that in the Eurasian crane, as in the sandhill crane, this may well serve to make the nesting bird less conspicuous in a dead-grass environment.

The same nesting area is used from year to year by experienced birds, and indeed the same site may be used again. Nest-building is performed by both sexes. The nest is always placed either in water or very near water that is generally only a few centimeters deep. The habitat used may be a bog, heath, marsh, mosse, or myr. The Scandinavian nesting biotopes are typically surrounded or nearly surrounded by forests of spruce, pine, birches, and some alders. The mosse of Sweden described by Walkinshaw (1973) are boggy areas surrounded by pines, while the more arcticlike myrs are sphagnum moss areas also often surrounded by pines or spruce. Nests in arctic Lapland seem to be smaller than those farther south, but the size and conspicuousness of the nest seem to vary greatly by region or habitat. Four nests found by Walkinshaw in Norrbotten were built in myrs with surrounding nesting territories of 50 to 400 hectares. All the nests were placed in low sedge or similar vegetation, and all but one were immediately adjacent to a pine or low dwarf birch. No nest was more than 100 meters from a forested area, and the water around the nesting ridges was from 14 to 61 centimeters deep. Of 20 Scandinavian nests, the average dimensions were 81.7×92 centimeters wide, and 12.58 centimeters high. The average water depth of 18 nests was 29.36 centimeters. Nests in the arctic areas seem to be associated with deeper water but are placed on dry ridges. Although some nests may be established more rapidly, two or three weeks may elapse between the arrival of the birds in the nesting area and the completion of the nest. Furthermore, sometimes several uncompleted nests are begun before a final choice is made (Glutz, 1973). Bylin (1980) reported a high proportion of 80 nest sites being on lakeshores or in dense offshore vegetation.

Egg-laying and Incubation

The clutches of this species normally contain two eggs (see table 16). Of 200 full clutches, only 5 contained a single egg, and, in another instance, of 93 clutches (perhaps not all full), only 10 had a single egg. There have also been rare reports of 3-egg and 4-egg clutches (Glutz, 1973).

The egg-laying interval of the Eurasian crane is normally 2 days, but less often it is a single day, and sometimes 3 or 4 days. The birds have a single brood, but replacement clutches following the loss of the initial clutch have been reported when such losses have occurred fairly early in the incubation period. The interval between nesting efforts in such situations is about 16 to 18 days. The incubation period averages 30 days, but ranges between 28 and 31 under natural conditions (Cramp and Simmons, 1980; Glutz, 1973).

Incubation begins with the first egg, and is performed by both sexes, with the female taking the greater share of the responsibility. Walkinshaw (1973) has observed the incubation behavior of a pair of Eurasian cranes in Sweden, and found that during a period of 18 hours the birds changed places only three times. With another nest, he watched for a 24-hour period. In the first case,

the nonincubating bird (a female) stood about 100 meters from the nest during the first night of observation, while on the second night the male stood about 500 meters from the nest after dark. In the case of the second nest the nonincubating bird roosted about 500 meters from the nest, where it was out of sight behind a tree-grown point. In a hatching nest that Walkinshaw also watched, he observed that the first egg hatched early on the morning of May 22, and the second one the following day in late afternoon. The first-hatched chick left the nest before the second egg had hatched, and apparently was attended by the female, while the male incubated the remaining egg until it too hatched. Evidently a one- or two-day interval between the hatching of the two eggs is normal, but at times the chicks may hatch almost simultaneously (Glutz, 1973; England, 1963).

If disturbed by humans during incubation, the birds perform intensive distraction behavior, which typically involves the drooping of one wing and a hunched, limping walk. Or, the bird may perform a slow, mammallike bounding run, with long strides, with its head and neck held hunched down below the shoulders, and with the bill open. Such behavior is probably limited to very dangerous enemies such as humans or dogs; many ground predators are instead overtly attacked with bill-stabbing, kicking, and wing-beating behavior (Moll, 1963; Cramp and Simmons, 1980).

Hatching and Postbreeding Biology

The chicks are quite helpless immediately after hatching, but after only a few hours they are able to crawl off the nest and hide when disturbed. They may be fed pieces of eggshell by the brooding bird fairly soon after they are able to stand up. They are able to swim very soon after hatching, and within 24 hours are also able to run actively about. At two days of age they can stand erect, run, and swim quite dexterously, without holding their wings out away from the body (Walkinshaw, 1973).

Chicks respond to danger by squatting and "freezing." By about three days of age they are starting to pick up food items for themselves from the substrate and to drink water. When running, the young birds use their stubby wingbuds to help them, and by nine weeks of age they are able to fly for short distances. By ten weeks of age they are fully able to fly, even though their flight feathers are not quite fully grown by then (Glutz, 1973).

The adult birds also undergo their postbreeding molt while the young are being raised. Not all adults molt their primaries every year; some birds molt them only every second year and perhaps some flight feathers may be held for as long as four years, independently of mating success. During the wing molt all the flight feathers are dropped within about two days, and the birds remain flightless for about five or six weeks.

During this same period the primary coverts, under wing coverts, much of the tail and axillaries, and some tertials, tertial coverts, and scapulars are also molted. At least in northern Germany, the flightless period occurs while the young are very small, during late May or early June. In July or August the molt of the greater wing coverts, most tertials, scapulars, and other tail feathers also occurs. Still later the upper wing coverts and remaining body feathers are lost, mainly between July and November. During those years when the flight feathers are not molted the plumage is otherwise replaced in the same sequence, but the tail, under wing coverts, and primary coverts may not be molted. Apparently nonbreeding birds molt at the same time as do breeders. Yearling birds molt in a similar sequence to adult birds, but more slowly, so that molt may not be completed before their second winter. There is apparently often no molting of the flight feathers in such birds, so these feathers may not be replaced until they are a full two years old, or (at least in semicaptivity) even until the following summer (Glutz, 1973; Cramp and Simmons, 1980).

RECRUITMENT RATES, POPULATION STATUS, AND CONSERVATION

There is still only a rather small amount of information available on the population dynamics of this species. Nest success rates seem to range from 50 to 77 percent, and hatching success also seems to be fairly high (table 19). Bylin (1980) reported that 38 Swedish pairs of birds raised 18 young, representing 24 percent of all the eggs that were laid. Further, about 20 percent of the successful pairs raised 2 young. In another Swedish study, Nilsson (1982) found that in one area 16 of 38 pairs had large young in late summer during a three-year study, while in another area 25 of 37 pairs during a two-year period had young. Of the former group, 2 pairs were leading two young, and of the latter 12 pairs had two young, for a collective total of 34 percent "twins."

The best estimates of annual recruitment rates for the European population seem to be those of Fernandez-Cruz (1979-1980), who reported that 11.42 percent of a sample of 17,240 wintering birds in Spain were juveniles. Furthermore, of 1,874 pairs, 47.65 percent were leading young, and 17.62 percent of the total pairs had two young. Such figures suggest a reproductive success rate similar to that of sandhill cranes, or possibly slightly higher.

The earlier summary of population status by countries would indicate that in most areas Eurasian crane populations are declining, especially on the edges of the breeding range. Yet at least in some areas of Sweden the crane population is now increasing, and apparently is returning to a formerly higher population density (Nilsson, 1982). The best opportunities for censusing the entire Scandinavian population would be at the Rügen Island staging area. In 1972 as many as 24,000 to 48,000 birds may have crossed the Baltic Sea in that area, but this number does not agree well with the estimates of the individual Scandinavian countries (Swanberg, 1981).

The Eurasian crane is protected by law in Scandinavia and Finland, but nevertheless there seems to be a substantial mortality rate in that population, especially on the wintering grounds. Of 115 cranes banded in Sweden before 1973, 13 were recovered by 1974. Further, of 21 cranes banded as young in central Sweden, 4 lost their lives in their first year, 1 in the second, and 1 in the third, or at least 28 percent mortality before their earliest possible nesting age (Swanberg, 1981). Such figures would suggest that improved protection of the birds on their Spanish and African wintering areas may be vital if the crane population is to maintain itself in the face of declining wetland habitats and increased human population pressures.

EVOLUTIONARY RELATIONSHIPS

According to Archibald (1975, 1976), the Eurasian crane is part of a species complex that also includes the whooping crane, the Japanese crane, and the hooded crane. In all of these species the female's calls are shorter than the males, and she normally initiates the unison call sequence. The male then begins with a series of short, low calls that are followed by a regular series of longer and louder calls. The amount of visual posturing varies with the intensity of the threat display, with increased wing elevation and tertial erection especially evident in the male. Typically the female utters about three notes for every note uttered by the male, and the male's calls are usually disyllabic. In common with the whooping crane, Eurasian cranes lower and expose their darker primary feathers during intense display.

Wood's (1979) cladistic studies confirmed Archibald's broader taxonomic conclusions, although he found that Eurasian, hooded, and white-naped cranes tended to cluster in the same phenetic group, and that the Japanese crane tended to remain isolated from these species.

I would suggest that the hooded crane is the Eurasian crane's nearest living relative, and that relationships with other *Grus* species are so far not very obvious.

ORIGINS OF SCIENTIFIC AND VERNACULAR NAMES OF CRANES

Anthropoides—from the Greek *anthropos*, a man, and *oides*, having the likeness of.

paradisea—from the Greek *paradeisos*, paradise. The vernacular name Stanley crane is based on "*Anthropoides stanleyanus*" proposed by Vigors in 1826, apparently in honor of E.S. Stanley, who was the president of the Zoological Society of London from 1831 to 1851.

virgo—from Latin, a maiden. The vernacular name demoiselle is French, a damsel.

Balearica—of the Balearic Islands, in the Mediterranean.

pavonina—from the Latin *pavo*, a peacock.

p. ceciliae—After Lady William Cecil, who donated to the Zoological Society of London the live specimens on which the form's description was based.

p. gibbericeps—from the Latin *gibber*, a hump, and *ceps*, head.

p. regulorum—from Latin, pertaining to royalty.

Bugeranus—from the Greek *bous*, an ox or bull, and *geranus*, a crane.

carunculatus—from the Latin *caruncula*, a caruncle or small piece of flesh.

leucogeranus—from the Latin *leukon*, white, and *geranos*, a crane.

Grus—from Latin, a kind of bird, especially a crane. The vernacular name crane may have originally been derived from the Greek *geranos*, and more recently is from the Old English "cran." The Old German *Kraen* and the Danish *trane* are also related names.

americanus—of America. The vernacular name whooping crane is originally from the cry "houp," to command a dog or horse.

antigone—named (by Linnaeus) for the daughter of Oedipus, who hanged herself (presumably in reference to the species' bare neck skin). The vernacular name sarus is from the local Hindi name, sārus.

a. argentea—from the Latin, *argenteus*, silvery.

a. sharpei—after R.B. Sharpe, English ornithologist.

canadensis—of Canada.

c. nesiotes—from Greek, an islander.

c. pratensis—from Latin, pertaining to a meadow.

c. pulla—from Latin, pertaining to young animals.

c. rowani—after William Rowan, Canadian ornithologist.

c. tabida—from the Latin *tabidus*, shrinking or wasting away.

grus—see *Grus* above. It is believed that *grus* might refer to the hollow, gutteral or grunting voice of most cranes.

g. lilfordi—after Lord T. L. Lilford, English naturalist.

japonensis—of Japan.

monachus—from the Greek *monachos*, solitary, a monk. The vernacular name hooded crane also refers to the monklike plumage pattern.

nigricollis—from the Latin *niger*, black, and *collum*, neck.

rubicundus—from Latin, becoming or remaining red. The vernacular name brolga is from the aboriginal name, buralga.

r. argentea—from the Latin *argenteus*, silvery.

vipio—from Latin, a kind of bird, especially a small crane.

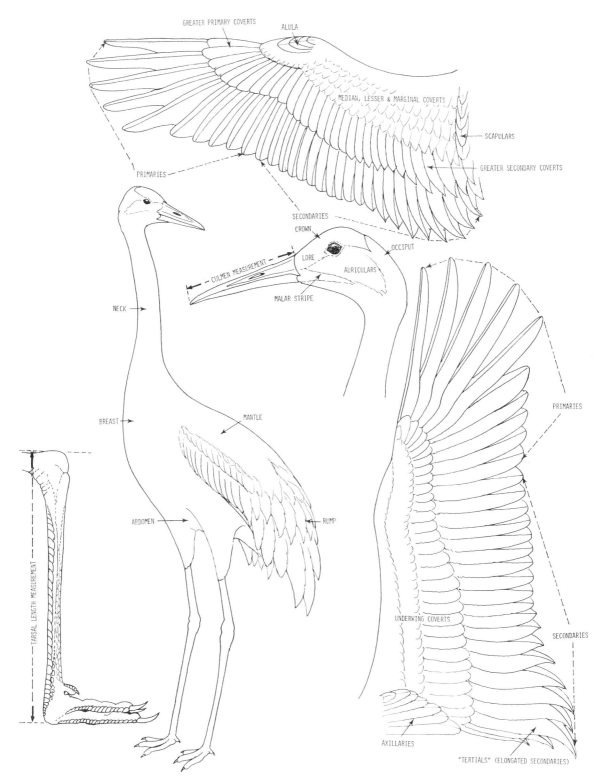

14. Topography and anatomical measurements of cranes.

KEY TO THE SPECIES AND SUBSPECIES
OF CRANES OF THE WORLD

Key to the Families of Gruoidea

I. Bill short, almost chickenlike, 10 rectrices .... Psophidae (trumpeters)
II. Bill elongated and tapering, 12 rectrices
    A. Hallux large, bill nearly as long as tarsus .... Aramidae (limpkins)
    AA. Hallux small, less than half as long as tarsus .... Gruidae (cranes)

Key to Cranes of the World*

A. Bill shorter and swollen toward tip, with oval nostrils; a cluster of strawlike feathers on crown (subfamily Balearicinae) .... Crowned crane (fig. 15F)
    B. Neck feathers dark gray, large throat wattle present
        C. Generally larger and paler, with a large white area on upper cheek ..... West African crowned crane.
        CC. Generally smaller and darker, with a small white area on upper cheek .... Sudan crowned crane.
    BB. Neck feathers light gray, a small throat wattle present
        C. Upper margin of cheek patch rounded and lacking a knobby process .... South African crowned crane
        CC. Upper margin of cheek patch extended into a knoblike process .... East African crowned crane
AA. Bill longer and tapering, with linear nostrils, crown not tufted (subfamily Gruinae)
    B. Head entirely feathered, crown feathers paler than rest of head, bill shorter than head (*Anthropoides*)
        C. Neck and face feathers black, contrasting with gray body, iris red .... Demoiselle crane (fig. 15A)
        CC. Neck and face gray, like rest of body, iris dark brown ...Blue crane (fig. 15J)
    BB. Head partially bare in adults, bill longer than head
        C. A feathered lappet on throat, and warty red skin extending to lappet and nostrils (*Bugeranus*, in part) .... Wattled crane (fig. 15I)
        CC. No feathered lappet, no skin extending forward to nostrils.
            D. Entire front of face bare of feathers, otherwise white with black primaries (genus *Bugeranus*, in part) .... Siberian crane (fig. 15E)
            DD. Front of face not entirely bare, usually not white with black primaries (*Grus*)
                E. Tail uniformly gray, with a darker tip, body also mostly grayish, never entirely white
                    F. Reddish bare area limited to crown
                        G. Napes, cheeks, and throat grayish white or black

---

*In part after Walkinshaw (1949), generally based on adult characteristics.

        H. Lower neck black in front, white behind .... Eurasian crane (fig. 15K)
          I. Plumage ashy gray throughout .... Western Eurasian crane
          II. Plumage more pearly gray, with lighter inner secondaries .... Eastern Eurasian crane
      HH. Neck entirely gray .... Sandhill crane (fig. 15B)**
        I. Wing averaging over 500 mm (min. 490 mm), culmen averaging over 130 mm (min. 113 mm) .... Greater sandhill crane
        II. Wing averaging under 500 mm (max. 525 mm), culmen averaging under 130 mm (max. 144 mm)
          J. Tarsus averaging under 200 mm (max. 228), culmen averaging under 100 mm (max 110 mm) .... Lesser sandhill crane
          JJ. Tarsus averaging over 210 mm (min. 203 mm), culmen averaging over 100 mm (min. 93 mm)
            K. Culmen averaging at least 125 mm (min. 110 mm) .... Florida sandhill crane
            KK. Culmen averaging under 125 mm (max. 127 mm)
              L. Limited to Cuba and Isle of Pines .... Cuban sandhill crane
              LL. Limited to North American mainland .... Canadian sandhill crane
     GG. Nape and throat pure white, lores blackish
       H. Foreneck dark gray, legs reddish .... White-naped crane (fig. 15H)
       HH. Foreneck white, legs blackish .... Hooded crane (fig. 15G)
   FF. Bare red or grayish skin covering all of head except for ear coverts
     G. Legs reddish, body plumage pale grayish blue to whitish .... Sarus crane (fig. 15L)
     G. With white collar and white inner secondaries .... Burmese sarus crane
     GG. Lacking white collar, inner secondaries gray .... Indian sarus crane
   FF. Legs blackish, body plumage uniformly gray .... Australian crane (fig. 15C)
     G. Darker above and below .... Southern Australian crane
     GG. Paler above and below .... Northern Australian crane
 EE. Tail either black or white, body pale gray to white, at least on underparts
   F. Tail black or blackish, no white on nape .... Black-necked crane (fig. 15D)
   FF. Tail white, white also present on nape or hindneck
     G. Secondaries black, neck mostly dark gray .... Japanese crane (fig. 15M)
     GG. Primaries black, neck and body entirely white .... Whooping crane (fig. 15N)

Key to Greater, Canadian, and Lesser Sandhill Cranes, by Sex

A. Adult males
  B. Total body index (wing + exposed culmen + tarsus) under 850mm
    C. Tarsus + culmen usually under 285 mm (max. 338 mm,), under 3.75 kg .... Lesser
    CC. Tarsus + culmen usually over 340 mm (min 312 mm), over 3.75 kg .... Canadian
  BB. Total body index over 850 mm
    C. Wing + culmen usually under 620 mm (max. 652mm), under 4.9 kg .... Canadian
    CC. Wing + culmen usually over 685 mm (min. 624 mm), over 4.9 kg .... Greater
AA. Adult females
  B. Total body index under 815 mm
    C. Tarsus + culmen usually under 275 mm (max. 302 mm), under 3.5 kg .... Lesser
    CC. Tarsus + culmen usually over 325 mm (min. 303 mm), over 3.5 kg .... Canadian
  BB. Total body index over 820 mm
    C. Wing + culmen usually under 575 mm (max. 606 mm), under 4.3 kg .... Canadian
    CC. Wing + culmen usually over 650 mm (min. 603mm), over 4.3 kg .... Greater

---

**If sex is known, see following key for separating *tabida, rowani,* and *canadensis.*

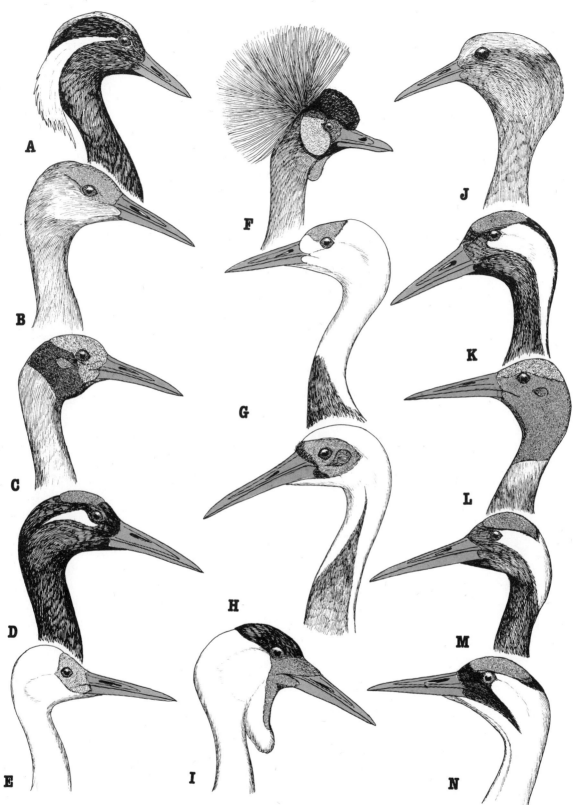

15. Heads of cranes of the world, including demoiselle crane (A), sandhill crane (B), Australian crane (C), black-necked crane (D), Siberian crane (E), crowned crane (F), hooded crane (G), white-naped crane (H), wattled crane (I), blue crane (J), Eurasian crane (K), sarus crane (L), Japanese crane (M), and whooping crane (N).

REFERENCES

The following list of more than 400 references is by no means a complete bibliography of cranes, but does include a few titles that for various reasons were not specifically cited in the text. Walkinshaw's (1973) monograph contains a large number of citations not found in the present list, and he additionally has recently (1981c) updated and supplemented his earlier bibliography. All told, his two citation lists include nearly 2,500 citations. Nearly 40 percent of the 1973 list deals with the whooping crane, 20 percent with the sandhill crane, 15 percent with the Eurasian crane, and 8 percent with the Australian crane. Each of the remaining nine species individually comprise no more than 4 percent of the citations, and the Siberian, Japanese, white-naped, demoiselle, and hooded cranes each make up no more than 1 percent. It is thus apparent that at least the English literature on cranes is strongly biased toward the whooping and sandhill cranes, and that many fundamental studies remain to be undertaken on the majority of the cranes of the world. It is especially unfortunate that the literature on four of the world's endangered or vulnerable species (Siberian, Japanese, white-naped, and hooded) is still so scanty, considering the importance of a proper understanding of their biology and management if they are to be preserved from extinction.

Akiyama, M. 1981. Countermeasures for the preservation of red-crowned cranes at present and in the future. p. 102, *in* Lewis and Masatomi, 1981.

Aldrich, J. W. 1979. Status of the Canadian sandhill crane. pp. 139-148, *in* Lewis, 1979e.

Alerstam, T. 1975. Crane *Grus grus* migration over sea and land. *Ibis* 117:489-495.

Alerstam, T., and Bauer, C. A. 1973. A radar study of the spring migration of the crane (*Grus grus*) over the southern Baltic area. *Vogelwarte* 276:1-16.

Ali, S. 1927. The Moghul emperors of India and naturalists and sportsmen. Pt. 2. *Journal Bombay Natural History Society* 32:34-63.

———. 1946. An ornithological pilgrimage to Lake Mānāsārowār and Mount Kailas. *Journal Bombay Natural History Society* 46:286-308.

———. 1958. Notes on the sarus crane. *Journal Bombay Natural History Society* 55:166-168.

———. 1976. Status and conservation of the black-necked crane (*Grus nigricollis*) and other wildlife in Ladakh. Unpublished manuscript report to the World Wildlife Fund.

Ali, S., and Ripley, S. D. 1969. *Handbook of the birds of India and Pakistan.* Vol. 2. Bombay: Oxford University Press.

Allen, R. P. 1952. *The whooping crane.* Research Report No. 2, National Audubon Society, New York.

———. 1956. *A report on the whooping crane's northern breeding grounds.* National Audubon Society, Supplement to Research Report No. 2, 1-60.

Andreev, B. N. 1974. (*Birds of the Vilvuysk Basin.*) Yakutsk: Yakutsk Book Publishers. (In Russian.)

Archibald, G. W. 1973. Cranes over Kyushu. *Animal Kingdom* 76(6):17-21.

———. 1974. Methods for breeding and rearing cranes in captivity. *International Zoo Yearbook* 14:147-155.

———. 1975. The unison call of cranes as a useful taxonomic tool. Ph.D. dissertation. Cornell University, Ithaca, N.Y.

———. 1976. Crane taxonomy as revealed by the unison call. pp. 225-251, *in* Lewis, 1976a.

———. 1978. Winter feeding programs for cranes. pp. 141-148, *in* Temple, S. (ed.). *Endangered birds: Management techniques for preserving threatened species.* Madison: University of Wisconsin Press.

———. 1981a. Cranes wintering in the Republic of Korea. pp. 66-69, *in* Lewis and Masatomi, 1981.

———. 1981b. Introducing the sarolga. pp. 213-215, *in* Lewis and Masatomi, 1981.

———. 1981c. Last call for the Siberian crane. *Natural History* 90(3):58-61.

Archibald, G. W., and Oesting, M. 1981. Black-necked crane: A review, pp. 190-196, *in* Lewis and Masatomi, 1981.

Archibald, G. W., Siigata, Y., Matsumoto, K., and Momose, K. 1981. Endangered cranes. pp. 1-12, *in* Lewis and Masatomi, 1981.

Archibald, G. W., and Viess, D. L. 1979. Captive propagation at the International Crane Foundation, 1973-78. pp. 51-74, *in* Lewis, 1979e.

Armstrong, E. A. 1943. The crane dance in East and West. *Antiquity* 17:71-76.

———. 1979. The crane in the British Isles and crane traditions as evidence of culture diffusion. pp. 237-248, *in* Lewis, 1979e.

Austin, O. L., Jr. 1948. The birds of Korea. *Bulletin Museum of Comparative Zoology,* Harvard College, 101(1):1-301.

Azarov, V. I. 1977. (Siberian cranes in northern Kazakhstan and Tiumen Province.) *Abstracts of the VII USSR National Ornithological Conference,* Cherkassy, the Ukraine, 27-30 September 1977, vol. 2, pp. 188-189. Kiev: "Naukova Dumka." (In Russian.)

REFERENCES

Baker, E. C. S. 1928. The game birds of the Indian Empire. *Journal Bombay Natural History Society* 32:397-407.

_____. 1929. The game birds of the Indian Empire. *Journal Bombay Natural History Society* 33:1-6.

Baldwin, J. H. 1977a. A comparative study of sandhill crane subspecies. Ph.D. dissertation, University of Wisconsin, Madison.

_____. 1977b. A comparative study of the sandhill crane subspecies. pp. 266-275, *in* DeWitt, C. B., and Soloway, E. (eds.), *Wetlands ecology, values and impacts.* Madison: Institute for Environmental Studies, University of Wisconsin. (Also published in Feldt, 1977, pp. 54-62.)

Bartlett, A. D. 1861. Notes on the breeding and rearing of the Chinese crane (*Grus montignesia*) in the Society's Garden. *Proceedings Zoological Society of London,* 1961, pp. 369-370.

Beddard, F. E. 1890. On the structure of *Psophia* and on its relations to other birds. *Proceedings Zoological Society of London,* 1890, pp. 329-340.

_____. 1898. *The structure and classification of birds.* London: Longmans, Green.

_____. 1902. Notes upon the osteology of *Aramus scolopaceus. Ibis,* series 8(2):33-54.

Beebe, C. W., Hartley, C. I., and Howes, P. G. 1917. *Tropical wild life in British Guiana.* Vol. 1. New York: New York Zoological Society.

Bennett, A. J., and Nauman, L. E. 1978. Summer populations of sandhill cranes in southeastern Wisconsin. *Passenger Pigeon* 40:349-357.

Bennett, E. T. 1831. *Gardens and managerie of the zoological society delineated.* Vol II. London: Zoological Society of London.

Benson, C. W. 1960. Breeding seasons of some game and protected birds in Northern Rhodesia. *Black Lechwe* 2:149-159.

Benson, C. W., Brooke, R. J., Woesett, R. J., and Irwin, M. P. S. 1971. *The birds of Zambia.* London: Collins.

Berg, B. 1930. *To Africa with the migratory birds.* New York: C. P. Putnam's Sons.

Berndt, R. 1938. Intrasternale Trachealschlingen bei Vögeln. *Gegenbaurs Morphologisches Jahrbuch,* 82:27-117.

Bieniasz, K. A. 1979. The greater sandhill crane in Routt County, Colorado, pp. 197-204, *in* Lewis, 1979e.

Bishop, M. A., and Blankinship, D. R. 1981. Dynamics of subadult flocks of whooping cranes at Aransas National Wildlife Refuge, Texas, 1978-1981. pp. 180-189, *in* Lewis, 1982.

Blaauw, F. E. 1897. *A monograph of the cranes.* Leiden: E. J. Brill.

Blackman, J. G. 1971a. Sex determination of Australian cranes (Gruidae). *Queensland Journal of Agriculture and Animal Science* 28:281-286.

_____. 1971b. Distribution of the sarus crane in northern Queensland. *Emu* 71:137-138.

_____. 1978. The swamp. pp. 147-183, *in* Lavery, H. J. (ed.), *Expedition North.* Victoria (Australia): Richmond Hill Press.

Blankinship, D. R. 1976. Studies of whooping cranes on the wintering grounds. pp. 197-206, *in* Lewis, 1976a.

Bliese, J. C. W. 1976. Some diurnal characteristics of sandhill crane flocks in southcentral Nebraska. pp. 157-165, *in* Lewis, 1976a.

Blyth, E., and Tegetmeier, W. G. 1881. *The natural history of the cranes.* London: Horace Cox.

Boeker, E. L., Aldrich, J. W., and Huey, W. S. 1961. Study of experimental sandhill crane hunting season in New Mexico during January 1961. U.S. Fish and Wildlife Service, *Special Scientific Report (Wildlife)* No. 63. 24 pp.

Boise, C., 1976. Breeding biology of the lesser sandhill crane — a preliminary report. pp. 126-129, *in* Lewis, 1976a.

_____. 1977. Breeding biology of the lesser sandhill crane *Grus canadensis canadensis* (L.) on the Yukon-Kuskokwim delta, Alaska. M. S. thesis, University of Alaska, College.

_____. 1979. Lesser sandhill crane banding program on the Yukon-Kuskokwim delta, Alaska. pp. 229-236, *in* Lewis, 1979e.

Bold, A. 1981. Cranes of the Mongolian People's Republic. p. 49, *in* Lewis and Masatomi, 1981.

Boothroyd, P. 1980. Whooping crane records for Manitoba, 1943-1979. *Blue Jay* 38:162-165.

Bravery, J. A. 1969. The sarus crane in northeastern Queensland. *Emu* 69:52-53.

Britton, P. L. (ed.). 1980 *Birds of East Africa.* Nairobi: East Africa Natural History Society.

Brodkorb, P. 1967. Catalogue of fossil birds: Part 3 (Ralliformes, Ichthyornithifomes, Charadriiformes). *Bulletin of the Florida State Museum, Biological Sciences* 2(3):99-220.

Brown, L. H., and Britton, P. L. 1980. *The breeding seasons of East African birds.* Nairobi: East Africa Natural History Society.

Buller, R. J. 1967. Sandhill crane study in the Central Flyway. U.S. Fish and Wildlife Service, *Special Scientific Report (Wildlife)* No. 113. 17 pp.

_____. 1976. Recent studies of age ratios of sandhill cranes in the Central Flyway. pp. 78-85, *in* Lewis, 1976a.

_____. 1979. Lesser and Canadian sandhill crane populations, age structure and harvest. U.S. Fish and Wildlife Service, *Special Scientific Report (Wildlife)* No. 221. 10 pp.

_____. 1982. Distribution of sandhill cranes wintering in Mexico. pp. 266-272, *in* Lewis, 1982.

Burke, V. E. M. 1965. A count of crowned cranes (*Balearica regulorum* (Bennett)) in the Kisii District, Kenya. *Journal East Africa Natural History Society and National Museum* 25:162-163.

Bylin, K. 1980. (Some aspects of the biology of the crane *Grus grus* during the breeding season). *Vår Fågelvärld* 3915-19. (Swedish, with English summary.)

Carlisle, M. J. 1982. Nesting habitat of sandhill cranes in central Alberta. pp. 44-52, *in* Lewis, 1982.

Carpenter, J. W. 1979. An outline of the treatment and control of crane parasites. pp. 101-108, *in* Lewis, 1979e.

Carpenter, J. W., and Derrickson, S. R. 1982. Whooping crane mortality at the Patuxent Wildlife Research Center, 1966-1981. pp. 174-179, *in* Lewis, 1982.

Carpenter, J. W., Locke, L. N., and Miller, J. C. 1976. Mortality in captive sandhill cranes at the Patuxent Wildlife Research Center, 1966-1975. pp. 268-283, *in* Lewis, 1976a.

Chekmenev, D. I. 1960. (On the biology of the demoiselle crane in Central Kazakhstan.) *Trudy Institute Zoologii Aka-*

demii Nauk Kazhjstoi SSR, Alma Ata. 13:142-147. (In Russian.)

Cheng, Tso-hsin. 1973. *A distributional list of Chinese birds.* Vol. 1, Non Passeriformes. Translated and published by NTIS, U.S. Dept. of Commerce, Springfield, Virginia.

————. 1981. Cranes in China. pp. 47-48, *in* Lewis and Masatomi, 1981.

Clarke, H. W., and Amadei, L. 1969. Breeding in captivity of the black-necked crowned crane. *Avicultural Magazine* 73:37-39.

Conway, W. G. 1957. Three days with a family of whooping cranes. *Animal Kingdom* 40(4):98-106.

Conway, W. G., and Hamer, A. 1977. A 36-year laying record of a wattled crane at the New York Zoological Park. *Auk* 94: 786.

Cosgrave, R. 1911. Notes on the cranes at Lilford Hall, *Avicultural Magazine*, New Series, 2:147-150.

Coues, E. 1874. *Birds of the Northwest. A handbook of the ornihology of the region drained by the Missouri River and its tributaries.* U.S. Geological Survey, Miscellaneous Publications No. 3:1-791.

————. 1892. Family Gruidae. In *North American birds.* Boston: Estes and Lauriat.

Cracraft, J. 1969. Systematics and evolution of the Gruiformes (Class Aves). I. The Eocene family Geranoididae and the early history of the Gruiformes. *American Museum Novitates* 2388:1-41.

————. 1971. Systematics and evolution of the Gruiformes (Class Aves). Additional comments on the Bathornithidae, with descriptions of a new species. *American Museum Novitates*, 2449:1-14.

————. 1973. Systematics and evolution of the Gruiformes (Class Aves). 3. Phylogeny of the suborder Grues. *American Museum of Natural History Bulletin* 151:1-127.

Cramp, S., and Simmons, K. E. L. (eds.). 1980. *The birds of the western Palearctic.* Vol. II. Oxford; Oxford University Press.

Crandall, L. S. 1945. We have two of the rarest chicks in the world. *Animal Kingdom* 48:119.

Crete, R. A., and Grewe, A. H. 1982. Greater sandhill cranes of Burnett County, Wisconsin. pp. 281-287, *in* Lewis, 1982.

Cyrus, D., and Robson, N. 1980. *Bird atlas of Natal.* Pietermaritzburg, Natal University Press.

Czekala, N., and Lasley, B. 1977. A technical note on sex determination in monomorphic birds using faecal steroid analysis. *International Zoo Yearbook* 17:209.

Dathe, H., and Neufeldt, I. A. 1978. *Atlas der Verbreitung palaearktischer Vogel.* 7 Lieferung. Berlin: Akademie-Verlag.

Davis, M. 1969. Siberian crane longevity. *Auk* 86:347.

Day, D. H. 1980. The crane study group, 1980. *Bokmakierie* 32: 90-92.

Deignan, H. G. 1945. The birds of northern Thailand. *U.S. National Museum Bulletin* 186:1-616.

Delacour, J. 1924. (Letter from Indo-China.) *Ibis*, Series II(6): 398.

————. 1925. Le grue à cour noir. *L'Oiseau* 6:233-236.

Dementiev, G. P., and Gladkov, N. A. 1968. *Birds of the Soviet Union.* Vol. 2 Translation published by NTIS, U.S. Dept. of Commerce, Springfield, Virginia. Originally published in Russian, 1951.

Derrickson, S. R. 1980. Whooping crane recovery plan. Report prepared by the whooping crane recovery team, U.S. Fish and Wildlife Service, Washington, D.C. 206 pp. (multlith).

Derrickson, S. R., and Carpenter, J. W. 1982. Whooping crane production at the Patuxent Wildlife Research Center, 1967-1981. pp. 190-199, *in* Lewis, 1982.

Dolan, B. 1939. Zoological results of the second Dolan Expedition to western China and eastern Tibet, 1934-36. Part 1. *Proceedings Academy of Natural Sciences, Philadelphia*, 90:159-185.

Douthwaite, R. J. 1974. An endangerd population of wattled cranes. *Biological Conservation* 6:134-142.

Dowsett, R. J., and Dowsett-Lemaire, F. 1980. The systematic status of some Zambian birds. *Le Gerfaut* 70:151-200.

Drewien, R. C. 1973. Ecology of Rocky Mountain greater sandhill cranes. Ph.D. dissertation, University of Idaho, Moscow.

————. 1978-1981. Whooping crane transplant experiments. Idaho Cooperative Wildlife Research Unit, University of Idaho, Moscow, unpublished Progress Reports No. 13-16.

Drewien, R. C., and Bizeau, E. G. 1974. Status and distribution of greater sandhill cranes in the Rocky Mountains. *Journal of Wildlife Management* 38:720-742.

————. 1978. Cross-fostering whooping cranes to sandhill crane foster parents. pp. 201-222, *in* Temple, S. (ed.), *Endangered birds: Management techniques for preserving threatened species.* Madison: University of Wisconsin Press.

Drewien, R. C., Derrickson, S. R., and Bizeau, E. G. 1982. Experimental release of captive parent-reared greater sandhill cranes at Grays Lake refuge, Idaho, pp. 99-111, *in* Lewis, 1982.

Drewien, R. C., Oakleaf, R. J., and Mullins, W. H. 1976. The sandhill crane in Nevada. pp. 130-138, *in* Lewis, 1976a.

Dymin, V. A., and Pankin. N. S. 1975. (Nesting and migration of storks (Ciconiidae) and cranes (Gruidae) in the upper Amur region.) pp. 263-267, *in* Ornithological Studies in the Soviet Far East. *Proceedings of the Institute of Biology and Pedology*, New Series, Vol. 29(132). (In Russian.)

England, M. D. 1963. Studies of less familiar birds. 124. Crane. *British Birds* 56:58-62.

Erickson, R. C. 1975. Captive breeding of whooping cranes at the Patuxent Wildlife Research Center. pp. 99-114, *in* Martin, R. D. (ed.), *Breeding endangered species in captivity.* New York: Academic Press.

————. 1976. Whooping crane studies at the Patuxent Wildlife Research Center. pp. 166-176, *in* Lewis, 1976a.

Erickson, R. C., and Derrickson, S. R. 1981. The whooping crane. pp. 104-118, *in* Lewis and Masatomi, 1981.

Faanes, C. A., and Frank. A. M. 1982. Characteristics of diurnal sandhill crane flocks in the Platte River valley, Nebraska. pp. 22-26, *in* Lewis, 1982.

Farner, D. S. 1955. Birdbanding in the study of population dynamics. In Wolfson, A., (ed.), *Recent studies in avian biology.* Urbana: University of Illinois Press.

Feduccia, A. 1980. *The age of birds.* Cambridge: Harvard University Press.

REFERENCES

Feldt, R. D. (ed.). 1977. *Eastern greater sandhill crane sympo-sium.* Proceedings of a conference held 24-26 October 1977. Wildlife Society (Indiana chapter), Indiana Conservation Council, Inc., and Division of Fish and Wildlife, State of Indiana. 123 pp. (multilith).

Fernandez-Cruz, M. 1979-1980. La micracion e invernade de la grulla comun *(Grus grus)* en España. Resultudos de Projecto *Grus* (Crane Project). *Ardeola* 26-27:1-164. (English Summary.)

Field, D. 1978. First aerial survey of wattled cranes. *Bokmakierie* 30:18-20.

Fisher, J., Simon, N., and Vincent, J. 1969. *The red book: Wildlife in danger.* New York: Viking Press.

Fjeldså, J. 1977. *A guide to the young of Europe precocial birds.* Tisvildelje, Denmark: Scarv Nature Publications.

Fleming, R. L., Sr., Fleming, R. L., Jr., and Bangdel, L. S. 1976. *Birds of Nepal, with reference to Kashmir and Sikkim.* Katmandu: Published by the authors.

Flint. V. E. (ed.) 1978a. (Birds.) pp. 90-149, *in* Vinokunov. A. A. et al. (eds.), *Red data book of the USSR.* Central Research Laboratory for Nature Conservation, USSR Ministry of Agriculture, Lesnaya Promyshlennost, Moscow. (In Russian.)

——————. 1978b. (Strategy and tactics for conservation of rare birds.) *Priroda* 756(8):14-29. (In Russian.)

Flint, V. E., and Kistchinski, A. A. 1975. (The Siberian white crane in Yakutia.) *Zoologicheskii Jhurnal* 5(8)1197-1212.

——————. 1981. The Siberian crane in Yakutia. pp. 136-146, *in* Lewis and Masatomi, 1981.

Flint, V. E., and Smirenskii, S. M. 1977. (New data on the distribution of the Japanese crane and the Far Eastern white stork.) *Abstracts of the VIII USSR Ornithological Conference,* Cherkassy, the Ukraine, 27-30 September 1977, vol. 2, p. 251. Kiev: "Naukova Dumka." (In Russian).

Flint, V. E., and Sorokin, A. G. 1981. The biology of the Siberian crane (sterkh) in Yakutia. pp. 146-149, *in* Lewis and Masatomi, 1981.

Flower, S. S. 1925. Contributions to our knowledge of the duration of life in vertebrate animals, IV. Birds. *Proceedings of the Zoological Society of London,* 1925, pp. 1365-1422.

Forbes. W. A. 1882. On the convoluted trachae of two species of manucode *(Manucodia atra* and *Phonygama gouldi):* with remarks on similar structures in other birds. *Proceedings Zoological Society of London,* pp. 347-353.

Frith, C. R. 1974. The ecology of the Platte River as related to sandhill cranes and other waterfowl in south central Nebraska. M.S. thesis, Kearney State College, Kearney, Nebraska.

——————. 1976. Crane habitat of the Platte River. pp. 151-156, *in* Lewis, 1976a.

Frith, C. R., and Faanes, C. A. 1982. Inventory of sandhill crane roosting habitat on the Platte and North Platte rivers, Nebraska. pp. 13-16, *in* Lewis, 1982.

Fritzell, E. K., Krapu, G. L., and Jorde, D. G. 1979. Habitat use patterns of sandhill cranes in the Platte River valley — A preliminary report. pp. 7-12, *in* Lewis, 1979e.

Fry, C. H. 1981. West African crowned crane status. pp. 251-253, *in* Lewis and Masatomi, 1981.

Fürbinger, M. 1888. *Untersuchungen zur Morphologie und Systematik der Vogel.* II. Allgemeiner Teil. Amsterdam: Van Kokkema.

Fuzhang, Z., Wenning, D., and Ziyu, W. 1981. (A large flock of white cranes, *Grus leucogeranus,* wintering in China.) *Acta Zool. Sinica* 27(2):179. (In Chinese.)

Garrod, A. H. 1876. On the anatomy of *Aramus scolopaceus. Proceedings Zoological Society of London,* 1876, pp. 275-277.

Gee, G. F., and Sexton, T. J. 1979. Artificial insemination of cranes with frozen semen. pp. 89-94, *in* Lewis, 1979e.

Gills, H. B. 1969. First record of the sarus crane in Australia. *Emu* 69:49-52.

Glutz von Blotzheim, U. N. (ed.). 1973. *Handbuch der Vogel Mitteleuropas.* Band 5. Weisbaden: Akademische Verlagsgellschaft.

Gole, P. 1981. Black-necked crane in Ladakh. pp. 197-203, *in* Lewis and Masatomi, 1981.

Goold, J. W. 1977. Status of the eastern greater sandhill crane in Indiana. pp. 18-23, *in* Feldt, 1977.

Gray, A. P. 1958. *Bird hybrids.* Farnum Royal (Bucks.): Agricultural Research Bureaux.

Greenberg, J. 1981. Sandhill cranes nesting in Illinois. *Wilson Bulletin* 92:527.

Greenway, J. C. 1958. *Extinct and vanishing birds of the world.* New York: American Committee for International Wildlife Protection, Special Publication No. 13.

Grewe, A. H. 1977. The current status of eastern greater sandhill crane in Minnesota. pp. 12-17, *in* Feldt, 1977.

Grigorescu, D., and Kessler, E. 1977. The Middle Sarmatian avian fauna of South Dobrogea. *Revue Roum. Géol. Géogr.* (Ser. Géol.) 21:93-108.

Griswold, J. A. 1962. Raising cranes in captivity. *America's First Zoo* 14:28-31.

Grote, H. 1943. Zur Biologie dreier seltener Kranicharten. *Beiträge zur Fortpflanzungsbiologie der Vogel* 19:33-36.

Grummt, W. 1961. Ornithologische Beobachtungen in der Mongolei. *Beiträge zur Vogelkunde* 7:349-360.

Guthery, F. S. 1972. Food habitats, distribution, numbers and subspecies of sandhill cranes wintering in southern Texas. M.S. thesis, Texas A & M University, College Station.

——————. 1976. Foods and feeding habitat of sandhill cranes in southern Texas. pp. 117-125, *in* Lewis, 1976a.

Guthery, F. S., and Lewis, J. C. 1979. Sandhill cranes in coastal counties of Texas: Taxonomy, distribution and populations. pp. 121-128, *in* Lewis, 1979a.

Harrison, C. J. O. 1978. *A field guide to the nests, eggs and nestlings of North American birds.* Cleveland: Collins.

Hattori, U. 1928. *Mythology of all races.* Vol. 8. Cambridge: Cambridge University Press.

Heinroth, O. 1922. Die Beziehungen zwischen Vogelwicht, Eigewicht, Gelegewicht, und Brutdauer. *Journal für Ornithologie* 70:172-285.

Heinroth, O., and Heinroth, M. 1926-1928. *Die Vogel Mitteleuropas.* 4 vols. Berlin-Lichterfeld: H. Bermühler.

——————. 1958. *The birds.* Ann Arbor: University of Michigan Press.

Hemmingsen, A. M., and Guildal, J. A. 1968. Observations on birds in northeastern China. *Spolia Zoologica Musei Hauniensis,* pt. II. 28:1-326.

REFERENCES

Hendrickson, H. T. 1969. A comparative study of the egg white proteins of some species of the avian order Gruiformes. *Ibis*111:80-91.

Herter, D. R. 1982. Staging of sandhill cranes on the eastern Copper River delta, Alaska. pp. 273-280, *in* Lewis, 1982.

Hickey, J. J. 1955. Some American population research on gallinaceous birds. *In* Wolfson, A. (ed.), *Recent studies in avian biology*. Urbana: University of Illinois Press.

Hinds. D. S., and W. A. Calder. 1971. Trachael dead spaces in the respiration of birds. *Evolution* 25:429-440.

Hoffman, R. H. 1977. The status of the eastern greater sandhill crane in southern Michigan. pp. 2-9, *in* Feldt, 1977.

———. 1979. Thickness and variablity of eggshells of southern Michigan cranes. pp. 181-188, *in* Lewis, 1979e.

Hopkinson, E. 1926. *Records of birds bred in captivity*. London: Witherby.

Howard, H. 1950. Fossil evidence of avian evolution. *Ibis* 92: 1-21.

Howard, T. J. 1977. The ecology of the greater sandhill crane in central Wisconsin. pp. 39-47, *in* Feldt, 1977.

Hunt, R. A., and Gluesing, E. A. 1976. The sandhill crane in Wisconsin. pp. 19-34, *in* Lewis, 1976a.

Hunt, R. A., Gluesing, E. A., and Nauman. L. E. 1976. The greater sandhill crane in Wisconsin: A preliminary report. Madison: Wisconsin Dept. of Natural Resources Research Report No. 86. 17 pp.

Ingersoll, E. 1923. *Birds in legend, fable and folklore*. New York: Longmans, Green & Co.

Innouye, M. 1981. A historical review of conservation of red-crowned crane (Tancho) in Hokkaido. pp. 99-101, *in* Lewis and Masatomi, 1981.

Iverson, G. C., Tacha, T. C., and Vohs, P. A. 1982. Food contents of sandhill cranes during winter and spring. pp. 95-98, *in* Lewis, 1982.

Jacob, J., Plawer, J., and Rosenfeldt, P. 1979. Gefiederwachsckompositionen von Kranichen und Rallen. Beitrag zur Systematik der Gruiformes. *Journal für Ornithologie* 120:54-63. (English summary.)

Jahn, H. 1942. Zur oekologie und biologie der Vogel Japan. *Journal für Ornithologie* 90:6-302.

Johansen, H. 1930. Zur Fortpflanzung des Monchskranichs. *Beiträge Fortpflanzungbiologie der Vogel* 6:105-112.

Johnsgard, P. A. 1971. Observations on sound production in the Anatidae. *Wildfowl* 22:46-59.

———. 1973. How many cranes make a skyful? *Animals*, December 1973, pp. 532-539.

———. 1981. *The plovers, sandpipers and snipes of the world*. Lincoln: University of Nebraska Press.

———. 1982. Whooper recount. *Natural History* 91(2):70-75.

Johnsgard, P. A., and Redfield, R. 1978. Sixty-five years of whooping crane records in Nebraska. *Nebraska Bird Review* 45:54-56.

Johnson, D. H. 1976. The status of the sandhill in North Dakota. pp. 69-77, *in* Lewis, 1976a.

———. 1979. Modelling sandhill crane population dynamics. U.S. Fish and Wildlife Service, Special Scientific Report (Wildlife) no. 222. 10 pp.

Johnson, J. 1976. Distribution of sandhill cranes in Minnesota. pp. 59-68, in Lewis, 1976a.

Kale, H. W., II (ed.). 1978. Rare and endangered biota of Florida. II. Birds. Gainesville: University Presses of Florida.

Katz, B. 1979. Breeding ethology of the hooded crane. pp. 217-222, *in* Lewis, 1979e.

Karlsson, A. 1980. (The cranes *Grus grus* at Lake Hornborgasjön.) *Vår Fågelvärld* 39:377-384. (In Swedish, with English summary.)

Kawamura, N. 1975. (Studies on the hooded crane at Yashiro, Yamaguchi Prefecture: Its roosting behavior.) *Miscellaneous Reports of the Yamashina Institute for Ornithology* 7(5):550-561. (In Japanese, with English summary.)

———. 1981. The hooded crane at Yashiro, Yamaguchi Prefecture. pp. 244-249, *in* Lewis and Masatomi, 1981.

Khacher, L. 1981. Conservation needs of black-necked cranes at Bhuta, Arunachal Pradesh, and Ladakh. pp. 204-211, *in* Lewis and Masatomi, 1981.

King, B. F., and Dickinson, E. C. 1975. *A field guide to the birds of south-east Asia*. Boston: Houghton Mifflin.

King. W. B. (ed.) 1979. *Endangered birds of the world: The ICBP red data book*. Reprinted in handbook form by Smithsonian Institution Press, Washington, D.C.

Kiracofe, J. 1964. The sarus crane *Grus collaris*. Successful breeding and other observations. *Modern Game Breeding* 1(2):12-18.

Klika, I. 1974. Ein Beitrag zur Brutbiologie des Saruskranichs (*Grus a. antigone* L.). *Zoologische Garten Zena* 44(1-2): 1-11.

Koga, T. 1975. On the cranes of Japan in the wild and captivity. *Der Zoologische Garten* (N.F.) 45:81-86.

———. 1976. Increasing captive production of Japanese and white-naped cranes. pp. 351-355, in Lewis, 1976a.

———. 1981. Wild and captive cranes in Japan. pp. 50-51, *in* Lewis and Masatomi, 1981.

Konrad, P. M. 1976. Potential for the reintroduction of cranes into areas of former habitation. pp. 317-326, *in* Lewis, 1976a.

———. 1981. Status and ecology of wattled crane in Africa. pp. 220-237, *in* Lewis and Masatomi, 1981.

Kozlova, E. V. 1975. (Birds of the zonal steppes and wastelands of Central Asia.) *Trudy Zoologischeskogo Instituta, Leningrad* 59:8-239. (In Russian.)

Krapu, G. L. 1979. Sandhill crane use of staging areas in Nebraska. pp. 1-6, *in* Lewis, 1979e.

Krechmar, A. V., Andreev, A. V., and Kondrat'ev, A. Y. 1978. (Ecology and distribution of sandhill cranes in northeastern USSR.) pp. 140-142, *in* Kretchmar, A. V., et al., *Ecology and distribution of birds of Northeastern USSR*. Moscow: "Izdatel'stvo Nauka." (In Russian.)

Kucheruk, V. V. (undated). (New data on the distribution of the white-naped crane.) Unpublished (?) manuscript. (In Russian.)

Kuyt, E. 1976a. Recent clutch size data for whooping cranes, including a three-egg clutch. *Blue Jay* 34:82-83.

———. 1976b. Whooping cranes: The long road back. *Nature Canada* 5:2-9.

———. 1977. The continuing story of the whooping crane. pp. 107-111, in *Canada's threatened species and habitats*, Canada Nature Federation, Ottawa.

———. 1979. Banding of juvenile whooping cranes and discovery of the summer habitat used by nonbreeders. pp. 109-112, *in* Lewis, 1979e.

REFERENCES

_____ 1981a. Clutch size, hatching success and survival of whooping crane chicks, Wood Buffalo National Park, Canada. pp. 126-129, *in* Lewis and Masatomi, 1981.

_____ 1981b. Population status, nest site fidelity, and breeding habitat of whooping cranes. pp. 119-125, *in* Lewis and Masatomi, 1981.

Kyu, K. H., and Oesting, M. R. 1981. Cranes in Korea. pp. 57-60, *in* Lewis and Masatomi, 1981.

Labuda, S. E., and Butts, K. O. 1979. Habitat use by wintering whooping cranes on the Aransas National Wildlife Refuge. pp. 151-159, *in* Lewis, 1979e.

Larue, C. 1980. Increasing fertility of crane eggs. *Avicultural Magazine* 86:10-15.

_____ 1981. Techniques for breeding cranes in captivity. pp. 15-18, *in* Lewis and Masatomi, 1981.

Larue, C., and Hoffman, K. 1981. Artificial incubation and hand-rearing of cranes. *International Zoo Yearbook* 21: 215-217.

Lavery, H. G. 1965. The brolga, *Grus rubicundus* (Perry) on some coastal areas in north Queensland: Fluctuations in population, and economic status. *Queensland Journal of Agricultural Science* 21:261-264.

Lavery, H. G., and Blackman, J. G. 1969. The cranes of Australia. *Queensland Agricultural Journal* 95:156-162.

Law, S. C. 1930. Fish-eating habit of the sarus crane (*Antigone antigone*). *Journal Bombay Natural History Society* 34: 582-583.

Leach, M. (ed.) 1972. *Funk and Wagnalls standard dictionary of folklore, mythology and legends.* New York: Funk an Wagnalls.

Leopold, A. 1949. *A sand county almanac.* New York: Oxford University Press.

Lewis, J. C. 1974. Ecology of the sandhill cranes in the southeastern Central Flyway. Ph. D. dissertation, Oklahoma State University, Stillwater.

_____ (ed.) 1976a. *Proceeding of the International Crane Workshop,* 3-6 September 1973, International Crane Foundation, Baraboo, Wisconsin. Stillwater: Oklahoma State University Publishing and Printing Dept.

_____ 1976b. Roost habitat and roosting behavior of sandhill cranes. pp. 93-104, *in* Lewis, 1976a.

_____ 1977. Sandhill crane. pp. 5-43, *in* Sanderson, C. E. (ed.), *Management of migratory shore and upland game birds in North America.* Lincoln: University of Nebraska Press.

_____ 1979a. Taxonomy, food and feeding habitat of sandhill cranes, Platte Valley, Nebraska. pp. 21-28, *in* Lewis, 1979e.

_____ 1979b. Factors affecting the spring inventory of sandhill cranes. pp. 33-40, *in* Lewis, 1979e.

_____ 1979c. Molt of the remiges of *Grus canadensis.* pp. 255-259, *in* Lewis, 1979e.

_____ 1979d. Field identification of juvenile sandhill cranes. *Journal of Wildlife Management* 43:211-214.

_____ 1979e. *Proceedings 1978 Crane Workshop.* Rockport, Texas, December 1978. Fort Collins: Colorado State University Printing Service.

_____ (ed.). 1982. *Proceedings 1981 Crane Workshop.* Tavernier, Fla.; National Audubon Society.

Lewis, J. C., and Masatomi, H. (eds.). 1981. *Crane research around the world.* Proceedings of the International Crane Symposium at Sapporo, Japan, in 1980, and papers from World Working Group on Cranes, International Council for Bird Preservation. Baraboo, Wisconsin: International Crane Foundation.

Libbert, W. 1969. Ueber das Verhalten der Kraniche auf Rast- und Sammelplatzen. *Beiträge Vogelkunde* 14:388-405.

Littlefield, C. D. 1976. Production of greater sandhill cranes on Malheur National Wildlife Refuge, Oregon. pp. 86-92, *in* Lewis, 1976a.

_____ 1981. The greater sandhill crane. pp. 163-166, *in* Lewis and Masatomi, 1981.

Littlefield, C. D., and Ryder, R. A. 1968. Breeding biology of the greater sandhill crane on Malheur National Wildlife Refuge, Oregon. *Transactions North American Wildlife and Natural Resources Conference* 33:444-454.

Littlefield, C. D., and Thompson, S. P. 1979. Distribution and status of the Central Valley population of greater sandhill cranes. pp. 113-120, *in* Lewis, 1979e.

Lovvorn, J. R., and Kirkpatrick, C. M. 1981. Roosting behavior and habitat of migrant greater sandhill cranes. *Journal of Wildlife Management* 45:842-857.

Lowe, P. R. 1931. On the relations of the Gruimorphae to the Charadriimorphae and Rallimorphae, with special reference to the taxonomic position of the Rostratulidae, Jacanidae and Burhinidae (Oedicnemidae *olim*) with a suggested new order (Telmatomorphae). *Ibis,* ser. 13, 1: 491-534.

Lu, Zong-bao, Yao, J., and Liao, Y. 1980. (Observations on the breeding habitats of black-necked cranes.) *Journal of Zoology* (China) 1980:19-23. (In Chinese.)

Ludlow, P. 1928. Dongtse or stray bird notes from Tibet. *Journal Bombay Natural History Society* 33:78-83.

Ma, G. E. 1981. Breeding habits of red-crowned cranes. pp. 89-93, *in* Lewis and Masatomi, 1981.

Ma, G., and Xu, S. 1980. (Preliminary study on counting methods for the population of the red-crowned crane *Grus japonensis.*) *Journal of Zoology* (China) 1980:4-7. (In Chinese.)

Macartney, P. 1968. Wattled cranes in Zambia. *Bokmakierie* 20:38-41.

Mackworth-Praed, C. W., and Grant, C. H. B. 1970. *Birds of West Central and Western Africa.* London: Longmans.

Madsen, K. K. 1981. Search for the eastern sarus crane on Luzon, Philippines. pp. 116-118, *in* Lewis and Masatomi, 1981.

Makatsch, W. 1970. *Der Kranich (Grus grus u. a.).* 2nd ed., Neue Brehm-Bücherei 229. Lutherstadt: A. Zeimsen Verlag.

_____ 1976. The status of the European crane in the German Democratic Republic. p. 350, *in* Lewis, 1976a.

_____ 1981. The status of common crane in Upper Lusatia. pp. 186-187, *in* Lewis and Masatomi, 1981.

Makowski, H. 1981. Common cranes in the German Federal Republic. p. 118, *in* Lewis and Masatomi, 1981.

Maroldo, G. 1980. Crip, the constant dancer. *Blue Jay* 38:147-161.

Marten, E. M. 1979. Hunting and harvest trends for migratory game birds other than waterfowl: 1964-76. U.S. Fish and

REFERENCES

Wildlife Service, *Special Scientific Report (Wildlife)* No. 218.

Martens, J. 1981. Zur Kenntnis des Vogelzuges im nepalischen Himalaya. *Die Vogelwarte* 26:113-128.

Masatomi, H. 1970-1972. (Ecological studies on the Japanese crane, *Grus japonensis.*) Senshu Agricultural and Industrial Junior College, Bibai, March 1970, March 1971, March 1972, and June, 1972. (In Japanese: translation summary in files of International Crane Foundation, Baraboo, Wisconsin.)

———— 1979. (Ecological studies on the Japanese crane, *Grus japonensis*, XI.) *Journal Senshu Agricultural and Industrial Junior College*, Bibai. 12:5-11. (In Japanese.)

———— 1980. (Ecological studies on the Japanese crane, *Grus japonensis*, XII.) *Journal Senshu Agricultural and Industrial Junior College*, Bibai, 13:1-7. (In Japanese.)

———— 1981a. The red-crowned crane. pp. 81-85, *in* Lewis and Masatomi, 1981.

———— 1981b. Populations of red-crowned cranes in Hokkaido, pp. 86-88, *in* Lewis and Masatomi, 1981.

Masatomi, H., and Kitagawa, T. 1974. Bionomics and sociology of tancho or the Japanese crane *Grus japonensis*. I. Distribution, habitat and outline of annual cycle. *Journal of the Faculty of Science, Hokkaido University*, Series VI, Zoology 19(3):777-802.

———— 1975. Bionomics and sociology of tancho or the Japanese crane, *Grus japonensis*. II. Ethogram. *Journal of the Faculty of Science, Hokkaido University*, Series VI, Zoology 19(4):834-878.

Mathiasson, S. 1964. Visible diurnal migration in the Sudan. *Proceedings XIII International Ornithological Congress*, Ithaca, New York, pp. 430-435.

Mauman, L. E. 1977. The status of the eastern greater sandhill crane in Wisconsin. p. 12, *in* Feldt, 1977.

McCoy, J. J. 1966. *The hunt for the whooping cranes.* New York: Lothrop, Lee and Shepard Co.

McNulty, F. 1966. *The whooping crane: The bird that defies extinction.* New York: E. P. Dutton.

Medway, Lord, and Wells, D. R. 1976. *The birds of the Malay Peninsula.* Vol. 5. London: H. F. and G. Witherby.

Meinertzhagen, R. 1927. Systematic results of birds collected at high altitudes in Ladak and Sikkim. Pt. 2 *Ibis*, series 12, 3:571-633.

———— 1954. *Birds of Arabia.* Edinburgh: Oliver and Boyd.

Meise, W., Schönwetter, M., and Stresemann, E. 1938. Aves Beickiana. *Journal für Ornithology*, 1938 (Sonderheft): 171-221.

Melvin, S. M. 1977. Migration studies of Wisconsin greater sandhill crane. pp. 27-38, *in* Feldt, 1977.

Melvin, S. M., and Temple, S. A. 1980. Migration ecology and wintering grounds of sandhill cranes from the interlake area of Manitoba. Unpublished manuscript report to the U.S. Fish and Wildlife Service. 60 pp.

———— 1982. Migration ecology of sandhill cranes: A review. pp. 73-87, *in* Lewis, 1982.

Merikallio, E. 1958. Finnish birds, their distribution and numbers. *Fauna Fennica* 5:1-181.

Miller, R. S., Hochbaum, G. S., and Botkin, D. B. 1972. A simulation model for the management of sandhill cranes. New Haven: *Yale University School of Forestry and Environmental Studies Bulletin* No. 80:1-49.

Mitchell, P. C. 1911. On longevity and relative viability in mammals and birds, with a note on the theory of longevity. *Proceedings Zoological Society of London*, 1911, pp. 425-548.

———— 1915. Anatomical notes on the gruiform birds *Aramus giganteus* Bonap. and *Rhinochetus kagu. Proceedings Zoological Society of London*, 1915, pp. 413-423.

Miura, J. 1981. Red-crowned crane in Nemuro District. p. 96, *in* Lewis and Masatomi, 1981.

Moll, K. H. 1963. Kranichbeobachtungen aus dem Mürutzgebiet. *Beiträge zur Vogelkunde* 8:221-253; 368-388; 412-439.

———— 1967. *Unter Adlern und Kraniche am Grossen See.* Wittenburg Lutherstadt: Ziemsen Verlag.

Moody, F. 1931. Death of an American whooping crane. *Aviculture Magazine*, series 4(9):8-11.

———— 1932. *Water-fowl and Game Birds in Captivity.* London: Witherby.

Mullins, W. H., and Bizeau, E. G. 1978. Summer foods of sandhill cranes in Idaho. *Auk* 95:175-178.

Nelson, E. W. 1896-97. Eskimos about Bering Strait. *18th Annual Report of the Bureau of American Ethnology*, part 1:1-518.

Nesbitt, S. A. 1977. The current status and future of the greater sandhill crane in Florida. pp. 24-25, *in* Feldt, 1977.

Nesbitt, S. A., and Williams, L. E., Jr. 1979. Summer range and migration routes of Florida wintering sandhill cranes. *Wilson Bulletin* 91:137-141.

Neufeldt, I. 1973. (The Manchurian crane.) *Okhoti i Okhotnich'e Khoziaistvo* 11:47-48. (In Russian.)

———— 1974. (The Siberian white crane.) *Okhota i Okhotnich'e Khoziaistov*, 12:26-27. (In Russian.)

———— 1977. (The distribution of the hooded crane, *Grus monacha*, in light of the available information.) *Ornitologiya* 13: 56-61. (In Russian.)

———— 1981a. The hooded crane in the USSR. pp. 239-243, *in* Lewis and Masatomi, 1981.

———— 1981b. The cranes must live. pp. 13-14, *in* Lewis and Masatomi, 1981.

Neufeldt, I., and Pukinsky, Y. B. (undated). (The hooded crane, *Grus monacha* Temminck, in the Soviet Union.) Translated from a Russian manuscript by Elizabeth C. Anderson for the International Crane Foundation.

Neufeldt, I., and Wunderlich, K. 1978. *Grus monacha* Temminck. *in* Dathe, H., and Neufeldt, I. (eds.), *Atlas der Verbeitung palaeartischer Vogel*, 7 Leiferung. Berlin: Akademie-Verlag.

Niemeier, M. M. 1979a. Early sternal and trachael development in *Grus canadensis* spp. pp. 223-228, *in* Lewis, 1979e.

———— 1979b. Structural and functional aspects of vocal ontogeny in *Grus canadensis* (Gruidae: Aves). Ph.D. dissertation, University of Nebraska, Lincoln.

Nilsson, S. G. 1982. Differences in the breeding success of the common crane *Grus grus* between south and central Sweden. *Journal für Ornithologie* 123:93-95.

Nishida, S. 1981. Wintering life of cranes in Kagoshima and Yamaguchi prefectures, Japan. pp. 52-60, *in* Lewis and Masatomi, 1981.

Novakowski, N. S. 1966. Whooping crane population dynamics on the nesting grounds, Wood Buffalo National

REFERENCES

Park, Northwest Territories, Canada. *Canadian Wildlife Service Report Series* No. 1. 20 pp.

Owre, O. T. 1966. The crowned crane at Lake Rudolf. *Bulletin British Ornithologists' Club* 86:54-56.

Parker, R. H. 1971. Priorities in bird conservation in Nigeria. International Union for the Conservation of Nature and Natural Resources, IUCN Publications (n.s.) No. 22:34-37.

Parker, W. K. 1868. A monograph on the structure and development of the shoulder girdle and sternum in the vertebrata. *Ray Society of London.*

Pennycuick, C. J., Alerstam, T., and Larsson, B. 1979. Soaring migration of the common crane observed by radar and from an aircraft. *Ornis Scandinavica* 10:241-251.

Perfil'ev, V. I. 1963. (New data on the ecology of the Siberian crane.) *Byulleten Moskovskogo Obshchevtva Ispytatelei Prirody Otdelenie Biologisheskii* 68(1):25-28. (In Russian.)

——— 1965. (The Siberian crane and its preservation in Yakutia.) *Priroda Yakutii i ee Ohkrana*, Yakutsk, 1965: 99-113. (In Russian.)

Peters, J. L. 1934. *Check-list of birds of the world.* Vol. 2. Cambridge: Harvard University Press.

Petrides, G. A. 1949. Viewpoint on the analysis of open season sex and age ratios. *Transactions 14th North American Wildlife Conference*, pp. 308-325.

Polivanova, N. N., Polivanov, V., and Shibaev, U. 1975. (*Grus japonensis* on Lake Khanka.) *Byulleten Moskovskogo Obshchestva Ispytatelei Prirody Otdelenie Biologisheskii* 80:49-58. (In Russian, English summary.)

Pomeroy, D. E. 1980a. Growth and plumage changes of the gray crowned crane *Balearica regulorum gibbericeps. Bulletin British Ornithologists' Club* 100:219-223.

——— 1980b. Aspects of the ecology of crowned cranes *Balearica regulorum. Scopus* 4:29-35.

Portenko, L. A. 1981. *Birds of the Chukchi Peninsula and Wrangel Island.* Vol. 1. Translated from Russian: Smithsonian Institution and National Science Foundation, Washington, D. C.

Portmann, A. 1959. Les organes respiratoires. *in* P. Grasse, ed. *Traite de Zoologie, Tome XV.* Oiseaux. Masson et Cie., Paris.

Poulsen, H. 1975. Antagonistic behavior in two species of cranes. *Dansk Ornithologisk Forenings Tidsskrift* 69:119-122.

Prezhwalsky, N. 1877. The birds of Mongolia, the Tangut Country, and the solitudes of northern Tibet, *in* Rowley, C. G., *Ornith. Misc.* 2(3):417-438.

Pukinskii, Y. B. 1977. (The hooded crane in Primor.) *Ohkota i Okhotnich'e Kozyaistvo*, 1977(1):28-30. (In Russian: English summary in *Bird-banding* 49:189-90.)

Pukinskii, Y. B., and Ilyinskii, I. V. 1977. (On the biology and behavior of the hooded crane in the nesting period, Primor District, Bikin River Basin.) *Byulleten Moskovskogo Obshchestva Ispytatelei Prirody Otdelenie Biologicheskii* 82:5-17. (In Russian, English summary.)

Putnam, M. S. 1982. Refined techniques in crane propagation at the International Crane Foundation. pp. 250-258, *in* Lewis, 1982.

Pycraft, W. P. 1913. *The courtship of animals.* 3rd ed. London: Hutchinson & Co.

Pyong-Oh, W. 1967. The present status of some threatened and rare birds in Korea, 1962-66. *Bulletin International Commission for Bird Preservation* 10:109-113.

Ramakka, J. M. 1979. Capturing sandhill cranes in Texas and Nebraska. pp. 75-80, *in* Lewis, 1979e.

Rand, A. L., and Fleming. R. L. 1957. Birds of Nepal. *Fieldiana* 41:1-218.

Rand, A. L., and Gilliard, E. T. 1968. *Handbook of New Guinea birds.* Garden City: Natural History Press.

Rasch, E. M., and Kurtin, P. J. 1976. Sex identification of sandhill cranes by karotype analysis. pp. 309-316, *in* Lewis, 1976a.

Reinecke, K. J., and Krapu, G. L. 1979. Spring food habits of sandhill cranes in Nebraska. pp. 13-20, *in* Lewis, 1979e.

Ridgway, R. 1941. The birds of North and Middle America, part IX. *U.S. National Museum Bulletin* 50:1-254.

Roberts, T. S. 1880. The convolution of the trachea in the sandhill and whooping cranes. *American Naturalist* 14:108-114.

——— 1932. *Birds of Minnesota.* Vol. 1. Minneapolis: University of Minnesota Press.

Roslyakov, G. E. 1977. (Rare birds of the lower Amur River.) *Abstracts of the VII USSR National Ornithological Conference*, Cherkassy, the Ukraine, 27-30 September 1977, vol. 2, pp. 241-243. Kiev: "Naukova Dumka." (In Russian.)

Rothschild, Lord W. 1930. Sarus crane breeding at Tring. *Bulletin British Ornithologists' Club* 50:67-68.

Rowland, B. 1979. *Birds with human souls. A guide to bird symbolism.* Knoxville: Tennessee University Press.

Rüppell, W. 1933. Physiologie und Akustik der Vogelstimme. *Journal für Ornithologie* 81:433-542.

Rutgers, A., and Norris, K. A. 1970. *Encyclopaedia of aviculture.* Vol. 1. London: Blandford.

Sasaki, M., and Takagi, N. 1981. Chromosomes in Guiformes, with notes on the chromosomal diagnosis of avian sex. pp. 19-23, *in* Lewis and Masatomi, 1981.

Sauey, R. T. 1976. The behavior of Siberian cranes wintering in India. pp. 326-342, *in* Lewis, 1976a.

——— 1979. Feeding biology of juvenile Siberian cranes in India. pp. 205-210, *in* Lewis, 1979e.

Sauey, R. T., and Brown, C. B. 1977. The captive management of cranes. *International Zoo Yearbook* 17:89-91.

Schäfer, E. 1938. Ornithologische Ergebnisse zweier Forschungreisen nach Tibet. *Journal für Ornithology* '86 (Sonderheft): 1-349.

Schneider, J. G. 1788-1789. *Requila librorum Frederici II. Imperatoris de arte venandi cum avibus. Cum Manfredi Regis additionibus. Accedunt Alberti Magni Capita de Falconibus Asturibus et Accipitribus.* Part 1-11. Leipzig.

Scott, D. A. 1981. Status and distribution of cranes in Iran and some observations in Iraq. pp. 70-72, *in* Lewis and Masatomi, 1981.

Serle. W. 1939. Field observations on some northern Nigerian birds. Pt. 1. *Ibis*, series 14(3):654-699.

Serventy, D. L., and Whittell, H. M. 1967. *Birds of Western Australia.* 4th ed. Perth: Lambert Publications.

Sharpe, R. B. 1894. *Catalogue of the Fulicarae and Alectorides in the collection of the British Museum.* London: British Museum (Natural History).

REFERENCES

Sheffeldt, R. W. 1915. On the comparative osteology of the limpkin (*Aramus vociferus*) and its place in the system. *Anatomical Record* 9:591-606.

Shibaev, I. V. 1975. (Crane migration in south Primore.) pp. 254-262, *in* Nechaev, V. A. (ed.), *Ornithological studies in the Soviet Far East*. Proceedings of the Institute of Biology and Pedology, new series, vol. 29(132). (In Russian.)

Shibaev, I. V., and Litvinenko, N. M. 1977. (Recent Soviet-Japanese research on migratory and/or endangered birds.) *Abstracts of the VII USSR National Ornithological Conference*, Cherkassy, the Ukraine, 27-30 September 1977, pp. 251-252.

Shroufe, D. L. 1976. Seasonal migrations of the greater sandhill crane through northwest Indiana. pp. 51-58, *in* Lewis, 1976a.

Sibley, C. G. 1960. The electrophoretic patterns of egg-white proteins as taxonomic characters. *Ibis* 102:215-284.

Sibley, C. G., and Ahlquist, J. E. 1972. A comparative study of the egg white proteins of non-passerine birds. *Peabody Museum of Natural History Bulletin* 39:1-276.

Sick, H. 1972. Trumpeters. pp. 124-124, *in Grzimek's Animal Life Encyclopedia*. Vol. 9. New York: Van Nostrand Reinhold.

Sieber, H. 1932. Beobachtungen über der Biologie des Kranichs (*Megalornis grus grus*). Beitr. Fortpfl. Biol. Vogel 8: 134-139, 176-180.

Skinner, M. F., Skinner, S. M., and Gooris, R. J. 1977. Stratigraphy and biostratigraphy of late Cenozoic deposits in central Sioux County, western Nebraska. *Bulletin American Museum of Natural History* 158:265-371.

Sludski, A. A. 1959. (On the distribution and biology of the Siberian white crane.) *Ornitologiya* 2:159-162. (In Russian.)

Smirenskii, S. M. 1980. (Ranges and numbers of Japanese (*Grus japonensis*) and white-naped (*Grus vipio*) cranes.) *Ornitologiya* 15:26-35. (In Russian.)

Smirenskii, S. M., and Shtilmark, F. P. 1977. (Significance of the middle Amur River area for preserving the Far Eastern stork, the Japanese crane, and the white-naped crane.) *Abstracts of the VII USSR National Ornithological Conference*, Cherkassy, the Ukraine, 27-30 September 1977, vol. 2, pp. 246-247. Kiev: "Naukova Dumka." (In Russian.)

Smith, E. R., Jr. 1979. A wintering flock of sandhill cranes in central Louisiana. pp. 149-150, *in* Lewis, 1979e.

Smythies, B. E. 1953. *The birds of Burma*. Edinburgh: Oliver and Boyd.

Snow, D. (ed.). 1978. *An atlas of speciation in African non-passerine birds*. London: Trustees of the British Museum.

Snyder, N. F. R., and Snyder, H. A. 1969. A comparative study of mollusk predation by limpkins, Everglade kites, and boat-tailed grackles. *Living Bird* 8:177-223.

Spitzer, P. R. 1979. The Siberian crane at Bharatpur. pp. 249-254, *in* Lewis, 1979e.

————. 1981. The lily of birds. *Animal Kingdom* 81(5):24-30.

Steel, N. R. 1977. Breeding the grey-necked crowned crane. *Avicultural Magazine* 83:63-68.

Stegmann, B. 1978. Relationships of the superorders Alectoromorphae and Charadriomorphae (Aves): A comparative study of the avian hand. *Publications Nuttall Ornithological Club* No. 17.

Stepayan, L. S. 1975. (*Composition and distribution of USSR avifauna. 1. Non-passerines.*) Moscow, Science Press. (In Russian.)

Stephen, W. J. D. 1967. Bionomics of the sandhill crane. Ottawa: *Canadian Wildlife Service Reports 2*.

————. 1979. Whooping crane sightings, prairie provinces 1977 and 1978. *Blue Jay* 37:163-168.

Stephenson, J. D. 1971. Plumage development and growth of young whooping cranes. M.S. thesis, Oregon State University, Corvallis.

Steyn, P., and Ellman-Brown, P. 1974. Crowned crane nesting in a tree. *Ostrich* 45:40-42.

Stresemann, E., and Stresemann, V. 1967. Ein Semmelplatz mausernder Kraniche (*Grus grus*). *Journal für Ornithologie* 108:81-82.

Sugita, H., and Suzuki, S. 1980. (Reproduction in the wattled crane.) *Animals and Zoos* (Tokyo Zoological Park Society) 32(11):6-10. (In Japanese, English summary.)

Sukilovskaya, A. M. 1963. (The change of ranges of the common crane, the white crane, and the demoiselle crane in the Soviet Union.) *Byulleten Moskovskogo Obshchestva Ispytatelei Prirody Otdelenie Biologisheskii* 68:125-127. (In Russian, English summary.)

Sutherland, C. A., and McChesney, D. S., 1965. Sound production in two species of geese. *Living Bird* 4:99-106.

Swanberg, P. O. 1981. Notes on the population of common crane in Scandinavia and Finland: A preliminary survey. pp.184-185, *in* Lewis and Masatomi, 1981.

Swenk, M. H. 1933. The present status of the whooping crane. *Nebraska Bird Review* 1:111-129.

Tacha, T. C. 1981. Behavior and taxonomy of sandhill cranes from mid-continental North America. Ph.D. dissertation, Oklahoma State University, Stillwater.

Tacha, T. C., and Lewis, J. C. 1979. Sex determination of sandhill cranes by cloacal examination. pp. 81-84, *in* Lewis, 1979e.

Tacha, T. C., Martin, D. C., and Endicott, C. G. 1979. Mortality of sandhill cranes associated with utility highlines in Texas. pp. 175-176, *in* Lewis, 1979e.

Takahashi, R., and Nakamura, K. 1981. Artificial incubation and rearing of red-crowned cranes in Kushiro crane park. pp. 97-98, *in* Lewis and Masatomi, 1981.

Taka-Tsukasa, N. 1967. *Birds of Nippon*. Tokyo: Maruzen Co., Ltd.

Tarboton, W. R. In press. The status and conservation of the wattled crane in the Transvaal. Proceedings Fifth Pan-African Ornithological Congress.

Taylor, W. E. 1976. Sandhill crane habitat management on the Hiawatha National Forest. pp. 44-50, *in* Lewis, 1976a.

————. 1977. Status of the greater sandhill crane in the Upper Peninsula of Michigan. pp. 10-11, *in* Feldt, 1977.

Tebbel, P. D., and Ankney, C. D. 1979. Biology of the sandhill cranes in the southern Algoma District, Ontario. pp. 129-134, *in* Lewis, 1979e.

Thiollary, J.-M. 1979. La migration des grues a travers l'Himalaya et la predation par les aigles royaux. *Alauda* 47:83-89.

Thompson, R. L. 1970. Florida sandhill crane nesting on Loxahatchee National Wildlife Refuge. *Auk* 87:492-502.

Thorpe, W. H. 1961. *Bird song: The biology of vocal communication and expressions in birds*. Cambridge: Cambridge University Press.

REFERENCES

Toepler, J. E., and Crete, R. A. 1979. Migration of radio-tagged greater sandhill cranes from Minnesota and Wisconsin. pp. 159-174, *in* Lewis, 1979e.

Topsell, E. 1972. *The fowles of Heauen, or history of birdes.* Edited by T. P. Harrison and F. D. Hoeniger. Austin: University of Texas Press.

Traylor, M. A. 1963. Check-list of Angolan birds. *Publ. Culturais Comp. Diamentes de Angola,* No. 61.

Trevor-Battye, A (ed.). 1903. *Lord Lilford on birds.* London: Hutchinson & Co.

U.S. Fish and Wildlife Service. 1981. The Platte River ecology study. *Special Research Report, Northern Prairie Wildlife Research Center,* Jamestown, North Dakota. 186 pp.

Urban, E. K. 1981. The Sudan crowned crane. p. 254, *in* Lewis and Masatomi, 1981.

Urban, E. K., and Walkinshaw, L. H. 1967. The Sudan crowned crane in Ethiopia. *Ibis* 109:431-433.

Uspenskii, S. M. 1961. Zur Verbreitung und Biologie des Nonnenkranichs in Nordost-Siberien. *Falke* 8:334-337.

Uspenskii, S. M., Beme, R. L., Priklonskii, S. G., and Veskov, V. N. 1962. (The birds of northeastern Yakutia.) *Ornitologiya* 4:64-86; 5:49-67. (In Russian.)

Valentine, J. M., Jr. 1979. the Mississippi sandhill crane: A status update. pp. 135-138, *in* Lewis, 1979e.

—————. 1981. The Mississippi sandhill crane, 1980. pp. 167-179, *in* Lewis and Masatomi, 1981.

—————. 1982. Breeding ecology of the Mississippi sandhill crane in Jackson County Mississippi. pp. 63-72, *in* Lewis, 1982.

Valentine, J. M., Jr., and Noble. R. E. 1970. A colony of sandhill cranes in Mississippi. *Journal of Wildlife Management* 34:761-768.

—————. 1976. The Mississippi sandhill crane. pp. 343-346, *in* Lewis, 1976a.

van der Ven, J. A. 1981. Common cranes in Europe. pp. 181-183, *in* Lewis and Masatomi, 1981.

van Doorn, C. 1966. Die Zucht von Mandschurenkranichen (*Grus japonensis*) im Rotterdam Zoo. *Freunde des Kölner Zoo* 9(2):39-45.

van Ee, C. A. 1966. Notes on the breeding behavior of the blue crane *Tetrapteryx paradisea. Ostrich* 37:23-39.

—————. 1981. Status of the blue crane in south and southwest Africa. p. 159, *in* Lewis and Masatomi, 1981.

Vaurie, C. 1965. *The birds of the Palaearctic fauna: Non-passerines.* London: Witherby.

Viniter, S. V. 1979. (The pearl of Asia, the Japanese crane.) *Priroda* 1979(4):96-100. (In Russian.)

—————. 1981. Nesting of the red-crowned crane in the central Amur region. pp. 74-80, *in* Lewis and Masatomi, 1981.

Vinokurov, A., Sapetin, Y., and Priklonskii, S. 1976. (*Rare, endangered, and little-known birds of the USSR.*) Moscow: *Transactions of Oksk State Reserve,* Ministry of Agriculture. 224 pp. (In Russian.)

Voorhies, M. R. 1981. Ancient ashfall creates a Pompei of prehistoric animals. *National Geographic* 159(1):66-75.

Vorobiev, K. A. 1954. (*Birds of the Ussuri area.*) Far Eastern Branch, Academy of Sciences of the USSR, Moscow. (In Russian.)

—————. 1963. (The birds of Yakutia.) Moscow. (In Russian.)

Voss, K. S. 1976. Behavior of the greater sandhill crane. M.S. thesis, University of Wisconsin, Madison.

Walkinshaw, L. H. 1949. The sandhill cranes. *Cranbrook Institute of Science Bulletin* 29:1-22.

—————. 1951. Nesting of white-naped crane in Detroit Zoological Park, Michigan. *Auk* 68:194-201.

—————. 1963. Some life history studies of the Stanley crane. *Proceedings XIII International Ornithological Congress,* Ithaca, 1962. pp. 344-353.

—————. 1964. The African crowned cranes. *Wilson Bulletin* 76:355-377.

—————. 1965a. One hundred thirty-three Michigan sandhill crane nests. *Jack-Pine Warbler* 43:137-142.

—————. 1965b. Territories of cranes. *Papers of the Michigan Academy of Science, Arts and Letters,* Vol. 50:75-88.

—————. 1965c. Sandhill crane studies on Banks Island, N.W.T. *Blue Jay* 23:66-72.

—————. 1965d. Attentiveness of cranes at their nests. *Auk* 82:465-476.

—————. 1973. *Cranes of the world.* New York: Winchester Press. (Supplement of range maps and egg records privately published as *The Cranes,* vol. 1, no. 1, 1973.)

—————. 1976. Sandhill crane on and near the Kissimmee Prairie, Florida. pp. 1-18, *in* Lewis, 1976a.

—————. 1978. Sandhill crane studies in Michigan's Upper Peninsula. *Jack-Pine Warbler* 56:107-121.

—————. 1981a. West African crowned crane observations. pp. 255-257, *in* Lewis and Masatomi, 1981.

—————. 1981b. The sandhill cranes. pp. 151-162, *in* Lewis and Masatomi, 1981.

—————. 1981c. Cranes of the world: a partial bibliography. pp. 24-45, *in* Lewis and Masatomi, 1981.

—————. 1982. Nesting of the Florida sandhill crane in central Florida. pp. 53-62, *in* Lewis, 1982.

Walton, H. J. 1946. On the birds of southern Tibet. *Ibis* 88:57-84; 225-226.

West, O. 1963. Notes on the wattled crane *Bugeranus carunculatus* (Gmelin). *Ostrich* 34:63-77.

—————. 1976. Notes on the distribution and status of the southern population of wattled crane in Africa. pp. 347-349, *in* Lewis, 1976a.

Wetmore, A. 1928. Additional specimens of fossil birds from the Upper Tertiary deposits of Nebraska. *American Museum Novitates* 302:1-5.

—————. 1956. A check-list of the fossil and prehistoric birds of North America and the West Indies. *Smithsonian Miscellaneous Collections* 131:1-105.

—————. 1960. A classification of the birds of the world. *Smithsonian Miscellaneous Collections* 139:1-37.

—————. 1965. Birds of the Republic of Panamá. Pt. 1. Washington: *Smithsonian Miscellaneous Collections* 150:1-483.

Whymper. C. 1909. *Egyptian birds.* London: Adam & Charles Black.

Wiley, S. 1978. A review of techniques in the maintenance and propagation of cranes. pp. 17-27, *in* Risser, A. C., Baptista, L.F., Wiley, S. R., and Gale, N. B. (eds.), *Proceedings 1st International Birds in Captivity Symposium.* North Hollywood: International Foundation for Conservation of Birds.

REFERENCES

Williams, L. E., Jr., and Phillips, R. W. 1972. Northern Florida sandhill crane populations. *Auk* 89:451-548.

Winterbottom J. M. 1971. *A preliminary check list of the birds of South West Africa.* Windhoek: South West Africa Scientific Society.

Won, P. O. 1977. (Present status of cranes wintering in Korea, 1976-77.) Kyung Hee University Institute of Ornithology. (In Korean, English summary.)

———. 1981. Status and conservation of crane wintering in Korea. pp. 61-65, *in* Lewis and Masatomi, 1981.

Wood, D. S. 1976. Phenetic relationships within the family Gruidae. M.S. thesis, University of Oklahoma, Norman.

———. 1979. Phenetic relationships within the family Gruidae. *Wilson Bulletin* 91:384-399.

Wyndham, C. 1940. The crowned crane (*Balearica regulorum*). *Ostrich* 9:45-48.

Yamashina, Y. 1978. (Current status of *Grus japonensis, G. vipio,* and *G. monacha* in the Asian continent.) *Miscellaneous Reports of the Yamashina Institute for Ornithology* 10(51):43-57. (In Japanese, English summary.)

Yarrell, W. 1827. Observations on the trachea of birds with description and representations... *Proceedings Zoological Society of London,* pp. 33-34.

Zhou, F. Z., Ding, W. N., and Wang, Z. Y. 1980. Black-necked cranes (*Grus nigricollis*) wintering at Cao-Hai, Guizhou Province. Manuscript of paper presented at International Crane Symposium, Sapporo, Japan, 21-22 February 1980.

Zimmerman, D. R. 1975. *To save a bird in peril.* New York: Coward, McCann & Geoghegan.

INDEX

This index is limited to the English vernacular and Latin names of crane species and subspecies, including fossil forms. Complete indexing is limited to entries for the English vernacular names of species as used in this book. The principal account of each species or genus is indicated by italics.

And as wee see strainge Crane are wont to doe
First stalke a while ere they their wings can finde,
Then soare from ground not past a yard or two,
Till in their wings they gathered have the winde;
At last they mount the very cloudes vnto,
Trianglewise according to their kind.

(Topsell, 1972).